Redirecting Human Rights

Global Ethics Series

Series Editor: Christien van den Anker, Reader, Department of Politics, University of the West of England, UK

Global Ethics as a field builds on longer traditions of ethical reflection about (global) society and discusses ethical approaches to global issues. These include but are not limited to issues highlighted by the process of globalisation (in the widest sense) and increasing multiculturalism. They also engage with migration, the environment, poverty and inequality, peace and conflict, human rights, global citizenship, social movements, and global governance. Despite fluid boundaries between fields, Global Ethics can be clearly marked out by its multidisciplinary approach, its interest in a strong link between theory, policy and practice and its inclusion of a range of work from strictly normative to more empirical.

Books in the series provide a specific normative approach, taxonomy, or an ethical position on a specific issue in Global Ethics through empirical work. They explicitly engage with Global Ethics as a field and position themselves in regard to existing debates even when outlining more local approaches or issues. The *Global Ethics Series* has been designed to reach beyond a liberal cosmopolitan agenda and engage with contextualism as well as structural analyses of injustice in current global politics and its disciplining discourses.

Titles include:

Anna Grear
REDIRECTING HUMAN RIGHTS
Facing the Challenge of Corporate Legal Humanity

Ivan Manokha *(editor)*
THE POLITICAL ECONOMY OF HUMAN RIGHTS ENFORCEMENT

Darrel Moellendorf
GLOBAL INEQUALITY MATTERS

Global Ethics Series
Series Standing Order ISBN 978–0–230–01958–4

You can receive future titles in this series as they are published by placing a standing order. Please contact your bookseller or, in case of difficulty, write to us at the address below with your name and address, the title of the series and the ISBN quoted above.

Customer Services Department, Macmillan Distribution Ltd, Houndmills, Basingstoke, Hampshire RG21 6XS, England

Redirecting Human Rights

Facing the Challenge of Corporate Legal Humanity

Anna Grear
Senior Lecturer in Law, Bristol Law School, Bristol UWE, UK

palgrave
macmillan

First published 2010 by
PALGRAVE MACMILLAN

Palgrave Macmillan in the UK is an imprint of Macmillan Publishers Limited, registered in England, company number 785998, of Houndmills, Basingstoke, Hampshire RG21 6XS.

Palgrave Macmillan in the US is a division of St Martin's Press LLC, 175 Fifth Avenue, New York, NY 10010.

Palgrave Macmillan is the global academic imprint of the above companies and has companies and representatives throughout the world.

ISBN-13: 978–0–230–54222–8 hardback

This book is printed on paper suitable for recycling and made from fully managed and sustained forest sources. Logging, pulping and manufacturing processes are expected to conform to the environmental regulations of the country of origin.

A catalogue record for this book is available from the British Library.

Library of Congress Cataloging-in-Publication Data
Grear, Anna, 1959–
Redirecting human rights : facing the challenge of corporate legal humanity / Anna Grear.
p. cm. – (Global ethics)
Summary: "This book explores the implications of human embodiment for human rights law and theory. It reflects on the ethical significance of the link between human embodiment and our quintessential ontological vulnerability in an attempt to problematise corporate human rights claims"–Provided by publisher.
Includes bibliographical references and index.
ISBN 978-0-230-54222-8 (hardback)
1. Juristic persons. 2. Human rights. I. Title.
K650.G74 2010
341.4'8–dc22 2009048529

10 9 8 7 6 5 4 3 2 1
19 18 17 16 15 14 13 12 11 10

Printed and bound in Great Britain by
CPI Antony Rowe, Chippenham and Eastbourne

I dedicate this work to Judah and Joshua, my beloved children;
to my 'quasi-sons', Hadlee, Guy and Luke;
and to my 'quasi-son-in-law', Peter.

To them and to the many others in whose co-presence
I have grown – and grow – I owe profound gratitude.

Contents

List of Abbreviations		ix
International Instruments and Committee Reports		x
Acknowledgements		xiv
Foreword by Upendra Baxi		xv
Introduction		**1**
Chapter 1	**Human Rights under Pressure?**	**7**
	The Universal Declaration of Human Rights paradigm under pressure	7
	A brief assessment of corporate accountability to human rights standards	18
Chapter 2	**Corporate Human Rights?**	**23**
	Liberal pragmatism and the corporate beneficiaries of the ECHR	23
	Re-assessing arguments in favour of corporate human rights	31
Chapter 3	**Law, Persons and Disembodiment**	**40**
	Quasi-disembodiment	41
	Reflections on legal personality	45
	Corporate personality theory	59
	Personhood and property	65
Chapter 4	**The Liberal Subject of Rights, Capitalism and the Corporation**	**68**
	Liberal law as a rationalising enterprise	68
	The genesis of liberal rights and the liberal legal subject	70
	The corporation and capitalism: Personification and ideology	84
	Corporations: The ultimate legal person?	89
Chapter 5	**A Genealogy of Quasi-Disembodiment in International Human Rights Law**	**96**
	Exclusions in the early construction of rights	98
	The UDHR paradigm: Paradoxes of dis/embodiment	102
	'The universal is male': The persistent marginality of women in international human rights law	104
	Two competing conceptions of human rights?	110

Chapter 6	**The Centrality of Human Embodiment**	**114**
	The centrality of embodiment	115
	Embodied vulnerability	126
Chapter 7	**Embodied Vulnerability and the Universal Declaration of Human Rights**	**137**
	Empathy, rights and embodiment: The eighteenth century	138
	Empathy, rights and embodiment: The universal declaration of human rights	140
	International rights: Bio-politics, sovereign power, bare life and the challenge for human rights: A critical reading of Article 14 UDHR	150
	Embodied vulnerability and the UDHR rights: Conceptual issues	156
	Towards the ethical reconstruction of human rights and the human rights subject	162
Chapter 8	**Embodied Vulnerability and the Limits of Privatisation: Reconsidering Property and Human Rights**	**168**
	Property and the bifurcation of human rights discourse	168
	Property: A contested concept under increasing pressure	171
	Excludability and exclusion: Separating the analytical from the ideological	181
	Re-imagining property: Inclusion, propriety and rights as 'what is due'	184
	A case study: The right to water	191
Chapter 9	**Some Brief Conclusory Thoughts and Future Research Directions**	**201**
	A brief aside on an important emergent and future challenge	202
	Embodied human vulnerability and the UDHR – 'Minding the gap'	204
Notes		207
Bibliography		252
Index		265

List of Abbreviations

AI	Artificial Intelligence
CEDAW	Convention on the Elimination of all Forms of Discrimination Against Women
CERD	Convention on the Elimination of all Forms of Racial Discrimination
CHR	Commission on Human Rights
CSR	Corporate Social Responsibility
CSW	Commission on the Status of Women
DEVAW	Declaration on the Elimination of Violence Against Women
ECHR	European Convention on Human Rights and Fundamental Freedoms
ECtHR	European Court of Human Rights
GATT	General Agreement on Tariffs and Trade
ICCPR	International Covenant of Civil and Political Rights
ICESCR	International Covenant of Economic, Social and Cultural Rights
IMF	International Monetary Fund
NAFTA	North American Free Trade Agreement
NGOs	Non-Governmental Organisations
OECD	Organisation for Economic Cooperation and Development
SLAPPS	Strategic Lawsuits Against Public Participation
TNCs	Transnational Corporations
TRIPS	Trade-related Intellectual Property Rights
TRMFHR	Trade-related Market-friendly Human Rights
UDHR	Universal Declaration of Human Rights
UNDP	United Nations Development Programme
WTO	World Trade Organisation

International Instruments and Committee Reports

African [Banjul] Charter on Human and Peoples' Rights, adopted June 27, 1981, OAU Doc. CAB/LEG/67/3 rev. 5, 21 I.L.M. 58 (1982), *entered into force* Oct. 21, 1986

The Brussels Declaration Concerning the Law and Customs of War, Brussels, 27 August 1874

Manual of the Laws and Customs of War on Land, Oxford, 9 September 1880

Convention Respecting the Laws and Customs of War on Land, 29 July 1899, 32 Stat 1803, Art XLVI

Convention du 12 Juin 1902 pour regler les conflits de loi en matiere de marriage

Convention du 12 Juin 1902 les conflits de loi et de jurisdictions en matiere de divorce et de separation de corps

Convention du 12 juin 1902 pour regler la tutelle des mineurs.

International Agreement for the Suppression of the White Slave Traffic, Paris, 18 May 1904

Conventions Respecting the Laws and Customs of War on Land, 18 October 1907

International Convention for the Suppression of White Slave Traffic, Paris, 4 May 1910, 211 Consol TS 45 1912 Gr Brit TS No 20

Convention No 3: Convention Concerning the Employment of Women Before and After Childbirth, Washington, 28 November 1919 (revised in 1948 (Convention No 103))

Preamble to the Constitution of the International Labour Organisation, as contained in the Treaty of Peace Between the Allied and Associated Power and Germany, Versailles, 28 June 1919

Convention No 4: Convention Concerning the Employment of Women during the Night, Washington, 28 November 1919

Recommendation No 4: Recommendation concerning the Protection of Women and Children against Lead Poisoning, Washington, 28 November 1919

International Convention for the Suppression of the Traffic in Women and Children, Geneva, 30 September 1921, 9 LNTS 415

International Convention for the Suppression of the Traffic in Women of Full Age, Geneva, 11 October 1933, 150 LNTS 431

Convention No 45: Convention Concerning the Employment of Women on Underground Work in Mines of All Kinds, Geneva, 21 June 1935

UN GAOR, Comm'n on Hum. Rts Drafting Comm. 1st Sess., 13th mtg., at 2, U.N Doc E/CN.4/AC.1/SR13 (1947)

UN GAOR, 3rd Sess., 181st–183rd plen.mtg. at 857, UN Doc A/C.3/SR.181–183 (1948)

Third Committee Records (U.N GAOR, 3rd Sess. UN Doc A/C.3/ (1948) 84th–180th mtgs

Universal Declaration of Human Rights GA res. 217A (III) UN Doc. A/810 at 71 (1948)

Convention on the Elimination of All Forms of Racial Discrimination GA Res 2106 (XX) Annex, 20 UN GAOR Supp. (No 14) at 47, UN Doc A/6014 (1966), 660 UNTS 195

International Covenant on Civil and Political Rights GA res. 2200A (XXI) 21 UN GAOR Supp. (No 16) at 52, UN Doc A/6316 (1966), 999 UNTS 171

International Covenant on Economic Social and Cultural Rights GA res. 2200A (XXI) 21 UN GAOR Supp. (No 16) at 49, UN Doc A/6316 (1966), 993 UNTS 3

Convention on the Elimination of All Forms of Discrimination Against Women GA Res 34/180, 34 UN GAOR Supp. (No 46) at 193, UN Doc A/34/46

CEDAW Committee General Recommendation No 12 (eighth session, 1990) GAOR, 44th Session, Supp. No 37, UN Doc A/44/38, 1989

Report of the Sub-Commission on Prevention of Discrimination and Protection of Minorities, in its forty-third session, Geneva, 5–30 August 1991, UN Doc. E/CN.4/Sub.2/1991/65 of 24 October 1991

Vienna Declaration and Programme of Action UN Doc.A/CONF.157/24 (Part 1) at 20 (1993)

Declaration on the Elimination of Violence Against Women GA Res 48/104, 48 UN GAOR Supp. (No 49) at 217, UN Doc A/48/49 (1993)

Human Rights Committee, General Comment 28, Equality of Rights Between Men and Women (Article 3), UN Doc CCPR/C/21/Rev.1/Add.10 (2000)

Norms on the Responsibilities of Transnational Corporations and other Business Enterprises with regard to Human Rights' (2003) UN doc E/CN/.4/ Sub.2/2003/12/Rev.2

Interim Report of the Secretary-General's Special Representative on the Issue of Human Rights and Transnational Corporations and Other Business Enterprises, 22 February 2006, E/CN.4/2006/97

National Legislation

Countryside and Rights of Way Act 2000

The Corporate Manslaughter and Corporate Homicide Act 2007

Table of Cases

Agrotexim Hellas SA and Others v Greece A 330-A (1995); (1996) 21 EHRR 250

Aguas del Tunari SA v Republic of Bolivia (ICSID Case No ARB/02/3)

Allan Singer v Canada [1990] 1 SCR 425

Allan Singer v Canada Communication No.455/1991 (UN Doc. CCPR/C/51/ D/445/1991)

Autronic AG v Switzerland A 178 (1990); (1990) 12 EHRR 485

Awas Tingni Community v Nicaragua, case no 79, Inter-Am CHR (Judgment of the Inter-American Court of Human Rights of 31 August 2001)

Buckley v United Kingdom (ECHR) Case No 23/1995/529/615, 1996-iv; 23 EHRR 101

CIN Properties Ltd v Rawlins [1995] 2 EGLR 130

Comingersoll SA v Portugal 2000-IV 355; (2001) 31 EHRR 772

Connecticut General Life Insurance Company v Johnson 303 US 77, 90 (1938)

County of Santa Clara v Southern Pacific Railroad 118 US 394 (1886)

Ex parte Royall 117 US 241 (1886)

R v Environment Secretary, ex p Davis (1989) 59 P & CR 306

First National Bank of Boston v Belotti 435 US 530 (1978)

Irwin Toy Ltd v Quebec [1989] 1 SCR 927

Case No. 06/13865 *Mazibuko and Others v The City of Johannesburg and Others*

Milirrpum v Nabalco Pty Ltd (1971) 17 FLR 141

Porter v Commissioner of Police of the Metropolis [1999] All ER (D) 1129

Soloman v A Soloman & Co Ltd [1897] AC 22

Société Colas Est SA and Others v France 2002-III 421; (2004) 39 EHRR 17

The Trustees of Dartmouth College v Woodward (1819) 17 US (4 Wheat) 581 at 636

Victoria Park Racing and Recreation Grounds Co Ltd v Taylor (1937) 58 CLR 479

Zino Davidoff SA v A & G Imports Ltd, Levi Strauss & Co v another v Tesco Stores Ltd and another; Levi Strauss & Co and another v Costco Wholesale UK Ltd (Joined Cases C 414/99–C 416/99 [2002] CMLR 1)

Other sources

DETR Consultation Paper (1998)

Web Addresses

http://www.ulla-loezter.de/article/362.susan_george_the_end_of_neo-liberalism_alternatives_to-finance_led_capitalism.html
http://www.ips-dc.org/reports/top200.htm
http://www.sociology.org/content/2005/tier1/ajana.html
http://www.thomhartmanncom/summary/shtml
http://www.unglobalcompact.org/ParticipantsAndStakeholders/index.html
http://www.commondreams.org/news2000/0725-08.html
http://www.alterinter.org/article2629.html?lang=fr

Acknowledgements

I would like to thank St Johns College, Oxford for awarding me a Visiting Scholarship at the University of Oxford in Summer 2007, and the University of Keele for awarding me with a Visiting Fellowship in February 2008 at the AHRC-funded Centre for the study of Gender, Sexuality and the Law – both pivotal times of reflection and research on themes relevant to the central concerns of this book.

I would like to thank those who have most inspired my work and set my mind on fire with a frequency I have found transformative: Upendra Baxi, Kevin Gray, Costas Douzinas, Ngaire Naffine and Dianne Otto.

I cannot put into words my debt to Upendra Baxi and Kevin Gray. I am deeply grateful to them both for their decisive influence on my intellectual formation, their continuing interest in my work and for their enriching encouragement and critique, including their comments on drafts or part-drafts of this book.

I am also especially grateful to Ngaire Naffine and Dianne Otto for their insightful work and their willingness to engage with mine.

I would like to thank Sarah Joseph, Patricia Elliot, Nick Buttle and Alice Belcher, in addition to those already mentioned, for their reflections and critique of draft chapters. For their comments on earlier work that formed the foundation of this book – I would like to thank Christopher McCrudden, Sandra Fredman, Neil Stammers, Leslie Kim Treiger Bar-Am, Peter Edge and Penelope Simons.

I would especially like to thank Sue Gibbons for her fabulous and detailed critique and long-time friendship and inspiration. She is one in a million, and a pivotal figure in my academic development.

Last, but not least, I would like to thank Richard Hart of Hart Publishing for the chance to review and copy-edit so many fine academic texts, and for his kind permission to use some brief quotations from *The End of Human Rights*.

Foreword

It is a privilege indeed to contribute a foreword to this pioneering, provocative, and promising work.

Pioneering because Anna Grear not only retrieves a lost continent of thought (peopled by jurists and social theorists who sought to solve the puzzle of the legal personality of corporations) but she also resituates it in the context of a 'critique of disembodiment' and in 'defence of embodied vulnerability as the proper foundation of human rights legal subjectivity'.

In this sense, this work marks some fresh starts towards understanding the *ontology* of human rights. It may also further excite the attention of those who continue to pioneer post-Lacanian approaches to law and jurisprudence, and also supplement Alain Badiou's *Theory of The Subject* (2009) within the contexts of his insistence concerning the forms of 'militant subjectivity', the variegated practices of 'democratic materialism.'

As concerns 'provocation,' controlled dictionary meanings guide us to understand this as that 'something', which 'incites, instigates, angers, or irritates.' To be sure, this work may irritate and even anger the votaries of globalization amongst the communities of corporate lawpersons (lawyers, justices, law academics and students) and specialists in international economic law. Yet any careful reading of this work may no longer fail to heed Grear's provocation. She fully suggests why the domains of 'international economic law' and 'international human rights law' may no longer remain hermetically sealed, if only because claims to access human rights by corporate and business entities are on the increase, as remain, also, transnational corporations' complaints of being 'victimized' by human rights and social movements.

The provocation of this work as 'incitement and instigation' enables us to rethink 'embodied vulnerability as a foundation of human rights'. In a sense, the early discourse concerning legal personality is framed by the libertarian human rights to the possession and ownership of property. In a vastly different conjuncture, the theory and praxes of human rights and social movements now reframe these very rights within the logics of new common property rights. In this way, Anna Grear thus provokes us all to revisit the aporia enunciated by Jacques Ranciere: 'They' [the communities of resistance and the revolutionary militancy of suffering people] *'acted as subjects that did not have the rights that they had and had the rights that they had not.'*

The oft-noted paradoxical and ambivalent character of human rights acquires an edge here both in terms of the power and error of human rights, if I may so put this. Despite her critical approaches to forms of human rights essentialism and human rights 'utilitarianism,' Anna Grear remains persuasive in reading the claims to corporate human rights as 'colonizing'. Far from being a polemical gesture, Anna Grear here echoes Kwame Nkrumah's withering description of 'neocolonialism' as *'power without responsibility and exploitation without redress'*. In thus specifically addressing struggle-based contradictions, she invites us all to rethink TNC conduct in all its awesome hot pursuit of the itineraries of 'neoliberalism'. In so far as this pursuit contributes to a never-ending reproduction of the 'Third Worlds' of suffering humanity 'corporate human rights' claims may not find much legitimacy.

Too many images crowd my mind as I read this precious text.

First, corporate human rights talk and action suggests many an inversion of what Hugo Grotius named as *appetitus societatis*, roughly put here, the desire to live in peaceful and just society/world orderings. The *recta ratio* (good reason) practiced by the state-like, yet state-transcendent, global corporations results primarily in the destruction of nature and human life-worlds, thus expanding biopolitical regimes that Michel Foucault poignantly named as comprising the prowess of both 'hyper-profit' and 'infra-power'. One way to further name this inversion – constituting a 'nacropolitics' of corporate human rights talk and action – invites attention in a Heideggerian moment as *'being towards death'*.

Second, and related to this, the regimes of immunity and impunity thus fully constituted in turn adversely affect the possibilities of a just world ordering because these constitute what Frank Pearce and Steve Tombs memorably described as 'toxic capitalism', which Anna Grear here differently reinforces via her analyses of the law and politics of disembodiment/embodiment. If so, at stake here remains more than the juristic and juridical categories of immunity and impunity, as this work amply shows. How far then, may we engage any reconsideration of corporate human rights in terms of what Martin Heidegger named as *'nonanswerability'* and that something which Jacques Derrida later re-frames not just as *'responsibility'* but as *'response–ability'*?

Third, it is precisely on these registers that the interrogation of the inauthenticity of some new forms of multifariously articulated 'corporate human rights' occurs. No matter howsoever framed, the grammars of corporate social responsibility, ethical investment, or even bioethics, continue to conceal from view the full excision of contemporary human rights values, norms, and standards from 'business ethics' and the 'good' corporate governance languages.

For all these related reasons, I read the promise of this work as mapping, or rather emplotting, some itineraries of 'future history' (to evoke a gifted and messianic phrase of Walter Benjamin) of contemporary human rights.

Not too many works concerning 'human rights' present so much by way of a recall of Heideggerian notions of *'concernful'* engagement that articulate both the *anxiety* and the *angst* here extended and adapted to corporate human rights talk and action. This reminder remains important if only because the now fully emergent new paradigm of trade-related, market-friendly human rights strives towards supplanting an earlier vision of the universal human rights of all human beings.

In sum, the narrative heights here scaled, and indeed in some munificently reader-friendly ways, summon admiration. Further, no critique of this work may now fully escape a new terrain of contestation thus constituted.

Upendra Baxi
Professor Emeritus
Warwick Law School
December 10, 2009.

Introduction

To some, the idea of corporate human rights will appear inherently contradictory – an oxymoron. Human rights, it is perhaps natural to assume, are for human beings – not corporations. How can it be possible that a global corporation, for example, can invoke, even discursively, a category of rights designed for the protection of living human beings and communities? To others, however, perhaps especially some lawyers, the concept of corporate human rights is relatively unproblematic. Corporations are, after all, legal persons. They represent important human interests, and there is no reason in principle why they ought not to have human rights as well as contractual, proprietary and constitutional rights. Law, as such lawyers understand, has an almost limitless facility for the production of new forms of personification, new forms of legal subjectivity. The extension of human rights to corporations is merely, in this light, another exercise of law's generative power – a not necessarily remarkable extension of human rights subjectivity that simply reflects law's facility for populating and categorising its own universe. Indeed, it has been noted that where companies have been granted 'victim status' in respect of certain human rights, 'the basis for that protection appears to have been the status of the company as a legal person'.[1]

While, however, it is true that the plasticity of legal subjectivity has some exciting possibilities for the generation of new rights bearers, it should be noted that throughout its history, law's talent for personification has become thoroughly imbricated with a complexly-related power and tendency to define 'humanity'. Legal subjectivity has been, to a decisive degree, shaped and conditioned by a deep legal anthropomorphism, and in a sense, law's award of legal subjectivity often amounts to an exercise of an anthropogenetic power. In fact, it is highly likely that a conceptually slippery and obfuscating conflation between legal subjectivity and humanity lies behind the emergence of corporate legal humanity – and accordingly this book will attempt to trace precisely how the conflation between legal subjectivity and humanity might be implicated in the whole idea of corporate human rights.

Although these concerns might seem rather technical to some readers, it is nonetheless vital to understand how the analytical and ideological closures of legal subjectivity form the complex conduits through which corporations move to inhabit human rights law as putative human rights claimants, beneficiaries, and even 'victims'. But these concerns, familiar to lawyers of a critical theoretical orientation, need placing within the framework of contemporary globalisation – a phenomenon that is far more than legal.

Globalisation is a context that lends pressing urgency to the need to question the very idea of corporate human rights, and it forms an indispensable backdrop to the argument of this book, for it is in the context of contemporary globalisation that the most troubling implications of corporate human rights discourse are most starkly revealed. Two major contemporary realities converge in this context. The first is the phenomenon of contemporary economic globalisation. The second is the globalisation and discursive ascendancy of rights discourse itself.

Contemporary economic globalisation, as we shall see, forms a context in which transnational corporations emerge as the dominant actors, possessing, in some cases, more economic clout and political influence than many nation-states. At the same time, globalisation has been shown to generate unprecedented levels of peril and risk for human beings and communities – and is linked to emergent new forms of systemic violence and the production and expansion of troubling forms of human vulnerability, as well as to environmental degradation.

Secondly, corporate human rights discourse needs to be considered against the backdrop of an ever-increasing global commitment to rights discourse. The discourse of human rights (arguably *the* ascendant ethical language of contemporary global law and politics),[2] presents an almost irresistible target for corporate desire. And, as we shall shortly see, globalised human rights discourse forms an overarching discursive domain that corporate actors exploit with ever greater influence. Indeed, so advanced is the global corporate human rights agenda that the entire Universal Declaration of Human Rights paradigm, it has been argued, is being progressively supplanted by a paradigm of trade-related, market-friendly human rights.[3]

There seem to be at least two results of corporate influence on international human rights discourse of profound relevance to the concerns of this book. First, the most cherished goals of the international human rights movement are reinterpreted in ways that serve a globalised capitalist agenda. In the process, human rights become less able to protect vulnerable human beings and communities from the excesses of the very same agenda. The very meaning of human rights changes, and is rendered open, at a paradigmatic level, to a globalised neoliberal ideology profoundly implicated in the production of intense human suffering, particularly in the global South. This is, as will be seen, a genuine problem facing the future of human rights. Secondly, powerful economic actors have, in this process, somehow 'acquired new or fuller legal identities as rights-holders, in turn influencing the character of legal systems and legal process'.[4] Specifically, corporations have invoked, through the discursive colonisation of international human rights law, a form of corporate humanity.

In response to the dangers presented by these complex shifts, it will be argued in this book that the very concept of human rights for corporations is now in need of urgent interrogation. It will furthermore be argued that human rights require protection from this development, and that human rights need *redirecting* towards the embodied, vulnerable human being, precisely in order to challenge the development of a form of corporate legal humanity. However, it is worth noting that the concept of human embodied vulnerability is an idea rich with possibilities for the future theorisation of human rights, and for the future theorisation of the legal and political subject more generally. Many of these possibilities, however, lie beyond the remit of the present work, though they will be briefly indicated where appropriate and particularly in the conclusory reflections offered at the end of the book.

The argument offered in this work will need to follow many twists and turns. Starting with the context of globalisation, we will need to examine the pressure that international human rights discourse is currently under (Chapter 1), before looking more closely at corporate human rights as a legal matter (Chapter 2). In order to understand law's receptivity to corporate human rights, we will need to explore the phenomenon of legal disembodiment and its ideological role in the construction of the liberal legal person: both human and corporate (Chapters 3 and 4). We will also need to look at how disembodiment functions in international human rights law (Chapter 5). Once the main elements of a critical thesis are established, we will explore the centrality of human embodiment (Chapter 6) and the related idea of human embodied vulnerability – particularly the potential of embodied vulnerability to provide a different grounding for international human rights law and theory – one resistant to corporate humanity (Chapter 7). Our reflections will also necessarily take us into a reconsideration of the property right – so foundational to liberal legal theory and so fundamental to the ideological function of liberal law's relationship with capitalism – and we will finish the substantive argument of the book by reflecting on how embodied vulnerability might function in legal and judicial reasoning concerning human rights claims in that most significant of legal contexts (Chapter 8).

In short, it will be argued that human embodied vulnerability, understood as the foundation of the human rights universal and the foundation of the human rights legal subject, embraced as the value underlying the ethical heart of human rights discourse, yields both a theoretical foundation for international human rights law, and a value for judicial deployment possessing vigorous potential for the protection of human beings and communities in the face of corporate rights claims. Embodied vulnerability also provides a limit concept against which the corporation-driven logics of privatisation and commodification can be evaluated and challenged by courts. So rich, indeed, are the theoretical possibilities provided by embodied vulnerability that, in its light, even the concept of property itself is rendered open to reformulation on the basis of a carefully recalibrated understanding of the relationship between property and human rights.

Preliminary caveats

When a legal theorist sets out to write a book that embraces so many different realms of thought and theoretical concern, it is extremely daunting to think of all the likely points at which the interdisciplinary nature of the work might result in misunderstandings or the unintended invocation of much more complex and specialist debates underlying, for example, the choice of a term. While it is impossible to anticipate the many ways that this work will be read and misread, it seems important to underline a few key caveats.

First, this is not an argument that corporations should not have legal rights, nor is it an argument that human beings should be the sole recipients of legal rights protection. In fact, it seems vital, in the light of increasingly urgent concerns to protect animals, eco-systems, and a host of other putative rights-subjects, to generate a broad and all-embracing theory of legal subjectivity. However, this important aim is not the aim of the present work – though it will be the subject matter for a future book: *Law, Persons and Vulnerability: A New Theory of Legal Subjectivity*. The present work is focused on one very particular problem: the issue of corporate legal humanity and how it might be resisted in human rights law and theory, most especially within the corporation-imperilled and highly symbolic UDHR paradigm.

Secondly, while the argument will focus on the ideological role of disembodiment and embodiment in the genesis and theory of rights, it is important to note that neither the human body nor vulnerability is intended to be read as monolithic or purely 'natural' categories. While embodied human vulnerability will be presented as an ontic matter and emphasis placed upon the body's complex incarnate materiality in its context-mediated location in material and social space, this emphasis should not be understood to entail a denial of the role of social construction in the forming of bodily life. Both the body and vulnerability emerge from a convergence between human social construction and the biological and material templates and conditions of ontic life. Both the human body and vulnerability are dynamic, mutable and capable of a whole range of variant and even competing conceptualisations. In a sense, both are moving targets with a complex core. The argument of this book is not, therefore, that the human body or human vulnerability are fixed or monolithic givens. But it *is* the argument of this book that human materiality, the ontic dimension of existence, and the vulnerability emerging from it, should be understood as being conceptually and ethically foundational to a satisfying theory of international human rights.

Thirdly, a focus on vulnerability should not be read as an attempted valorisation of human suffering, despite the ethical urgency that human suffering brings to the task of this work. Embodied vulnerability can also be embraced and celebrated as a value intrinsic to multiple forms of human flourishing, as will be seen. Additionally, vulnerability is not a uniquely human condition, although there may be uniquely human forms of vulnerability. Ontic vulnerability seems to provide a theoretical value that unites human beings with other putative rights-holders: other living species, the environment, social institutions – even corporations. But vulnerability also reflects clusters of characteristics and nuances that enable us meaningfully to speak of relevant distinctions between bearers and putative bearers of rights. Minimally, and focally in the context of the present argument, human embodied vulnerability is, in central and decisive ways, of a different order and kind to any putative corporate vulnerability – as will become clear – particularly, it will be argued, for the purposes of human rights attribution.

Fourthly, it is not the argument of this book that the 'human' is a fixed category. The emergence of post-human discourse, the advent of genetic enhancements, cybernetics, and so on, challenge our ability to think about the already blurred boundaries of the human – even as an ontic matter. But, notwithstanding the deepening complexity of the notion of the human, this book focuses on the continuing urgency of protecting the billions of clearly recognisable, central-case, living human beings and communities who remain in a profoundly material and thoroughly incarnate vulnerability to exploitation, exclusion and immiseration. These themes, again, are particularly compelling in the context of contemporary globalisation – a reality that produces new forms and intensities of human vulnerability. Indeed, it may even be the case that precisely *because* of the emergence of the discourse of the gene, cybernetics, robo-culture etc, that those human beings who are not admitted, for economic or other reasons, to the privileged interior of an emergent post-human techno-culture will require new forms of legal protection and ever greater levels of ethical attentiveness.

And so we begin

It is now time to begin our exploration of the nature and sources of corporate legal humanity and its relationship with rights discourse, especially international human rights discourse. The urgency of challenging corporate humanity is underlined by the stark fact that if international human rights discourse is not rescued, somehow, from the plausibility structures and agendas of global corporate power, then entities as powerful, in some cases, as quasi-states, will effectively have become dominant international human rights 'insiders'. Human rights have long been ambivalent in their relationship with power, especially, the power of property and capital – but the commodified colonisation of international human rights discourse in the context of economic globalisation, at the height, arguably, of the global power of rights discourse itself, is a deeply troubling contemporary reality with urgent implications.

What we now face is the danger to human rights futures presented by the genesis of a corporation-friendly human rights legal sensibility. It is entirely possible that human beings, vulnerable and embodied, may find themselves almost irreversibly unprotected in the face of global corporate self-interest and the burgeoning political power of corporate humanity. Something has to change. This is but one modest theoretical contribution to a far wider and deeply urgent critical task.

1
Human Rights under Pressure?

The Universal Declaration of Human Rights paradigm under pressure

The matrix of globalisation

This book is primarily a response to deeply troubling contemporary shifts in international human rights discourse in favour of corporations[1] and to the related idea that the corporation is an appropriate beneficiary of human rights.[2] The very idea that international human rights discourse could be colonised by the interests of corporate entities, and the related idea that the corporation can be thought of as some kind of human rights 'victim'[3] are, to most non-lawyers, genuinely puzzling and counterintuitive. There are various complex factors that come together to explain the law's openness to corporate human rights discourse. Some of the most important of these factors will be explored in this book. But before we explore them, it is essential to grasp the seriousness of pressures facing international human rights law through the development of corporate human rights discourse. In order to do this, we need to locate corporate human rights discourse within the matrix of contemporary globalisation.

We live in an era of rapidly accelerating globalisation. Although globalisation and its meanings, implications and processes are the subject of fierce contemporary contestation, there is a sense in which globalisation is nothing new. Historically, processes of globalisation can be traced back to well-established transnational flows of people, goods and religious ideas, from at least the sixteenth century,[4] in a period of marked European expansion – and perhaps even earlier, to the thirteenth century emergence of the Mongol Empire.[5] However, the marked contemporary intensification of transnational interactions has led a range of commentators to see a qualitative departure from earlier forms of global interaction.[6] What seems to characterise the contemporary phase of globalisation (which arguably began with European colonial domination in the nineteenth century) is the sheer scale, speed, density and content of the transnational flows.

Overviews of the available studies on globalisation reveal it to be a multifaceted phenomenon, 'with economic, social, political, cultural, religious and legal dimensions intertwined in most complex ways'.[7] The term 'globalisation' captures, therefore, a wide and dizzying range of diverse and even contradictory processes, events and developments.[8]

The contemporary intensification and increased complexity of global transnational flows takes place, moreover, in the context of a widening global gap between rich and poor, a global population explosion, the looming threat of environmental disaster, the emergence of new anxieties about global security post-9/11, the privatisation of organised violence, fears about 'peak oil' and a range of apocalyptic misgivings about the future survival of the human race. Indeed, themes of escalating violence and deepening human vulnerability have been compellingly linked to the dynamics of globalisation.[9]

The range and pace of transnational interactions is reflected in a disorientating 'rush of products, ideas, persons and money [stimulated by] jet transportation, electronic telecommunication, massive decolonization and extensive computerization'.[10] Add to this the flows associated with techno-scientific progress (including bio-technologies and nanotechnology), popular culture and global commodity brands, and what emerges is a fairly comprehensive and familiar snapshot of some of the more immediately recognisable plausibility structures of the pivotal phenomenon of contemporary globalisation: the ascendency of transnational corporations (TNCs).[11] It is notable that while the complexities of contemporary globalisation have generated an industry of commentators and analysts and while reductive or unilateral accounts of globalisation will be inadequate to capture its nature, it seems broadly accepted, nonetheless, that *economic* globalisation is a significant (for many, the dominant) strand of its contemporary meaning. In fact, contemporary globalisation is widely recognised as being dominated by TNCs, which function in meaningful respects as the 'key agents of the new world economy'.[12]

It cannot be denied that the recent financial crisis has added an additional dimension of complexity to debates concerning the contemporary character and trajectory of globalisation. But there are no signs that global TNC dominance is on the wane. Indeed, recent moves in response to the crisis by the globalised economic institutions (the International Monetary Fund, the World Trade Organisation etc), themselves 'both a symptom of and a stimulus for globalisation',[13] suggests that there is no room for optimism concerning the future implications of the contemporary financial crisis for any genuine power shift in the world economic order. More than one commentator has noted that while leaders such as Merkel and Sarkozy have called for a re-invention of capitalism, redistribution in favour of capitalism's dominant institutions is intensified. There are reasons to suspect that the current crisis is not so much a crisis *of* neoliberalism but a crisis *within* neoliberalism concerning the best way to retain and protect some of its fundamental tenets, structures and institutions. Meanwhile, the cost of the crisis is being 'socialised' by a strategy in which the private risks of the owners of capital are underwritten by the state, the losses of corporations and banks are mitigated and the ordinary tax-payer is left holding future debts that in effect, simply pass the impact of the crisis to ordinary citizens.[14]

The globalised economic institutions widely regarded as the engines of the neoliberal world order (particularly the International Monetary Fund (IMF) and the World Bank) continue to remain linked to an ideologically informed institutional separation between politics and economics in the service of the agenda of global capitalism, in which the state continues to play a facilitating role. Gill has argued that the worldwide amendment of old constitutions and the formation of new ones under the influence of the IMF, the World Bank and other institutional agencies of global capitalism, amounts to the construction of a '*de facto* constitution for global capital', operative in a range of contexts: international, regional and national.[15] Pointing to the collapse of the Eastern bloc and the emergence of arguments about the 'end of history', Gill suggests that '[t]o a greater or lesser extent new forms of possessive individualism re-emerged worldwide and social institutions were re-defined to create an emergent market civilization – a monoculture of both social development and mind that is associated with a new political economy of disciplinary neoliberalism'.[16] Beck, however, suggests a more fractured reality in which the power of global business is engaged in a meta-power struggle with nation-states – a reality in the light of which 'globalisation needs to be decoded' in rather insidious terms – as 'a creeping, post-revolutionary, epochal transformation of the national and international state-dominated system governing the balance of power and the rules of power'.[17]

The emergence of a relatively hegemonic capitalist global political economy is, therefore, a principal feature of contemporary globalisation. And while this form of globalisation is not unopposed by countervailing conceptions,[18] nor untroubled by its own internal crisis to a contestable and as yet undetermined extent, it presents a profound and complex challenge to the future of human rights. The sheer reality of global corporate dominance has produced a situation in which human rights discourse struggles to retain critical distance from the human rights-colonising activities of formations of global capital. So profound is this problem that some scholars accuse human rights discourse of being, in effect, a Trojan horse for neoliberal capitalist values.[19] Evans and Ayer, for example, have argued, along similar lines, that the idea of universal human rights is currently forced to serve a hegemonic neoliberal approach to rights which has effectively 'co-opted' human rights 'in support of processes associated with capitalist globalisation'.[20]

Quite simply, it is essential not to underestimate the influence of TNCs in the current world order. Beck characterises contemporary globalisation as 'one of the most important changes there has been in the history of power'[21] – a complex set of shifts and struggles in which TNCs emerge as 'private sector *quasi-states*'[22] wielding unprecedented levels of power and influence. Despite all the theoretical complexity and variation in scholarly understandings of globalisation, the one thing that scholars of the global political economy are almost univocal on '...regardless of their disciplinary, analytic or ideological inclinations... [is the fact that] corporate global rule is already here'.[23]

Transnational corporations, quite simply, dominate the current world order. In 1996, of the world's 100 largest economies, 51 were corporations – outnumbering the 49 states included on the list.[24] The top 200 corporations generate 27.5 per cent of the world gross domestic product and 'their combined annual revenues are greater than those of the 182 states that contain 80 per cent of the world population'.[25] More than one third of the world's industrial output was produced by TNCs in as early as 1995, and although 'the organizational novelty of the TNCs may be questioned from a world system perspective, it seems undeniable that their prevalence in the world economy, and the degree and efficacy of centralized direction they manage to achieve, manage to distinguish them from older forms of international business enterprise'.[26] TNCs have increasingly shaped the global economy. They have exercised *de facto* political power over a wide range of international institutions, processes and discourses – and continue to – and that includes, troublingly, the semantically overstretched but ethically ascendant language of human rights.

TNCs and human rights discourse

Such is the decisive influence of TNCs on human rights discourse that Baxi has argued that the entire Universal Declaration of Human Rights (UDHR) paradigm stands imperilled by the development of a new paradigm of 'trade-related, market-friendly human rights (TRMFHR)'. In fact, he suggests, the UDHR paradigm is 'being steadily, but surely, *supplanted*' by the new paradigm and that it

> seeks to demote, even reverse, the notion that universal human rights are designed for the attainment of dignity and well-being of human beings and for enhancing the security and well-being of socially, economically and civilizationally vulnerable peoples and communities. The emergent paradigm insists upon the promotion and the protection of the collective human rights of global capital, in ways which 'justify' corporate well-being and dignity even when it entails continuing gross and flagrant violation of human rights of actually existing human beings and communities.[27]

And this process is not in its infancy. Baxi insists that human rights discourse has already been 'critically appropriated by global capital' – and that a comparative sociology of human rights 'leaves us with no other credible option' in terms of a conclusion.[28] This is a stark claim. It implies that the 'human rights of global capital'[29] pressurise the UDHR paradigm in a way that effectively threatens to displace it, perhaps even irrevocably.

It is important to contextualise this claim by briefly noting the key characteristics of the UDHR paradigm and some inherent weaknesses that make corporate encroachment on the paradigm all the more problematic. The international human rights regime is built around the UDHR, and its two related covenants, the International Covenant of Civil and Political Rights (ICCPR)[30] and the International Covenant of Economic, Social and Cultural Rights (ICESCR).[31] It comprises a system of standards and implementation procedures centred on the United Nations – in particular the Human Rights Council, supported by a small group of regional human rights regimes, key among which is the European Convention on Human Rights (which will be discussed in more depth in the next chapter). Fundamentally, the UDHR paradigm, which emerged in response to the Nazi holocaust,[32] produced the invocation of an 'international consensus on substantive norms with high moral voltage'[33] and a re-conceptualisation of national human rights violations which transposed them into matters of international concern. However, the rights regime spawned by this moral outrage emerged (perhaps predictably[34]) with a strong commitment to state sovereignty and concomitantly weak enforcement mechanisms. The much-vaunted commitment to the high-minded ideals of the human rights standards promulgated by the UN still, in fact, await the genesis of strong implementation and enforcement practices. The UDHR is, accordingly, 'a regime with extensive, coherent and widely accepted norms, but extremely limited international decision making powers – that is, a strong promotional regime'.[35]

The fact that the international human rights law regime is, in effect, predominantly a *promotional* regime makes the undermining of that regime by the appropriation of human rights discourse by global corporations all the more troubling. The regime is being subverted at its only real point of purchase: its ethical and rhetorical appeal. This ethical and rhetorical appeal has in any case a poor track record of preventing human rights abuses, as the global record of human rights violations reveals. When nation-state interests or the paramount imperative of national sovereignty seem to require the violation of human rights, then the apparent normative consensus around human rights tends to collapse,[36] and the language of human rights is exploited by the state in the service of its own interests. The inherent state-centrism of the regime means that it is ill-equipped to prevent human rights violations justified, for example, in the name of national interest or 'national security' objectives,[37] a tendency dramatically exacerbated post 9/11.[38] Furthermore, as the concepts of national interest and national security are colonised by the market-friendly agenda of the powerful global economic actors that dominate the current world order, it is likely that 'enhanced competition for markets and for production niches in the current global restructuring of capital accumulation [will] fragment the conceptions of national self-interest even further, and augment the political aggressiveness that defends them against competing states'.[39] State-centrism is a doubly problematic flaw in a context where the modern state 'is not only (asymmetrically) subject to, but also agent of, the forces and logic of global capitalism'.[40] Not only is national sovereignty robustly defended and linked to weak human rights enforcement mechanisms, but the traditional defence of state justifications for the limitation or violation of human rights based on the discourse of national security and national interest now operates in a setting where national interest is increasingly read in the light of the imperatives of the globalisation of the economy. This renders those human rights that collide with these imperatives even more profoundly vulnerable. The UDHR emerges from such an analysis as structurally compromised. When we speak of the corporate subversion of the UDHR paradigm we are therefore speaking of the exploitation of a regime already exhibiting key weaknesses in its design.

Given the stark reality of ongoing global human rights abuses,[41] the suggestion that the UDHR regime is being further undermined by interpretive distortions favouring TNCs gives much cause for alarm concerning the future of human rights. TNCs, in the globalised context, have enormous economic and political power. And as Santos points out, '[b]ecause of their private character, these economic actors can commit massive violations of human rights with total impunity in different parts of the world.... [and b]ecause such actors are at the core of the loss in economic national sovereignty, their actions, no matter how offensive to human rights, are unlikely to collide with consideration of national interest or security that might otherwise prompt the corrective or punitive intervention of the state'.[42] These are indeed troubling times for human rights proponents concerned to protect human beings and communities from these powerful economic actors.

The task for human rights proponents is daunting. Baxi suggests that in the context of contemporary globalisation human rights proponents can, at best, hope to mitigate the harshness of neoliberal globalisation, but from an essentially captive position 'within the general imperatives of [the] ideology'[43] – an observation that remains as yet undeflected by the recent emergence of a crisis internal to neoliberalism. And arguably, even if the current crisis in neoliberal ideology were to shake faith in neoliberalism to any significant degree, it remains unclear that this will result in a post-neoliberal global order,[44] or challenge the sense in which the very notion of the 'global' continues to carry, in Baxi's words, 'connotations of the commercialization of humanity'.[45]

Global capital wields enormous power. Beck suggestively notes, moreover, the complex nature of such power. One of the strategic advantages enjoyed by capital is the power to refuse investment – a power that transforms economic power into an elusive politics of 'side-effect' – a form of 'domination by nobody' – in which the political meta-power of global capital is increased by the sense in which '"Nobody" is doing politics... and they are doing so in a very effective and often deliberate way'.[46] This deliberate politics as side effect, however, does not imply that the power of global capital is a centrally coordinated campaign of domination. In fact, it could be argued that matters are made more complex by the very *heterogeneity* of actors involved in the process of 'domination by nobody'. As Beck points out, 'the political meta-power "of capital" results from the collective impact of very heterogeneous actors, markets, capital flows, supranational organisations and so forth, each of which understands itself to be making decisions in its own interest on the basis of economic considerations'.[47] The ideological convergence inspiring such a heterogeneous collection of actors nonetheless seems to produce a high degree of homogenisation at the level of choice – particularly in relation to the policy choices of governments.[48]

In seeking to understand the distortion of the UDHR paradigm there are two particularly salient contexts that need to be considered. Both relate to the broad reconfiguration of the relationship between state and capital: 'the end of the nation-state and the reproduction of "soft"/failed' states. Baxi suggests that the end of the nation-state thematic is intrinsically linked to the emergence of contemporary human rights in the form of the host of self-determination claims made at the end of the colonial era that marked the end of the Westphalian state form and led to the emergence of a multiplicity of new states. He notes that what the gurus of globalisation mean by the end of the nation-state is that 'the state becomes a point, perhaps, not even a nodal one, in the network of intensified international economic relations in a "borderless world"'[49] – a borderless world 'for global capital' – but not for violated communities and human beings.

Moreover, globalisation has meant a transformation in the characterisation of the 'soft state'. The 'soft' state was previously characterised as a state unable to fulfil its disciplinary role in relation to welfare, the control of corrupt political practices, and its lack of a civic culture. This has, however, under the auspices of the new world order, been re-conceptualised as a state that fails to provide adequate spaces for capital. The 'progressive' state is a state that provides a stable, governance-centred location for global capital. Beck conceptualises this in terms of the neoliberalisation of the state – the 'economic self-transformation of politics in the sense of self-colonisation'.[50] The state itself legitimates the power of capital. Indeed, so extensive is this reconstruction of the role of the state that Gill has discerned the emergence of what he calls a 'new constitutionalism'. His central argument is that deepening global inequalities have coincided with a *redefinition of the political on a global scale*. This development resulted from the softening of traditional political constraints and the production of frameworks specifically designed to ensure a long-term commitment to the neoliberal path of development. Moreover, Gill identifies this new form of constitutionalism as the 'political-juridical counterpart to "disciplinary neoliberalism"', defined as 'a discourse of political economy that promotes the power of capital through the extension and deepening of market values and disciplines in social life, under a regime of free enterprise'.[51] A central objective of this new constitutionalism is precisely to set the future in capitalist terms by preventing future governments from undoing commitments to the neoliberal pattern of accumulation. The new constitutionalism is thus the '*political/juridical* form specific to neoliberal processes of accumulation and to market civilization'.[52] Although it is, as yet, impossible to predict where the current crisis within neoliberal ideology will lead, it is difficult to shake the conviction that TNCs will continue to exert a decisive influence on the world order or that states will, by and large, continue to serve the imperatives of the global economic institutions. Indeed, the recent dispensing of billions of dollars by the G20 to the IMF raises the spectre of the strengthening influence of such institutions as governments and transnational economic actors scramble to protect the fundamental commitments of the existing world order.[53]

The form of constitutionalism identified by Gill echoes Baxi's analysis of the emergence of a new paradigm of human rights. The UDHR paradigm, as we have noted, assigned to states the principal responsibility for upholding human rights standards and of meeting the basic needs of human beings. But the new trade-related market-friendly paradigm calls upon the state (as a member of the new world order) to serve capital by pursuing '*de-regulation, de-nationalization and disinvestment*' – thus significantly reducing the state's redistributive role. While the state may become more interventionist to control market excesses in response to the financial crisis, there is no cause to anticipate the resurrection of the re-distributive state. In fact, the evidence thus far seems to reflect intervention to mitigate the worst effects of the crisis on financial institutions and corporations, while ordinary citizens struggle in a situation of spiralling unemployment and record levels of personal debt. For Baxi, the 'end of the nation-state' is, in fact, really only the end of the '*re-distributive state*', marking 'in some important ways ... the end of the processes and regimes of *human rights-oriented, redistributionist governance practices* in ways that convert the mandate of "progressive realization" of social, economic, and cultural rights of the people into an ongoing cruel hoax'.[54]

The progressive state remains, in short, a good host state for global capital.[55] And the human cost of that is likely to remain high. The growing inequality linked to the maximisation of economic growth in favour of TNCs results in the reduction in real income for the bottom 40–60 per cent of families[56] and the denial of economic and social rights to those most in need of them. This can be directly related to the ideological primacy given to a particular neoliberal reading of civil and political rights as being 'the freedom of individual action, non-interference in the private sphere of economics, the right to own and dispose of property, and the important principle of laissez-faire'.[57] The recent gathering of G20 handed an unprecedented amount of financial power to the IMF, deeply implicated in the invention and imposition of the Washington Consensus and the structural adjustment programmes that have ravaged many developing countries, to lend to cash-strapped nations on the basis, presumably, of further conditionality packages.[58] This does not bode well for the poor inhabitants of cash-strapped nations. Beck notes that the few countries in the global South that have attempted to reject neoliberal strictures have been effectively forced to submit under pressure from the World Bank and Western funding bodies,[59] and Richardson has argued that the World Bank and the IMF have most pressurised those marginalised societies where poverty is most rife – insisting on structural adjustments such as deregulation, privatisation and the removal of protective policies.[60] Such developments raise a genuine question concerning the degree to which UN organisations such as the IMF, World Bank, World Trade Organisation (WTO) and so on have simply acted as 'midwives' to the neoliberal order of power.[61] It is troubling to think that the WTO rules were extensively influenced by corporations and have been described as a formalisation and strengthening of global corporate power.[62] The ongoing influence of TNCs and their interests in the operation of the world economic system, in short, continues to be a subject of deep concern to anyone concerned for the poorer inhabitants of the earth. Indeed, it is arguable that just as the state and politics have been redefined in the context of neoliberal constitutionalism, human rights themselves have been re-interpreted as constructs dependent for their realisation upon an order of rights for corporations.

Baxi's argument is that human rights now exist within a trade-related market-friendly paradigm (a claim which must necessarily be located within the context of the complex materiality of contemporary globalisation).[63] He substantiates his claim by a careful argument that includes a range of examples concerning the interpretive distortion of human rights. He notes, for example, that the war against hunger, in the 1998 Rome Declaration on the Right to Food, becomes implemented as an integrated system of food security dominated by a small group of multinational food corporations; the struggle against homelessness, in the 1998 UN Social Summit, becomes a set of 'mandates authorizing a whole range of human rights violative practices of the construction industries and urban developers'; sustainable development becomes the launch pad for massive projects primarily benefiting the imperatives of foreign investment and the 'promotion and protection of corporate governance "greenwashing practices"'; while the United Nations Development Programme (UNDP) inspired Global Sustainable Development Facility is supported by money from 'some of the most egregious multinational enterprise corporate human rights offenders'.[64] Furthermore, he argues, TNCs infiltrate human rights discourse by seeking, increasingly, to have their rights instantiated in treaty regimes, such as the WTO agreement, which we have already noted, and the agreement on trade-related intellectual property rights (TRIPS). The World Copyright Treaty 1996, for example, protects corporate ownership of electronic and genetic databases (including the database infrastructure supporting the human genome project). In fact, as Evans and Ayers note, 'property and investment rights are protected in "exquisite detail" under [the North American Free Trade Agreement (NAFTA), the General Agreement on Tariffs and Trade (GATT)] and more recently the WTO – with 20,000 pages of GATT/WTO regulations and 1,400 articles within NAFTA specifying exact rules to protect the rights of capitalist corporations'.[65] The rights of corporations, in other words, are extensively protected, to the point where the 'the promotion and protection of some of the most cherished contemporary human rights becomes possible only when the order of rights for global capital stands fully recognized'.[66]

Ironically, the trade-related market-friendly paradigm means that human rights themselves stand in danger of being recast as obstacles to be overcome in the name of guaranteeing their own future (particularly, for example, in the context of the Draft OECD-sponsored Multilateral Agreement on Investment).[67] Baxi argues that the new order of international rights for global capital has 'profound[ly] destructive impacts on the human rights of human beings everywhere'.[68] These harms include the way in which corporations have: corrupted national regimes aimed at social and human development; engaged national authorities in the cooption, corruption, or coercion of human rights communities whose activities subvert the imperatives of globalisation; influenced law, medicine, media, science and education; and created 'human, bio, eco and genetic hazards...without undue obligation for reparation, restitution and rehabilitation'.[69] A wide range of commentators has, of course, routinely decried such corporate harms. Jochnick, for example, has argued that the impact of TNCs on human rights 'ranges from a direct role in violations, such as abuses of employees or the environment, to indirect support of governments guilty of widespread repression'. He notes, perhaps unsurprisingly, that the conduct of global corporations can also 'have a dramatic impact on poverty, either by directly undermining human welfare (for example, limiting a community's access to land or food) or influencing relevant government policies and laws (eg, relating to agriculture, technology, employment and subsidies)'.[70] Kinley and Joseph note that, while there is genuine scope for corporations to have a positive impact, corporate activity has had a genuinely detrimental impact on human rights protection. The most egregious abuses have occurred in the developing world, abuses including complicity in the brutality of the police and military in host states, the use of forced and child labour, the suppression of human rights to free association and expression, violations of rights to cultural and religious practice, infringements of property rights (including the infringement of intellectual property rights), and environmental violations. Turning their attention to the developed world, Kinley and Joseph point out that abuses also occur in this context, most typically concerning the violation of environmental rights, privacy rights, consumer rights to health and information and violation of rights to freedom of association.[71]

Frustratingly, moreover, when contemporary social movements attempt to make corporate power accountable to human rights standards, they risk the conversion of 'human rights movements into [human rights] markets',[72] thereby simply further extending the reach of the corporation-driven paradigm. Baxi notes the tendency, for example, for human rights movements to organise themselves in market-led terms, with NGOs themselves operating as economic actors in competition for economic resources, producing in the process and in combination with other actors such as funding bodies something approaching a 'human rights market rationality'.[73] While NGOs also maintain some degree of autonomy from markets, it is clear that the market-led discourse has more than superficial levels of purchase on human rights movements, producing in the process ethically fraught practices such as the commodification of human suffering.[74]

The corporate invocation of human rights languages is deeply troubling. Corporations are quite capable of visiting damage upon human populations without needing any additional empowerment from the concept of corporate human rights. There are great dangers in legitimating corporate interests by using the language of human rights. Indeed, it seems likely that such legitimation can make it more difficult for individuals to hold corporations to account and render the human rights of human beings less potent as a form of protection for them. One example of this is the impact of the 'corporate human rights' of commercial free speech, privacy and honour as expressed in corporate Strategic Law Suits Against Public Participation (SLAPPS). SLAPPS have been described by Pring and Canan as a form of law suit aimed at 'effectively denying the equality of citizenship so fundamental to informed decision making... [a strategy that amounts to] an ideologic argument for economic interests as the superior voice in determining public policy'.[75] In effect, SLAPPS silence the rights of expression of human beings in favour of corporate interests. This argument brings us back to our earlier considerations of the emergence of a new constitutionalism. The use of legal, constitutional and constitution-like limitations to prevent governments or citizens from intervening in the smooth operation and prioritisation of the market has been, at least until lately, an intensifying trend – the idea being to insulate 'key aspects of the economy from the influence of politicians or the mass of citizens by imposing, internally and externally, "binding constraints" on the conduct of fiscal, monetary, trade, and investment policies'.[76] While much talk of the end of *laissez-faire* may give the impression that such programmatic global institutional privileging of the public policy interests of powerful economic actors will be curtailed, the underlying commitments and power bases seem unlikely to be significantly reconfigured in the current context. At the international level, the WTO and the IMF seem set to remain as influential as ever, and arguably as neoliberal as ever in their fundamental commitments. Indeed, George argues that it looks as if the international system, 'the G20 and the EU in particular, are absolutely determined to *save* neoliberalism at all costs'.[77]

A brief assessment of corporate accountability to human rights standards

Arguably, the mutation in the UDHR paradigm identified by Baxi is all the more troubling because the phenomenon has been accompanied by a deficit of corporate human rights accountability. In general terms, TNCs have been remarkably successful at evading UN attempts to make them accountable to human rights standards – though the recent adoption of the Norms on the Responsibilities of Transnational Corporations and Other Business Enterprises with Regard to Human Rights[78] by the Sub-Commission on the Protection and Promotion of Human Rights is an important, though not entirely convincing, development.

TNCs have successfully resisted UN-based efforts, since the 1970s, to hold them accountable to human rights standards. For example, the UN attempt to produce a universal Code of Conduct for Transnationals was a notable and much lamented failure.[79] Corporations are also exempted from the jurisdiction of the International Criminal Court.[80] The UN Norms, however, promise to mark a distinctive break with the ideology of voluntarism that has, until now, dogged attempts to apply human rights standards to global corporations.[81] But while the Norms announce a zero-tolerance approach to the most blatant human rights abuses, and for the first time, attempt to impose the disciplinary regimes of international human rights law upon business enterprises, the likely future success of the Norms should not be overestimated. First, early signs seem to suggest that the Norms will be contested by corporations, both directly and indirectly.[82] Kinley and Chambers have pointed out that when the Norms came before the UN Commission on Human Rights, at its 60th Session in 2004, 'they encountered a frosty reception from member states already primed with the concerns of the corporate sector'.[83] The Norms were put on hold at that stage by the Commission, which later (in 2005) recommended that the UN Secretary-General appoint a Special Representative to review the whole question of corporations and human rights. The Special Representative published an Interim Report in February 2006, which concluded that the Norms should be abandoned[84] – which is not an encouraging outcome for those who hope that the Norms will prove a positive step in the development of international corporate human rights accountability.

Secondly, we should not overlook the implications of the fact that such corporate contestation of the Norms will take place within the inescapable overarching global economic context in which the UDHR paradigm is in the process of being supplanted by a paradigm that already systemically advantages corporations. It is arguable that even if the Norms (or another non-voluntaristic regime for the human rights accountability of corporations) were to be fully established, such a regime would struggle to reverse the existing interpretive distortion of human rights meanings and might even be undermined by a related (and possibly parasitic) mutation in the meaning of human rights accountability. Thirdly, the complex task of holding corporate entities accountable to the UN Norms will be further complicated by what Baxi has termed the 'dense intertexuality' of the Norms.[85] The text of the Norms refers to at least 56 pre-existing instruments, producing, because of the inherently open-textured nature of human rights norms, a profound indeterminacy. This raises the spectre of future difficulties concerning the intelligibility, authoritativeness and future enforceability of the Norms.

The Norms, beset as they are with these and other problems,[86] are nonetheless a rare instance of a sustained attempt to move beyond corporate voluntarism in relation to the application of international human rights standards to the operations and activities of TNCs. However, it should be remembered that TNC human rights accountability is further limited by the traditional state-centric focus of international human rights law – a focus which tends to mean that it is ill-equipped in structural and ideological terms to hold TNCs accountable for human rights abuses. Moreover, 'the continuation of a state-centric logic in the field of human rights will represent a growing impediment to an efficient and morally decent human rights policy'.[87] This problem becomes even more acute in a situation where states are reconstituted as agents of the logic of global capitalism,[88] as discussed above. Evans and Ayer argue that the state is now effectively an administrative unit for managing the global economy; while Panitch suggests that states should be understood as 'the authors of a regime that defines and guarantees, through international treaties and constitutional effect, the global and domestic rights of capital'.[89]

The state-centric focus of the traditional paradigm, however, does not mean that a basis for corporate human rights accountability is entirely absent. Within the traditional paradigm the state has a duty not only to respect, but also to protect and ensure the enjoyment of human rights within the state's national jurisdiction. This includes a responsibility to control private entities within the state's borders – an interpretation of international human rights law obligations now endorsed by international human rights jurisprudence.[90] Such a duty is, for example, explicitly enumerated by Article 2(e) of the Convention on the Elimination of all Forms of Discrimination against Women (CEDAW), and was, in any case, arguably implicit in the preamble to the

UDHR (which states that 'every organ of society' is bound to abide by its provisions), in Articles 28 and 30 of the UDHR,[91] and in the provisions of the two International Covenants.[92] In addition, as Baxi has recently argued, '[m]any ... United Nations summit declarations and programmes of action and environmental treaties and arrangements are open to a reading that cast certain human rights responsibilities upon global corporations'.[93] However, as yet (with the exception of the UN Norms) it is fair to say that there is little sign of any direct and binding international human rights law addressing the human rights responsibilities of corporations. One possible reason for this – to be discussed later in this book – is the underlying ideological orientation of liberal law and the effect of its genealogical links to the UDHR paradigm.

Some direct duties are, however, imposed on non-governmental bodies in the relatively constricted field of universal crimes. Customary international law, for example, prohibits non-governmental bodies from committing universal crimes under international law – a reality consistent with the fact that the Nuremberg International War Crimes Tribunal held two leading German industrialists accountable for their role in crimes against humanity. However, the extent of the liability of non-governmental bodies under customary international law remains deeply uncertain, arguably limiting its effectiveness as a source of accountability.[94] In this context, we should note, for the second time, the absence of TNC liability to the jurisdiction of the International Criminal Court. Moreover, in respect of the UN Norms on the Responsibilities of Transnational Corporations, Joseph argues that instead of being enforced 'in toto' the Norms will be confined in any case, in terms of any future international enforceability, to '...the small category of universal crimes ... [because] [i]t is difficult to imagine the creation of an international tribunal with the capacity to deal with all potential human rights abuses by TNCs, given the range of duties outlined in the Norms and the vast number of TNCs in the world'.[95]

As it stands, then, when the various factors noted here are taken into account, it seems that TNCs can continue to exploit international human rights norms in their own favour, while still largely evading attempts to hold them liable within an international human rights law framework which is, at present, structurally and ideologically ill-suited to the task.

The UN Global Compact

Nor is this depressing picture alleviated by the discourse of corporate social responsibility (CSR), of which the UN Global Compact is perhaps the foremost contemporary international expression. The Global Compact was established from its inception as an initiative 'intended to increase and to diffuse the benefits of global economic development through *voluntary* corporate policies and actions'.[96] It was introduced by Kofi Annan, the then Secretary General of the UN, at the 1999 Davos World Economic Forum.

The Compact, initially nine principles, now enlists corporate adherence to ten principles concerning human rights, labour rights, environmental responsibility, and finally, the latest addition, anti-corruption. Williams notes that while there has been a generally enthusiastic response to the compact from the business sector,[97] the US is a notable exception.[98] This US exceptionalism (by no means atypical in the international human rights field) is suggestive of the problematic nature of the Compact's voluntarism and the concomitant absence of an adequate accountability structure. Indeed, on this latter ground alone, the Global Compact has attracted trenchant criticism, but there are also other telling criticisms. For a start, not everyone is prepared to accept that globalisation in its current form can ever bring genuine development to the poor, or genuine human rights progress. In fact, it can be (and has been) argued that official UN support for the ideology of corporate-driven globalisation as a way of delivering human rights outcomes is a sell-out: that it undermines the work of those actors who argue that a relatively unregulated market is incompatible with environmental sustainability and social justice, and provides nothing more than a convenient 'bluewash' for corporations who simultaneously seek to improve their corporate image without significantly changing their behaviour.[99] The defence sometimes offered to this criticism – that the Compact is not intended to be a code, but is designed to '...serve as a (frame) of reference to stimulate best practices and to bring about convergence around universally shared values'[100] – misses the point. Code or non-code – in either case – the Compact provides a public forum for corporate self-presentation concerning commitment to certain principles, including the importance of human rights, without delivering an accountability mechanism capable of testing and ensuring corporate compliance with those same principles. The Compact therefore cannot guarantee integrity. No wonder then that Baxi, among others, laments the raising of resources from global corporations, including some of the worst violators of human rights, and in particular isolates the Global Compact as rendering 'legitimate' a partnership between the UN and some 'offending multinationals'.[101] Unsurprisingly, perhaps, and almost certainly correctly, Monshipouri, Welch and Kennedy conclude that TNCs will simply 'not address specific human rights violations if assigned only to a voluntary set of principles set up in the UN Global Compact'.[102]

In summary

The overall picture of the relationship between corporations and human rights at the global level gives much cause for anxiety concerning the future of human rights. At present, the state-centrist UDHR paradigm stands imperilled by corporate global dominance to the extent that human rights must now be read as trade-related and market-friendly constructs to a troubling degree. This interpretive mutation accompanies a situation in which

TNCs have shown scant concern for human rights, particularly in the global South.[103] The developments that imperil the UDHR paradigm are inextricably linked with contemporary globalisation and cannot adequately be understood without reference to its complex materiality. The role of the state in the prioritisation of corporate interests is notable, and in any case the state-centric framework of international human rights law remains ill-equipped to hold powerful private entities to account, particularly where there is a lack of political will among states to do so.

It will be argued later in this book that some aspects of the contemporary crisis in human rights reflect complex links between the suppositions of the UDHR paradigm and the structural and ideological closures of liberal law – law which, it will be argued, inherently favours the corporate form. Worryingly, the distorting effects of the imperatives of economic globalisation are increasingly coupled with the rights-threatening and progressively more coercive state in the post-9/11 world order in the name of national security and national interests. In the light of such threats, whether or not human rights can survive as constructs genuinely capable of protecting vulnerable human beings and communities is, as yet, by no means clear.[104]

This book is written in full awareness of the discursive vulnerability of human rights, and the vulnerability of human beings in the contemporary world order. In the light of the developments traced in this chapter it is especially important to subject the protection of corporations by human rights discourse, norms, laws and other protective instruments to renewed and sustained critical scrutiny, and to find a theorisation of human rights that protects their humanitarian critical core from dilution in the interests of powerful economic actors. This book is dedicated to the pursuit of that goal.

2
Corporate Human Rights?

In the last chapter the dangers of corporate human rights distortion in the context of globalisation, and the incipient danger of such developments for the protection of human beings were examined – and it was concluded that it is vital to interrogate the very notion of corporate human rights. In this chapter, accordingly, the beginning of that task will take the form of an examination of some of the arguments in favour of conceptualising corporations as the putative victims of human rights violations, and, importantly, a critical reflection on the fact that corporations are explicitly included within the protective mantle of the European Convention on Human Rights and Fundamental Freedoms.

In the course of his argument, Baxi notes that proponents of corporate human rights might maintain that any attempt to deny human rights to corporations would stand 'exposed to an indictment of enormously inaccurate misreading of human rights norms and standards'.[1] He suggests that this assertion would be based largely on the importance of associational rights (to be discussed below in the section addressing Addo's arguments) in combination with the protection offered to the right to property within the international framework (which will be addressed at points in the argument here but most specifically in Chapter 8). Furthermore, proponents of corporate human rights protection might argue that human rights are stated to belong not just to human beings, but to 'persons'; and, in some contexts, this would clearly include 'legal persons'.

Liberal pragmatism and the corporate beneficiaries of the ECHR

The inclusion of 'legal persons' as the beneficiaries of human rights is most notably true of the European Convention on Human Rights and Fundamental Freedoms (ECHR): Article 1 of Protocol 1 explicitly grants the right to peaceful enjoyment of possessions to legal as well as natural persons. Moreover, in an important departure from the individualist construction of civil and political rights in the UDHR framework, the ECHR recognises both collective and individual aspects of such rights.[2] Thus, while within the UDHR framework the rights of the individual predominate ('All the rights in the Universal Declaration and the Covenants, with the exception of self-determination of peoples, are rights of individuals, not corporate entities'[3]), in the ECHR framework the notion of corporations as the *beneficiaries* of human rights protection finds explicit support, both textually and judicially (as we shall see below). This makes the ECHR of particular significance in any reflection on the notion of corporate human rights as a normatively defensible and desirable legal development.

The ECHR is also a particularly strategic target because of its internationally respected status. The European Convention system is widely thought to be the most juridically mature of the supranational human rights regimes and there is a widespread perception that the ECHR is the 'most developed and successful international human rights instrument'.[4] Moreover, the pervasive conviction that the European Court of Human Rights (ECtHR) is 'the only institution of [its] kind and ... an inspiration in other continents',[5] gives the ECHR, and the jurisprudence generated by the court, particular importance in the battle for human rights meanings. Indeed, so influential is the ECtHR that it has been described by one scholar as a 'sort of world court of human rights'.[6] (In this context, for example, it should be noted that the International Covenant on Civil and Political Rights and the American Convention of Human Rights Systems are also facing increasing corporate use of their respective civil and political human rights[7] and, moreover, that the reasoning and interpretive methodologies of the ECtHR have been increasingly adopted by the Inter-American Court of Human Rights.[8]) The ECHR is highly likely, therefore, to be influential on the development of international human rights law in relation to corporate human rights protection. It seems vital, in the light of this, to note that TNCs (the focus of critique in international human rights discourse) are *not* the paradigmatic case of corporate entity heard at the Strasbourg court. They are, in fact, 'rare visitors' to the ECtHR.[9] This fact alone should call the appropriateness of contemporary ECHR jurisprudence as an appropriate guide to the development of international human rights law in response to global corporate dominance into sharp question: TNCs present threats and accountability problems that smaller or sole-proprietor companies simply do not. It could therefore be a mistake to allow ECHR jurisprudence to shape and dictate international legal development of human rights protection in respect of TNCs – certainly without accounting for the difference between the smaller companies seeking ECHR protection and the global corporate giants currently dominating the world order and distorting the UDHR paradigm.

Emberland has relatively recently concluded the first major study of the protection of companies under the ECHR.[10] His work is a rare and sustained study of corporations as the *beneficiaries* of human rights, singling out the

ECHR as unique among international human rights documents because '... it offers wide-ranging protection for business entities such as companies in addition to not-for-profit organisations and natural persons'.[11] Arguably, what makes the ECHR unique in this respect is the fact that companies were always intrinsically favoured by the framers of the Convention. Indeed, the preamble of the Statute of the Council of Europe, the body from which the Convention emerged, has as one of its stated aims the achievement of 'a greater unity between its Members for the purpose of ... facilitating their economic ... progress'.[12] It is not without significance that the ECHR is the progeny of the same heritage that generated the treaties that founded the European Economic Community (and its successors). Emberland points out that this fact and the associated 'arguments relating to the European Liberal project [mean that] company claims should theoretically expect a favourable response from the [European Court of Human Rights] since such claims are part and parcel of the order sought to be realised by the Convention'.[13] The corporation-friendly construction of the ECHR reflects the fact that the text of the ECHR is intimately informed by the 'core values of a capitalist system [and]... the value system of the liberal state, in which the company as protagonist of private enterprise has a natural place'.[14] So intimate is the relationship between liberal capitalism and the ECHR that Emberland insists that '[i]t would be meaningless to disconnect the Convention's democratic model from [the] core values of a capitalist system'.[15] All this makes the ECHR a particularly constructive subject of critical reflection when considering corporations as human rights beneficiaries and examining the underlying commitments assumed to render such a position normatively sustainable.

It should be noted that Emberland is *not* himself concerned with mounting a normative defence of corporate human rights. He is primarily interested in analysing and explaining the doctrinal response thus far developed by the European Court of Human Rights (ECtHR) to claims for protection by companies/corporations (he uses the terms interchangeably[16]) under the ECHR – and by so doing, revealing the distinctive structure of the ECHR – a distinctiveness that, again, renders the fittingness of the ECHR as a template for the future development of international corporate human rights law a subject of particular complexity. Emberland's methodology is to scrutinise the ECtHR's response to corporate litigation on matters within its competence by analysing the structures within which the Court is situated, in particular the legal framework of the ECHR, and the underlying values of the treaty. His examination is therefore a useful insight into the ideological orientation of ECHR as a whole. Crucially, the underlying liberal values of the treaty itself emerge as pivotal to understanding the Court's response to corporate claims for protection under the Convention.

We should also pause to note that the underlying liberal capitalist paradigm of the ECHR has a degree of resonance or complex continuity with the neoliberal paradigm currently driving contemporary globalisation. Although it is true to say that traditional European liberalism cannot be said to be entirely neoliberal in that European liberalism tends to embrace a social and regulatory dimension, it should not be forgotten that the ECtHR undertakes its interpretive task in the context of the current global political economy and its plausibility structures. On the one hand, it is impossible for the court to be immune to the influences already identified within the marketised *zeitgeist* of our age in relation to human rights interpretations. On the other hand, although the ECHR has no formal authority beyond the liberal European public order it shapes, there is substantial and growing judicial use of the Convention in a range of jurisdictions far beyond the boundaries of Europe[17] – a manifestation of what Slaughter has suggested is a form of legal globalisation which is both a 'cause and consequence of economic globalisation'.[18] While some longstanding continuities between liberalism, law and corporate power will emerge in more detail in the following chapters, it is important, at this stage, to note the suggestive linkage between liberal values, capitalism, economic progress and contemporary globalisation as the matrix within which corporate human rights claims and strategies are currently emerging. The significance of liberalism and its relationship with human rights law will emerge more fully in argument yet to come (as will the significance of a critique of certain key traditional liberal legal suppositions to a defence and ethical reinvigoration of human rights law and discourse).

In the ECHR system, corporate claims thus far make up a relatively small percentage of the case law overall – a mere 3.8 per cent over the five-year period from 1998–2003, for example.[19] It should also be noted that, to date, companies have tended to focus their claims within a relatively narrow band of human rights provisions (although some of them are rights traditionally assumed to belong to individual human beings, as we shall shortly see). Despite the small number of claims and the relatively narrow range of human rights invoked, it is nonetheless important to interrogate the whole notion of corporate human rights as a normative matter. The relatively small number of claims does not undermine the significance of the fact, that, in conceptual terms, an established and influential human rights court is actively defending companies as human rights beneficiaries. Nor is the importance of interrogating the notion of corporate human rights deflected by the fact that text of the ECHR, certainly in Article 1 of Protocol 1, explicitly grants the right to peaceful enjoyment of possessions to 'legal' as well as natural persons. The mere fact that a legal text instantiates a right grants neither the existence, nor the formulation of the right, immunity from normative critique. On the contrary, such normative critique of corporate human rights, and the human rights texts and jurisprudence that support them, is an increasingly urgent matter.

If the ECHR, as a highly influential human rights structure, is especially protective of corporate entities, it seems essential in the light of Baxi's thesis, to interrogate this, and the degree to which such protection of the corporate form is *normatively* justified within the reasoning of the ECtHR. In fact, it will be argued that far from revealing a normative justification for corporate human rights protection, Emberland's analysis demonstrates that the Court's reasoning is profoundly pragmatic and teleological – and decisively shaped by what the Court perceives to be the object and purpose of the ECHR. The Court, in making its determinations, draws on the text of the treaty itself, its drafting history, and, crucially, the liberal value system underlying the text and 'other aspects of the nature of human rights protection that find their expression in the treaty or follow by implication from it'.[20] The judicial interpretation of the ECHR thus relies to a decisive extent upon the ideological underpinnings of the Convention, revealed particularly in its preamble, which suggest the pivotal influence of a constellation of commitments at the core of European liberalism in which 'companies concerns' can be seen by the court as 'largely compatible with the treaty's ideology'.[21]

It is precisely in the light of this liberal capitalist structural context that Emberland attempts to rationalise the Court's reasoning in response to corporate litigation. He explores three issues regarded as doctrinally unresolved or debatable by the Court. The first is whether corporate shareholders can claim 'victim' status (pursuant to Article 34 of the ECHR) for matters that in formal terms have befallen the companies in which they hold shares. This is answered, in principle, in the negative unless it is impossible for the company itself to apply for relief or the company is merely a 'vehicle' for the individual shareholders' business activities.[22] The second issue, close to the heart of this book, is whether corporate entities can successfully invoke rights provisions thought to apply only to individual human beings. This is answered, in principle, in positive terms (thus far) in relation to select aspects of Articles 8(1), 10(1) and 41 of the ECHR.[23] The third issue is whether, once protected by rights-provisions, for-profit entities' interests should be subject to a lower standard of judicial scrutiny concerning governmental interference than the standard applied to scrutiny of interferences with the rights of individuals outside the for-profit setting.[24] Emberland notes that the Court's justification for applying a less intense review standard is based on a 'characteristically brief' justification and that '[i]n fact, the Court's introduction of low-intensity protection standards in the business context is almost devoid of explanation'.[25]

Perhaps most revealingly in relation to interrogating the court's normative justification of corporate human rights protection, Emberland finds himself forced to explore 'how the Court's reasoning might be made structurally coherent, since the judgments and decisions themselves intimate only vaguely their underlying rationale'.[26] Generally, the Court's motivations remain veiled beneath 'brief and enigmatically phrased reasoning'.[27] What Emberland's study reveals is the profound sense in which the reasoning of the ECtHR emerges as brief and essentially pragmatic. The Court simply does not engage in a fully explicated, normative assessment of whether or not companies are appropriate beneficiaries of human rights protection. Nor, interestingly, as Dignam and Allen point out, has the court engaged 'in a technical legal sense with the question of whether the artificiality of the corporation imposes limitations on its ability to be the victim of a rights violation'.[28] The issue seems a 'non-issue' – decided almost by ideological *fait accompli*. Emberland points out that 'under the Convention the notion of companies enjoying rights protection is not disputed in principle: The Court does not *per se* regard corporate litigation with suspicion'.[29] Emberland defends the *coherence* of the Court's approach given the underlying liberal capitalist teleology of the Convention extremely well. However, the pragmatism of the Court's approach is deeply unsatisfying from a critical perspective – even more so once this pragmatism is juxtaposed to the human rights imperilling international paradigm shift currently underway. Moreover, no amount of doctrinal coherence can, by itself, answer the underlying normative question.

It is interesting, and perhaps suggestive, to pause to reflect on the fact that the essentially pragmatic response of the ECtHR carries echoes familiar to those critical of the legal origins of corporate personhood. The original attribution of legal personhood to the corporate form was marked by a profound lack of judicial contestation. In fact, Finnis evocatively describes the original judicial attribution of personality to corporations as a *ukase*.[30] This is because, faced with the question of 'whether the 14th Amendment's provision forbidding any state from denying the equal protection of its laws to all persons within its jurisdiction applied to corporations', the US Supreme Court, in *Santa Clara County v Southern Pacific Railroad Co*[31] prefaced its judgment with the perhaps startling statement that '[t]he court does not wish to hear argument on the question .... We are all of the opinion that it does'. But, as

> Justices Black and Douglas observed in 1949, 'there was no history, logic, or reason given to support that view. Nor was the result so obvious that exposition was unnecessary'. But though this dissenting judgment of Black and Douglas JJ deploys powerful reasons against that 'result' ... neither the Court itself nor any Justice supporting the result has ever added even a single sentence of justification to the ukase of 1886.[32]

Thus it was that the 14th Amendment, originally intended to protect slaves, was interpretively extended, *without argumentative justification*, to protect corporations. Tellingly, the lack of principled justification where corporate rights attribution is concerned has continued in the American constitutional jurisprudence. Meyer, for example, argues that the increasing application of the Bill of Rights to corporations in the United States has coincided with the abandonment of corporate theory, and that this amounts, in effect, to a 'prosaic legitimation' of a contestable development – perhaps unsurprisingly because: '[t]his pragmatic approach is a less controversial guarantor of corporate rights than a theoretical methodology that raises fundamental questions about the nature of a corporation and its role in society'.[33]

Likewise, although the ECtHR clearly deliberates in a socio-legal context within which corporations are now already well-established in their possession of legal personality – and explicitly granted the right to peaceful possession of property by Article 1 of Protocol 1 – there is nonetheless an analogous lack of contemporary judicial grappling with the underlying normative question of whether a company *should* enjoy *human rights* protection. No matter how pragmatically consistent the ECtHR's response may be in relation to the liberal ideological and legal content and background of the ECHR, when it extends, for example, Article 8 protection (the right to respect for one's private and family life, home and correspondence) to a company, such *pragmatic coherence* cannot *per se* provide a *normative* defence of corporate human rights. In other words, the 'soundness of the Court's response to corporate litigation from a pragmatic view point' simply cannot – as Emberland rightly concedes – 'outweigh the importance of ideological, political or other informed critique of the very notion that a company may "have" human rights'.[34]

Notwithstanding this important and logically necessary concession, and despite his general agnosticism on the normative desirability of corporate human rights, Emberland does briefly pause to criticise what he calls the 'conceptually inspired critique' of corporate human rights protection, particularly with reference to the ECHR.[35] He points out, first, that it would be difficult to find much evidence to support the view that any principled opposition to the notion of corporate protection under the ECHR is a 'manifest feature of the case law'. This may be explained, perhaps, by a combination of the marginality (in numerical terms) of corporate claims and the pragmatism which apparently renders corporate human rights uncontroversial in principle. Dissent, he notes, 'tends to be encountered on the normative plane'.[36] His focus is on the dissent offered in the United Kingdom's ECHR discourse, rather than more broadly. And, although he notes that the arguments against corporate ECHR enjoyment are broadly similar to arguments found in relation to comparable regimes of fundamental rights, such as US constitutional law or EU law, he does not address the systemic critique offered by critics of corporate human rights protection in wider international human rights law or anti-globalisation discourse. Nor (perhaps understandably given his focus) does he refer to the distortion of the UDHR paradigm identified by Baxi.

Turning to a particularly recurrent theme, Emberland addresses the argument that companies having human rights is a 'conceptual oxymoron' – that a company, unlike a human being, 'has "no soul to be damned, and no body to be kicked"'.[37] Emberland argues that such conceptually inspired critique fails to take into account the fact that the ECHR protects not just human rights, but fundamental freedoms. He argues that the term 'fundamental freedoms' lacks, in linguistic terms at least, the 'intimate bond with the qualities of natural persons that characterises "human rights"'.[38] He also suggests that the argument that human rights cannot apply to companies rests on a classical liberal interpretation of human rights as being zones of protection, in particular for the weak and vulnerable, from state power and governmental excess.

In response to these arguments, three main points can be made. First, Emberland seems to concede the very position he criticises in relation to the conceptual critique. The fact that he has to insist that fundamental freedoms lack the intimate bond with human beings that the term 'human rights' invokes suggests that he concedes something central to the conceptual critique: the notion that human rights and the human being share, conceptually and linguistically, such a close bond that the notion of 'corporate' human rights indeed seems oxymoronic. The conceptual critique of corporate human rights is not defeated by arguing that 'human rights' for corporations must, in the ECHR context, be translated as 'fundamental freedoms' for corporations. In fact, by relying on the utilisation of a sister concept that diminishes, at least linguistically, the bond between humanity and human rights, Emberland concedes, to a degree, the *force* of the conceptual critique. Secondly, although Emberland's criticism works better if understood as an insistence that corporations do not in fact have human rights under the ECHR, but instead enjoy fundamental freedoms, it is by no means clear that any such distinction can easily be drawn. Indeed, it is likely that the two terms are synonymous.[39] Emberland never seems fully to explicate or defend his attempted distinction. Thirdly, it may be the case that some conceptual critiques of corporate human rights emerge from the presuppositions of classical liberalism. But it is also the case, as will be argued in this book, that classical liberalism can be exposed as part of the complex basis upon which corporate human rights find ideological sustenance in law. This is a line of analysis that facilitates an attack on corporate human rights by critiquing rather than simply endorsing the presuppositions of classical liberalism.

Finally in relation to the conceptually inspired critique of corporate human rights, Emberland argues, relying on Addo (with whose argument we shall shortly engage), that the notion that human rights are for natural persons fails to take into account the fact that human rights have become more influential, and that the generation of the legal order no longer rests upon the archetypal traditional interaction between individuals and states. Certainly, it is true that human rights have become more influential. It is also true that there is a wider range of juris-generative actors in our pluralistic contemporary legal communities. However neither of these points intrinsically supports the notion of human rights for corporations, as will be argued shortly. In sum, Emberland's treatment of the 'conceptually inspired critique' of corporate human rights fails to be fully convincing.

Moving away from the 'conceptually inspired' critique, Emberland examines, first, some ideological and political arguments against corporate protection by the ECHR. While accepting that it is 'wholly legitimate to argue against corporate ECHR enjoyment on ideological or political grounds', Emberland stresses the Convention's basis in European liberalism, a response entirely consonant with his aim of rendering the responses of the ECtHR *structurally coherent*.[40] In addressing the argument that corporations might enjoy disproportionate litigious advantages, Emberland argues that the Convention system does not permit adjudication on the 'basis of the real or presumed strength of the applicant person' and that the treaty's provisions apply universally regardless of status – again, a response entirely consistent with his pragmatic concern to reveal the structural realities of the ECHR system. The same is true of his arguments in relation to questions of symmetry and merit.[41] In response to those critics who argue that ECHR protection is 'conditional' – that is, that companies should be disqualified from relying on human rights standards because they have historically threatened the rights of other persons, Emberland suggests that such merit-based arguments are not compelling in relation to the ECHR. This is because the past or present conduct of the actual person applying to the Court does not have bearing on the right to benefit from ECHR protection; nor does treaty protection depend on 'proclivities for human rights abuse in the generic group which the applicant represents'. The symmetry argument is that 'having no responsibility to respect the human rights of others, companies ... deserve no ECHR protection'.[42] However, while conceding the logical defensibility of the symmetry argument, Emberland's response focuses, yet again, on the realities of the EHCR, suggesting that the argument fails to take adequate account of the main design of Convention protection. In other words, as in most of his careful and well-researched work, Emberland, when faced by such anti-corporate human rights arguments, focuses on the reality of the ECHR values and structure to defend corporate human rights protection as *pragmatically and ideologically consistent* with the treaty and its underlying values, rather than as *normatively defensible per se*.

Re-assessing arguments in favour of corporate human rights

Perhaps the best known proponent of corporate human rights as a normative matter is Addo. His chapter entitled 'The Corporation as a Victim of Human Rights Violations'[43] contains a set of key arguments which will be addressed here.

Addo begins his argument by suggesting that the notion that corporations have duties is now familiar, and that these duties (such as duties towards employees, the environment and to be transparent and accountable in various matters including product liability) are 'evidently human rights duties'.[44] (This in itself is a contestable assertion, because it seems to assume without argument that various forms of legal duty, because they involve duties to people, groups or society, amount to human rights duties. However, this is by no means clearly correct or straightforward as a claim. It seems to make human rights duties synonymous with any legal duty owed to a human being – without argument on the point.) Addo then suggests that 'it is however odd that the suggestion that corporations can also be victims of human rights violations is not so readily appreciated'.[45] He suggests that unease about the idea of corporate human rights victims is based on three things. The first is the artificiality of corporations as entities 'with no inherent ability to suffer harms associated with human rights violations'. Secondly, past experience reveals that 'the management, personality and ethos of corporations are guided by legal and moral rules which generally have very little to do with human rights at all'. Thirdly, corporations are driven by market-oriented principles in the private sphere, while human rights are conceptualised as directed, primarily, to state action in the public sphere.[46]

Addo's first attack on this 'conventional wisdom' is to argue that the wider context of human rights is influenced by 'traditional principles of doctrine and an excessive overlay of the historical basis of human rights'; which, he submits, 'has ceased to be relevant today'.[47] It will be argued in this book, *contra* Addo, that the historical basis of human rights remains deeply relevant, particularly from a critical perspective. For, it is the ideological contours of liberalism in the genealogy of human rights that lay the foundations for corporate human rights discourse. However, it will also be argued that that part of human rights history that registers normative horror at human violation should be reaffirmed as being foundational to the distinctive ethical character of human rights. Arguably, this part of the historical basis of human rights remains as sharply relevant as ever in the light of the catalogues of forms of suffering visited upon humanity throughout the twentieth and into the twenty-first centuries. Moreover, that part of the historical basis of the UDHR paradigm that lies in the reaction to the Nazi holocaust has particular relevance when understood as a reaction to the imposition of suffering upon 'embodied' personalities. To anticipate argument to come, once we focus on human 'embodied vulnerability' an ethically important space opens up between the corporation and the human being for the purposes of human rights attribution. It becomes clear that (as Addo puts it) corporations have no inherent capacity to 'suffer harms associated with human rights violations'. But, unlike Addo's argument, it will be argued in this book that this particular distinction (with others) between human beings and corporations has critical normative consequences for how we should conceptualise human rights beneficiaries.[48]

Addo, while acknowledging that corporations are artificial legal entities without the capacity to suffer the same order of harms as human beings, nonetheless suggests that the corporation is a suitable beneficiary of human rights in the special sense that it represents human interests. The corporate form rests upon a human sub-stratum whose interests are perceived to be, in reality, the interests at stake:

> 'It is true that corporations are artificial legal entities but they are organised, operated by and for the benefit of human beings. There is thus a sense in which policies and activities directed at corporations can actually affect the human beings behind the corporation'.[49]

The first point to note in relation to this is the rather trite one that the human beings behind the corporation retain, at all times, their human rights and that these human rights attach to them as human persons and are not dissolved by the corporate veil. Secondly, it is by no means clear at all that any alleged or actual 'harm' done to a corporation would necessarily trigger the human rights of the human beings in the corporate substratum. But crucially, while it is possible to claim that the human rights of human beings may in some circumstances be affected by activities directed at a corporation, this is a very different claim from the claim that the human rights of the persons affected by policies and activities aimed at corporations attach *to the corporation itself*. The argument that human beings are affected by actions affecting corporations does not logically imply that the corporation itself ought to have human rights. In a sense, Addo's claim relies on the essentially Hohfeldian notion that 'transacting business under the forms, methods and procedure pertaining to so-called corporations is simply another mode by which *individuals* or *natural persons* can enjoy their property or engage in business'.[50] This may be so, but the corporate form is an important intermediary construct. The claim that the corporate form represents the rights and interests of human beings does not, in either logic or law, justify a claim that the corporate form itself should benefit from those same rights and interests.

It is important to note that, despite the fact that some important human interests are represented by the corporate form, the corporation is not straightforwardly interchangeable with its human sub-stratum for the purposes of human rights attribution. Addo acknowledges the artificiality of the corporation, but allows that artificiality no analytical weight in his argument. Yet, it is important to take seriously our own legal constructs. The corporation is, in law, an independent jural entity capable of ownership and action in its own right – in a sense, that is the very point of forming a corporation. And, despite being the outcome of autonomous human choices exercised in the context of associational rights the corporation is not reducible, in any straightforward way, to the human sub-stratum beneath it. The fact that the legal personality of an institution grants the institution an existence independent of its members has decisive implications. For example, the corporate entity does not terminate with the death of its human members. It can be sued in its own name. It, rather than its shareholders, has an insurable interest in its own assets. It can own property in its own name and that property does not, thereby, become the property of the human beings who at any moment make up the human sub-stratum. These facts alone should alert us to the absence of any simple continuity between the corporation and its human substratum for the purposes of attributing human rights to corporations as beneficiaries based on arguments about the effect on individual human beings behind the corporate form of actions that affect the corporation.

In response to such objections concerning the translation of the interests of individual human beings into a corporate human right, proponents of corporate human rights might seek to argue that corporate human rights are a special form of group right, and on this basis form a *group* 'human' right. This too is a contentious claim. It rests, in part, perhaps, on the assertion of the importance of the human right to free association. However, although the corporation can be conceptualised as the result of a pre-existing exercise of an associational human right, it by no means follows that the entity formed by this exercise itself possesses human rights. It is helpful, at this point in the argument, to bear in mind the distinction between 'collective' and 'corporate' conceptions of group rights. Jones, for example, insists that what 'distinguishes a group right is its subject rather than its object – who it is that holds the right, rather than what it is a right to' and, furthermore, that 'if a right is to have a serious claim to be a human right, it must be a right that we can plausibly ascribe to human beings as such and one that we can plausibly ground in their humanity'.[51] The argument that the corporate right is a group human right therefore needs closer examination.

Jones suggests that, in the collective conception, a group right is a 'right held jointly by those who make up the group' and that in this conception 'the group *qua* group has no standing that is not reducible to the moral standing of its members'.[52] By contrast, the corporate conception of group rights 'ascribes moral standing to the group as such'.[53] Under the corporate conception of group rights 'the holder of the right is the group conceived as a single, integral entity. Morally, the group might be said to constitute a right-bearing "individual"', and – the key point for present purposes – the 'right is held not jointly by the several individuals who make up the group, but by the group as a unitary entity: the right is "its" right rather than "their" right'.[54] It is clear that a corporation holds its rights as a unitary legal entity, rather than as a collective. The interests of the corporation are its own interests and exist for it as a significant identity in its own right. The bottom line, as Jones insists, is that 'if we conceive of group rights as corporate rights, then we cannot represent them as human rights.... Corporate rights cannot be human rights because they are rights held by corporate entities rather than by human beings'.[55] This point becomes more potent, arguably, when we recall the nature of the paradigmatic actors at the heart of international human rights subversion: TNCs are usually formed by groups of corporate entities – a feature that arguably renders the TNC's identity more remote from its human sub-stratum. In fact, for Jones, the distinction between collective and corporate group rights is crucial to the question of whether the rights in question are *congruent* with the morality of human rights or 'whether they belong to a quite different and potentially *conflicting* morality'.[56]

Addo argues that human rights fail in their 'primary purpose of protecting against abuse' if they are limited to a focus on direct effects on individuals. Here he enlists the support of a principle that he calls the 'principle of effective protection'. He links this, in the context of protecting corporations, to a 'principle of derivative entitlement'.[57] What is interesting is that the two cases that he cites in support of this principle do not quite grant corporations free-standing human rights in the way that Addo's earlier argument suggests.

Additionally, the first case on which Addo seeks to build a principle of derivative entitlement may not quite establish it in the way that he hopes. A closer look at the case reveals that Addo's discussion of it is potentially misleading. Addo cites the case of *Allan Singer v Canada*[58] in which the UN Human Rights Committee, he argues, reasoned in a way that 'endorsed [the] principle of derivative entitlement'.[59] The case involved an author who ran a stationery and printing business in Montreal. His clientele were predominantly but not exclusively English speaking. Starting in 1978, the author received numerous summons from the Quebec authorities, requiring him to replace commercial advertisements in English outside his store by advertisements in French. Singer contended that the Charter of the French Language (Bill No. 101) discriminated against him because it restricted the use of English for commercial purposes. The reasoning Addo cites is as follows:

> The State party has contended that the author is claiming violations of rights of his company, and that a company has no standing under article 1 of the Optional Protocol. The Committee notes that the Covenant rights which are at issue in the present communication, and in particular the right to freedom of expression, are by their nature inalienably linked to the person. The *author* [emphasis added] has the freedom to impart the information concerning his business in the language of his choice. The Committee therefore considers that the author himself and not only his company, has been personally affected by the contested provisions....[60]

The conclusion that the Committee endorses the principle of derivative entitlement is made, using this paragraph as the only evidence offered in support. It should be noted, however, that the inclusion of the company in the wording of the paragraph that Addo cites reflects the fact that the State of Canada, forwarding a submission by the Government of Quebec, sought to render Singer's claim inadmissible precisely by characterising it as being presented on the basis of violations of the rights enjoyed 'by his company' Allan Singer Ltd (with reference to the fact that Article 1 of the Optional Protocol to the ICCPR and paragraph (a) of Rule 90 of the Committee's rules of procedure establish that only individuals may submit a communication to the Human Rights Committee). To suggest that the Committee is endorsing a principle of derivative entitlement when the question of corporate standing was only introduced by the impugned State party as an attempted strategy for excluding the human applicant's claim seems somewhat opportunistic. Singer made his claim as an individual and resident of Montreal and his claim was that he was the victim of language discrimination by the State of Canada because the Charter of the French Language Bill restricted his use of English for commercial purposes. Accordingly, it would be more accurate to argue that it was the author's human right to express himself in a language of his choice in the context of his commercial expression that was protected, rather than that the Committee endorsed any form of derivative human rights entitlement to a corporate entity *per se*. The fact that the Committee's reference to Singer's company is triggered by the State's attempt to exclude Singer's claim hardly offers a ringing endorsement of any principle of derivative entitlement.

The second case used by Addo to support the principle of derivative human rights entitlement for corporate entities is *Thompson Newspapers Limited v Canada*.[61] That case concerned s. 1 of the Canadian Charter and an alleged violation of rights by s. 17 of the Combines Investigation Act. The appellant was a corporation – and several of its officers, as individual appellants, were served with orders to appear before the Restrictive Trade Practices Commission to be examined under oath and to produce documents. The orders were issued pursuant to s. 17 of the Combines Investigation Act in order to determine if there was evidence that the corporation had committed the offence of predatory pricing contrary to s. 34(1)(*c*) of the same Act. The appellants applied to the Ontario High Court for a declaration that s. 17 and the orders were inconsistent with the guarantee to fundamental justice in s. 7 of the Canadian Charter of Rights and Freedoms and the guarantee against unreasonable search or seizure in s. 8 of the Charter. The precise reasoning in the relevant passage cited by Addo states that

> If s. 17 of the ...Act violates these individual's rights and cannot be justified under s. 1 of the Charter, it is rendered of no force or effect as a result of s. 52 of the Constitution Act 1982. Since the Combines Investigation Act does not provide for separate treatment of corporations, it

follows that if s. 17 is of no force or effect in respect of human beings it must also be of no force or effect in respect of corporations.

Again, this case does not entirely support Addo's argument in the way that he might wish. Two points are key. First, the crucial distinction between the earlier case (*Irwin Toy Ltd v Quebec*)[62] in which a corporation was ruled *not* to have standing under s. 7 of the Canadian Charter of Rights and the *Thompson* case was the presence of human applicants. In other words, without the human applicants, *Irwin Toy Ltd v Quebec* would suggest that the corporation would *not* have had standing. Secondly, and *crucially* in analytical terms, the impugned legislation did not 'provide for separate treatment of human beings and corporations'. This is pivotal to the reasoning, and it does not amount to a claim that the Canadian Charter of Rights allows for corporate human rights standing, even in a straightforwardly derivative way.

Even if corporations are granted standing by courts within various human rights regimes, as Addo suggests they are,[63] this does not amount to a normatively satisfying argument in favour of accepting corporate human rights. It should be noted that Addo places considerable reliance upon the example of the ECHR. But, as we have already seen, the pragmatic teleology of the ECtHR simply does not establish that the notion of corporate human rights beneficiaries is a normatively desirable or defensible development.

At the heart of Addo's argument in favour of corporate human rights lies the conviction that both the effective protection of individuals behind the corporate form and the credibility of human rights now require the recognition of corporate human rights.[64] He points to existing judicial recognition of corporate human rights (particularly by the ECtHR) and suggests that 'this development...is commendable because it is likely to contribute beneficially to the calls on corporations to take their human rights duties and responsibilities seriously'.[65] While Addo's plea for greater corporate responsibility is welcome and laudable, his argument seems to rest on a dubious premise. Baxi's work, and the catalogue of corporate human rights abuse evidenced by academics and NGOs the world over suggest that Addo's assertion is naïve. It is far more likely that, by interpreting human rights in favour of corporate entities, we simply risk equipping powerful artificial legal entities with a discourse that imbues them with a problematic moral equivalence with the living human being – a discourse that corporations already exploit while simultaneously resisting the imposition of human rights standards.

Addo explains that seeking to 'allow corporations to claim benefits under human rights standards is what may be termed the double-edge value of human rights'.[66] He suggests that in 'seeking to give credibility to corporate duties in the field of human rights, it is also important to recognise the *corresponding* claims and entitlements of these corporations...For after all, it would be insincere for corporations to claim rights under the human rights regime and yet deny their duties and responsibilities in that field'.[67] In response to these suggestions it may be argued, first, in the light of widespread corporate human rights abuses and the powerful (and frequently distorting) effect of the profit-imperative, that it seems questionable that sincerity can simply be taken to be a prime motivational characteristic of corporate entities. Second, there is no logical or legal necessity for a correlative understanding of human rights entitlements and human rights duties in Addo's terms. For example, the state bears primary responsibility for the fulfilment of human rights norms; yet states are not possessors of correlative human rights claims and entitlements. Nor does analytical correlativity between rights and duties in Hohfeldian terms support the assertion that any entity that possesses a *duty* with respect to a matter ought also to have *rights* in relation to that same matter. It is logically and legally possible for *A* to have an obligation towards *B* in respect of something without *A* having an equivalent entitlement. The relevant correspondence is between *A*'s duty and *B*'s right – it is *B*'s right that *correlates* to *A*'s duty. Addo's correlativity point thus appears to be misplaced as a defence of corporate human rights.

An additional argument presented by Addo concerns the importance of human rights protection developing to reflect contemporary social realities – by which he means, in the context of his argument, the recognition that corporations play a central role in our societies. He makes the point that the 'credibility and the effectiveness of human rights law depend on the dynamic approach to its interpretation taken by courts' in response to social change.[68] This is true. But given the social reality, particularly in the globalised context, of the extensive power of transnational corporations (some corporations have greater resources even than states as we saw in Chapter 1) the credibility of human rights (one of Addo's primary concerns) would arguably be far better protected if the need for correlative entitlements when placing such powerful entities under human rights responsibilities were *denied*. A socially responsive interpretation of human rights could, in fact, ensure that such powerful artificial entities will not be conceptualised as human rights beneficiaries. In fact, if saving the credibility of human rights is the issue at stake, it is increasingly clear that this goal is not best served by extending human rights entitlements to powerful artificial entities with a record – both historically and contemporaneously – of being egregious human rights violators – violators, moreover, that share few, if any, of the vulnerabilities usually associated with human rights violations.

There is yet a further argument against corporate human rights that reticulates with Addo's argument yet again leads to the opposite conclusion. This argument, reflecting Addo's concern for the need for human rights to be interpreted in socially responsive ways, follows from the fact that human rights frequently emerge as a result of social construction ('that is to say, created, re-created and instantiated by human actors in particular socio-historical settings and conditions'[69]) as concepts of resistance to forms of power that oppress human beings. Stammers, for example, has argued that '[a] good *prima facie* case...can be made to show that many of the key innovations in the socio-historical development of human rights were constructed and articulated, in the first instance, in the context of social movements seeking to challenge extant relations and structures of power'.[70] In this globalised age the power of economic actors requires human rights to operate as critical concepts of resistance. It seems particularly poignant, in this light, that the UDHR paradigm should have been colonised by such powerful, frequently rights-violating entities. Baxi's assertion that 'increasingly, global capital claims a new order of international rights for itself in ways that have profound destructive impacts on the human rights of human beings everywhere'[71] suggests that it is *this* social reality to which human rights interpretations need to become fully responsive.

The task of challenging the implicit conceptual shift from recognising corporate 'personhood' to the notion of corporation as human rights beneficiaries, or 'victims', to use Addo's more emotive terminology, is in urgent need of interrogation. This is notwithstanding the fact that human rights law seems to render human rights norms open to the corporate form, and notwithstanding the interpretive shift in that direction that Addo espouses. In fact, it seems essential to problematise the 'human' rights of corporations if human rights are to survive as constructs capable of adequately protecting human beings and communities *from* such powerful economic legal actors. This problematisation will be further developed in this book, principally through the argument that human embodied vulnerability should be regarded as the foundational characteristic of a human rights beneficiary. However, in order to appreciate the full significance of embodiment to human rights theory, we will first need to examine a key conduit for the reception of corporate human rights claims: the operation of a form of disembodiment in legal rationality – and some related conceptual slippages in the concept of legal personhood.

3
Law, Persons and Disembodiment

Introductory remarks

Thus far we have identified a particular problem in international human rights discourse: a distortion of the Universal Declaration of Human Rights paradigm driven in large part by global corporate entities in the context of contemporary globalisation. We have also reflected on the case offered for corporate human rights and found it wanting in both normative and conceptual terms. The interim conclusion offered at the end of the last chapter stressed the importance of problematising the 'human' rights of corporations if human rights are to survive as constructs capable of adequately protecting human beings and communities *from* such powerful economic legal actors – particularly in a globalised context.

Since law, including international human rights law, seems amenable, in certain ways, to corporate human rights claims – whether as the direct beneficiaries of the ECHR or as the more complexly-constituted beneficiaries of the discursive exploitation of the UDHR (and the economic 'preconditions' for the fulfilment of human rights goals) as traced in Chapter 1 – it seems essential to examine why international human rights law lends itself so readily to corporate claims. The openness of international human rights law – of all forms of law – to corporate discursive colonisation is particularly challenging because, as the shock registered by many lay-people when confronted by the idea of corporate human rights reveals, the idea that a disembodied legal person can claim a category of rights centred upon living human beings appears deeply counter-intuitive. It is, after all, entirely natural, when thinking of the possessors of international human rights, to think of human beings.[1] Indeed, it was the catalogue of gross inhumanity and genocide in the European holocaust that led to the birth of the UDHR paradigm at the end of the Second World War. Underlying the moral outrage driving the UDHR drafters there is arguably an unmistakeable emphasis on the embodied nature of the human suffering. (That claim will be fully defended in Chapter 7). The founding impulse of international human rights law was captured in the embodiment-centred shock symbolised by iconic images of the mounds of naked, emaciated bodies found at Auschwitz and other concentration camps. Such realities offer incontrovertible evidence of the stark, bottom-line, inescapable materiality of human existence. They underline with savage clarity the fact that human beings are, fundamentally, body-persons – embodied personalities – key among whose characteristics is a fundamental vulnerability. How then, could the human rights regime birthed in response to such iconic bodily violations and their precursors in Nazi social and political organisation[2] prove itself so susceptible to global corporate exploitation?

A principal part of the answer lies, arguably, deep within the cognitive architecture of law itself. It will be argued here that what is at work can be characterised as a particularly potent fusion between legal disembodiment and liberal capitalist ideology. Accordingly, in the next three chapters, beginning with this one, we shall explore the links between these ideas and international human rights law. This is a complex argument and will take us through some challenging territory. In this chapter we shall introduce the links between disembodiment (or what will be called quasi-disembodiment) and legal personhood. We will focus on the debates surrounding the nature of legal persons (including corporations) in order to defend the interim conclusion that liberal law is ideologically and structurally tilted in favour of disembodied property owners and accumulators of capital – and that the corporation is an almost perfect fit for this formulation. In Chapter 4 we will explore more fully the content and implications of liberal legal personality in particular, and link this even more clearly with the structural and ideological advantages enjoyed by corporations over human beings in law. Then, in Chapter 5, we will trace the argument into the heart of international human rights law.

Quasi-disembodiment

Turning first to the important idea of legal disembodiment, it needs to be emphasised that the full significance of the fact of human material embodiment, on which law ultimately relies for its effect, has been systematically suppressed in law and legal theory. This suppression has certain complex implications, even for international human rights law, as we shall see. The heart of the problem of legal disembodiment lies, arguably, deep in the philosophical foundations of liberal legal rationality.

Law (including human rights law) is typically conceived of in the West as a discourse of reason and Western reason is conceived of as being disembodied to such a degree that the very structure of rationality itself 'is regarded as transcending structures of bodily experience'.[3] The fundamental Cartesian insistence on the supremacy of reason over nature entails – or presupposes – that the rational self has an internal aspect – the mind – and an external aspect – the body – and it is this body which rationality both transcends and defines.

Accordingly, the body is conceived of as being a part of 'nature', separated from rational mind as an object to be controlled and mechanised.[4] Kant, building on the foundation of the Cartesian mind/body dualism, moreover, identified reason with morality. Kantian moral theory (which is deeply influential in mainstream accounts of international law and human rights) is the paradigmatic case of purely rational morality. The Kantian moral subject is defined precisely by its possession of abstract and universal characteristics that transcend embodied particularity,[5] and Kant's universally binding moral principles can only be derived from 'pure practical reason'. Disembodiment, in this framework, therefore, is a key theme in relation to reasoning morally, because the foundations of morality, on this view, 'can have absolutely nothing to do with either human feeling or the fact that we have bodies'.[6] The body, in this Kantian approach, is viewed as a part of 'nature' and identified with emotions, conceptualised as external 'forms of determination and a lack of freedom... taking us away from the path of pure reason'.[7] The transcendental Kantian moral person thus entails *the exclusion of the body*.[8]

Such disembodiment is foundational to the conceptualisation of the 'juridical person' of liberal legal theory:

> The liberal understanding of person, property and the physical body relies upon an important conceptual structure: the radical dichotomy between subject and object. Kantian ... theories are premised on the decontextualisation of the subject from the world of objects, including the body. These theories accept the body as an object rather than as *integral* to personhood. The separation of subjects from objects, by shearing all distinguishing embodiment or particularity, permits the formal equality of legal subjects.[9]

Law, as – *archetypically* – a discourse of reason, functions as both product and producer of this disembodied rationalism. This is both reflected by and explains the suppressed status of human embodiment in law, and the related fact that '[r]ationalist legal theory [has systematically underplayed] the mundane fact that in order for the law to function at all it must first and foremost have a hold over bodies'.[10] Yet, despite law's elevation of disembodied rationalism, the body is presupposed by law. The body operates within mainstream liberal rights theory, for example, as the 'corporeal boundary to support fundamental personal rights'.[11] The body is radically muted in terms of its theoretical significance for law's conceptualisation of persons; yet, simultaneously – paradoxically – the law uses the body (especially the female body)[12] as a focal site of regulation and control.

Law's discourse of disembodiment seems fundamentally at odds with the embodied materiality that seems so central to the inception of international human rights law.[13] The relationship between legal disembodiment and human materiality has, moreover, a complex ongoing existence that operates in an almost subterranean way. Law, including human rights law, mediates relations in a context wherein embodied persons interact with each other and the things and constructs operative in our socio-cultural and material worlds. Yet, at the same time, law's sub-stratum of embodied, concrete existence is radically muted by law's self-presentation as a form of abstract reason.

In liberal legal systems, moreover, this muting of concrete particularity is intrinsic to law's claim to do justice. Liberal legal justice is, in formal terms, conceived of as abstract, general, universal, relatively 'blind' to concrete particularities. Indeed, liberal rights theory severs itself from the body precisely *because* legal justice is achieved through a formal equality achieved through a universalism addressing legal subjects as *abstract* wills or personalities – 'made possible by [the] separation of will from any particular form of embodiment'.[14] As Douzinas and Gearey have argued, '[f]ormal justice as fairness reduces the concreteness of the other, minimises differences of need and desire, and emphasises similarities and homologies between subjects. The moral worth of the other's demand is to be sought more in what self and other share than in those differences and specificities that make the other a concrete historical being'.[15] Accordingly, liberal legal thought has tended to characterise the legal actor as a rational, universalised, unitary subject – a subject constructed as a homologous abstract individual – an individual directly descended from a rigid bifurcation of the world reflecting the longstanding dualistic divisions drawn in Western philosophy and science between reason and nature.

At this early stage in our discussion we should pause to make explicit the fact that the presumed subject/object relations emerging from this bifurcation of the world produces profoundly gendered results. In fact, even the nature of rationality itself has been, traditionally and historically, gendered:

> Having divided the world into two parts – the knower (mind) and the knowable (nature) – [western] scientific ideology goes on to prescribe a very specific relation between the two ... Not only are mind and nature assigned gender, but in characterising scientific and objective thought as masculine, the very activity by which the knower can acquire knowledge is also genderised. It is that between a subject and an object radically divided ... masculine ... connotes, as it so often does, autonomy, separation and distance.[16]

The bifurcation in Western thought posits the relationship between aspects of reality as being intrinsically oppositional. Relatively obdurate divisions were drawn very early on between male/female, mind/body, reason/emotion, nature/culture. These constructs continue to be negatively defined by each other (and, in that sense, are mutually dependent in analytical terms). These binaries, moreover, have had particular implications for the mediation of power: 'From Plato to Descartes, the scene was set in which body/women/

emotion/nature coalesced into that which was rightfully governed by mind/men/reason/culture as the basis for the development of civilised society'.[17] Western thought thus amalgamated mind/reason/culture and maleness. Nature was conceptualised as being an object and gendered as female. The female, at the same time, was immersed in the body and both were consigned to relative irrationality. The body, moreover, was conceptualised as being antithetical to abstract reason: '[t]he body, notoriously and ubiquitously associated with the female, regularly has been cast, from Plato to Descartes to modern positivism, as the chief enemy of objectivity'.[18]

The disembodiment of Western rationalism is therefore profound in its implications. It is also ultimately *impossible* (this will be argued in detail in Chapter 6). Its impossibility, moreover, produces a deep and enduring paradox. Although rationality is constructed as quintessentially *disembodied* (it transcends the structures of bodily experience) and *male* (the female, as the mutually-constitutive opposition, is immersed in embodiment), to be recognised as *male*, a person is typically identified by the possession of a particular *morphology*. There is, in other words, a body smuggled into Western disembodied rationality. As Ahmed has put it, '[t]he disembodiment of the masculine perspective is itself an inscription of a body, a body which is so comfortable we needn't know it was there, a body which is simply a home for a mind, and doesn't interrupt it, confuse it, deceive it with irrationalism, or bleeding, or pregnancy'.[19] Accordingly, the identification of the archetypal possessor of rationality has been historically dependent upon the identification of a male morphology. Objectivity, it turns out, far from being neutral, is gendered male – and the disembodiment of rationality is never complete.

This paradoxical state of affairs is fully reflected in the construction of law's archetypal subject. The central case legal subject is also in an important sense disembodied – *and* simultaneously male: the very paradigm of the rational agent. In fact, the paradoxical disembodiment common to Western rationalism and to law is better termed *quasi-disembodiment*. This term makes clear the incomplete emptiness of the formally empty subject. It reveals the sleight of ideological hand invoked by the notion of abstraction in this context. Accordingly, the term will be used throughout this book. A related point is worth making briefly: Bodies never completely disappear in law. But when the law *does* have a human body in mind, that body is 'the bounded heterosexual male body', 'immutable', a construct that operates as 'a means of denying bodily integrity to women (and to men who refuse to behave like "true" men who are deemed to lack clear boundary definition)'.[20] In fact, it has been noted that the male body of the law is defined precisely through the mechanism of exclusion, and those bodies that are excluded are those bodies that present an irreducible challenge to legal individualism – bodies assumed to lack definition, to be fluid, and most problematically – those bodies capable of morphing to become two bodies in one.[21]

The idea of quasi-disembodiment, and its gendered implications, has a potent role in the dominant constructions of legal subjectivity, both in relation to the conceptualisation of the human 'person' in law, and to the conceptualisation of the corporate 'person'. Quasi-disembodiment is, accordingly, crucial to a critical reading of international human rights law and its related openness to corporate human rights discourse.

Reflections on legal personality

Human rights, law and legal personality

Although it is most apt, when thinking of *human* rights, to think of human beings, it will be argued here that the same cannot, and *should not*,[22] so confidently be asserted of the possessors of legal personality or of the bearers of legal rights in general.

One of the many tensions besetting human rights discourse is the rupture between human rights as standards of ethical critique – as a teleologically-driven aspiration for a justice not-yet-here that seems to focus, archetypically, on the human condition[23] – and human rights as instantiated in law. When human rights ideals become law, they inevitably become embedded within, and form part of, a web of multiple, interpenetrating jural concepts, constructs and judicial rationalities. In this web, legal personality is of pivotal importance. In fact, the implications of the quasi-disembodiment associated with legal rationality and the complex nature of legal personality become *particularly* important in the human rights context, because human rights law is 'the *paradigmatic* place in which humanity, subject and law come together'.[24] While human rights may be the paradigmatic site of convergence between humanity, subject and law, this convergence is far from unproblematic. A particularly challenging intellectual terrain results from the fact that legal subjectivity and legal personality (the two will be distinguished shortly) are concepts embedded in apparently intractable and long-standing intellectual contestations concerning, in large part, their relationship with the nature of humanity (itself a constructed notion) and other things that are taken to make up our world, such as corporations. In short, the jurisprudence relevant to the theme of the entities that populate law reveals not just deep tensions but 'considerable confusion',[25] rendering the convergence of humanity, subject and law within human rights law a site of considerable intellectual complexity.

A particularly pertinent theme for the purposes of the present work is the tendency to *conflate* legal subjectivity with humanity. Consider, for example, the statement that

> ... legal subjectivity has not been exclusively bestowed on humans; its use as an economic strategy indicates that the distinction between humanity and others is not strict and unchangeable. The meaning of humanity was

> not conclusively settled when we abandoned classical thought or settled for a weak sense of natural law *a la* Hart.[26]

Even as the writer here emphasises the fact that legal subjectivity has been bestowed on the other-than-'natural'-human, he relates that bestowal to the *changing meaning of the human*. This arguably reflects not only law's anthropogenetic power but also the longstanding and almost inseparable link between legal subjectivity and the designation of 'humanity'. This conflation is persistent in legal thought – and has rightly been sharply criticised for its obfuscating effect, particularly in the context of corporate personality theory, but the conflation of legal subjectivity (or personhood – a closely related concept) with humanity is also a particularly important theme, possibly an ever more important theme – in the context of theorising human rights and in relation to the hyper-extension of human rights claims. It seems highly likely that legal quasi-disembodiment, taken together with the conflation of legal subjectivity/personhood with humanity, forms a complex conceptual conduit through which corporations move to claim what arguably amounts to 'legal *humanity*' through the invocation of human rights law.

In the context of such conceptual slippage it becomes important to interrogate the nature of legal subjectivity/personhood and to examine the ways in which it could usefully be *distinguished from* the notion of the human being. Must it always be the case that to expand the inclusivity of legal subjectivity, we somehow expand the notion of humanity? Surely the conflation of legal subjectivity and humanity is conceptually muddled and normatively undesirable – dangerous even – particularly in relation to the hyperextension of human rights discourse, as the corporate subversion of human rights discourse suggestively illustrates.

In reality, human beings are but one candidate for legal subjectivity,[27] and while the designation of the 'human' becomes ever more complex in relation to 'post-human' discourses and realities,[28] it is nonetheless arguable that there is no intrinsic need for all actual or putative legal subjects or persons to be conceptualised as human legal subjects or as the *bearers of human rights*. On the contrary, much might be gained by nuanced and careful attention to the uniqueness and complexity of – and the commonalities, analogies and distinctions between – legal subjects and/or candidate legal subjects in order to provide a suitably responsive and carefully calibrated theory of legal rights to protect, for example, animals, the environment or even individual entities within the environment such as trees, to evoke Stone's memorable discussion.[29] The extension of legal subjectivity to include entities such as artificial intelligences and robots is also a subject of growing importance.[30] This important inclusory agenda should, it is submitted, be carefully *liberated from* the tendency to conflate legal subjectivity and humanity. The conflation reflects (and produces) an anthropomorphism that is as dangerous in its implications for human beings as it is to non-human beings and entities. For example, while it is increasingly challenging to even think about the blurred boundaries of the human[31] there nonetheless remains a compelling social justice case for the maintenance of a strong human rights focus on the central case embodied, vulnerable human being discernible at the heart of the UDHR paradigm (see Chapters 6 and 7) who will doubtless be (as the post-human future unfolds) disproportionately represented by the most disempowered and impoverished human beings on the planet – those who lack access to the privileged discourses and technologies of the post-human and will be pressed to the excluded margins. There is grave danger in stretching the semantic structure of human rights to the point where they become a meaningless, all-embracing reference for anything thought to have ethical importance or a claim for inclusion within the legal community of concern.

Corporate rights, animal rights, the rights of eco-systems, 'post-human' rights and human rights need not be reduced to one monolithic category of reference. Indeed, the requirements of justice would imply that what is required is a language and conceptual framework with the complexity, responsiveness and intellectual power to embrace a multiplicity of meanings, sites, characteristics, vulnerabilities and capacities in our ever more complex legal and political ecology. The challenges we face require nothing short of a rights theory able to respond dynamically to constant shifts and new claims while steering a meaningful path through complexity to ensure liberating, context-responsive outcomes in our material lives and locations. The conflation of legal subjectivity and humanity seems to offer nothing but obfuscation to this important challenge.

Turning to the task of challenging the conflation of legal subjectivity and humanity, it is, as has already been suggested, reasonable to conceptualise the human being as the archetypal subject of human rights. Indeed, it is the argument of this book that, as an urgent ethical matter, the human being (understood as *vulnerable* and *embodied* – a view to be defended later) should be the inclusively conceptualised and distinctive beneficiary of human rights law. In other words, as an urgent ethical matter, it needs recognising that the conflation of emergent claims for legal subjectivity (for animals, the environment, artificial intelligence (AIs) etc) with *human rights* claims is as conceptually muddled, misleading, unhelpful and potentially dangerous in its implications as the conflation of legal subjectivity with humanity.

At the heart of the problems just enumerated there lies a widespread and *inaccurate* assumption that human beings are the archetypical *legal person* and that legal personality most naturally reflects 'natural persons'. There are two aspects to this assumption, both of which need examining. The first is that the human being, of all the potential candidates for legal personality, is the prototype legal person. The second is that so-called 'natural' legal persons reflect a pre-existing 'natural' human person who exists, as it were, in nature, unmediated by social construction. Both aspects of the assumption need to be challenged. When they are, what emerges from an analysis of legal persons is not the dominance of the human being as a species being but rather the dominance of the 'natural' (broadly liberal) construct of the 'person' – which has historically taken a reductive form: that of the quasi-disembodied, rational, acquisitive actor. Moreover, the construction of this legal actor matches, to a high degree, the template of the corporate actor.

To be explicit, and to remind readers where the overall argument is going in the next three chapters of this book, it will be argued that there is a remarkable degree of correspondence between law's person, particularly as exemplified by its dominant template – a template that forms the submerged but archetypical beneficiary of liberal law – and the corporation. This argument, once fully made, suggests that law's tendency towards abstraction and disembodiment, combined with its ideological elevation of property (intimately linked, as we shall see, to the construction of law's person) means that law is *better suited,* in structural and ideological terms, to the corporation than to the human being. This, in turn, will be linked to the openness of human rights law to corporate human rights discourse – underscoring the fact that, rather than simply *subverting* the UDHR paradigm, global corporate actors are exploiting *an ambivalence* in it – or even a paradox at its heart concerning a rupture between embodiment-centred energy and the quasi-disembodiment of the universal bearer of human rights. That particular part of the argument is yet to come – but at this stage we need to bear in mind the fact that human rights, when they become law, become subject to law's closures in a way that tends to complicate the relationship of the idea of human rights with both legal subjectivity *and* with the human being, and that the key legal construct implicated in this process is that of the legal person. Different theories of the legal person, however, reflect differing degrees of abstraction and liberal ideological tilt. Accordingly, we will now explore an overview of legal and corporate personality, before, in the next chapter, moving to a critical analysis of the dominant construction of legal personhood operative in liberal law.

Some preliminary clarifications

In theoretical discussions of law's persons different terms are used, sometimes interchangeably. Writers variously refer to legal persons, legal personality, legal subjects (and subjectivity) and legal entities. It will be helpful to attempt at the outset to distinguish these terms from one other. The term 'legal subject' will be taken, following Nekam,[32] to mean a unit (whether a plant, an animal, a human being, a spirit, or a group) regarded as important enough to merit juridical protection and thus the subject of legal rights.[33] Legal subjectivity is accordingly constituted by the bearing of rights, and rights only exist where there is a subject. Subject and rights, on this view, are mutually constituting[34] – one cannot exist without the other. Nekam prefers, however, the term 'legal entity', because it has a neutral implication that suggests the artificiality of both law and the rights-bearing unit of law more effectively than the other usual terms – 'subject/person'. Thus although the terms legal subject/person and legal entity are, in essence, alternative ways of describing the same thing – that is, the basic rights-bearing unit, as an analytical matter, of a legal system – the term 'entity' avoids any suggestion of subjectivity in its broader sense (with its implication of self-reflective consciousness and other incidents taken to accompany the modern notion of the subject or the person more broadly understood).

Before we examine the notion of the legal 'person' and its profound conceptual complexities,[35] we should also pause to draw out a distinction between legal personhood (personateness) and legal 'personality'. Despite the fact that again the terms are often used interchangeably in legal writing, it is possible to distinguish them: 'the distinction is between legal personateness as the constant unit in the logic of a legal system' (the rights-bearing-unit or entity albeit designated as 'person' rather than 'entity/ subject') and 'legal personality as referring to the sum total of the legal relations, actual or potential, of a legal person'.[36] Thus, legal *persons* (as units of reference within legal rationality: corporations, states, individuals etc) have legal *personalities* (constituted by the density and nature of the rights and duties (actual and potential) attributed to them as legal persons) which makes the idea of *categories* of legal persons legally intelligible. (This idea of the intelligibility of *categories* of legal person is important to the argument of this book, which relies, in part, on the suggestion that differences between corporations and human beings as notional units of legal reference should be especially important in human rights law for reasons yet to be fully defended).

The complex notion of the legal 'person'

It is often assumed that the 'person' is the paradigmatic legal subject – and, moreover, the archetypical subject of human rights law. However, the term 'person' is problematic in legal theory because of the profound degree of almost inevitable conceptual convergence between the notion of the person and the notion of the human being. This convergence is not in any way straightforward and certainly not always justified or necessary. Accordingly, it needs examination in the interests of conceptual clarity, not only because the term legal 'person' invokes enormous complexity but because it plays such an important role in law, including human rights law. For the purposes of the broad argument of this book it is important to tease out this complexity if we are to render transparent the conceptual slippages involved when corporate persons claim (arguably) a form of legal 'humanity' by the invocation of human rights law in their favour.

The notion of the person has generated a contested jurisprudence articulated by way of, broadly speaking, two major theoretical positions. On the one hand there is the 'positivist' insistence on the emptiness or formality of the notion: The term 'person' is just a misleading label driving at formal legal subjectivity – the legal entity. On the other hand, there are those who are more 'naturalist' in their orientation, linking the notion of legal persons with the notion of pre-legal 'natural' persons. This draws into the debate some complex philosophical discussions of personhood that link legal and moral status and, in some accounts, political status and the notion of civic inclusion. These two broad understandings of legal personality sit in uneasy relation to each other. And it is worth noting that with one or two exceptions, the study of legal personality 'as it applies to humans', once a key theoretical theme, 'tends no longer to be the subject of sustained theoretical analysis'.[37] Accordingly, the notion of the 'human' legal person or subject of law has become relatively neglected theoretical terrain, perhaps particularly in relation to the 'subject' of human rights law. In the light of this, it becomes all the more important to reflect on legal personhood's complexity – not least because of its potential role in the corporate subversion of human rights.

Turning first to the positivist understanding of the term legal 'person', the term functions in an identical way to the terms 'subject' and 'entity' and is simply used to denote the basic unit of law. The explanation usually given for the role and nature of the legal person in this context is that any system or organised structure of thought with its own internal logic requires a set of reference points – constants upon which the system depends. As Derham puts it: 'Just as the *concept* 'one' in arithmetic is essential to the logical system developed and yet is not one something (eg: apple or orange, etc.), so a legal system... must be provided with a basic unit before legal relationships can be devised which will serve the primary purpose of organizing the social facts. The legal person is the unit or entity adopted'.[38] This unit, as a pure unit of legal logic, is conceptualised in positivist theories as being functionally independent of any pre-existing social reality.

Naturalist scholars, by contrast, insist that there is a pre-legal person, a 'natural' human subject, with certain intrinsic qualities, for whom rights and duties are a 'natural' and inevitable augmentation of that underlying nature. Legal rights, in other words, operate as an overlay placed upon a natural subject whose nature renders such rights apposite and intelligible. Rights seen from this perspective, 'inhere in the natural condition of being a human'.[39] This naturalist view has been characterised as axiomatic for human rights lawyers. But as we shall see, this view is not immune from critique. For, it possesses certain identifiable ideological contours that make it an ambivalent foundation for human rights. The 'natural' person behind this view is not socially unmediated. It is a constructed person that takes two main forms. Both of these forms of 'natural' person reflect liberal suppositions – and one of them, in particular, has especially intimate links with the character and role of the corporation, as will be argued below and in the next chapter.

The term 'person' invokes complexity because it comes laden with a fraught social and philosophical history that is difficult to excise from discussions of legal personhood, whether positivist or naturalist. A brief examination of the historical journey of the term 'person' indicates, moreover, its entanglement with the ideological construction of power in liberal political and legal theory, most notably the power to exclude certain classes of human being from inclusion in the inner circle of actors endowed with legal and civic rationality and – in particular – the status acquired through the institution of property.[40] Davies and Naffine, for example, map the central legal division between personhood and property in terms that reveal how the two concepts mutually define each other in negative terms. This reveals the intimate and paradoxical sense in which personhood is defined and constituted by property in the liberal conception of the person: '[t]o be a person is to be a proprietor and also to be property – the property of oneself'.[41] The theme of the centrality of property in the constitution of the liberal legal person – and its attendant exclusions – will emerge more clearly as our discussion of legal personhood develops.[42] For now we shall trace the evolution of the term 'person' in more general terms.

The original meaning of *persona* was a mask.[43] As Radin explains, '... there can be no doubt that "person" is the Latin persona, the Greek *prosopon* , and that originally these words meant a "theatrical mask", familiar to us as one of the devices of Greek and Roman theatre. From this, the meaning of "role" was derived and by an almost inevitable metaphor, the dramatic role became that which any person plays in the drama of life'.[44] The term was thus used to 'denote ... the part played by a man in life, and still later, the man who plays it. ... Last of all, the term comes to denote a being capable of sustaining legal rights and duties'.[45] Naffine draws out a rather different nuance in relation to this point, suggesting that although the term 'person' began with an inherent sense of artificiality in its meaning (as a reference to the notion of a 'mask' or 'role'), as we approach the modern meaning of the term 'person' we 'acquire a sense of a sovereign, reflective subject, a being with his own self-determining personality'.[46] Despite the fact that the concept of a 'person' gained a 'modern' content reflecting a more self-determining individualism, the use of 'person' simply to mean a 'human being' had long in fact co-existed with the more technical use of the notion of the 'person' in the sense of 'role'. Radin argues, for example, that the meaning of 'person' as meaning human being 'remained in constant usage side by side with *persona* in the original sense of "mask" or "role" or "function", and both senses are to be found in literary and legal writings'.[47]

The concept of a 'person' is generally taken to have been first elaborated as a *legal category* in Roman law where, incidentally, the concept of the person was also distinguished from the concept of property. The term 'person' in Roman law meant a natural person. It was not used to denote the basic legal unit or subject of law. Slaves were persons, but not legal subjects for most purposes, for example. At the same time, abstract entities were capable of legal relations, but were not known as 'persons'. Thus there was, in Roman law, no amalgamation of the concept of personhood and legal subjectivity: 'the Roman law while recognising a slave as a natural being, and therefore one who had to be considered in a general classification of persons, regarded him as utterly devoid of legal existence ... he only acquired a civil status on the day of his manumission'.[48] Accordingly, in Roman law there was an inbuilt resistance to the potential for confusing human beings and legal persons – since human beings and legal persons clearly were not coterminous. The confusion between personhood and legal subjectivity seems to have arisen at a later point in history. Derham argues that the

> more lasting confusion grew from the attempts of the early Christian theologians to grapple with the doctrine of the Trinity in the light of Greek (principally Aristotelian) metaphysics... By the sixth century Boethius was able to produce a definition of *persona* as "the individuality of a rational being", and the primary use of the word to refer to the "part played" was obscured. The ambiguity and confusion produced is with us yet.[49]

It was with the historical emergence of liberal individualism that the word 'person' was chosen as the '*terminus technicus* to designate the subject of rights'.[50] Individualism emerged in its modern form with the shift from feudal 'status'-driven relations to modern social and legal relations predicated on 'contract' in which the individual became the fundamental unit of law.[51] The emergence of the primacy of contract entailed an emphasis on the rights of the individual over their property and their own persons – as espoused in the political theories of the seventeenth century: most notably those of Hobbes and Locke. Their accounts of society as being founded on a putative founding contract based on free assent captured the imagination of the age and aptly supported the market orientated freedoms of the emergent liberal capitalist socio-political order with a potent founding myth. In fact, Macpherson has described the emergence of contract-driven social relations in terms of the emergence of the 'possessive individual', firmly linking the rise of the new liberal social order to a conception of personhood predicated upon the decisive importance of ownership – both of property and self.[52] Individualism thus implicates an element of exclusivity of proprietary control – which is linked in liberal theory to the very notion of humanity itself.[53]

Accordingly, Nekam argues that it is with the emergence of individualism that an anthropomorphic assumption entered the discourse of the legal subject. Nekam argues that the language of the 'person' after the rise of individualism complicated legal reasoning about rights-bearing entities. Although (as noted above) Radin has suggested that the term 'person' had long had a dual usage in legal writings (as a reference both to a 'role' and a natural person) Nekam argues that, with the rise of individualism the term 'person' came to bear a problematic dual meaning. His argument seems to suggest that this dual usage is problematic because 'person' was now used to designate the legal subject (the entity who was the beneficiary of rights) but at the same time it was also used to designate the human individual and the physical, psychological and metaphysical qualities that human communities think they are justified in assigning to it.[54] In other words, Nekam seems to be responding to the fact that when, with the rise of individualism, a set of assumptions concerning the nature of natural persons came into play, there is a sense in which the underlying notion of the individual 'person' became almost fully blended with legal subjectivity. We might add, from the point of view of a more contemporary critical awareness, that this legal subjectivity was a liberal subjectivity, and that, with the development of liberal political and legal theory, the anthropomorphic assumption that Nekam identifies came to assume the form of the liberal legal subject. The result is not only that the gravitational pull between the two senses of 'person' became almost irresistible, but that the content of the natural person took on identifiable ideological contours. The individual, construed in a highly particular way, became the archetypal legal subject, as we shall see.

The near fusion between the two senses of 'person' causes genuine problems from a positivist perspective on legal personhood because '[t]he expressions "subject of rights", "person" and so on, which are used to designate the artificial legal concept have ... different meanings when not used in a strictly legal sense and these involuntarily come into the mind whenever one uses them'.[55] For Nekam, '[t]he use of the idea of *personality* to explain the *subject-of-rights* character of a thing, and the consequent use of the word "person" to designate the legal entity, are both as inappropriate as they are dangerous. While from one point of view they say far too much, from another they say far too little'.[56] The too much inheres in the implication that the human person is a natural subject of rights and in the occlusion of the artificiality and abstraction of law (a point we shall later explore from a critical perspective). The too little inheres in the lack of information contained in the notion of personality to indicate why and when a thing will be taken as a legal entity, or to begin to indicate (much less explain) the fundamental legal fact that there is a gradation among legal entities in terms of the density of rights attributed to them. In fact, the fraught question of the degree to which the concept of the rights bearing entity of law invokes an underlying concept of a 'natural' person (and indicates or reflects the nature of that person) lies behind some of the most fractious and complicated theoretical disagreements in the jurisprudence of legal personality. This contested notion of an underlying 'natural' beneficiary (whose legal image is its legal abstraction) besets not just the theory of legal personality as it relates to natural persons (so called) but also the theoretical readings of the nature of corporate legal personality, as we shall see.

Three conceptions of law's person

Naffine has recently offered a fresh analysis of what it is to be a legal person.[57] Her review of the jurisprudence of the legal person sets out to analyse the longstanding tensions in the jurisprudence of persons and to identify the different uses of the term 'person' in law. Importantly for present purposes, Naffine seeks to 'discover whether law's persons necessarily derive their meaning from metaphysical conceptions of the person'.[58] Naffine's overview is extremely useful and reflects her long term engagement with the question of the nature of legal personality. Her scheme will be borrowed here, and the theme of quasi-disembodiment will be mapped onto her analysis at pertinent points.

Naffine's wide-ranging analysis of the jurisprudence of persons reveals three different identifiable conceptions of legal personhood. Although it is fair to say that she focuses predominantly on 'natural' persons in her discussion, and does not really attend to the nature of corporate personality, we shall do so shortly.

The first conception of law's person identified by Naffine is designated as 'P1'. This is legal subjectivity in Nekam's sense of the rights-bearing-abstract-legal-entity, which Naffine characterises as legal personality as a bare analytical construct, 'nothing more than the formal capacity to bear a legal right and so to participate in legal relations'.[59] By contrast, 'P2' is the definition applied to the 'animate being' and coheres around the concept of 'any reasonable creature in being'. P2 is linked with 'biological and metaphysical definitions of humanity'.[60] 'P3' is the 'responsible subject', or the 'rational and therefore responsible human legal agent or subject – the classic contractor'[61] – the archetypal political and legal actor of liberal theory. Naffine's analysis reveals that legal subjects, understood in the P1 sense, as we would expect from our brief foray into Nekam's theoretical argument, need not be human at all (and therefore, she suggests, includes the corporation). P2 legal subjects are the conception most intimately related to the biological identification of a natural living human being. P3 further constricts the notion of the underlying human being by elevating a characteristic (rationality) taken to qualify someone for the status of 'person'. This has the result that, as 'we move from P1 to P2 to P3, there is a progressive exclusion of beings from the privileged status of person and thus the legal circle or legal community steadily diminishes'.[62]

P1, as the 'formal capacity to bear a legal right and so to participate in legal relations' is essentially 'empty', in the sense that 'anything can be a legal person because legal persons are stipulated as such or defined into existence'.[63] For this view – perhaps most famously encapsulated by Kelsen – a 'legal person is the unity of a complex of legal obligations and rights.

Since these obligations and rights are constituted by legal norms (more correctly: *are* these legal norms), the problem of "person" is in the last analysis the problem of the unity of a complex of norms'.[64] Disembodiment in this legal person is complete because the 'so-called physical person ... is not a human being, but the personified unity of the legal norms that obligate or authorise one and the same human being'.[65] This legal person is completely abstract. The human being comes before law, not as a flesh and blood entity, but as a legal construct – a juristic person – and in that sense cannot be a human being in the law at all. The legal person is purely a product of law and has no existence beyond law's normative order. Naffine, however, points out that, although P1 might appear to be the 'least interesting, most colourless and abstractly formal type of legal person',[66] this very blankness means that the construct has profound plasticity. Furthermore, law can multiply at will both the persons it creates or recognises and variations in the relations between them. The P1 facility for multiple extensions of legal subjectivity, taken seriously, implies not only that the legal person need not rely on any underlying notion of a human being at all, but that P1 is potentially the most inclusive conception of legal personality available to us. This then is Nekam's conception of a legal 'entity' – the formal, logical unit presupposed by rights and duties as legal categories. This legal person's genesis is entirely jural. The supposed independence of this conception from any pre-existing or underlying account of the person means that it is conceptualised as radically undetermined by any antecedent subject. Yet this fundamentally positivist account of the legal person as being a mere abstract 'entity' raises genuine questions concerning the degree to which P1 can avoid materialisation – and an ideologically uneven materialisation at that.

Materialisation seems inescapable given law's nature as practical reasoning designed to yield outcomes in an actual social world. Even Nekam, for example, acknowledges that the beneficiary of legal rights (the legal entity – law's subject) is 'always something in whose experimental (by which he seems to mean empirical) existence the community believes'; although he insists that the 'legal entity' is only the legal image of this beneficiary, that the legal entity will only possess those characteristics which the abstraction of law imbues it with, and that 'all the other eventual qualities of the beneficiary will be totally immaterial from [the law's] point of view'.[67] Radin adopts a more complex view of the relationship between P1 and human beings – one that attempts to make materiality internal to law. He acknowledges, without using the terminology, the tendency in law towards disembodiment. He notes, for example, the emphasis laid on documents in the later Roman administration of law which meant that legal judgment could dispense with the embodied presence of parties at hearings at any stage after the preliminary examination. He also notes the feudal and medieval multiplication of 'personalities' ('roles') that might cohere in the life of any one man.[68] However, despite the very real role of disembodiment and artificiality in law Radin suggests that the human legal personality is not *entirely* a construction of law. Radin argues that human personality can only be conceptualised as a purely legal construction if legal relations are taken to be the ultimate units of law. He acknowledges that there is a sense in which they are taken to be so because law is 'the statement of those relations which the various regulative institutions of the community recognise and protect'.[69] Nevertheless, he notes that, when we consider the nature of Hohfeldian powers,[70] we encounter the fact that the physical actions of human beings in the world produce (frequently unintended) legal results and that there is 'scarcely an example of the exercise of a physical power which is not at the same time the exercise of a legal power, that is, which does not result in a change in the legal relations of the persons affected'. In other words, we are forced to 'take into account the real concrete human being as a prolific source of relations'.[71] Radin's argument suggests that P1 theories, if they insist on regarding legal persons as purely conflations of abstract legal relations – a mere convergence of norms or a point of formal logic – fail to account for the very real *legal* (jurisgenerative) presence of materiality.

Additionally, it is submitted, the materialisation of the P1 conception has seemed, historically at least, inexorable. Yet such materialisation is not as an unconstructed 'natural' person. A critical reading of law assisted by a focus on social history as a method of ideological critique[72] reveals that the materialisation of P1 seems to take a form predominantly reflecting the ideological dominance of another conception of the legal person: the quasi-disembodied rational male actor of liberal legal theory (P3). Frustratingly perhaps, as Naffine has noted, positivist theorists have 'tended to cease their theorising at the very point at which it becomes most interesting and so have simply not engaged with the question of the *form* of law's personification'.[73] In their insistence on the idea of the legal person as a formal concept, Naffine argues, positivists have, in fact, 'demonstrated a wilful blindness' to the empirical character of law's personification and have thereby inhibited the possibility of fertile theoretical dialogue on the subject, removing, moreover, the 'analysis of the legal person from its socio-political context'.[74]

The positivist assertion that legal personhood is purely a technical device occludes not only the socio-political *context* of legal personhood but also the socio-political *function* of legal personhood.[75] From a critical perspective, this foreclosure serves the ideological role of attempting to render 'neutral', and thus unproblematic, the nature of legal personhood as a construct bearing implications for the exercise of exclusory power. The excision of context, and the related lack of engagement with the question of the empirical shape of P1's personification when the conception is operative in legal reasoning, can be read as – in itself – a contestable ideological closure operative within positivism. The question of power is always implicated in such closure, and the fact that P1 is forced to materialise means that the socio-political context is never actually transcended. Accordingly, positivism has been characterised as 'the philosophical consciousness of knowledge-as-regulation.... Through positivistic order... society can be controlled so that it can be made predictable and certain'.[76] The related fact that P1 tends to materialise as P3 (another construct, but one with quite specific contours that serve to advantage certain groups more than others) is suggestive of law's fundamental commitment to disembodied rationalism and its simultaneous elevation of the quasi-disembodied beneficiary of liberal legal theory as being the construct in whose favour law's predictability and certainty tend to operate. (It should be noted that P3 has an intimate and mutually constitutive relationship with private property – as will be argued later).

Turning from an account of the P1, broadly positivist account of legal personhood, Naffine turns to the broadly naturalistic conceptions P2 and P3. These conceptions both presuppose a 'natural' human being as being some form of sub-stratum to the construct of the legal person. In the P2 and P3 conceptions of legal personhood it is clear that the ascription of some form of 'natural' *humanity* is a central concern. Both conceptions, in their distinctive ways, attempt to identify a human person as being the foundation of the legal person – and both conceptions, arguably, reveal the presence of the identifiable ideological factors associated with liberal political and legal theory.

Recall that, for naturalist theorists, there is, beneath the legal person, a 'natural' human subject, with an intrinsic character. The P2 accounts of legal personality focus directly upon the 'natural condition of being human'.[77] The position presupposes a living human being. That human being 'becomes a legal person in this P2 sense at birth, which is also legally defined, and stops being a legal person at whole brain death, legally defined'.[78] For P2 theorists, legal rights are quintessentially an augmentation of the innate moral attributes of 'natural' persons – a conception described as 'almost axiomatic' for human rights lawyers.[79] P2 thus relies on biological definitions of the human but melds biology with certain metaphysical assumptions concerning 'natural persons' such as freedom, equality and dignity. Indeed, Article 1 of the Universal Declaration of Human Rights can be read as a paradigmatic statement of the metaphysical commitments underlying the P2 conception – which (as we shall see in Chapter 5) can in turn be linked to the exclusory assumptions underlying the liberal conception of the person.

While P2 has the virtue of being more *potentially* inclusive of human beings than the P3 conception, it is important to note that the paradigmatic naturalism of Article 1 of the UDHR is expressed in abstract universal terms – and that the abstractionism that tends to beset the dominant readings of the human rights universal has been linked to a distinct *deficit* in the putative inclusiveness of the P2 conception. In particular, it will be argued in Chapter 5 of this book that the quasi-disembodiment operative in P2's abstract universalism, particularly as it emerges in the UDHR paradigm, has proved exclusory in international human rights law and discourse – and that those exclusions reveal a submerged rights beneficiary in the form of something approaching P3. This critique will be more fully developed in the context of tracing quasi-disembodiment in the conceptual genealogy of international human rights law (in Chapter 5), when the nature of the human rights universal is further interrogated.

P3, Naffine's other 'naturalistic' conception of legal personhood, stands firmly in the classical 'natural' rights tradition of the liberal theorists. The P3 conception draws out specific human characteristics taken to qualify someone to be a 'rights holder'. Reflecting its central emphasis on rationality, the conception relies on the notion of the 'mentally and legally competent human adult',[80] and constructs the legal person as a rational, choosing, will-exercising 'discrete possessor of rights'.[81] In this sense, Naffine suggests that P3 is 'a conspicuous departure from ordinary-language meanings of the term "person"'. In this sense it is more akin to P1 than P2: 'it is a technical legal term whose meaning may be regarded as interior to law'.[82] While the P3 construct is undoubtedly 'interior' to law, it is arguable that P3's legal 'interiority' reflects the influence of the fundamental commitments of classical liberalism in modern law. Thus, while P3 can be regarded as a 'technical' legal concept in one sense, it is nonetheless a concept with a far more pervasive political and philosophical currency than a focus on the technical confines of law might convey. P3 is in fact an instance of a powerfully naturalised ideological construction of the person – so 'natural' *precisely because* it is strongly influenced by broader assumptions about the nature of the human being that permeate our traditional socio-political culture.

This point is borne out by a closer look at the contours of P3. Naffine argues that '[i]n P3 we have the rational and therefore responsible human legal agent or subject: the classic contractor, the individual who is held personally accountable for his civil and criminal actions ...'.[83] She suggests that this legal subject 'is ... impossibly self-possessed and self-reliant, will-driven, clinically rational and individualistic. Certainly he is never pregnant, for this would threaten his physical integrity. Also he is not to be thought of as a wife'.[84] P3 is the quasi-disembodied liberal legal actor *par excellence,* a construction of law's person which gives legal form to the privileging of the male, property-owning, hyper-rational classical contractor – the archetypal 'natural' man of classical Western liberal philosophy (and intimately related to its private property construct).[85] In fact, the P3 construct – and the mythic 'natural' actor represented by it – has drawn incisive critique and has been comprehensively unmasked by a range of critical theorists as being the submerged primary beneficiary of law in Western cultures. This gives P3 particular importance in a discussion of the legal person. The importance of P3 also rests on its usefulness as a site in which the underlying historical orientation of a dominant strand of liberalism comes most fully into the open for the purposes of critique.

To summarise briefly, it seems that the quasi-disembodiment of the legal actor finds expression in different and sometimes complex ways in all three conceptions of law's person. P1 is radically disembodied – a construct with no necessary connection to social facts. It reflects a closure that renders the positivist project problematic in two central respects: the closure itself may reflect the prevalence of disembodied rationalism (with all that it implies); and the closure cannot, in any case, convincingly resist either the juris-generative role of human action in the world, nor can it resist materialisation – which, when it occurs, seems to favour the P3 conception. P2 is biologically based, but subject to metaphysical and cultural assumptions which tend to be combined with an abstractionism that renders the related human rights universal problematically quasi-disembodied and exclusory along P3 lines (of which more later). P3 is not only a quasi-disembodied person but appears to be inseparable from the possessive individualism of a particularly dominant strand of liberalism as articulated in the context of emergent capitalism and the elevation of contract. All three constructions are therefore ideologically tilted, though to differing degrees. Thus, it is possible to conclude, with Naffine, that the concept of legal personality (which she uses interchangeably with legal personhood) 'fairly *systematically* helps to support a quite particular interpretation of the person, and one which has an intimate connection with its companion concept, property'.[86]

Corporate personality theory

Turning to our other key protagonist for the purposes of this book, the corporation, we find that P2 and P3 do not directly address the other-than-natural-human legal subject. In relation to P2 in particular, Naffine comments that 'there tends to be a general amnesia about corporations as legal persons when P2 is invoked; or the corporation is – wrongly to P1 theorists – distinguished as an artificial person'.[87]

As Naffine suggests, P1 theorists can easily account for the legal personality of corporations. For such theorists, legal persons are simply formal – analogous to '... mathematical equations devised for the purpose of simplifying legal calculations'.[88] Since legal persons are a mere point of convergence for a set of legal relations in mutual dependence, the only reality they have is as jural constructs. Thus, legal personality, conceived of as being a formal device of great plasticity, is as easily applied to the corporation as to the human being or any other thing that the legal system in question chooses to endow with legal subjectivity. However, although P1 has the explicit theoretical capacity to account for the legal personhood of the corporation, it seems that P2 and P3 nonetheless have their analogues in theories of corporate personality. Indeed, the question of corporate personality has long been embroiled in debates, analogous to the positivist/naturalist divide in the general theory of legal personality, concerning whether or not the corporate person is 'real' or 'fictitious', 'natural' or 'artificial'.[89] Given the complexity of the topic and the apparent intractability of the contention between different theoretical positions it is not proposed here to offer any kind of answer to the quandary. However, issues in corporate theory will be mapped out below, utilising Naffine's P1, P2, P3 formula, to draw out certain relevant aspects of corporate theory for the present purpose of tracing the theme of quasi-disembodiment in law and liberal legal theory.

There are, according to Schane, three main views of corporate personality.[90] Schane calls these theories the 'creature, the group and the person theories'. Here, however, the terms 'fiction, group, and natural entity theory' respectively will be adopted, since these names seem to be more widely used in corporate theory. (It should be noted, however, in the interests of clarity that 'group theory' is also sometimes known as 'symbolist' or 'bracket' theory, and sometimes, in another variant, as 'purpose' theory[91]).

The key question animating theories of corporate personality concerns the degree to which the corporation ('the word "corporation", derived from the Latin *corporatus*, made into a body, designates a body of men joined together for a common purpose'[92]) has rights distinct from the individuals composing it. We shall take each of the three main theories in turn and attempt to relate themes emerging from our reflections on P1, P2 and P3 to them.

Representing, perhaps, the apotheosis of artifice, the fiction theory insists that the corporation is only a legal entity in the mind of the law – a *persona ficta* – invisible and intangible. In this view, '[p]ersonality is not the reflection of a pre-given object reflected in the mirror of law ... This personality is nothing more than a trick of the law ... nothing more than a consequence of the deployment of a stratagem ... subjectivity as pure legal invention'.[93] A classic statement of this position is found in the judgment of Chief Justice Marshall in *The Trustees of Dartmouth College v Woodward*: 'A corporation is an artificial being, invisible, intangible, and existing only in contemplation of law. Being the mere creature of law, it possesses only those properties which the charter of its creation confers upon it....'[94] This is clearly a completely disembodied notion of the corporate form. It sees the corporation as simply an invented legal reality – a jural entity with no pre-existing reality, a person purely carved out and structured by the cognitive activity of law as a system. As Radin points out, 'the term "fiction", as applied to a corporate person, was meant to carry over the notion of a legal fiction, which in Roman Law as in English was the deliberate assumption of the thing which was not, a definite and quite unconcealed make-believe'.[95] The fiction theory, however, tends to distinguish between natural and artificial persons, emphasising the artificial nature of the corporation as a person by carefully distinguishing it from 'natural' persons.[96] In this sense the fiction theory, despite resonance with the P1 theory of the legal person, is in fact a departure from P1, because P1 theorists would maintain the equally artificial status of *all* legal persons.

However, the fiction theory has been criticised for being 'untrue to the living society [it is] meant to fit': Hallis, for example, insisting that 'we should drop the term "fictitious" when referring to the juristic personality of a group' on the basis that it simply fails to reflect the social facts underlying the legal system.[97] The two main alternative theories on offer both focus on the social reality of groups in one way or another. Group theory emphasises associative rights, whereas natural entity theory tends to suggest that human associative groups take on a life of their own. Turning first to group theory (which, as noted above, seems sometimes to be known as the 'symbolist' or 'bracket' theory, or, in another variant, 'purpose' theory),[98] the argument is that the right to join together and conduct business under an assumed name does not give rise to a separate entity. Persons are human beings and 'only human beings can have interests and rights... a corporation is only a legal device or formula which will enable very complex jural relations to be comprehended simply'.[99] For this theoretical position the rights of the corporation as a legal unit are, in reality, merely the rights of the members who make up the group behind the corporate name – and 'consequently, a corporate name can never be the name of any artificial being; it is simply a useful label for identifying the members of the group'.[100] Here, then, 'natural' actors, who are simply associated for the purpose of conducting shared business, are viewed as being entitled to the same protection of law as is guaranteed to them as individuals. (This is the view implied by Addo's argument concerning corporate human rights which we discussed in Chapter 2 – recall that he argues that the rights of corporations, in the end, are the rights of human beings.)

The group theory of the corporation has been criticised for, in effect, doing away with the concept of corporateness altogether. It lacks explanatory force when faced with the fact that 'a corporation or society may endure indefinitely, [nor can it] account for a corporation representing an endowment or instrumentality which does not even offer individual rights'.[101] Derham points out that the deductions drawn from this theory, at least in its symbolist or bracket theory variants, 'have been rejected repeatedly by courts in common law jurisdictions on both sides of the Atlantic. The academic puzzle of generalizing the conditions under which a court may "pierce the veil of incorporation" would not have presented itself had they not been so rejected'.[102] In essence, the group theory simply fails to account for pivotal features of the corporation such as corporate immortality and limited liability and cannot, as a result, offer a satisfactory theory of corporate personality. If the fiction theory fails, with its focus on the artificiality of the corporation, to take materiality seriously enough, group theory fails to take the interpretive practices and artificial conceptual constructs of law adequately into account.

The third major theoretical position concerning the legal personality of corporations is known as 'natural entity' theory, 'person' theory or 'realist' theory. Here the corporate personality is based on the idea of an underlying 'real person'. However, rather than this 'real' person being the 'natural individual', this theory insists that this 'real' person is constituted by social reality of groups as 'real' entities. The best-known advocate of this position is Otto Von Gierke. Gierke rejected fiction theory and focused on the old Germanic conception of the reality of the group-entity.[103] According to natural entity theory, the corporation is neither a legal fiction created by state law, nor a contract between individuals, but instead a natural person with a pre-legal existence. Gierke conceived of the corporate body as a real group person, a living social force.[104] Therefore the state merely *recognises*, rather than *creates*, the legal association – the corporation, in other words, 'is a legal person *naturally*, as much as any human being'.[105] Importantly, a group has a will of its own (a common will) and pursues its own goals. As Maitland put it: '[i]tself can will, itself can act; it wills and acts by the men who are its organs as a man wills and acts by brain, mouth and hand. It is not a fictitious person; it is a *Gesamtperson*, and its will is a *Gesamtwill*; it is a group-person, and its will is a group-will'.[106] Thus a real corporation could come into existence independently of any state concession 'just as it could be credited with a fuller legal capacity since as a real person it could be held liable not only contractually but also delictually'.[107]

This theory has been criticised for failing to account for the one-man company, including the corporation sole – and cannot, accordingly, account for the shift achieved in the landmark dictum in *Soloman v A Soloman & Co Ltd*[108] – the case 'credited with having articulated the founding propositions of company law'[109] – in which it was established that a company can have a single owner and that that single owner, as much as any group, could use the corporate form to shelter from personal liability for the conduct of the company. This is a significant explanatory gap – perhaps a gap made symbolically all the more telling for the fact that this dictum has been credited with laying down the 'essential prerequisites for the development of the corporate conglomerates which are now such a dominant feature of business enterprise'.[110] An equally telling criticism of the theory is delivered by Stoljar who points out that the theory raises the same intellectual difficulty as the fiction theory it criticised – 'it again confronted us with a person, virtually a super-person, with a mysterious "will" of its own, a person making no less demand on our credulity than its fictitious rival'.[111]

Drawing these brief accounts of the rival theories together with Naffine's template we can note that P1 has its partial analogue in the fiction theory, but simultaneously offers critique to the presupposition of that theory that the corporation is to be distinguished from the 'natural' legal person on grounds of its artificiality. For P1 *all* legal persons are equally artificial. In terms of P2, we see the widespread assumption of 'natural' humans variously at work in the fiction theory, the group theory, and natural entity theory. But it is a moot point as to what kind of 'natural' person is in play in each of the theories. Gierke's natural entity theory draws attention to the idea of 'corporality': emphasising 'that in order to understand the terms of production and ascription of legal capacity to the group or institution, it is important to recognise the incorporated subject as a body with an idiosyncratic materiality'.[112] Gierke, in positing the real presence of a group entity as a pre-legal natural person with a certain corporate materiality, creates, arguably, an analogue of sorts to the P2 conception. Natural entity theory thus resonates with a central aspect of the P2 account of legal personality – its emphasis on a pre-legal, 'natural' materiality. But this 'super person' does not share the same order of material vulnerability as the embodied human being (as even proponents of corporate human rights, such as Addo, have been forced to admit by implication).[113] Arguably, in fact, the actors associating to form the idiosyncratic materiality of the incorporated subject may best reflect the P3 conception of the 'natural' legal subject.

It is interesting, in this connection, to note that Gierke's theory was decisive in the development of state-independent corporate personality in North America in the nineteenth century when the legal basis for corporations changed and corporations broke away from the state in a movement towards privatisation as the values of industrial capitalism took hold.[114] Natural entity theory played a vital conceptual role in the 'personification' of corporations – arguably also the 'personification of capital' as Neocleous has put it, arguing that between 1844 and 1914 the corporate form was established as 'the legal subjectivity of capital', a legal subject which took to the stage, moreover 'as a fully-fledged persona as capitalist states were at pains to clarify in the late nineteenth century'.[115] This connection is brought out even more explicitly, perhaps, by Federman, who notes that

> [t]he corporation of 1886 represents the production of the normal understanding of the new American man, the bodily expression of male power, the individual self liberated from the constraints of the past and 'the molestations of society or state...'. It is now the construct of a well-placed, self-interested enterprising group of persons willing to stake their lives and livelihood for economic success. As such, the corporation meets the requirements of the 'balanced character,' that psychological trait necessary (and applied only to elite males) for the emerging commercial economy of the late nineteenth century.[116]

The construct of the corporation as being the corporal expression of (male) acquisitive power[117] has obvious ideological continuities with the P3 legal person as the archetypical personification of liberal legal culture. If the P3 conception of law's person is, in essence, the rational liberal man of property, then the corporation emerges as that person writ large – the rational (male/ disembodied) liberal *persona* of capital. Additionally, the corporation, as the 'personification of capital', the 'new American man', emerges as a construct ideally suited to industrial capitalism. For the corporate form is constituted precisely as 'a person for the purposes of capital accumulation and not for the purposes of justice'.[118]

Space does not permit a fuller elaboration of the theories of corporate personality. Clearly the subject is deeply complicated and each position contains some element of a complex truth. But each position, because it captures elements of a multifaceted reality, tends to invite contestation from theorists committed to the elevation of some competing aspect of the problem. The argument concerning the true nature of corporate personhood has quite simply never been settled.[119] In all the theories, however, as we noted above in relation to theories of legal personhood more generally, there is an element of ideological masking or mystification that tends to obscure the fact that the corporation, however conceived in corporate theory, has telling similarities to the P3 'natural' legal person. The question of materialisation and the politics of power are thus as persistent in relation to how we conceptualise the corporation as they are in relation to how we conceptualise the 'natural' legal person. Derham, for example, notes of corporate theories that 'all [the] theories, and their variations, have been used for social and political ends'.[120] Horwitz has argued that the theories function as elucidations of the issues surrounding corporate growth and the nature of changing attitudes to the nature of corporations.[121] Putting it bluntly, shifts in corporate theory reflect underlying economic and political imperatives.

At the beginning of the nineteenth century in America, fiction theory was conceptually ascendant. However, new economic needs rendered the premises of fiction theory out of kilter with changing realities. This led to calls for free incorporation – which lay closer to the explanatory framework of group theory. Group theory, however, 'treated corporations in terms familiar to partnership law',[122] and this theory, accordingly, struggled to 'accommodate the special features of corporate immortality, limited liability and distribution of power'.[123] Crucially, natural entity theory emerged triumphant because it was the most useful theory to account for the needs of American corporations. In short, the theory, 'in its treatment of the corporation as a bearer of rights and duties, freed corporations from those restrictive notions that were built into the [fiction] and group theories'.[124] We have already linked natural entity theory to the constitution of the idealised capitalist legal actor. The theory that occluded other theories of corporate personality was ultimately a theory in which the P3 quasi-disembodied legal actor can be read, writ large. In the next chapter this link between the 'natural' and corporate person in liberal law will be more fully traced – and the underlying political and economic motivations for various theoretical positions will be more fully traced out.

Personhood and property

Before moving on to explore the implications of the dominance of the P3 conception of legal personality in the next chapter, it is important to note, in a little more detail, its links with the liberal concept of property. This is because property has a complex and ambivalent position in the lexicon of human rights. This ambivalence arises, in part from the nature of the traditional liberal legal construction of property – and we should note that property, like liberalism itself, is the subject of competing interpretations. Property discourse, like human rights discourse, is frequently caught between formulations and interpretations that can be described as broadly exclusory and inclusory in social terms (an argument to be more fully traced in Chapter 8).[125] It is true to say, however, that liberal legalism and the related legal interpretation of the nature of property have constructed a mutually reinforcing discourse in which private property and the private liberal legal actor mutually constitute each other in broadly exclusory terms, radically contiguous with the contours of the P3 legal actor and his interests.[126]

P3 has emerged from our analysis thus far as being the archetypal legal person of liberal law. Not only does P1 tend to materialise as P3, but P3 is in a sense a more ideologically explicit and augmented form of the presumptions operative in P2. The dignity and freedom of P2, and the presuppositions about physical autonomy operative in its insistence on live birth to qualify for personhood, reveal certain philosophical continuities with the P3 construct. P3, conceptualised as the 'free person', emerges then as 'the basic legal unit'[127] – and while 'non-human beings and abstract entities can also be legal persons ... a certain conception of the human being, as a free and possessive individual, provides the template for legal being'.[128] P3 is therefore intimately linked with the concept of property – and this link emerges quite clearly and persistently in liberal legal theory. Revealingly, we have also linked P3, in particular, to corporate personality.

Davies and Naffine offer an analysis of the relationship between persons and property in liberal theory and law that reveals the two concepts to be in a state of radical mutual interdependence. Accepting the modern legal orthodoxy concerning the separation between the two concepts, in which 'to be a person, it is said, is *precisely* not to be property',[129] Davies and Naffine note that not only do the two concepts negatively define each other, but that the purity of the distinction is open to question, noting in particular various ways and points at which law 'commodifies' people. Along similar lines, Halewood has argued that

> [c]ommodification, the process of transforming an object, quality, or capacity into something with a recognisable market value, occurs in several ways. The human body is commodified by wage labor, by advertising, by commercial exploitation of women's bodies, by biotechnology's reduction

> or fragmentation of the body into marketable parts, and by the conceptual and ideological shift in our society toward thinking of the body as something marketable or alterable.[130]

For Halewood, commodication is a *necessary* result of the conceptual structure of the liberal legal view of the property relationship. The mind/body dualism intrinsic to the foundations of liberalism regards the body, as we have already seen, as an object – as a base materiality separated from the subject. The subject is therefore 'bare', 'stripped of all particularity so that each possesses a similar moral weight. But the subject, having become thus fungible, assumes the principal characteristics of an object (ie: fungibility) and thus opens itself to commodification'.[131] For Halewood, the 'property paradigm and its instrumentalism have become reified and naturalised as the only possible explanation of the relation of self to embodiment'.[132] The body is used in liberalism as that which defines the boundaries of rights-holders. But beyond that, the body is devalued and objectified – a mere container or outer limit for the rational subject. The body in liberal discourse, in this analysis, is therefore quite naturally a target for commodification.

Not only is there a sense in which liberal theory renders the body a commodifiable object, but the liberal self is constituted at a fundamental level by self-ownership. This in turn provides a foundation for the ownership of the external world – which is, like the body, relegated to object status. Locke, for example, asserts that we have property in ourselves, and so in our labour, and that whatever we mix our labour with becomes 'proper' to us – we gain property in it.[133] Hegel, likewise, developed an account of property that linked it inextricably with the notion of self-ownership. For Hegel, however, we do not begin as self-owning. We become free subjects by taking the world into ourselves – that is, we become self-owning by externalising ourselves through the appropriation of objects: 'the person therefore becomes both pure subject and object. Similarly, the object, which starts as a mere thing, having no end-in-itself, becomes invested with the will and spirit of the appropriator'.[134] Hegel's theory attempts to provide 'a unified self and object, wherein an understanding of property is contained in legal personality itself',[135] rendering the imbrication of legal personhood and property radically intimate.

Davies and Naffine argue that a paradox arises from these formulations. The paradox resides in the simultaneous insistence in liberal philosophy that persons and property are radically distinct and yet that we are 'self-proprietors' – a concept that logically entails ownership of the self – that is to say, a conceptualisation of the self as property.[136] What this amounts to, as O'Donovan has asserted, is the fact that '[t]o be a full individual in liberal society one must be an appropriator, defined by what one owns, including oneself as a possession, not depending on others, free'.[137] Property interests, in other words, articulate and guarantee the autonomy of the individual. They constitute their personhood. We should note, moreover, that the notion of the person as proprietor lends itself particularly well to the ideological orientation of a market society. This is a key insight provided by Macpherson, who coined the term 'possessive individualism' to suggest the highly individualistic and acquisitive construction of the person entailed by liberal theory, and particularly that of Locke.[138] Macpherson encapsulates his critical argument in the following terms:

> The individual was seen neither as a moral whole, nor as part of a larger social whole, but as owner of himself. The relationship of ownership, having become for more and more men the critically important relation determining their actual freedom and actual prospect of realising their full potentialities, was read back into the individual.... [F]reedom is a function of possession. ... Society consists of relations of exchange between proprietors. Political society becomes a calculated device for the protection of this property and for the maintenance of an orderly relation of exchange.[139]

Taking all of our preceding observations and arguments into account, it is possible to draw the interim conclusion that liberal law is ideologically and structurally tilted in favour of disembodied property owners and accumulators of capital: quasi-disembodied possessive individuals. The corporation (including its 'gender') is an almost perfect fit for this formulation.

In the next chapter the P3 legal person and the nature of rights in the liberal legal system will be further examined from a critical theoretical perspective, as will the nature of the corporation as P3 writ large. After that, the central theme of quasi-disembodiment and liberal ideology will be linked, through a genealogical reading, to international human rights law in Chapter 5, suggesting the possibility that the UDHR paradigm is inherently open to corporate subversion. Fortunately, however, the paradigm also contains the theoretical basis for developing a resistance to corporate human rights claims –an idea that will be fully explored in Chapters 6 to 8 of this book.

4
The Liberal Subject of Rights, Capitalism and the Corporation

We have been exploring the link between legal persons and law's underlying liberal orientation in order to clarify a possible explanation for the inherent openness of modern human rights law to corporate beneficiaries. We noted in the last chapter that, while it is entirely natural when thinking of the possessors of human rights to think of the human being, when human rights claims take the form of legal claims, they inevitably become imbricated with the web of constructs that populate law's matrix and become subject to law's systemic closures. In relation to this, we saw how all three of law's conceptions of the legal person according to Naffine's typology, P1, P2 and P3, reflect, albeit with differing nuances, the presuppositions of legal liberalism. We were able to conclude that, in general terms the concept of legal personhood supports a relatively specific reading of the 'person' as the liberal legal subject – a subject inextricably connected to the notion of private property. Furthermore, we saw how this subject can be linked to the corporate form in a way that suggests that the corporation is the liberal legal actor writ large and, in all likelihood, the most perfect form of the quintessential legal actor.

In this chapter, we shall develop a critical and socio-historical reading of the construction of the liberal subject of rights in order to reveal more fully the reasons for the openness of law (including human rights law) to the incipient privileging of the corporation.

Liberal law as a rationalising enterprise

In the argument thus far Western liberal law has been characterised as being both a product and producer of a particular form of disembodied rationalism. This rationalism, moreover, as already implied, can be conceptualised as the operative discourse of a *rationalising project* aimed at the *excision* of socio-political context. This rationalising project, as we shall now see, can be linked at a systemic level to liberal law's enmeshment with liberal capitalism. That enmeshment explains not only law's distinctive ideological tilt towards the P3 classic liberal legal actor in particular, but also the more covert tilt involved in the construction of P2 and P1 legal persons. In fact, the argument to come reveals that all three conceptions can accurately be described as liberal legal persons – although the differing conceptions operate more problematically (in terms of their tendency towards exclusive readings) in some contexts and for some purposes than for others.

Mainstream liberal legal scholarship has tended to present the rationality of law as the manifestation of formally neutral and relatively consistent principles and rules, the operations of which are mediated by the application of dispassionate, detached logic in the pursuit of justice and formal equality. However, as Horwitz has argued, such legal scholarship has tended to be ahistorical, and 'derives from [an] attempt to suppress the real contradictions in the world'.[1] In reality, law is a social product, and it emerges from a social struggle for power.[2] While the dominant juridico-legal account of rights and law tends to suppress their socially contingent and paradoxical nature, an account sensitive to socio-historical context reveals a narrative fraught with contestation and inequalities. In such a reading the rationalising enterprise of law emerges as an historically contingent exercise, and rights emerge as profoundly contradictory concepts that are 'neither self-generated nor self-enforcing but rather summarise, make concrete, and depend for any protective effectiveness they may possess on, the nature of wider sets of social relations and developments within them'.[3] Accordingly, in this chapter we shall trace the historical emergence of the liberal subject of rights. This reading of the liberal subject reveals its paradigmatic closures as *historically contingent closures* reflecting a particular set of social relations and developments, and exposes modern law as being the facilitator of 'the mechanism by which capital dominates civil society'.[4]

Because, as we have already seen, subject and rights operate as co-dependent constructs in an analytical sense, the liberal subject of rights emerges as pivotal to the justification of a liberal legal order based on rights. The liberal subject and the nature of liberal rights, accordingly, mutually constitute each other, and this fact has certain implications for the liberal conception of human rights – particularly for their translation into a form of legal right. But the genesis of human rights, despite the dominance of the liberal subject of rights in mainstream accounts, should not be understood as a monolithic or simple process. Indeed, both natural rights and human rights, as we shall see in this chapter and the next, are best understood as being paradoxical – even bifurcated.[5] It is therefore unhelpful and deeply inaccurate to read human rights through an optimistically constructed mono-logical account. This point is particularly salient when reflecting on the complex relationship of human rights to power, their openness to corporate exploitation, and their complex relationship with capitalism.[6]

The genesis of liberal rights and the liberal legal subject

Natural law to natural rights

According to Douzinas, the story of rights begins in the original natural law conception of 'right' as being an objective relationship of justice and a methodology of transcendent critique. The classical natural law tradition used the notions of 'nature' and 'right' as revolutionary concepts of resistance to authority, to 'judge the real in the name of the ideal': What is 'right by nature' was used to challenge the extant authority of ancient custom, and deployed as 'an independent tool for critique'.[7] However, this revolutionary use of 'natural right' was countered by a directly related oppositional strategy utilised by the established powers. The critical energy of the concepts of 'nature' and 'right' were, perhaps predictably, subverted in favour of supporting power structures of the status quo.[8] There are thus elements of both closure and critique in natural law and the origins of the notion of right – a dynamic tension between emancipatory discourses and discourses devoted to consolidation of the existing social power structures. Accordingly, there is a longstanding and fractious ambiguity in the relationship between rights and power – with rights claims frequently emerging as forms of claim adopted by social movements pressing for transformation and just as frequently co-opted by the interests of the status quo, the interests of which tend to crystallise rights in predominantly exclusory forms at the moment of institutionalisation.[9] Thus, the original tension in the concept of 'nature' is carried forward into the discourse of natural rights and into the discourse of international human rights.

For Finnis, rights-talk predominantly reflects its juristic origins.[10] He argues that the modern vocabulary of rights began its genealogical journey in the classical language of European culture as '*jus*'[11] derived from Roman law. But it is most usefully articulated in the work of the natural law philosopher Aquinas – who presents the primary meaning of *jus* as 'the just thing itself'.[12] *Jus* is the 'what's right', the 'what's fair', the objective pattern in a relationship of justice, the 'what's due' – 'that which is just in a given situation', the ensemble of juridical relationship established by rules, between two or more persons in relation to some subject-matter (act, thing, or state of affairs)'.[13] For Douzinas, however, Aquinas' formulation of justice is a pallid construct. It amounts to nothing more than the just application of existing laws, rather than 'a rational and dialectical confrontation of institutional and political common sense'.[14] Douzinas argues that, as a direct result of Aquinas' teaching the 'new legislative powers of church and state were legitimised and natural law teaching was absorbed by theology'.[15] Justice thus became a 'cold virtue' rather than a critical concept.[16]

The next crucial shift, vital to understanding modern rights (and the related subject of those rights) is the process through which the objective classical concept of 'right' mutated into 'rights'. Finnis identifies this 'watershed' development in the evolution of rights as being Suarez's treatise on law written around 1610 AD: 'Here, the "true, strict and proper meaning" of "*jus*" is said to be: "a kind of moral power [*facultas*] which every man has, either over his own property or with respect to that which is due to him"'.[17] This shift is also reflected in the language of Grotius, who describes *jus* as meaning 'a moral quality of the person enabling [*competens*] him to have or do something justly'.[18] Finnis suggests that a way of understanding this shift is as '...Aquinas's primary meaning of *jus*, but transformed by *relating it exclusively to the beneficiary* of the just relationship, above all to his doings and havings'.[19] The crucial point is that the rights-bearing subject has moved to centre stage. *Jus* is now something that a subject *possesses*. Grotius is credited by Santos with being the most sophisticated expositor of the rationalist natural law of the seventeenth century, and in Grotius' theory we find, as in so many elements of the history of rights, closure and critique in uneasy, fractious co-existence – a mirror perhaps of contradictory impulses at work in the extant socio-historic context. Grotius' work *De Jure Belli ac Pacis* combines (in the words of Tuck) 'the language of both absolutism and liberty', and it is 'well known [that] the rationalist natural law served to legitimate both the "enlightened despotism" and the liberal and democratic ideals that led to the French Revolution'.[20]

The 'watershed' transition in which the objective justice of natural law transmuted into subjective, individual rights achieved its most iconic expression in the classical natural rights theories of the seventeenth century. Importantly, the sense in which *jus* could be conceived of as the 'just outcome of distribution, the calculation of the just proportion amongst external things shared by the citizens'[21] was lost. In its place, the seventeenth century political philosophers erected 'right' as a claim to individual liberty in a political theology divested of God or classical nature, and they constructed a foundation myth for the new socio-political order in the form of social contract theory:[22] 'Epicurean ideas, according to which the *polis* was the outcome of an original contract, and the Stoic belief that the law should be in harmony with the reason of the world, acquired renewed importance ... [T]his was the natural law of modern merchants ... [and] it attributed contemporary legal and social arrangements to a primordial assembly and a freely-entered contract'.[23]

Social contract theory

Socio-political context is foundational to an adequate understanding of the origins of liberal legal rights and their archetypal subject. Santos argues that Rousseau, Hobbes and Locke, the founding fathers of social contract theory, represent 'distinct parts of an intellectual constellation', and that they are 'best understood as part of a large project for the rationalization of social life'.[24] For Santos, the rise of social contract theory, variously nuanced by the three founding liberal political philosophers, is a manifestation of what he describes as the 'tension between regulation and emancipation at the origin of the modern legal field'.[25] Although Santos focuses on the wider project of modern law as a complex, systemic whole, his conception of the tension between regulation and emancipation echoes the historic tensions that we have already alluded to between emancipation and the consolidation of extant power, closure and critique, in the history of rights.

The idea of a social contract as a justificatory device aimed at defending a given set of political arrangements can be traced back as far as the eleventh century. The innovation offered by Hobbes, Locke and Rousseau is in a sense produced by the context of their theorising. For it emerged against the background of the debate from rationalist natural law and, *crucially*, for Santos, from their perception that they were part of an emergent socio-political order and exponents of a new scientific approach to the analysis of the world: 'In one way or another the universality of a new legal and political obligation is connected with the truth claims of modern science'.[26] (This is perhaps particularly true of Hobbes, who was convinced of the potential of science to create a rational social order.[27])

All three philosophers employ the 'state of nature' as a construct through which to posit the pre-contractual existence of humankind – the state of nature in which 'men' lived before entering into the state – or society. As Douzinas suggests, this differs from the view of the 'ancients, for whom nature was a standard of critique transcending empirical reality'. By contrast, 'the nature of Rousseau, Hobbes and Locke was an attempt to discover the common elements of humanity, the lowest common denominator behind the differing individual, social and national characteristics and idiosyncrasies'.[28] In other words, in the process of constructing liberal political theory the impulse towards disembodiment and decontexualisation played a foundational role. In order to establish the identity of the 'man' of natural rights, Rousseau, Hobbes and Locke sought out the universal elements of humanity by *subtracting* from embodied persons whatever made them unique, situated, distinctive and nuanced – in order to strip them down to their most basic underlying 'nature'. The mythical 'man' thus produced was 'an artificial construct of reason, a naked human being endowed only with logic, strong survival instincts and a sense of morality'.[29]

All three philosopher's writings can be viewed as foundational to liberalism, each revealing a distinctive element of liberal thought, or 'an archetypal dimension to a global revolutionary project'.[30] For Santos, each of the axiomatic principles of modernity is represented by the philosophers: the principle of the state (Hobbes); the principle of the market (Locke); and the principle of community (Rousseau).[31] Of the three, however, it is Locke and Rousseau who have been most often credited by liberal theorists with the genesis of the liberal democratic tradition, in part because aspects of Hobbes' theory make him less flattering to liberalism.

For the purposes of the argument here it is important to focus on Hobbes and Locke. Locke is important to the present analysis because his is the form of liberalism that gained ascendancy in the context of emergent capitalism, and because his discussion of property is considered foundational to the justification of the inequalities of capitalist society. A wide range of liberal apologists rely on allegedly Lockean foundations. Although it may be going too far to suggest that Locke was the conscious author of contemporary liberal capitalism,[32] it is nonetheless possible to argue that contemporary liberal capitalism owes much to the use (and/or abuse) of Locke's theory as a justificatory foundation for later ideological positions. Hobbes is important for present purposes because, although, as Douzinas argues, the influence of Hobbes may have waned in politics, he was nonetheless the first philosopher completely to replace the notion of justice with the idea of rights. Moreover, if this aspect of Hobbes' work is properly understood, 'legal positivism becomes the necessary accompaniment and partner of rights discourse'.[33] In other words, it is in Hobbes that we find a strong conceptual link between liberalism and positivism – a link which invokes an important strand of critique concerning the rationalism of law and the related excision of social context (a point noted analogously in the last chapter in the discussion of positivist theories of legal personality in particular).

Given the implications of Hobbes' philosophy for both the philosophy of modern rights and the centrality of legal positivism, it is worth briefly drawing out some relevant aspects of his account. Hobbes presents natural rights as the power to do anything, as an expression of an unlimited, undivided sovereignty of the individual.[34] In Hobbes' state of nature,[35] a state of unconfined desire and untrammelled action, natural equality means that this unlimited, unencumbered power is shared by all. This equality, however, is grounded in the equal capacity to kill: 'Nature hath made men so equal, in the faculties of body, and mind... the weakest has strength enough to kill the strongest...'.[36] This unappealing conception of equality (combined with Hobbes' amoral way of reading morality in which pleasure defines good and pain defines evil) leads to war between individuals because, 'when the individual becomes the centre of the world, when fear, hate and love are the only ends of action, everyone is entitled to self-preservation and to the means to achieve it'.[37] Regulation therefore becomes the only escape. Hobbes is (in the words of Santos) the 'archetypal expounder of the modern principle of the state' because, for Hobbes, the social contract is the device by which this war between individuals is curbed by a civil society based on 'the absolute sovereignty of the state'.[38] That sovereign, moreover, is presented as a personification of the individual as the illimitable self – as a mortal god – its only limit being death, the 'absolute master'. Thus, the power of the sovereign is total, without limit – taking 'the characteristics of natural man and his right'.[39] In Hobbes' formulation, therefore, rights are rendered profoundly dependent upon the absolute power of the state because rights, after the social contract, ultimately derive from the will of the sovereign. This is the theoretical position which produces legal positivism as the 'inevitable accompaniment of the individualism of rights'.[40]

The tendency towards positivism in Hobbes is linked to Hobbes's seduction by modern science, and above all, 'by science's potential to achieve incontrovertible order' in both knowledge and politics.[41] But, as Santos notes, 'such an epistemology leads to reductionism: politics is separated from ethics; morality becomes a function of self-interest; good and evil are reduced to objects for which there is either an appetite or aversion.[42]

Hobbes wrote in a context where old certainties were being radically shaken. New social developments and movements were generating a changing world in which the pre-existing consensus about the common good was dissolving. What Hobbes observed was the emergence of a divided society in which individuals could 'articulate and pursue their own conceptions of the good in the face of variant and competing conceptions advanced by others'.[43] Hobbes foresaw civil breakdown and strife, the 'war of every man against every man' – and turned, in response, to the social contract and a strong sovereign in an attempt to provide some form of control. Hobbes' thinking can therefore be interpreted as anticipating and arguably facilitating a state-centric reductionist form of modern regulation.[44] Arguably, at the same time it also unconsciously prepares the way for the later elevation of positivism as a technique for cloaking the inequalities produced by the capitalist state order.

Macpherson insists that the only consistent view of society that emerges from an analysis of Hobbes' theory is a theory of society which provides 'non-violent ways by which every man can constantly seek power over others without destroying the society' – in other words, a 'possessive market society'.[45] For Macpherson, the inequalities of such a capitalist society are, in Hobbes' theory, produced by two rather distasteful kinds of equality: equal insecurity and equal subservience to the market.[46] This logic implies an inexorable moral reductionism. As Macpherson puts it, 'Hobbes saw, accurately, that in a possessive market society all values and entitlements are in fact established by the operation of the market, and all morality tends to be the morality of the market'.[47] In this regard, argues Macpherson, Hobbes was more perceptive than those who argued in defence of a more traditional morality. Hobbes was correct to predict that, once the market system was established no individual in it would be able to escape its logic, and that 'all rational men in it had to accept the market concept of justice as the only one'.[48] Given the centrifugal nature of the forces of market self-interest, the power of a centralised state becomes a necessary antidote – necessary, above all, to protect individual property rights. Hobbes was thus 'far ahead of any contemporary philosopher in the depth of his insight' concerning the inevitability of centralised state power in a possessive market society.[49]

Hobbes can accordingly be credited with the conceptualisation of a legal system based on individual rights, market relations, contract, a supreme state and its law.[50] In this juridico-political configuration, the sovereign state is illimitable, made in the very image of the market individual, and arising by necessity in response to conflictual, ever-shifting desire.[51] For Douzinas, this produces a savage and enduring paradox: 'the precondition of individual property rights is the absence of political and human rights, subjection the precondition of freedom. This is the tragedy of individualism, mitigated by the introduction of democracy but still present in the various forms of neo-liberalism'.[52] Individualism in the possessive society produces individuals whose drives bring them into market competition, thus creating the necessity for an overbearing external state power, and in this sense, 'Hobbes caught both the freedom and the compulsion of possessive market society'.[53] However, Hobbes' view of the society he sought to justify was, in a sense, deeply unflattering – and his view of the sovereign equally unappealing. For the English propertied class, as Macpherson points out, such unfavourable exposure, even presented as science, was unlikely to be popular.

This may well explain the preference for Locke's more 'ambiguous' doctrine.[54] Locke, in contrast to Hobbes, rejects the idea of absolute sovereignty. Accordingly his work is usually presented as the seminal foundation of liberalism. Locke clearly connects the legitimacy of government with its observance of certain limits. Government exists to protect natural rights and is only legitimate if natural rights are respected. Locke therefore places government under law, and conceptualises the rule of law as being the safeguard against tyranny and the abuse of power.

Despite some clear differences, Locke and Hobbes share certain key assumptions – especially the primacy of desire.[55] Santos certainly sees in Locke the privileging of the principle of the market.[56] In fact, Hobbes and Locke have both been read as defending the emergence of a market society populated by possessive individuals.[57] Locke's theory would at least have been appealing to the propertied classes of his time. Locke conceptualised the preservation of property as the 'great and chief end... of men's uniting into commonwealth and putting themselves under government',[58] but without the unflattering view of man's possessive nature presented by Hobbes. Locke's state of nature, rather than being a construct reflecting the brutal competitiveness of men, is inhabited by men in a more conducive state of, in Santos' words, 'perfect freedom, of equality and independence and, in general, a state of peace and goodwill and mutual assistance'.[59] However, Santos' reading of the state of nature arguably overlooks important arguments made by Macpherson as to the existence of inequalities in the state of nature and the implications of that for the normative justification of capitalist accumulation.

Although Macpherson has been accused of a certain degree of revisionism in his reading of Locke, reading Locke 'as if the future had already happened'[60] his reading is particularly useful to us because it seems to reflect a strong reaction to the ideological use to which Locke's theory was later put, particularly in the context of legal property theory. There is much dispute about the true nature of Locke's theory. But central to his theory, and widely accepted as such, is his assertion (and defence) of a *natural* individual right to property. Wood, for example, has argued that, for eighteenth century jurists Locke was 'the classic theorist of landed society and the landowners'.[61] This emphasises again the reticulation between Locke's theory and the interests of the dominant propertied class. The centrality of property to Locke's account is indisputable and has been thoroughly exploited by variant interpretations. Early nineteenth century socialists used it to defend the notion of worker's rights, for example, while, in the twentieth century, Locke was cited as the archetypal defender of private property – first, limited private property and then unlimited private property.[62]

Macpherson's analysis offers a particularly useful lens through which to understand the subsequent use of Locke's theory to justify the notion of unlimited capitalist appropriation. According to Macpherson,[63] Locke used natural right and natural law to found his property right. Crucially, he then removed all of the natural law limits from the right of property[64] but, equally crucially, did so in the state of nature – before the social contract founding civil society.[65] Initially, Locke's natural property right is limited, in that 'Man' can mix his labour with the earth to produce only what is useful and necessary for his self-preservation and happiness, and must avoid unnecessary waste. However, with the introduction of money, these restrictions are relaxed. The decisive shift occurs in section 36 of the *Second Treatise* where Locke explicitly argues that the natural law rule which limited the amount that anyone could appropriate to whatever that person could use no longer applies because 'the *Invention of Money*, and the tacit Agreement of Men to put a value on it, introduced (by Consent) larger Possessions, and a Right to them'.[66] Thus, in Locke's theory, the emergence of money dramatically transforms the social relations of property because the natural law rule – which limited the amount any person could appropriate within a proportionate, use-sensitive property order – is explicitly rendered inapplicable.[67]

Moreover, the introduction of money is read by Locke as a tacit agreement to inequality of possessions: a man can now accumulate as much property as he wants.[68] The earlier limitation based on waste or spoilage does not apply to money, because money ('gold and silver' in Locke's language) does not deteriorate. Nor, for that matter, does land. Macpherson points out that Locke's prime focus was on the utilisation of money and land as capital. Moreover, the value of money, as capital, 'is created by the fact of its unequal distribution .... What Locke has done ... is to show that money has made it possible, and just, for a man to accumulate more land than he can use the product of before it spoils ... Locke has justified the specifically capitalist appropriation of land and money'.[69] Importantly, the consent implied by the introduction of money predates the social contract and is established in the state of nature (which in Locke's theory amounts to a 'curious mixture of historical imagination and logical abstraction from civil society').[70] Crucially, this theory of property was used as a justification not only of inequality of property, but of '*unlimited individual appropriation*'.[71]

Douzinas argues that Locke's teaching on property had unforeseen but pivotal effects – placing the individual at the centre of the moral and political universe as its progenitor, a progenitor who is at the same time liberated from both nature and the social bonds that existed before the social contract. In this new order '[s]elf reliance and creativity become the hallmarks of human achievement, acquisitiveness the mark of self-realisation and dignity'.[72] It is not difficult to see how this image of the natural man might serve the socio-economic interests of an emergent capitalist class. Macpherson concludes that Locke had successfully erased the moral limits placed on unlimited capitalist appropriation, justifying and producing a positive moral foundation for capitalist society.[73] While the attempt to justify the *particular* ideological formation of capitalism at the sharp end of Macpherson's critique may not have been conscious in the writings of Locke (as Macpherson's critics have argued) – Locke's attempt to justify the new socio-political order of his day *was* a self-conscious task. Indeed, both Hobbes and Locke (like Rousseau) saw themselves as engaged in the justification of a new social and political order.[74]

What this brief examination of Hobbes and Locke reveals is that the foundations of modern legal rights and the genesis of legal positivism – notwithstanding the presence of 'contending liberalisms'[75] in the seventeenth and eighteenth centuries – cannot easily be separated from the distinctive ideological journey of early liberal capitalism. Liberal legal individualism and the property-rationalising project of liberal law emerged with the interests of a new social class, a class well-served by the social contract philosophers for whom the individual stood at the centre of the world, wielding rights in the name of individual self-interest.[76] In this light, the liberal concepts of free individualism and the centrality of rights, so often viewed ahistorically, as being intrinsic to the triumph of reason and progress as part of an enlightenment project, are revealed as rather more contingent in their orientation. They reflect a particular ideological tilt that coincided well with the service of certain social interests.[77] Liberal law arguably reflects the ultimate dominance of these interests over the various more radical, critical strands of liberalism that sought to challenge the consolidation of property and power in the hands of the emergent propertied classes.[78]

The nineteenth century: The ascendancy of legal positivism

Liberal capitalism reached its next important stage of development in the nineteenth century when capitalism became the dominant mode of production – a point from which the modern law and the paradigm it inhabits became entangled more profoundly, inextricably perhaps, with the unfolding of capitalism.[79] A key development in the nineteenth century for present purposes is the level of the state's responsiveness to the needs of liberal capitalism – reflected in the rise of legal positivism. Santos, for example, has argued that 'the rise of positivism in the epistemology of modern science and the rise of legal positivism in law and jurisprudence belong together as ideological constructs aimed at reducing social progress to capitalistic development'.[80] Modern science and modern law were produced as related facets of a rationalistic discourse. Within legal discourse rationalistic jurisprudence served to cloak the exclusionary implications of the elevation of the hyper-rational acquisitive property owner as being the proto-beneficiary of the new legal and political order. Accordingly, 'the violence at the heart of law and of public and private power, which had helped re-organise the world according to the new political and economic orthodoxies, was written out of the texts of the law, which became obsessed with normative questions, with the meaning of rights, sovereignty or representation'.[81] This masking of the operations of exclusory power through the use of an abstractionist cloaking technique has already been mentioned in relation to the construction of legal personality, both 'natural' and corporate. But this abstractionism is arguably most explicit in relation to the P1 (and its ideologically related P3) conception of legal personhood.

Recall that P1 theories insist on the empty formality of the legal person, denying any necessary analytical connection to a notion of a pre-legal entity or person. We can now see more clearly that this positivist insistence on constructing P1 as an autonomous logical form reflects a historically contingent liberal commitment to the presentation of law as a form of scientific rationality. While, as we saw above, this emerged in the work of Hobbes, during the nineteenth century law was re-constituted as a supremely rational state law in a context in which the disciplinary power of the state was united with science to produce new forms of social control.[82] New disciplinary technologies of power accompanied a relatively hegemonic positivism as law turned towards science. Law was accordingly conceptualised as a rational, technical formalism aimed at logical coherence, seamless coverage and certainty, the effective fusion of scientism and statism – producing what Weber characterised as formal legal domination, a domination 'legitimated by the rational system of state-enacted universal and abstract laws, presiding over a bureaucratic and professional administration, and applied throughout society through a form of justice based on logical formal rationality'.[83]

The positivistic commitment to law as a rational, technical, autonomous formalism is problematic. Law cannot completely excise the social – and nor can techno-legal logic remain pristine when applied to the social world. We have already noted two ways in which P1 is inadequate in theoretical terms. First, it fails to account for the ways in which material relations produce jural outcomes. Secondly, P1 theories tend to neglect consideration of the form that the legal person takes on materialisation – which is almost invariably the P3 rationalist liberal legal subject, as argued in Chapter 3. Ironically, the attempted positivist excision of social context is what ruptures the pure rationality of law. While rationality and liberal legality are inextricably intertwined, the attempted excision of the social produces legal *irrationality* – a point that becomes particularly clear in Norrie's critical reading of criminal law.

Liberal legality depends on logic, because the rule of law, the guarantor of formal justice between formally equal social actors, depends on the non-arbitrary application of rules. Accordingly,

> [legality] depends upon a system of norms that do not contradict each other, that are consistent and coherent. It requires that judges recognise and obey already existing rules through a system of precedent. All these things can only happen if the 'glue' that holds a system of laws together is logic or reason. Rationality is fundamental to legality.[84]

However, as Norrie has argued, once one looks beyond the self-presentation of law as rational, one tends to discover contradictions that disrupt the internal logic of the system. Writing in the context of a critical examination of criminal law, Norrie points out that a reading of certain key passages in legal judgments reveals that a commitment to rationality is both proclaimed *and* denied: 'Rationality is both a central legal virtue and an impossibility. Lawyers, both practising and academic, make their arguments on the assumption that logical reasoning is a central requirement, but in their moments of doubt, or when pushed to a position they do not accept, they jettison logic or insist on its limits.'[85] The jettisoning of logic at the fractured boundaries of rationality is not, however, understood as a response to the kind of limits that Norrie suggests they are. They are not seen or acknowledged as '*historical and social* limits on a reasoning process that is necessarily contradictory'.[86] Moreover, these limits, arising from a social world fraught with conflict, do *not* lead to the restructuring of legal discourse to take them into account – lawyers and legal theorists remain fully committed to a task of the rational reconstruction of the law.

Norrie argues that to understand the internal tension between rationality and irrationality in the law, one must look, primarily, at the intellectual structure of law and at the context in which that structure was developed – namely, in the crucible of specific social relations in an identifiable historical context.[87] The key to understanding law's tension is thus to be found in the socio-historical emergence of legal and liberal individualism. Norrie identifies the relevant historical context as being the late eighteenth and early nineteenth centuries – the period when legal individualism became dominant and liberal capitalism was in the process of gaining social dominance. Horwitz argues that mainstream liberal legal scholarship is also a part of this rationalising enterprise, part of an 'attempt to suppress the real contradictions in the world, to make the existing world seem necessary ... to be part of the nature of things'.[88]

Norrie's critical reading of the development of criminal law in the nineteenth century reveals that the emphasis placed on individual rights in liberal legal theory was a bulwark utilised to defend emerging middle class interests in new forms of property and wealth that characterised mercantile and then industrial capitalism. The criminal law was developed, by the nineteenth century criminal law reformers, *precisely* to safeguard these emergent property-orientated interests. The non-property owning class and the rising working class had to be taught that property rights were exclusive. Accordingly, in that period traditional 'customary rights' over land were submerged by an extensive series of land enclosures[89] and the introduction of new intensive capitalist agricultural methods, while the invasion of landed private property rights was labelled as 'crime'. Likewise, the old practise of tolerated pilferage was reconstituted as 'theft'.

The consequence of these new, 'objective', criminal laws was the production of a subject, a

> knowing individual subject, responsible for his actions. The reformers represented middle class interests and expressed these in the individualist ideology of their intellectual spokesmen, the political economists. The individual was conceived of as a rational economic actor, able to calculate what was in his own best interests. Just as the market regulates individual economic actors, so the criminal law regulates social conduct as an adjunct to the market.[90]

In other words, the legal subject produced to inhabit the criminal law of the nineteenth century was a significant instantiation of the P3 liberal actor – a translation of the economically astute market-man of possessive individualism into the form of a criminal subject who could calculate the costs and benefits of crime and punishment – a position clearly reflected by the development of utilitarian theories of deterrent punishment.[91] The new objective, rational criminal law and its calculating subject were birthed together in the age of industrial capitalism precisely to protect the forms of property and wealth produced by capitalism.[92]

This legal subject was, however, an abstraction. Disembodied and decontextualised, the 'juridical man' of the reformers was hyper-rational in his ability to calculate costs and benefits. He was also constructed, as Norrie notes, 'at the cost of every social circumstance that actually brings individuals to reason and calculate in particular ways'.[93] Norrie points out that crime was a social problem arising out of particular social conditions and constructed in the context of social conflict between classes with opposing views of morality. But, for the law reformers, the world was populated by atomistic individuals operating freely in a consensual context. The market and the law were conceived of as zones of rational exchange and neutrality rather than as conflict-ridden sites of power struggle between different classes. In Norrie's view '[i]ndividualistic ideological abstractions triumphed over bitter social realities, but the realities did not thereby obligingly disappear'.[94] The period of liberal capitalism in the nineteenth century is thus aptly described as setting in motion 'the social process of exclusion and the concentration of modernity'.[95] Law and legal theory played a crucial role in this powerful exclusory process, systematically suppressing the gap between the inequality-ridden reality of the emergent social relations and the juridical presentation of social relations.[96]

> In legal theory, the contradictions were kept at bay so long as the logic of abstract individualism and the myths of the political economy were adhered to. In theory, each individual was the same as every other. All were potential possessors of property rights, all potential offenders against them. That in reality the possessors and the offenders came from different social classes constituted hardly a ripple on the millpond of theory.[97]

The liberal legal subject of rights

At the root of the emerging liberal economic/juridical person of law lay a very particular conception of the individual – an abstraction that emphasised self-interest, rationality and calculation: the quintessential (or 'central case' or, in Weberian terms, 'ideal') liberal legal subject: P3. The gap between the messy, conflictual social circumstances of human life and the mythic legal construction of social relations as being consensual and rational parallels a corresponding gap between the legal subject and the human being. The liberal legal subject is an 'empty' or 'thin' subject: 'the caricature of the real person, a cartoon-like figure which, as all caricature, exaggerates certain features and characteristics and totally misses others'.[98] The gap takes the form, suggests Douzinas, of 'both excess and lack, and becomes fully visible when people start legal proceedings'.[99] The excess is constituted by the law's ascription to the subject of an extreme rationalism – the ability to reason and calculate, to make rational socially unencumbered choices – and this exercise of unencumbered choice is attributed to the legal person regardless of whatever constraining social circumstances might operate to hinder reason, calculation and choice. On the other hand, in terms of lack, the legal subject is stripped of the characteristics that create human identity. This subject is disembodied, decontextualised and devoid of a complex emotional interiority.

Quasi-disembodiment plays a crucial role in the liberal construction of the hyper-rational legal person. This is because, as noted in the last chapter, disembodiment is a feature of Western rationality in general and law in particular: 'law, as *nomos*, has always been predicated as a function of the mind and therefore in a hierarchical opposition to materiality which law serves to order and govern'.[100] The law's dualistic division between body and mind means that 'anything to do with the body or the senses is not part of the realm of reason and must be bracketed or excluded'.[101] The liberal legal subject can be read as a radical 'emancipation of the self from its contexts' (especially social and material realities). Such a reading performs a function of ideological closure, enabling the self 'to be emancipated from all forces and influences other than law itself'.[102] The liberal legal subject is, in the words of Douzinas, 'an isolated and narcissistic subject that perceives the world as a hostile place to be either used or fended against through the medium of rights and contracts [and] she is also disembodied, genderless, a strangely mutilated person'.[103] (The argument thus far renders Douzinas' use of the feminine pronoun misleading and inapt. The legal person or subject may be conceptualised as abstract, and in that sense 'genderless'. However, the disembodiment operative in liberal legal rationality is a form of quasi-disembodiment. Thus, in reality, the legal person bears the imprint of the presumed gender of rationality itself – *maleness*.) Liberal legal ideology constitutes the legal person as the quasi-disembodied entity who stands at the centre of the legal universe. As Schlag argues, that legal person is a 'metaphysical or calculating, self-interested being, conceived in an asocial way in a world whose sociality was no more than the coming together of individuals in a social contract... the law knew no real individuals, only their mystical abstractions'.[104]

Within this logic rights are pivotal elements. Rights operate as vehicles through which individual self-interest is expressed in forms of publicly exercised capacity: 'modern law made rights its building blocks' and human beings, the possessors of rights, are, particularly in the P3 conception, 'creatures of will and desire'.[105] Liberal legal logic is thus a logic of individual right and self-interest which produces a strange juxtaposition between the desiring self and its individualism and the abstract universalism foundational to the liberal legal mythology of justice. This leads to a contradiction between liberal claims to a universal inclusiveness and the realities of socio-historical exclusion. For

> [a]s a logic of individual right, law sets up requirements of universality and equality in its application. If all individuals are the same, then they should all be treated the same... Yet law is at the same time directed to the defence of the interests of wealth and power in society.... [T]he law entails 'a logic of equity', a tendency to seek 'to transcend the inequalities of class power which, instrumentally, it is harnessed to serve'.[106]

According to Douzinas, contemporary rights theories improve upon earlier versions by recognising the context-dependent nature of effective rights implementation, thus allowing for explicit consideration of the material and institutional resources available for the implementation of rights. Notwithstanding this improvement, though, 'the "ontology" of rights remains fully wedded ... analytically tied to rule-governed behaviour; rules create rights and rights belong to people, they exist only with the support of a subject'.[107] The precise nature of that subject is, accordingly, fundamental.

The liberal subject of rights: A recent elaboration

As we have already seen, rights logically require (or presuppose) a subject, but law's subjects are always a 'constructed *subjectus*' – a legal creation. Notwithstanding the central function of the construction of the subject in law, there has been, as noted in the last chapter, a general 'jurisprudential abstinence on the subject of the subject'.[108] According to Douzinas, however, Nino's writings afford a notable exception to this silence.[109] We shall briefly introduce some key themes in Nino's writing for the purpose of bringing the construction of the legal person closer to the key concern of this book – namely, the construction of the subject of human rights.

Nino defends a specifically liberal vision of the subject of human rights which relates to a justification of 'the normative principles underlying a liberal view of society'.[110] For Nino, legal subjects are 'not tied to any end, they are an originating source of valid claims, and they are responsible for their ends'.[111] Douzinas suggests that '[i]n this important formulation, we find the main elements of legal subjectivity'.[112] What emerges as being the most important characteristic of the liberal legal subject is the ability to choose. The liberal legal subject is the origin of his own interests and desires – the originating source of valid claims as Nino puts it – and this power to choose is what makes the legal subject responsible. The world is, accordingly, populated by unfettered persons whose freedom (and legal accountability) is constituted by free choice. The social world thus formulated is one in which rights are foundational building blocks, and in which '[t]he ability to choose is the most important characteristic and "the person constituted by it is prior to any end, interest and desire". This implies that when we refer to an interest or a desire, we presuppose a subject, and that the identity of that subject, the moral person, does not change with its ends, interests or desires'.[113] The will is the substratum or permanent force that constitutes the subject of rights, a formulation that conceptualises rights as conduits for the legalisation of the choices of the wilful, desiring self: 'rights legalise individual will and materialise individual desire'.[114]

Nino's emphasis on the nature of liberal rights is important. It links the public capacity to legally enforce private will to the P3 legal person (in particular) as the choosing, calculating, self-interested legal actor in a way that renders rights discourse an ideal tool for the expression of capitalist desire. And, if rights operate as 'public capacit[ies] given to the individual to allow him to attain his private objects of desire',[115] we can discern the way in which human rights, translated into a liberal form of legal right, are in an important and central sense, inherently open to being formulated as conduits for the mediation of capitalist desire, including corporate 'desire'/ 'preferences'.

The corporation and capitalism: Personification and ideology

Throughout this chapter there has been, in one way or another, an emphasis on the unfolding of modern positive law as a rationalising enterprise aimed at the protection of a broadly liberal capitalist political and economic order. Neocleous develops this argument further by focusing critical attention specifically on the corporate form, choosing the 'corporate *persona* worn by capital' to illustrate the argument that 'modern law has facilitated the mechanism by which capital dominates civil society'.[116] If we examine law's ideological tilt through the lens of *personification* we again find a telling confluence between the construction of the criminal subject (already briefly noted), the interests of the capitalist class, and the construction of the corporate personality.

Unsurprisingly, the nineteenth century emerges as a decisive period. Taking Marx's notion of personification, but reinterpreting it for strategic purposes, Neocleous argues that 'what is at stake in the process of personification is the juridical as well as the socio-economic conditions which enable *things* to appear as *non-human persons*'.[117] Neocleous demonstrates that this transmutation of 'things' into non-human persons was achieved in the nineteenth century when company law was modernised. Moreover, he argues, this personification of things as non-human persons has been decisive for the entrenchment of the social power of corporate capital.

Noting that anti-capitalist resistance to corporate power barely ever focuses on the *corporate form*, Neocleous proceeds to analyse the implications of the reformulation of corporate status in the nineteenth century, referring to the Joint Stock Companies Registration and Regulation Act 1844, the Joint Stock Companies Act 1856 and the Companies Acts 1862.[118] These were the Acts that paved the way for the momentous decision of the House of Lords in *Salomon v Salomon and Co Ltd*[119] – the case that 'formally defined and recognised the private company as the legal form of capital'.[120] As we noted in the last chapter, this case has been credited with establishing the constitutive preconditions of the corporate conglomerates which are now so dominant.[121] Correspondingly, Neocleous argues that the historic significance of the case for the 'intensification of capital accumulation was enormous ... what was being developed was a special legal subjectivity for capital, arising from the nature of capital itself'.[122]

To understand the special nature of this subjectivity, the corporate form requires a nuanced appreciation that draws a careful distinction between its economic and legal aspects. Neocleous argues that the legal subjectivity of the corporate form has two components: first a new legal body, the incorporated company. He argues that the 1862 Companies Act contained wording that effected a shift from persons forming 'themselves' into an incorporated company to the notion of persons forming a company 'by them' but not 'of them'. From that point, he argues, 'companies have been referred to as "it" rather than "they"'.[123] Secondly, there was the constitution of a new form of property – the share – which now stood conceptualised as property in its own right. Rather than 'ownership of a share of the compan[y's] assets... in a host of cases the courts found that shareholders in incorporated companies had interests only in the profits and not the assets'.[124] The shareholder had no property in or right to any company asset other than to the share. The company assets were now the company's property: 'In effect the development of company law had produced a new form of legal subject, the private corporation, and a new form of property, the share'.[125]

What these developments achieved was the establishment of the corporation as 'a new and independent legal subject, every bit as real in law as the new personal subjects of the classic legal form, *though totally removed from those subjects*'.[126] It is the corporation as subject that has ownership of capital as property, but the corporation is also nothing but capital – thus rendering capital both subject and object. It is this legal subject which 'took to the stage as a fully-fledged *persona*, as capitalist states were at pains to clarify in the late-nineteenth century'.[127] In Britain, the Interpretation Act 1889 stipulated that, in that Act and every Act passed after its commencement, the expression 'person' should (unless the contrary intention appears) be interpreted to include any body of persons – corporate or unincorporated. Meanwhile, in America, in 1886, the US Supreme Court interpreted the 14th Amendment of the US Constitution to include the corporation as a legal person.

This nineteenth century development in the personification of corporations is intimately related to the shifts in liberal law that we have already noted in relation to nineteenth century criminal law reform in Britain, and to law's role as a rationalising project aimed at the protection of middle class property interests by the concomitant production and control of new notions of criminality. Federman offers an account of the virtually simultaneous construction of corporate and criminal persons in America,[128] an account consistent with Norrie's reading of the ideological structure of English criminal law, and which supports the argument already introduced in this book, but soon to be made more fully, that liberal law is tilted in favour of the corporation and its interest in capital accumulation.

It was also during the nineteenth century that corporations broke away from the state in America[129] – and, as in England, the 'radical rethinking of the role of the corporation ... was but one aspect of a newly emerging society'.[130] This was an era in which there was a move towards privatisation as the values of industrial capitalism took hold in a context of increasing technological and social complexity. (It should be noted that the nineteenth century American conceptualisation of the corporation has been decisively influential on our understanding of the corporation today.)

Federman's analysis of the emergence of the corporate person in the jurisprudence of the American Supreme Court, and the simultaneous construction of the 'criminal' in American law, both suggest that the American judiciary, like the law reformers in Britain, were constructing a mechanism through which to disperse the new and conflicting interests generated by industrial capitalism. The shifting interests of a capitalist class also explain, to a large degree, the shifting fortunes of the various theories of the nature of the corporate form, as noted in the last chapter.

Federman reads the production of different kinds of persons (corporate and criminal) in 1886 in America as being the discursive production of criminal and corporate bodies. He begins by noting the two-pronged nature of the construction of an entity by using the analogy of mental illness provided by Hacking. Hacking argues that 'a "feature of a new mental illness is that it embeds itself in a two-headed way in a culture" producing two versions of the same thing: one healthy, the other ill'.[131] Hacking argues that to stabilise the two-pronged entity it is necessary to separate its aspects – the idealised rationalist image of the self from the deviant image of the self 'such that both versions become understood, explainable, and classifiable'. This bifurcation mechanism, applied to the construction of the legal subject, in turn produces an ahistorical self which the law rapidly comes to possess. The two selves are united by an oppositional relationship. This is the template, argues Federman, within which the corporate and criminal persons produced in 1886 in America should be understood.

Federman identifies two cases, *County of Santa Clara v Southern Pacific Railroad*[132] and *Ex parte Royall*,[133] both heard in the Supreme Court in 1886, as being the first emergence within US jurisprudence of the judicial classification and assessment of personalities using 'extra-legal signs of health and illness and productivity versus inefficiency'.[134] What is telling in Federman's analysis is the way in which the law, in a double move, categorises the corporation as the model American citizen, and the criminal as the deviant who poses a dark threat to private economic well-being. Corporate and criminal persons, accordingly, were almost simultaneously constructed. The Supreme Court awarded corporations the status of persons for the purposes of the 14th Amendment, while excluding criminals seeking federal remedies for unlawful imprisonment by state courts on habeas corpus from the national privileges extended to corporations, and 'both cases ... fed off each other: the "privileged norms" of corporate personhood were "reinforced by the reaction against the transgressor"'.[135]

Interestingly, Federman notes that, '[f]or the first time in American constitutional law, the legal person takes shape not simply as a bearer of traditional English liberties, with all that implies regarding personal autonomy, but as a corporate "person", who is not dissimilar to the bearer of traditional English liberties, and yet is structurally different'.[136] The corporate person, as suggested in the last chapter, seems to be a manifestation, in an important sense, of the P3 construct of the legal person in ideological terms. The corporation emerged in the nineteenth century as 'the new American man, the bodily expression of male power'.[137] In one sense this is unsurprising. The social changes and historical shifts leading up to the personification of the corporation in America reflect the shifting strategies of corporate lawyers protecting the developing business community interest groups.[138] This observation fits with the well-known feminist critique of rights – that rights tend to entrench the competitively asserted rights of privileged groups because those groups (predominantly male, white property-owners) have more effective access to the legal system than socially and economically disempowered groups.[139] The shift to corporate personhood was nothing more than the product of an influential group imposing its values and interests on American society during a time of economic revolution.[140] The shift also reflected the inadequacies of the fiction and group theories of the corporation to account for the growing functional economic autonomy of the corporation, itself driven by changing political and functional realities in a shifting social context.[141] These shifts played a pivotal role in the arguments concerning corporate autonomy played out before the courts.[142]

Mayer notes, in a similar vein, how the US Supreme Court has increasingly conferred Bill of Rights protection on corporations. At the same time, it is significant that the Court has ceased to theorise and, according to Mayer, currently possesses no coherent or defensible theory of the corporation.[143] The Supreme Court's failure to engage with and reflect upon the underlying normative suitability of the corporation to be a beneficiary of Bill of Rights protection is, moreover, entirely consistent with the unsatisfying lack of judicial reflection on the suitability of granting corporations the protection of a constitutional amendment originally designed for freed slaves in the 'ukase' in the *Santa Clara* case. The effect of this argumentatively undefended granting of status to corporations was predictably problematic: 'By 1938 Justice Hugo Black observed with dismay that, of the cases in which the Court applied the fourteenth amendment during the first 50 years after *Santa Clara*, "less than one half of 1 per cent invoked it in protection of the Negro race, and more than 50 per cent asked that its benefits be extended to corporations"'.[144] This corporate trend of seeking constitutional protection has continued, and expanded, shifting focus from the invocation of 14th amendment protections to the pursuit of due-process orientated protection of property and, later, more intangible protections such as protection for commercial and political free speech, privacy and the rights to government licenses or contracts.

It is clear from Mayer's analysis that such legal developments have been driven by the evolving political economy – led by corporate assertions of Bill of Rights privileges for themselves in direct response to increasing governmental attempts to develop regulation aimed at the protection of the environment, society and the consumer. In fact, opposition to modern regulation 'has become a unifying point for corporate interests opposed to reforms passed at the behest of labor, consumer and public interest groups'.[145] The increasingly successful corporate invocation of Bill of Rights protection has, unsurprisingly, brought about significant adverse consequences for individuals, particularly with regard to the aggressive assertion, by corporations, of commercial free speech rights. Mayer cites, as just one example, the corporate defence of cigarette advertising as a form of commercial free speech – an assertion involving the concomitant willingness to override the individual's right to be protected from tobacco advertising. He notes evidence of intimidation aimed at individuals who argued for the restriction of advertising. He concludes that 'the corporation's invocation of the Bill of Rights to protect Modern Property (the ability to advertise) and to thwart Modern Regulation (federal measures to protect health and the environment) impinges on individual liberties'.[146] He also observes how corporations utilise first amendment protections of political speech to subvert or derail government regulation.[147]

It is revealing that these developments have been directly accompanied by the demise of the theorisation of corporate personhood. Mayer notes that the US Supreme Court abandoned theorising about corporate personhood after about 1960, and that, while in some ways, this 'drastic doctrinal reversal is extraordinary, especially considering the frequency with which corporate constitutional rights are now asserted', in other respects this 'modern, pragmatic, antitheoretical approach is the prosaic legitimation of the corporation's constitutional status'.[148] Again, the widespread tendency of judges to avoid engagement with the normative status of corporate claims is conspicuous. This has distinct resonance with Norrie's assertion that the judiciary itself is embedded within law as part of a systemic rationalising enterprise in which legal reasoning involves the excision of social realities and the devaluing of claims that counter or contest the capitalist interests so intimately woven into the genesis of modern law. Mayer hits the ideological nail on the head when he suggests that the absence of judicial attention to the theoretical questions underlying corporate use of the Bill of Rights avoids difficult questions: '[t]his pragmatic approach is a less controversial guarantor of corporate rights than a theoretical methodology that raises fundamental questions about the nature of a corporation and its role in society'.[149] He also notes that, despite various reasons for the demise of corporate theory, including concern on the part of the US Supreme Court about whether it has any legitimate claim to define the nature and purpose of the corporation, 'the lack of a consistent basis for according corporations constitutional guarantees is all the more puzzling as the demand for corporate protection increases'.[150]

Corporations: The ultimate legal person?

We have noted, both here and in the previous chapter, the tendency of law's person towards disembodiment and abstractionism, accompanied by an emphasis on the legal person as a possessive individual, hyper-rational, calculating, and whose most important characteristic is the ability to choose. We have linked P1 and P3 to this in more explicit terms than P2 (which we shall attend to more closely in the next chapter) and have explored the nature of P1 and P3 as intimately related manifestations of a fairly consistent construction of liberal legal personhood. We have seen that the liberal legal person bears all the ideological hallmarks of an inextricable association with historically contingent and identifiable interests reflecting the emergence and contours of liberal capitalism, and consolidated throughout the nineteenth century when corporations emerged as fully-fledged legal persons in their own right.

It is arguable, in fact, that it is the corporation rather than the human being who emerges as the ideal legal person of liberal law. This appears to be so in two key respects. First, the corporate actor fits law's disembodied reading of legal personhood. Secondly, the corporate actor reflects the ideological characteristics, in particular, of the P3 legal actor, almost seamlessly.

Law's disembodiment and the abstractionism of legal discourse mean that the corporation, as a disembodied jural entity (as distinct from the human sub-stratum beneath it), perfectly fits the template of legal personhood in a way that the concrete, embodied, socially-situated human being simply cannot. This alone gives the corporate form a distinct advantage over the living human being. For it both fits law's template for the ideal legal actor, benefitting from this correspondence, while, at the same time corporate disembodiment means that the corporation is a particularly complex target for legal accountability, especially in the context of criminal accountability for harms committed against human beings. Although corporations can be said to possess a complex 'corporality' which is conceptually dependent upon legal concepts of embodied personhood,[151] it is clear that, in key respects, the corporate form stands in direct contrast to certain material aspects of embodied humanity. The corporation is, for example, immortal – a fact that stands in stark contrast to the all too evident vulnerability of the human being to death. Human beings are at risk from random perils in a material world in which either accident or the exercise of malign intent can result in their physical and absolute termination as material beings. Bodies can be killed. This is precisely what the law relies on when, for example, some legal systems impose the death penalty. Although it can be argued that company law permits companies to wind up voluntarily and that this can be said to constitute a kind of death, it has been argued that this is more equivalent to suicide in which the assets have been distributed before death, rather than, for example, the imposition of a death penalty.[152] And although the distinction between the imposition of death and the notion of suicide is a useful illustration of one aspect of corporate relative invulnerability to criminal sanction, the suicide analogy is not, in any case, on all fours with human suicide. This element of disparity arguably reflects the contrast between disembodiment and embodiment in material terms.

Although both the corporation and the human body can be viewed as social constructs,[153] corporate bodies do not share the same range of vulnerabilities as human beings. This becomes particularly clear and relevant in at least two contexts. One of these, as has just been implied, is the criminal law. The other *should* be, as will be argued in this book, human rights law.

The human body is the reason for human vulnerability to physical death, physical pain and law's punitive body-directed coercion. These are a set of vulnerabilities that that the corporate form simply does not share. Even Addo, arguably a foremost proponent of corporate human rights, admits that corporations are artificial legal entities without the capacity to suffer the same order of harms as human beings, as we noted in Chapter 2. Emberland likewise notes in his study of corporations as human rights beneficiaries that corporations have less at stake in terms of vulnerability within the social order, suggesting that '[c]orporate human rights issues may be judged trivial when compared with alleged violations of an individual human being's dignity, security or participation in political life'.[154] It is clear that corporations simply do not share the same order of vulnerabilities as do embodied human beings. While the vulnerabilities of human beings are inextricably related to their physical embodiment in a material world, the relative invulnerability of corporations to the same order of harms stems from their relative disembodiment. Although they have a corporeality of their own, predicated on an analogy with legal notions of human embodiment, corporations suffer none of the key disadvantages of material embodied vulnerability. Put simply, '[corporations] can live forever. They can change identity in a day. They can cut off parts of themselves and from them grow new selves. ...They don't need fresh air or clean water and don't fear illness or death.'[155]

This key distinction is revealed quite starkly in the context of the criminal law. We have already noted Federman's analysis of the simultaneous construction of two kinds of person, corporate and criminal, in nineteenth century America, and also Norrie's critique of the contiguous rationalising project of the nineteenth century British law reformers who produced new forms of criminality to defend the property interests of the emergent middle class. The tensions inherent in these discursive moves still remain embedded in the criminal law. The criminal law is a site where certain key differences between categories of legal person become explicit. In criminal law, human embodiment underpins the archetypical forms of law's disciplinary power. Criminal process, from arrest through to incarceration, presupposes and acts upon an identifiable material body – that of a human being. It is ultimately the body that is fulcrum point of the law's force, the body that enables the forces of the state apparatus to identify, capture and inhibit the freedom of the criminal.[156]

How then, does the criminal law deal with the crimes and harms committed by corporations? Here, two major issues arise: one is the problem encountered with locating the corporate mind for the purposes of attributing intention to the corporate form – a fact stemming from the complexity of the relationship between the corporate person and its human sub-stratum. The other problem is precisely the absence of a material body. In relation to the first point, there is a genuine conceptual difficulty that has led the courts to identify the mind of the corporation by identifying the minds of its actual human controllers.[157] The difficulty with this attempted solution is that the law requires us to speak of corporations as if they were agents operating with intentions of their own. Consistency with the notion that corporations possess legal personhood means that corporate actions cannot be coherently conceptualised as the actions of human individuals within the sub-stratum of the corporate form:

> For a corporation to be treated as [an] agent it must be the case that some things that happen, some events, are describable in a way that makes certain sentences true, sentences that say that some of the things the corporation does were intended by the corporation itself. That is not accomplished if attributing intentions to a corporation is only a shorthand way of attributing intentions to the biological persons who comprise [it].[158]

On top of these conceptual quandaries, the corporation, as a disembodied jural entity, has no physical body capable of incarceration or corporal or capital punishment. A company cannot therefore be tried for murder in the UK at the present time, as the only punishment available is life imprisonment. The criminal law centrally relies on bodies as the ultimate basis of its coercive ordering function. But the corporate body is simply not amenable to the force of law in this way.[159] Corporate disembodiment, taken together with the difficulties in attributing intention to the corporation as a person, seems to result in a situation where, 'although corporations appear to be persons, they escape any suggestion that they have agency when it comes to harms for which *some* person should be identified as responsible'[160] and, at the same time, they escape the archetypal operations of the punitive force of criminal law.

Corporations are arguably a particular combination of P1 and P3 legal persons. They are quintessentially disembodied as pure legal construct (P1) yet are also assumed to be rational, self-interested, capital accumulators, thus reflecting and magnifying the contours and characteristics of the P3 legal actor. But although they have rational, possessive intention, and are taken to be rational actors, they prove difficult to fix with the type of will and intention necessary for the straightforward imputation of criminal liability[161] as a corporate *person*. Consequently, although corporations appear in law as persons they manage to evade important implications of both embodiment and agency when it comes to being held accountable for harms as persons:

> The law, in other words, works in a way which is far more accommodating to corporate persons than human ones ... the corporation is a person when it comes to the advantages of law, but a 'non-person' when it comes to crimes seemingly committed by it ... the state personalizes capital, but doesn't punish it as a person. It punishes it (when it does) as capital – as something different to (human) persons ... Capital has used the corporate form to its advantage by avoiding some of the most obvious disadvantages of being a legal person, namely responsibility for one's acts. *A propos* of attacks on 'welfare scroungers' and 'the idle poor', one might say that it is the corporation that has acquired plenty of rights but few responsibilities.[162]

This analysis clearly demonstrates that the corporation is in some sense a much closer match to law's persons than human being; but despite this, disembodiment means that corporations escape, in an important way, vulnerability as persons to law's accountability mechanisms. Legal disembodiment thus operates in such a way that corporations enjoy structural advantages in law over human beings.

For human beings, by contrast with the corporation, there is a marked gap between the 'thin' persons of the law and the 'thick' human beings who inhabit the socio-material world which law co-ordinates and controls. This gap, moreover, is a problematic gap in which suffering can and has emerged through mechanisms of exclusion. This is particularly apparent in the case of the P3 construction of the legal person. (We have already noted that liberal legal personality, even P1 – the most formal conception – most often materialises as the systematic advantaging of the P3 legal actor.) There are a set of very real and specifically contoured socio-historic exclusions operative in liberal legal personality that come into the open in social history. Unsurprisingly, there is a vast literature on exclusion in law. Critical legal scholars, race theorists, queer theorists, feminists and others have all consistently argued that social life is far more complex, partial and irrational than liberal law and legal processes portray, and that law's ideological foreclosure disguises the profoundly selective partiality of its viewpoint. As we have already seen, liberal law's claim to neutrality and dispassionate analysis disguises the law's privileging of particular historically contingent interests and ways of conceptualising social relations. The liberal capitalist viewpoint privileged by liberal law has operated as a deeply exclusory construction. Speaking of the way in which a partial viewpoint, when dominant, operates to exclude non-privileged categories of people, MacKinnon argues that liberal law operates as a medium for making such dominance *invisible.* MacKinnon, as a feminist, picks up on the profoundly gendered dimension of this exclusion:

> ... the male standpoint dominates civil society in the form of the objective standard – that standpoint which, because it dominates in the world, does not appear to function as a standpoint at all. Under its aegis, men dominate women and children, three-quarters of the world. Family and kinship rules and sexual mores guarantee reproductive ownership and sexual access and control to men as a group. Hierarchies among men are ordered on the basis of race and class, stratifying women as well. The state incorporates these facts of social power in and as law. Two things happen: law becomes legitimate, and social dominance becomes invisible. Liberal legalism is thus a medium for making male dominance both invisible and legitimate by adopting the male point of view in law at the same time as it enforces that view on society.[163]

P3's historical manifestation as white, gendered, and classed is complex – but nonetheless identifiable. While privileging certain characteristics associated with the rational, acquisitive male citizen, the template of the legal actor operative in liberal law has operated to exclude those who cannot or do not fit the template. Social history is the site in which these exclusions surface in forms of social injustice. For example, while women were theoretically included in the liberal social contract theory underlying the early genesis of modern law, social history reveals that most women were not allowed to sign a contract until a much later time.[164] MacKinnon has made explicit the argument that '[n]o woman had a voice in the design of the legal institutions that rule the social order under which women, as well as men, live':[165]

> [T]he political theory which formed the principled backdrop for the new American republic certainly did not encourage [the visibility of women]. Hobbes grounded natural equality in the ability to kill. Locke argued that whoever did not leave a regime consented to it. Rousseau once posited the primitive passions as 'food, a female, and sleep'.... The exclusion of all women as such from the polity was so far a given that the absence of half the population from the founding process was not

> seen as qualifying its legitimacy – a legitimacy claimed on behalf of 'we, the people' no less.[166]

MacKinnon also notes that many men in the United States were also excluded from the official founding process of the new nation. Her list of excluded groups – women, men and women of colour, indigenous peoples – and the related disqualification from the process of non-property owners, together mark out the specific exclusions corresponding to the construction of the P3 liberal legal actor. Revealingly, the traditional targets for hate-speech of various kinds are radically continuous with the groups implicitly excluded by the cryptic 'insider' template of liberal law. This lends additional weight to the analysis of ideological exclusion in the law, not only in terms of the existence and detailed contours of the insider/outsider construct, but also as regards the seriousness of its consequences for excluded groups. The almost univocal critique generated of the liberal law's insider construct, P3, underscore the crucial fact that, as Friedman has argued, 'law discriminates... the rules themselves... are by no means totally impartial even when impartially applied. They come out of the struggle for power'.[167]

These fundamental exclusions operative in liberal law have not gone uncontested. From beyond the closures of positive law and liberal capitalist rights discourse, critical rights discourse has produced a countervailing set of claims for inclusion – a struggle which has enjoyed varying degrees of success. Returning to our theme of critique and closure in the history of rights introduced at the beginning of this chapter, it is apparent that, at various times, social movements have acted as midwives to rights claims as forms of protest against the extant power structures of their day.[168] In fact, Stammers and Baxi alike, in differing ways, endorse the idea that rights, including human rights, are authored primarily by communities in struggle, by social movements imbued with critical energy.

However, rights are all too frequently co-opted in the service of the powerful. Natural right, as we saw, began as a form of critique, only to be subverted into new forms of authoritarian closure. Natural rights, which emerged in part as the justification of a new social order, were flawed by the emergence of the rationalist possessive individual as the revolutionary potential of natural rights was both recognised and resisted by the propertied class. By the nineteenth century, the century that saw the rise and consolidation of the power of industrial capitalism, natural rights were treated by some as a 'dangerous, revolutionary doctrine which could be effectively utilised by the emerging democratic and socialist opposition movements' to the monarchies of the age.[169] However, natural rights were ideologically compromised (from a critical perspective) by their own quasi-disembodied formulation – and in any case, declined in popularity. They were not only assaulted by the extant powers, but also subjected to the ferocious philosophical onslaught of an ascendant legal positivism, and by the Marxist critique of their bourgeois nature.[170]

Natural rights came into profound disrepute with the dominant political and social forces of the nineteenth century. Arguably, this happened in a way that reveals the outworking of the implications of the quasi-disembodied universal man of rights – and his alter ego, the citizen. Douzinas argues that

> [a]ll assertions of ... rights by the groups and classes excluded from citizenship, women, blacks, workers or political and social reformers, were dismissed as selfish attacks against the common good and the democratic will. This was the era of state and empire-building, of utilitarianism and social engineering, the time of emergence of nationalism, racism and sexism. It was not that these ideas and practices were unknown before the nineteenth century but they now became theorised and respectable elements of European culture.[171]

Thus, there is a problematic gap between the thin person of legal rights and the thick human who lives in the material and social world. The human being is not disembodied, nor is she necessarily the template of the P3 legal actor. The gap that emerges between the formally equal universal bearer of rights and the complex particularity of embodied lives is a gap in which injustice has historically flourished. Corporations emerge in this light as, in a sense, the ideal beneficiaries of rights themselves and as almost archetypical instantiations of the P3 legal subject.

In the light of the analysis offered in this chapter and the last, we are now in a position to offer the interim conclusion that legal disembodiment and the construction of liberal legal subjectivity operate together as a form of complex conceptual conduit through which corporations enjoy distinctive structural advantages over the natural human being in law. Additionally, the intimate linkage between liberal capitalism and the structure of liberal law means that the corporation is arguably the most obvious and powerful beneficiary of the law's ideological tilt towards the possessive individual. As a disembodied, possessive accumulator, the corporation almost perfectly matches the liberal subject of rights, a reality in the light of which the receptivity of international human rights law to corporate human rights discourse becomes entirely less surprising, though it remains as troubling. In order to strengthen the interim conclusion reached here, we shall, in the next chapter, link the liberal subject of rights to international human rights law by exploring how quasi-disembodiment renders even international human rights law (putatively a human rights discourse with human embodiment at its core) open to corporate colonisation.

5
A Genealogy of Quasi-Disembodiment in International Human Rights Law

Introduction

A key theme thus far has concerned the discourse of quasi-disembodiment, a discourse intimately associated with Western rationality and embedded within liberal law. Disembodiment has also been characterised as a defining feature of the construction of the legal person, even in its more 'natural' formulation as the 'human legal person'. In particular, the idea of quasi-disembodiment has been introduced as a gendered ideological mechanism that privileges the submerged primary beneficiary of law: the (male) rational legal actor. In relation to this, it has been suggested that the corporation is arguably the paradigmatic legal person, both structurally and ideologically. The structural and ideological advantage of the corporate form over the human being in legal rationality accordingly provides an important critical backdrop for understanding the receptivity of human rights law to corporate human rights claims.

It is now necessary to link the theme of quasi-disembodiment more directly to the Universal Declaration of Human Rights[1] (UDHR) paradigm. It seems likely that human rights suffer from closures related to quasi-disembodiment at two levels. First, there is a closure invoked by the *abstraction* of the 'universal' possessor of rights. Secondly, a related set of closures are invoked when human rights become positivised as law and the human being becomes the human *legal* subject. In relation to this second level, it seems likely that a challenging convergence between anthropomorphism (a genuine problem in theories of the corporation as well as theories of legal subjectivity more generally) and the closures arising from quasi-disembodied conceptions of the 'natural' legal person (and the related rational 'man' of liberal philosophy) produces a complex but crucial conceptual conduit through which corporations move beyond legal personality to claim inclusion in a notion of something approaching 'legal humanity' through the invocation of human rights law.

Looking at the second level first, we have already covered much argumentative territory in relation to this point. We have noted the nature and pervasiveness of quasi-disembodiment in legal discourse, the privileging of the P3 liberal legal actor in law, the gap between the human being and the legal subject, and the almost perfect fit between the legal subject and the corporation in both analytical and ideological terms: the corporation is both quintessentially disembodied and the archetypal construct of capitalism. By contrast, when the full complexity of embodied human personality meets law a gap exists between the living person and the legal subject. This is a gap, moreover, with significant ethical implications. For, '...the legal subject is a persona or mask put on real people who, unlike the abstractions of moral philosophy, hurt, feel pain and suffer'.[2] We could equally well say that the legal subject is a persona or mask put on real people who are embodied and vulnerable, unlike the abstractions of legal discourse – including the corporate form. While the corporation can be conceptualised as idiosyncratically embodied and as vulnerable in certain respects, it simply does not share the same order of vulnerability, suffering or pain as human beings. This was argued in Chapter 2, where we also saw that the corporation is not a human individual and cannot coherently be reduced to its collective human substratum for the purposes of human rights attribution.

Human rights law is the paradigmatic jural site for the convergence of humanity, law and the legal subject.[3] The implications of the disembodiment associated with legal rationality and the reductionism of legal personality therefore become particularly salient in the human rights context. When human rights ideals are translated into law, human rights become legal rights, albeit of a rather special kind, and the subject of human rights becomes, in this sense, a legal subject – invoking the complexities and closures of legal discourse. This means that living human beings find themselves in an ironic relationship with human rights law. As human beings they live in a material world, are ontologically vulnerable, suffer from material harms and enjoy material benefits. Yet, as human legal subjects, human beings, once they become internalised within legal rationality, become enmeshed in a discourse in which the human person is conceptualised, particularly in liberal law (which has had and continues to have an important impact on international human rights law), as the quasi-disembodied legal subject. This means that, even in international human rights law – arguably the very site where 'humanity' is given notionally central normative status – the full implications of human embodiment are systemically suppressed. The rich complexity of human personality in its psychosomatic matrix and the implications of human physical situatedness (socio-cultural, geographical and environmental) are all, in an important sense, 'lost in translation'.

This chapter briefly explores the role of quasi-disembodiment in rights discourse, particularly in relation to the first level of closure: the abstraction of the human rights universal. However, although this chapter will emphasise quasi-disembodiment in the universal, and a related set of exclusions flowing from it, it is important to note that the body has historically had a complex role in the genesis of rights discourse. The quasi-disembodiment inherent in the abstract universal sits at odds with the role of the body both in the production of the empathy that produced the widespread adoption of rights language in the eighteenth century and in the genesis of the UDHR paradigm. Hunt has demonstrated, in relation to the emergence of the revolutionary language of rights in the eighteenth century, that changing social perceptions of the body and the development of empathy based on a new understanding of our shared condition of vulnerability – the realisation that others share our pains and emotions – formed a crucial part of the important socio-cultural shifts that birthed rights discourse.[4] At the same time, however, the notion of the body as a fundamentally bounded thing – a notion contributing to the development of the concept of autonomy that, together with empathy, formed the basis of the expanding rights-imagination – is intimately linked to the problematic exclusions of the liberal property concept[5] at the heart of law's ideological closure and to its concept of the person. The body, in other words, is deeply complex in its relationship with the foundational impulses of human rights discourse. This complexity will be explored more fully in Chapter 7, when we examine more fully the role of the body and embodied vulnerability in the genesis of rights in the eighteenth century and in the foundations of the UDHR paradigm. However, notwithstanding the fact that the body plays an important but often submerged role in rights discourse, the body is obscured from view by the abstraction of the universal 'man' or 'human' (as appropriate) of rights discourse. Quasi-disembodiment thus plays a complex and continuing role in the exclusions and closures associated with human rights.

Exclusions in the early construction of rights

Earlier, we noted the persistent tension between critique and closure in the history of 'nature', 'right' and later, 'rights'. We saw, for example, how the classical natural law tradition used the notions of 'nature' and 'right' as critical concepts of resistance to ancestral authority – and that this was always countered and subverted by the extant established powers in defence of the status quo.[6] We also noted the longstanding ambiguity of the relationship between rights and power, and the tendency of rights to emerge in the crucible of social movement struggles only to crystallise in somewhat exclusive forms at the moment of their institutionalisation,[7] in the power interests of the propertied classes.[8] These fractious ambiguities can be linked to an underlying rationality that imports quasi-disembodiment into the heart of human rights discourse. Indeed, we have already noted some elements of the role of quasi-disembodiment in the formulation of natural rights. It was argued in the last chapter that Rousseau, Hobbes and Locke, in positing their new vision of the emergent liberal social order, utilised the construct of 'natural man'. That construct emphasised the universal elements of humanity by subtracting from embodied persons whatever made them unique, situated, distinctive and nuanced to produce a universal 'man' as the proto-beneficiary of a new rights-based social order. The fact that this 'natural man' was conceived of as being an *abstract* universal means, inevitably, that the quasi-disembodiment emerging from the radical imbrication of rationality (the central characteristic of 'natural man'), abstraction and masculinity in Western philosophy and history was fully operative. The discourse of the universal, for all its inclusory rhetorical power, was thus constructed around a figure fully consistent with the exclusory interests of an identifiable socio-economic group. The exclusions accompanying the promulgation of the new rights-based social order produced, almost like a photographic negative, an archetypal beneficiary of natural rights – the construct of a natural man who was unmistakeably male, property-owning, European and white.[9]

While this construct certainly did not prevent others from invoking the universalistic language of rights, it nevertheless reflects a resistance to their claims for inclusion – particularly, and especially revealingly, as we shall see, in the case of women.[10] History reveals that, although modern rights, at their revolutionary birth, were based on a universalistic logic containing truly radical inclusive potentialities, these potentialities were noticeably muted. Natural man as a philosophical trope produced a universal but quintessentially abstract bearer of rights who, quite clearly, reflects the hallmarks of Western philosophical quasi-disembodiment. Accordingly, when the thin, abstract man of rights materialised, he possessed a highly specific morphology (male). He also had a specific socio-political status (property owning).

The discourse of the universal soon became, in the majority (rationalist) tradition at least, an almost inevitable accompaniment to capitalism. The political myth of the social contract, so influential in rights theory, gained its early plausibility precisely from the importance of contract and property rights to early capitalism, as was argued in the last chapter. The rights of 'man' were initially granted paradigmatically (and predictably) to the male (quasi-disembodied/rational) property-owning citizen – the political template of the P3 legal subject. Even in revolutionary France, where rights talk was at its most universalistic,[11] the initial institutional settlement strongly reflected the priority of 'the rights of propertied men'.[12] This is unsurprising in the light of the suppositions at work in the logic of the time and in its philosophical antecedents. Hunt notes, for example, that, when the natural rights theorist Locke wrote at the end of the seventeenth century, he simply did not have the rights of the propertyless, women or slaves in mind. He only saw rights as the entitlement of the white European (notably the

English) property-owning male and citizen.[13] While Rousseau's vision was more inclusive than Locke's, in the sense that Rousseau assumed that rights reflected the 'rights of *all men* to participate in making the social contract',[14] his work reflects the same impulse towards conceptualising the rights holder as quintessentially quasi-disembodied.[15]

The social exclusions reflected in such intellectual closures did not go uncontested in the debates leading up to the French revolutionary settlement. The rights of slaves, Calvinists, Jews and homosexuals were all openly debated and discussed,[16] with the question of citizenship in particular fuelling passionate claims from excluded groups.[17] But, while the universalistic logic of the Declaration had the potential to support such claims it did not inaugurate an inclusory socio-political structure. Perhaps the clearest reflection of the operation of quasi-disembodiment is augured by the widespread conviction that women were intrinsically unsuited to political life as a result of their female nature.[18] The abstract universal was constructed as autonomous, empty and masculine in a way completely continuous with the dualistic suppositions of Western thought, and the bearer of the rights of the Citizen, the bearer of active as opposed to passive rights, was a clear instance of the same dogmatic template. As Scott has argued:

> Maleness was equated with individuality, and femaleness with otherness in a fixed, hierarchical, and immobile opposition (masculinity was not seen as femininity's other). The political individual was ... taken to be both universal and male; the female was not an individual, both because she was non-identical with the human prototype and because she was the other who confirmed the (male) individual's individuality.[19]

The imbrication of rationality and nature underpinning the alleged unfitness of women for a role in the (rational) public sphere fully reflects the nature of quasi-disembodiment and its implications. Rationality – perhaps especially public political rationality – was emphatically the preserve of men. Accordingly, despite important arguments for the equality of women in the polity, offered perhaps most influentially by Condorcet, '[n]one of the national assemblies ever considered legislation granting political rights to women (who could neither vote or hold office), and on the few occasions on which the possibility arose, however tentatively, the deputies greeted it with widespread derision and incredulity'.[20] The French Declaration, like the American Constitution, excluded women from participation in political life, and 'women and propertyless individuals remained at the margin of English, American and French societies'.[21]

The links thus exposed between property, rationality and gender thoroughly reflect the set of ideological closures related to the elevation of the P3 legal subject in liberal law. The privileging of the juridico-political template of P3 can quite clearly be seen in the abstract universal of rights discourse. There is a sense in which rights discourse, from its very inception, was fractured by contestation – a contestation out of which the interests of the dominant capitalist class, reflected in law by the ascendancy of P3 as the ultimate legal person, emerged to trump the interests of those 'others' engaged in the social struggle for inclusion. In revolutionary France, as elsewhere, the more progressive elements of the struggle for liberal freedom and equality were ultimately overborne by the interests of a propertied, commercial class.[22] This was nothing new. The French Revolution had important historical antecedents and accompaniments. The English Civil War, for example, which coincided with the development of fundamental rights to life, freedom of opinion and property, reveals the exclusory results of early rights struggles, in particular, the tendency of rights struggles to capitulate to the interests of the propertied class. Ishay notes, for example, that '[t]he emergence of radical groups like the British agrarian communists the Diggers, who strove to be recognised as full-fledged citizens under the British sky, attested to the exclusive character of the revolution; their hopes for civil equality were soon thwarted by the political ascendancy of the men of property'.[23] Likewise, the American Revolution culminated in an 'inequitable resolution'[24] with Jefferson complaining that 'the property of this country is absolutely concentrated in very few hands'.[25]

The early rights Declarations, by enshrining an abstract universal as their beneficiary, import a hidden structure of exclusion within the universalistic logic of rights. Quasi-disembodiment operates as a core mechanism of this structure of exclusion – a potent closure reflecting a set of related ideological exclusions and unequal social power relations. The centrality of disembodied rationality and its inescapable fusion with masculinity produce a smuggled male morphology, which, apart from being gendered, also emerges, through the lens of a critical historical reading as radically associated with profoundly racist and classist assumptions. These elements combine in a complex way to produce the quintessential rights bearer – so intimately related to the P3 legal subject – as being white, male and property-owning in an intellectual context in which personhood and property function as co-constituting notions.[26] The abstract universal, in this sense, no matter how many claims for inclusion are made, possesses a stubborn subterranean tendency to privilege the quintessential liberal legal actor and his characteristics. His construction as white, male and propertied has long rendered later claims for inclusion conceptually problematic – none more so than in the case of women, who are quintessentially associated with embodiment. Even Condorcet, would-be defender of women's rights, utilised a rationalistic conception of the man of rights, elevating rationality as his defining characteristic: natural rights were the possession of abstract man because 'they are derived from the nature of man' – and key to this is the capacity 'of reasoning'.[27] The inconsistency in his position is clear. He consciously wants to defend women's rights, yet the very construct of natural man that he expounds is founded on a conception of rationality that inherently and irredeemably excludes women.

Quasi-disembodiment operates to produce a thinly cloaked resistance to the full extension of the logic of universalism to those with bodies whose contours and associated characteristics could not fit the abstract template of universal 'man'.[28] The related elevation of the property right (and its complex connection with notions of citizenship)[29] meant that, while maleness was inherently privileged by the abstract universal, not all males could initially take advantage of this privileging. For propertyless males, inclusion was to be somewhat delayed – certainly in relation to the construction of citizenship. But for women, the days following the success of the Revolution were among the bleakest in their history.[30] It took far longer for them to gain inclusion in the active rights of citizenship. To this day, the inclusion of women in the abstract universal of international human rights law remains a vexing and difficult issue – and still has not been achieved – as we shall shortly see. The exclusory effects of quasi-disembodiment remain clearly discernible in present day human rights struggles.

The emergence of rights as a central part of political and legal discourse accordingly presents a set of contradictions. While the body and empathy played an important role in the emergence of rights discourse in the eighteenth century, the dominant philosophical conception of the universal bearer of rights was quasi-disembodied and rationalistic. The liberationist revolutionary aspiration of the time and the logic of universalism both contained the radical promise of rights for all. But the conception of rational human nature operative in the philosophical assumptions underpinning rights theory meant that the paradigmatic proto-beneficiary of the new order of rights was inevitably quasi-disembodied. The centrality of property rights to the eventual legal formation of the new social order meant that law, possessive individualism, capitalism, the prominence of contract, the construct of the freely choosing rational actor and quasi-disembodiment all converged in a potent conceptual matrix to form the horizons, fundamental characteristics and quintessential orientation of the liberal legal and political order. The abstract universal man of the rights declarations was radically continuous with these themes. It is unsurprising, in the light of this analysis, that rights were, and remain, even in their later incarnations as 'human rights', hospitable to the interests of capitalist power – and, in time, to the corporation as the disembodied jural entity created precisely for the purposes of capital accumulation.

The UDHR paradigm: Paradoxes of dis/embodiment

Certain crucial continuities between liberal legal rights discourse and rational natural rights discourse are also reflected within the UDHR paradigm. Of particular importance for present purposes is the fact that the UDHR paradigm retains important elements of disembodied rationalism in its conception of the 'universal' bearer of human rights. This is reflected most obviously in the textual and philosophical continuities between the UDHR and the earlier declarations of the rights of man and the citizen. Marks, for example, has argued that the proclamation of rights during the French Declaration has had 'a major impact on the form and content of the UDHR proclaimed 160 years later, and subsequently on the current codex of internationally recognized human rights'.[31] He locates the criticism of human rights, made by a range of scholars, as tools of a 'Western, liberal, individualist, egoistical, dominating ideology' in the 'historical and philosophical essence of the accusation' – the French Revolution. (Human rights and the legacy of the French Revolution are both more internally contradictory than the accusation of the critics of human rights just noted implies, but, at this stage of our analysis we are interested in tracing one particular theme of critique – that of quasi-disembodiment and its related ideological tilt.) The assertion that all 'men are born and remain free and equal in rights' (Article 1 of the French Declaration of the Rights of Man and Citizen (1789)) becomes, in Article 1 of the UDHR, the statement that all 'human beings are born free and equal in dignity and rights' – an almost identical formulation, but for the exchange of 'human beings' for 'men'.[32] The UDHR, in other words, like the French Declaration, enshrines its rights as the inheritance of a being conceived of as an abstract universal.

As we have already noted, the logic of universalism reflects an important inclusory aspiration – and the UDHR, in particular, attempts to inaugurate the important notion of protecting human beings as *species-beings*,[33] but still in essentially in *abstract* terms. Douzinas has argued that, '[o]nce the slightest empirical or historical material is introduced into abstract human nature, once we move from the declarations onto the concrete embodied person, with gender, race, class and age, human nature with its equality and dignity retreats rapidly'.[34] Of course, it should be clear from the analysis thus far that abstract human nature was never truly empty to start with, and that the submerged beneficiary of such 'emptiness' would indicate a predictable and historically repetitious set of exclusions that expose, by negative imprint, the contours of the proto-beneficiary of the abstract formulation of the universal. This is, however, particularly problematic in international human rights discourse, because such critique, as Otto suggests, 'goes to the heart of the post-World War II discourse of universal human rights which, *as its most fundamental premise*, purports to apply *equally, without distinction*, to "*everyone*" [(Art 2 UDHR)]. [But notwithstanding this radical inclusory agenda] [t]he allegedly universal subject of human rights law ... reproduces hierarchies, including those of [gender], race, culture, nation, socio-economic status and sexuality...'.[35] In international human rights law, the abstract 'man' – now conceptualised as the abstract 'human' – still remains too abstract. He also remains, importantly, quasi-disembodied.

In international human rights law though, this quasi-disembodiment has notably contested effects. We have seen particularly revealing critical struggles around the materialisation of the abstract universal, especially as the bold vision of the UDHR has been increasingly positivised and, in the process, explicitly and increasingly criticised for its exclusions. Law is 'the terrain on which abstract nature acquires concrete form'.[36] When human rights become mediated as law, that which is abstract simply cannot remain abstract. The legal subject functions as a conduit through which the abstract (complete with its submerged ideological content) becomes concrete, frequently with, as will be seen, profoundly exclusionary results. As we have already observed, when the abstract materialises, the consistently patterned nature of its materialisation reveals its lack of true 'emptiness'. In international human rights law this is a point noted time and time again by critics who are troubled by the marginalisation of various groups and categories of human beings. The contemporary human rights movement is profoundly conscious of such exclusions and the contradiction between these and the logic of universalism.[37] Critiques of the dominant construction of the universal bearer of human rights have come from various quarters. But the most relevant for present purposes is the critique mounted by feminists,[38] since this gets to the heart of quasi-disembodiment and its intimate relationship with the dualisms of Western philosophy more directly than any other form of exclusion. In fact, the exclusion of women has arguably consistently proved to be the most problematic and intractable exclusion of all, amply reflecting the primordial status of the bifurcation between male and female in the closures of rationality.

'The universal is male': The persistent marginality of women in international human rights law

The abstract universalism of human rights law presents the bearer of those rights as 'gender neutral' – a formally open conception designed to represent the whole of humanity as a *species being*.[39] The UDHR, with its two related Covenants, the International Covenant on Civil and Political Rights (ICCPR)[40] and the International Covenant on Economic, Social and Cultural Rights (ICESCR)[41] (collectively known as the 'International Bill of Rights') provide that 'everyone' is entitled to the rights contained therein without distinction on grounds of, among other things, 'sex'. From this formulation we can see that international human rights law, as an analytical matter, recognises various particularities (race, sex, colour, religion, etc) related to the universal human being. Paradoxically, however, the traditional abstract formulation of the universal of human rights law has granted such variations in human embodiment and experience negligible weight in the construction of its central rights-bearing entity, reproducing, instead, familiar hierarchies and producing 'subjects that bear the markings of complex histories of subjugation and resistance'.[42] The persistent marginality of women in particular in international human rights law is especially revealing testimony to the ongoing exclusory effects of quasi-disembodiment. As we have already argued, quasi-disembodiment produces a submerged masculinity related to an ancient Western dualism, at the core of which lies an oppositional binary construction of sex/gender. A genealogical reading of international human rights law exposes the ongoing effect of such patterns and exclusions, as Otto's recent well-constructed genealogical reading of the female subjects of international human rights law demonstrates.[43]

Otto's detailed account reveals the construction in international human rights law of three recurring female subjectivities: the figure of the wife and mother (the binary opposite of the 'head of the household'); the formal equal with men (the binary opposite of the 'masculine standard' against which equality is measured); and the 'victim' subject (the binary opposite of the 'masculine bearer of "civilisation" who rescues "native" women from "barbarian" men'). These dualities, Otto argues, have displayed an enduring persistence and resilience in international human rights law, leading her to the 'unsettling observation that women's full inclusion in universal representations of humanity may be an impossibility so long as the universal subject (the "standard") continues to rely for its universality on its contrast with feminized particularities (the "other")'.[44]

Otto argues that women function as a necessary 'other' (*a la* Derrida)[45] in the constitution of a quintessentially masculine universal: male and female in international human rights law operate in a dualistic or oppositional relationship, in which one side (the male) is the dominant side of the duality (the 'standard'). The female operates as the subordinate 'other'. The categories are interdependent and mutually constituting. Otto argues that, for as long as a binary construction of humanity persists, it becomes extremely difficult to see how the universal can function as anything other than a 'masculine standard'. This argument places the binary construction of sex in oppositional terms at the heart of the problem. In other words, although Otto does not address quasi-disembodiment, it is possible to agree with her that the intransigent dualism inherent to quasi-disembodiment renders women's full inclusion in the human rights universal *conceptually impossible*. This is an important argument. It implies that any abstract (disembodied) conception of the human rights universal will necessarily and always exclude women precisely because of the operation of quasi-disembodiment (and the inescapably related co-imbrication of the body with femaleness). The nature of the intransigence of the sex binary is a subject of enormous complexity requiring an ongoing engagement, the details of which lie beyond the ambit of this particular book. But, minimally, the foregrounding of embodied vulnerability – the approach to be offered here for the redirecting of human rights to human beneficiaries and away from the corporate form – has interesting theoretical possibilities for the potential re-imagination of the sex binary (see Chapter 9).

Returning to our present critical task of tracing quasi-disembodiment in the UDHR paradigm, the evidence used by Otto and other feminist critics to expose the incipient masculinity of the universal is the textual, institutional and historical unfolding of international human rights law itself. The sheer difficulties, resistances to and complexities of accommodating women within international human rights law have been used to compel an underlying sexual ideology into the open. The evidence presented includes the record of the difficulties surrounding the inclusion of the female sex in the UDHR itself. As Otto emphasises, advocates for women's rights in the 1940s, faced with the drafting of the UDHR, did not start from a blank page. Women were already produced as the necessary 'other' by antecedent representations of their sex in earlier international treaties, such as those treaties regulating the conduct of war, the international labour standards developed during the years of the League of Nations and a set of instruments aimed at regulating trafficking for the purposes of prostitution.[46] Otto identifies the persistent presence of gender stereotypes (taken as 'natural') that present women as vulnerable subjects in need of male protection. She comments, moreover, that there is a

> remarkable stability in the female subjects produced by ... early legal instruments, who were valued for their chastity, their prioritization of motherhood and domesticity, their acceptance of the heterosexual family hierarchy and the paternal protection of the state, its laws and its wars. In contradistinction, male figures were produced as women's defenders and moral superiors (apart from the racialized criminals who trafficked them) and the active, public, protecting masculine subject was fashioned as the marker of full humanity, autonomous and self-determining, and in no need of special rules for his protection.[47]

Feminist accounts of international human rights law include a range of critical observations on the nature of the exclusions operative against women. For example, one problem of fairly obvious significance is the dominance of male voices in human rights discourse,[48] including their dominance on the drafting committee of the UDHR.[49] This was despite the active role of the Commission on the Status of Women (CSW), which attempted, during the drafting process, to 'elevate the equal rights and human rights status of women, irrespective of nationality, race, language, or religion, in order to achieve equality with men in all fields of human enterprise'.[50] As Otto points out, the views of the CSW clashed with the majority of the Commission on Human Rights (CHR), including Eleanor Roosevelt, the only woman on the CHR. The majority of the drafters felt that a general prohibition against discrimination based on sex would be sufficient to guarantee women's equal enjoyment of universal human rights.[51] They argued that protecting and preserving the universal nature of the term 'everyone' necessitated the avoidance of specific references to women. Feminists, however, have pointed out that this strategy failed lamentably to produce a genuine universality. The fatal flaw, according to Otto, was the failure to recognise that the universal was *already gendered*,[52] as her analysis of the antecedent documents palpably bears out. But there is a deeper sense in which the universal was already gendered, as the analysis in this book thus far suggests: the abstract universal is always inescapably gendered because it is quasi-disembodied – a term capturing, as we have seen, the incipient masculinity of disembodied rationalism and the related binary oppositional construction of women as somehow uniquely embedded in embodiment, and the sub-rational.

Returning to our reflections on the drafting process of the UDHR, the CSW drew attention to the use of masculine pronouns as generic terms for humanity in the early drafts of the UDHR – viewed as symptomatic of male dominance and the inscription of a masculine 'standard' in the UDHR. Eventually, under pressure from the CSW, the terminology used was shifted from 'all men' to 'all human beings'[53] – but this was instead of the more explicit 'all people, men and women' favoured by CSW activists.[54] As Otto notes, however, the victory of the CSW on gendered language was at best only partial: the masculine pronoun remained stubbornly dominant throughout.[55] This resulted, quite predictably, in the entrenchment of traditional gender hierarchies. There is, in fact, only one direct reference in the main text of the UDHR to the equal rights of women. But the significance of this, notwithstanding its apparently progressive gloss, is undercut by the fact that the reference appears, revealingly, in the context of the family (Art 16: Equal Marriage Rights). It is further muted by the impact of the liberal public/private divide (a 'major conceptual barrier to women's enjoyment of human rights'[56]) which has rendered the protection of women in the domestic sphere obdurately problematic.[57]

Feminists have also pointed out that the UDHR is silent on the issues of gendered violence and reproductive rights. Such crucial oversights, Otto suggests, reveal 'the powerful way that protective gender narratives work to prevent the abuses perpetrated by putative protectors – husbands, doctors and religious leaders – being classified as human rights violations'.[58] Beveridge and Mullally point out, in relation to this, that although the guarantees set out in the International Bill of Rights (the UDHR and its two companion Covenants) *could* be interpreted so as to protect gender-specific injury to women, there has been a marked failure to do so.[59] The paradigmatic human rights violation has archetypally reflected the experience of men – not women. Accordingly, the cloaked masculinity of the 'universal' tends to occlude the distinctive harms enacted on the gender-specific particularity of women.[60]

The disappointing masculinist construction of the bearer of universal human rights provoked feminists to vary their strategy – moving from the notion of generic inclusion to focus on women's *specific* protection in an attempt to redress the failures in international human rights discourse. As a result of such efforts, a separate institutional structure, explicitly devoted to violations of women's human rights, was established with the UN Convention on the Elimination of All Forms of Discrimination Against Women (CEDAW)[61] and its related Committee. Paradoxically, of course, the need for its adoption simply confirmed the general exclusion of women from human rights law and institutions.[62] The CEDAW regime, besides underlining the marginality of women, is notoriously undermined by an exceptionally high number of State reservations to the Convention and by the fact that the only enforcement mechanism it establishes is a reporting procedure. In this sense it compares unfavourably with its putative prototype, the 1966 Convention on the Elimination of All Forms of Racial Discrimination[63] (CERD), which has an individual complaints mechanism as well as a mechanism for inter-state complaint. In respect of State reservations, no procedure is established for ascertaining whether such reservations are compatible with the 'object and purpose' of the Convention – again, unlike CERD – and it is apparent that the number and extent of state reservations significantly undermine whatever normative force CEDAW might otherwise possess, and perhaps even legitimise violations of the rights contained therein.[64]

A fundamental theoretical flaw of CEDAW is its ongoing commitment to the 'equal treatment' approach that adopts a masculine 'standard' against which equality is to be measured.[65] As Beveridge and Mullally point out, this is a reiteration of the mistaken belief that 'distinction is the problem and lack of distinction the solution... [which] ... serves only to reinforce existing norms and values without in any way subverting the inherently gendered nature of the existing rules'.[66] Moreover, there is no explicit engagement with the issue of violence against women, and no attempt to articulate a right to bodily integrity. The Convention is generally silent concerning women's bodies, an obvious (and somewhat predictable) exception being the references to reproduction and the needs of pregnant women in the workplace.[67] This can perhaps be interpreted as part of what Otto refers to as the simultaneous attempt to treat women differently within the framework of equality – a project that she sees as demanding 'some re-conceptualisation of the universal subject'.[68] But it is a very limited form of inclusion, and hardly succeeds in reconceptualising the universal, since women are simply never conceived of as being genuine instances of the universal in the first place. These limited references to reproduction and pregnancy are quite compatible, in fact, with paternalism, and do nothing, moreover, to undermine the exclusionary oppositional construction of the sex binary so implicated in the exclusions of the abstract universal.

CEDAW's more promising attributes are that it addresses both direct and indirect discrimination[69] and the role of affirmative action.[70] It also indirectly addresses the problem of the public/private divide with a prohibition against discrimination that can be interpreted to include the private sphere.[71] There is also a sense in which CEDAW attempts to effect a shift forward to a partially reconstituted subject of international human rights law, albeit unsatisfactorily – producing a subject 'subtly positioned between a universal conception of human rights and a woman-centred political focus'.[72] Despite this (flawed) attempt to produce a more gender-inclusive universal subject, Otto's analysis reveals that all three marginalised subjectivities of women, noted earlier, remain stubbornly in existence.[73]

In the late 1980s, there was widespread dissatisfaction with the CEDAW strategy. Feminists noted the continued marginalisation of women from the universal frame of human rights. Notwithstanding CEDAW and the efforts of the CEDAW Committee to promote a substantive understanding of equality, women remained peripheral to mainstream human rights discourse – a dilemma that produced yet another attempt to re-evaluate feminist inclusion strategies.[74] This time, the claim made was that 'women's rights are human rights'.[75] This claim reflected a renewed attempt to conceptualise women's specific rights as human rights. The strategy had two main goals: first to ensure that gender-specific violations of rights were recognised as violations of the rights of the human rights universal; and secondly, to 'mainstream' women's human rights.

The first goal has not really been achieved. Attempts to conceptualise reproductive and sexual rights as being universal rights has met strong resistance – particularly from religious groups – although the attempt to focus on gender-specific violence has been relatively successful.[76] The identification of gender-based violence as a violation of women's human rights eventually culminated in the adoption of the Declaration on the Elimination of Violence Against Women (DEVAW).[77] Crucially, however, despite its recognition of gender-specific injury, DEVAW does *not* recognise violence against women as a violation of *human rights*. Yet again, the argument, much as in the drafting process of the UDHR, seems to be that recognising the specificity of women's harm would diminish or undermine the 'universality' of human rights.[78] This exposes the underlying logic in which the injuries of men are the quintessential human rights abuse: the injuries of men are assumed to be representative of injuries to the universal human being but the injuries of women are not. One notional half of humanity can fully represent the other notional half, who, for such representational purposes, are deemed ill-fitted to the template of the human being, and thus incapable of representing genuine instances of the universal. The abstract universal thus remains intransigently constituted in such a way as to exclude women from full inclusion in humanity.

The second strategy, that of 'gender mainstreaming' (the attempt to make gender issues visible within all mainstream human rights agendas and processes) has seen some success. In particular, Otto highlights the Human Rights Committee's General Comment no 28,[79] issued in 2000, as an example of a groundbreaking interpretation of equality issues. She notes that it 'includes the "sexed" issues that the women's-rights-are-human-rights strategy has been concerned with, for example in identifying backyard abortions as a threat to the right to life, but it does not confine itself to these issues, 'recognizing that "poverty and deprivation" may also pose a threat to women's right to life'.[80] However, notwithstanding these important signs of progress, 'all the dangers that attend the inclusion of women by reference to their specificities remain'. In particular, the focus on female vulnerability – on 'helplessness rather than agency' – has had the effect of further confirming the masculinity of the human rights universal 'who needs no special enumeration of his gender-specific injuries'.[81]

It can be seen from this survey that quasi-disembodiment remains as problematic in the constitution of the subject of international human rights law as it was in the constitution of the natural man of natural rights theory. The ongoing and intractable challenges attending the genuine inclusion of women in the universal reflect highly patterned forms of exclusion indicating the contours of the underlying template of 'full humanity'. Gender intersects with other hierarchies based on race, culture, nation, sexuality, and socio-economic status producing, it is suggested, further evidence that the submerged beneficiary of liberal rights is still an intransigent haunting presence in the abstract universal. The exclusions of the abstract universal, and the ideological tilt associated with it in terms of the interests of the white, male, propertied individual of liberalism, can be vigorously contrasted with the countervailing inclusory pressures from excluded groups who call upon the logic of the universal as the basis of their critique. Indeed, the contrast between the exclusory and inclusory constructions of human rights is so acute that it is possible to speak, in fact, of *two* distinct notions of human rights that co-exist in international rights discourse. This raises the distinct possibility that corporate human rights beneficiaries are simply extending the logic of *one* notion of human rights in their favour, and that, rather than distorting the *entire* UDHR paradigm, they are merely exploiting a clearly identifiable strand of rights-discourse descended from antecedent closures that arose historically to protect the interests of the (male) propertied classes.

Two competing conceptions of human rights?

Baxi has characterised the underlying ambivalence of human rights in terms of the existence of two competing conceptions or notions of human rights. He introduces the notions of 'modern' and 'contemporary' human rights, arguing that the two notions differ in four major respects: (1) their respective encapsulation of the logics of exclusion and inclusion; (2) the distinctive languages of human rights utilised; (3) in what he calls 'ascetic versus carnivalistic rights production'; and (4) in their contrasting relationships between human rights and human suffering.[82] What is interesting, for the purposes of the present argument, is the strong link between Baxi's 'modern' conception of human rights, the familiar closures of liberalism, and our theme of quasi-disembodiment.

Baxi suggests that the 'modern' notion of human rights is productive of exclusion and, even more worryingly, that historically the notion has produced 'justified' forms of human suffering. Bearing out the argument presented thus far in this book concerning the liberal construction of the legal subject of human rights, Baxi argues that

> [t]he criteria of individuation in the European liberal tradition of thought furnished some of the most powerful ideas in constructing a model of human rights. Only those beings were to be regarded as 'human' who were possessed of reason and autonomous moral *will*. What counted as reason and will varied in the course of the long development of the European liberal tradition. However, in its major phases of development 'slaves', 'heathens', 'barbarians', colonised peoples, indigenous populations, women, children, the impoverished, and the 'insane' have been, at various times and in various ways, thought unworthy of being the bearers of human rights.[83]

Note here the exclusory function of a notion of rationality – linked, of course, to will. Rationality is clearly constructed as being a gateway construct for admission to the 'human', but it is clear from Baxi's list of those thought unworthy to be human rights bearers that the exclusions reveal the precise contours of the submerged 'insider' cloaked by the mechanism of liberal legal disembodiment: the quasi-disembodied (white, male, property owning) agent, so intimately linked to the P3 legal subject. For Baxi, the principal historical role performed by the 'modern' construction of human rights was, in fact, to accomplish the imposition of 'justified' suffering in the cause of colonialism and imperialism: 'The "modern" human rights cultures, tracing their pedigree to the Idea of Progress, Social Darwinism, racism and patriarchy (central to the "Enlightenment" ideology) justified global imposition of cruelty as "natural", "ethical" and "just"'.[84] In the process, the suffering of the 'other of European imperialism' was ideologically suppressed. The suffering of female bodies, black bodies, the bodies of workers and the bodies of indigenous peoples was in an important sense constructed as both an inevitable sacrifice in the interests of progress, and made invisible – again reflecting the excision of questions of power through the invocation of discourses of rational neutrality. Indeed, Baxi goes so far as to suggest that '[m]aking human suffering *invisible* was the hallmark of "modern" (liberal) human rights formations'.[85] Thus, the ontology of the 'human' embedded in the 'modern' notion of human rights is a Western ideological construct whose foreclosing effect is intimately related to the historical imposition of 'justified' (invisible) suffering on the 'other'.

The foreclosing effect and precise contours of the 'human' of the 'modern' conception are further revealed (*and contested*) by the characteristically 'carnivalistic' production of new categories of human rights within the 'contemporary' human rights paradigm. The contemporary production of documents specifying the human rights of 'the girl child, migrant labour, indigenous peoples, gays and lesbians (...), prisoners and those in custodial institutional regimes, refugees, and asylum-seekers children'[86] amounts – in significant part – to an assertion of the foundational status of *embodied difference* in the construction of 'contemporary' human rights claims – and implicitly links embodied difference to the *imposition of suffering*. What this points up, again, arguably, are the explicit contours of the historically real exclusions forged by the *quasi-disembodied* universal subject of human rights once he materialised as their all-too-specific beneficiary. These contemporary attempts to name previously excluded groups as being the specifically enumerated beneficiaries of human rights instruments can be read as repeated and analogous critiques of the closures of the abstract universal; as – in fact – repeated and analogous critiques of the outcome of *quasi-disembodiment*.

The construction of 'modern' human rights reveals the radical and mutually constituting interdependence between personhood and property (noted earlier in relation to liberal theory), and the related elevation of the private property right:

> ...at the point in time when [French Declaration and the American Bill of Rights (1791)] were written and even today, especially in the United States, economic inequality was and is unchallenged ... because as both compendia make explicit, property ownership represents the principal mode of securing one's life and pursuing happiness.[87]

Indeed, Baxi argues that the 'absolutist right to property' forms one of the two constitutive elements of the 'modern' paradigm (along with 'the collective human right of the coloniser to subjugate "inferior" peoples').[88] This has clear implications in relation to the corporate use of human rights discourse. Indeed, it can be argued that corporate subversion of human rights is radically continuous with the commitments of early liberalism as expressed in the 'modern' notion of human rights. Thus,

> [l]ong before slavery was abolished, and women got recognition for the right to contest and vote at elections, corporations had appropriated rights to *personhood*, claiming due process rights for regimes of property denied to human beings. The unfoldment of ...'modern' human rights is the story of near-absoluteness of the right to property as a basic human right. So too is the narrative of colonisation/imperialism which began its

> career with the archetypal East India Company (which ruled India for a century) when *corporate sovereignty was inaugurated.*[89]

Coming to the end of this genealogical reading of human rights it is apparent that human rights, and their precursors in the rights of man, emerge as being deeply enmeshed with the presuppositions of liberal legal and political theory – and especially with its central commitment to the legal person as quasi-disembodied, abstract, rationalistic and possessive. Legal human rights subjectivity emerges as enmeshed with the closures of liberal capitalism, and human rights law emerges as intrinsically open to a corporation-friendly construction. 'Modern' human rights discourse is intimately linked to the historical and current elevation of property and to corporate sovereignty – a sovereignty linked to the related ideological suppression of the embodied suffering of countless human beings.

A genealogical reading of human rights thus reveals quasi-disembodiment, and the abstraction of legal rights discourse, to be ongoing sites of exclusion for human beings in human rights law, especially for those human beings who do not fit the submerged template of 'full humanity' implicated in the abstract universal. Meanwhile, the corporation closely approximates it. A key task, therefore, in redirecting human rights, will hinge on reconstituting the 'universal' of human rights in terms that do full justice to the embodied complexity and vulnerability of human beings, and in a way that is capable of being genuinely inclusive. One way of doing so, it will be argued, is by the foregrounding of embodied vulnerability in both the bearer of human rights and in the ethical foundation of human rights as a legal and political discourse. Accordingly, we now turn to the task of 'redirecting' human rights.

6 The Centrality of Human Embodiment

Thus far a central theme in this book has been a critique of a particular form of disembodied rationality along with its ideological implications and operative exclusions, exclusions that have attracted trenchant criticisms from and on behalf of excluded groups and categories of people. As noted earlier, history is the place where ideology comes into the open. A key mechanism for such exclusions in law seems to be the operation of a particular form of disembodiment operative in liberal legal rationality,[1] more accurately referred to as quasi-disembodiment. This is because, as has been argued, disembodiment is never total.[2] The traditional and dominant form of Western rational abstractionism, so central to law and legal reasoning, is inextricably linked to dualism – the binary construction of reality – and in particular the separation of the mind from the body (and the related oppositions between nature and culture, reason and emotion). This is a long-standing separation, 'dating as far back as Plato's deliberations in the *Phaedo*, Aristotle's musings in *De Anima* (on the soul), and exemplified *par excellence* in Decartes' famous dictum "*Cogito ergo sum*"'.[3] This dualism is, moreover, profoundly gendered. Disembodied reason, as we have seen, is inextricably linked with masculinity. It is radically implicated in 'man's' domination of nature through science,[4] and traditionally, the realms of culture and public life have been identified as the preserve of men. Women, meanwhile, have been viewed as deeply embedded in embodiment, virtually synonymous with nature and have been relegated to the private domestic sphere and to reproductivity.

It has been argued that this rationalistic dualism and its accompanying quasi-disembodiment are implicated in the exclusions operative in international human rights law and in the construction of the human rights universal.[5] Indeed, the centrality of quasi-disembodiment is fundamental to understanding the legal privileging of the corporate form, and the way in which human rights law is (perhaps counter-intuitively) open to the protection of corporate interests.[6] It has been argued already that the corporation is a disembodied jural construct, whereas the human being is an embodied, complex, organic being rendered quasi-disembodied within law's rationalising matrix. In a structural sense, then, as we have seen, the corporation is a far more precise fit for legal personhood than the human being, with her concrete and messy materiality that always eludes the boundedness of legal personification. Moreover, it has been argued that in ideological terms, the corporation (as a personification created precisely for the accumulation of capital) operates as the classic liberal contractor writ large, meaning that the ideological tilt of liberal law is also particularly accommodating to the corporation and its interests.[7] The paradoxical anthropomorphism that besets much corporate theory combined with the relative disembodiment or hollowing out of the human being in legal rationality produces the corporation as, in a sense, the *quintessential* legal subject. As has been suggested above, corporations have been able to move, facilitated by law's operative closures, to make a claim for something approaching legal humanity through the invocation of human rights law as *beneficiaries*. Aiding them have been the ideological orientation of liberal law towards capitalism and the related privileging of the private property construct, both of which are thoroughly implicated in Baxi's critique of the 'modern' notion of human rights, and which tend to enhance law's systemic openness to the privileging of the corporate form. These factors are also fundamental to the paradoxical conceptual structure of international human rights law – certainly in so far the UDHR replicates and employs the 'modern' conception of human rights,[8] as discussed in the preceding chapter.

It is now time to consider the centrality of human embodiment, its foundational role in reasoning and law, and the relevance of embodied vulnerability to the law and discourse of human rights. (In the next chapter we shall explore embodied vulnerability more fully and link it to the UDHR paradigm in depth.)

The centrality of embodiment

As we have already seen, the classical abstract rational account of meaning, thought and understanding renders the body external to the nature of rationality. Mind and body are taken to be neatly separable and rationality is taken to transcend bodily structures. However, it should be noted that the body does play a role, even in such an approach, through its perceptual mechanisms. But these bodily perceptual mechanisms merely serve rationality. They do so by gathering information, and have only an attenuated role in the assessment of information. In the language of Lakoff, '[p]erception is viewed as the means by which we establish correct correspondences between external reality and the symbol system in terms of which we think'.[9] It should be understood, however, that although the body can play this strictly defined role of mediation between the external world and a rational system for interpreting and understanding it, it nonetheless adds nothing essential to concepts. The body, in other words, plays no essential role in the provision of meaning. Certainly, it plays 'no role in characterizing the nature of reason'.[10] Reason – the nature of reason – is quintessentially disembodied. And, as Lakoff points out, while the assumptions behind such a view of the relationship between the mind and reality may not lead us into too much difficulty when thinking about tables and other everyday objects, such assumptions, extended to other domains, do lead to problems – and contribute to problematic outcomes.[11]

The disembodiment of reason thus relies on a fundamental mind/body dichotomy. This dichotomy is fundamental to the intractable dichotomies that we have already encountered concerning inclusion and exclusion in international human rights law (and elsewhere) – the central problematic of which focuses on the construction of gender and other hierarchies of embodiment and the intransigent and related problems produced by the public/private divide (so central to traditional liberal theory).

Since quasi-disembodiment and the mechanisms of disembodiment associated with rationality and law are so profoundly implicated in human rights paradoxes underlying the development of corporate legal 'humanity' it becomes essential to address quasi-disembodiment with a theoretical counterweight. Accordingly, it is a central argument of this book that human embodied vulnerability should be recognised as foundational to an ethically satisfying theory of human rights. In fact, the argument will go further than that, and insist that embodiment is inescapably central to an adequate understanding of rationality (and of law) itself. Accordingly, we shall now introduce the implications of embodiment for philosophy, for rationality, and for our understanding of the very foundations of law as an enterprise, before turning to some further reflections on the implications of embodiment and its concomitant vulnerability for human rights law and theory in particular.

The Western philosopher who is credited with having done more than any other to transcend the limitations of a disembodied conception of rationality and its related mind/body dichotomy is Merleau-Ponty.[12] His approach to embodied perception and its centrality to an adequate explanation of both rationality and our understanding of reality provides an apt philosophical foundation not only for a critique of disembodiment but also for a related defence of *embodied vulnerability* as the proper foundation of human rights legal subjectivity.

Merleau-Ponty foregrounds embodiment by providing a phenomenological account of perception as being embodied experience. In other words, bodily perception is not conceived by Merleau-Ponty as external to the structure of rationality or as a mere vehicle for information-gathering that the disembodied mind uses in establishing a correspondence between concept and reality. On the contrary, in Merleau-Ponty's philosophy, perception, knowledge and rationality are revealed as being *inescapably embodied*. Accordingly, the mind/body dualism is transcended, though dualities remain (higher level conceptualisation takes place but never ultimately leaves behind its embodied perceptual foundations – nor is it reduced to them).[13] Merleau-Ponty, therefore, embraces neither idealism nor empiricism understood in their reductive forms.[14] Instead, he retains the insights of both, transcending and uniting them in a more integral view in which he discovers 'in the experience of the perceived world a new type of relation between the mind and truth'.[15]

Merleau-Ponty's main thesis is presented in *The Phenomenology of Perception*[16] and then more concisely captured in his essay 'The Primacy of Perception'.[17] Fundamentally, in place of the traditionally disembodied mind of the dominant Western tradition, he offers us a thoroughly embodied incarnate subject in whom mind and body are inseparably intertwined – co-constituted, even: 'The perceiving subject is not this absolute thinker; rather it functions according to a natal pact between our body and the world, between ourselves and our body'.[18] Perception is always an embodied experience. Even our higher level reasoning, perceptual experience and cognition can never ultimately escape its foundations in our embodied perception. Merleau-Ponty thus completely rejects the ontological separation of body and mind offered by the traditional Cartesian view of reality. By a sustained study of the nature of perception as *embodied* perception he offers a radically alternative philosophy, treading a middle road between traditional empiricism and traditional idealism (and their respective treatments of perception), and in the process directly undermining the dominant Western conception of the disembodied intellect.[19]

For Merleau-Ponty, perception (which he points out has been the unquestioned basis of science and philosophy, functioning as that which 'opens a window onto things... [and] ...directed, quasi-teleologically, towards a truth in itself in which the reason underlying all appearances is to be found'[20]) is *always* and *inescapably* embodied. So intimate is the relationship between the body and perception, he suggests, that '[t]he theory of the body is already a theory of perception' – '[o]ur own body is in the world as the heart is in the organism: it keeps the visible spectacle constantly alive, it breaths life into it and sustains it inwardly, and with it forms a system'.[21] The body, in other words, as a living, perceiving body, is in an inherently open, systemic relationship with the world. Perception cannot be *merely* an interior representation of an external world which includes the body itself (as an external object) because perception is an embodied continuity with the world, and *thoroughly incarnate*. Merleau-Ponty argues that '[w]e have relearned to feel our body; we have found underneath the objective and detached knowledge of the body that other knowledge which we have of it in virtue of its always being with us and of the fact that we are our body... we are in the world through our body... we perceive the world with our body'.[22]

This theory of perception has important consequences. One of these is the emphasis it requires us to place on the perspectival nature of perception. This is because embodied perception is always located, has a position in space.

The idea of the objective, dislocated viewpoint – the view from 'nowhere' so central to disembodied Western abstractionism – is challenged. In Merleau-Ponty's words:

> [An object] is given as the infinite sum of an indefinite series of perspectival views in each of which the object is given but in none of which is it given exhaustively. It is not accidental for the object to be given to me in a 'deformed' way, from the point of view [*place*] which I occupy. That is the price of its being 'real'. The perceptual synthesis thus must be accomplished by the subject.... This subject, which takes a point of view, is my body as the field of perception and action [*practique*].[23]

Williams and Bendelow point out that the perspectival nature of perception 'is a primary expression of our embodiment', and that perception is also grounded in behaviour (such as looking, hearing, touching) as a quintessentially 'practical relationship to and involvement in the world'.[24] Again, this suggests that the body is always positioned, located, imbricated in materiality. Our everyday perceiving, moreover, involves an intimate bodily continuity between ourselves and the world, a bodily intimacy that takes place at a level below the threshold of our conscious awareness. We inescapably participate in an ongoing interaction with the world – such that 'the body's intimate continuity with the world means that it is part of a single *reversible* fabric or *flesh*'.[25] This again, has important implications from which further implications flow. First, we should re-emphasise that the body's relationship with the world is practical, sensory and involved. Adams suggests that Merleau-Ponty's view of the lived body is that it is naturally '"ethesiological" – sensing, feeling, libidinal, erotic, desiring, empathic. Spontaneously, "[t]he body asks for something other than... its relations with itself" ... [and that] [w]ith these insights, Merleau-Ponty emphasizes the interrelational structure of our embodied existence'.[26] (This point will have particular significance for a theory of human rights as we shall see below.)

Secondly, Merleau-Ponty's emphasis on the body as part of a single reversible flesh with the world points to the important notion of 'intercorporeality' – the idea that 'all being is interbeing, intertwining – and such interrelating is intrinsic to the very structure of subjectivity and lived reality'.[27] This is a very important idea. It completely undermines the radical separation between mind and body, self and other, body and other, human and world, so intrinsic to the dominant Western worldview, and will have further ramifications for the theorisation of human rights offered in this work. Dualistic language, understood in this light, will always be inadequate because it simply fails to recognise the dynamic, participatory, interrelational nature of reality. For Merleau-Ponty, subject and object are never separated. Rather, they are 'two abstract "moments" of a unique structure which is *presence*'.[28] If perception is always an interplay between the perceiving body and that which it perceives, and if there is an inherent mutual coupling between body and world, then the language of separation invokes an illusory distance.

Dualism and the disembodied perspective thus turn out to be lacking in both existential and epistemological terms. Towards the end of his life, Merleau-Ponty began to explore and develop his ontological position, arguing that the perceived world is also ontologically primary.[29] This is explored in *The Visible and the Invisible*, particularly in his chapter on 'The Intertwining – the Chiasm' – a chapter which introduces concepts through which to 'explore the production of visibility and "the metaphysical structure of our flesh"'.[30] The 'flesh' is Merleau-Ponty's most important philosophical idea – of which he says 'there is no name in traditional philosophy to designate it'.[31] Enlarging on the nature of 'flesh' he suggests that it is

> not matter, is not mind, is not substance. To designate it, we should need the old term "element", in the sense it was used to speak of water, air, earth and fire, that is, in the sense of a *general thing*, midway between the spatio-temporal individual and the idea, a sort of incarnate principle that brings a style of being wherever there is a fragment of being.[32]

On the nature of this style of being, Adams remarks that Merleau-Ponty endorses Heidegger's affirmation of the 'dynamic quality of being: being is be-ing.... [T]he flesh is a dynamic happening or transpiring or presencing – or ... a process of interrelating'.[33] Merleau-Ponty describes a 'chiasm', a dynamic crossing-over, inter-permeation, a 'shared world of *intermundane* space which crosses over and intertwines with that of similarly embodied human beings'.[34] Moreover, he explains that the visible (so central to traditional Western philosophy) and the tangible belong to the same order, since both seeing and touching are done by the same body – and that the imbrication of the visible in the tangible, and the tangible in the visible, mean that vision is a 'palpation with the look'.[35] And since it *is*,

> it must also be inscribed in the order of being that it discloses to us; he who looks must not himself be foreign to the world he looks at... he who sees cannot possess the visible unless he is possessed by it, unless he *is of it*, unless, by principle, according to what is required by the articulation of the look with the things, he is one of the visibles, capable by a singular reversal, of seeing them – he who is one of them.[36]

There is no disembodied, radically separate viewer to survey the world from a dislocated height. We are always inescapably interwoven with that which we observe. Adams sums up Merleau-Ponty's view on the flesh by arguing that the flesh is the chiasmic intertwining that reveals our essential being as a form of inter-being. Interrelationality (the interrelational coupling between self with the world and world with self) is the most real. Our subjectivity, thus understood, is more accurately an *inter*-subjectivity.[37] The flesh, in other words, can be understood as a radically non-dual reversible interpermeation of self and world – as inter*corporeality*. As Williams and Bendelow put it, '[i]ntersubjectivity... is carnal through and through, forged as it is by the intercorporeal relations of sentient body-subjects and their primordial bonds with a common reversible world'.[38] For Adams, this means that both knowledge and reality are quintessentially interrelational: the 'real world is the perceived world is the lived world is the phenomenal world is the participatory world is the interrelational world'.[39]

Dualism, in this view, is revealed as being an entirely inadequate formulation in both epistemological and ontological terms because there is no separate, independent, substantial self and no separate, independent, substantial world. There is no ultimate reality to a division between 'subject' and 'object': 'To even speak independently of self and world (or self and nature) is misleading. Since both of these are secondary theoretical abstractions removed from our every day (inter)existence, neither can claim priority'.[40] Embodied perception is the inescapable basis of all our knowing, all our being. Merleau-Ponty's philosophical exploration of this fact, and his subtle and beautiful exposition of the implications of embodiment – the way that the body is lived in its temporal and spatial location in the world – produces a philosophical view of reality that directly challenges the mind/body split (in existential, epistemological and ontological terms) and, logically, its related bifurcations (although Merleau-Ponty never addresses the gendered dimension of the binary). Disembodiment is, in this light, a great impossibility – a misleading illusion. Reading the term 'quasi-disembodiment' in the light of Merleau-Ponty's philosophy, it can be seen that the term neatly captures the sheer impossibility of disembodied rationality or perception while suggestively hinting at the ideologically conditioned nature of that impossibility.

Not only is the notion of disembodied rationality impossible, but it is unscientific – and in that sense – *irrational*. This becomes clear when we add the insights of cognitive science to our argument. There are now strong reasons for suggesting that the concept of disembodied rationality is *empirically unsound*. This is most clearly reflected in the work of Lakoff and Johnson.[41] Opening their book *Philosophy in the Flesh*, Lakoff and Johnson assert that the three major findings of cognitive science are: 'The mind is inherently embodied. Thought is mostly unconscious. Abstract concepts are largely metaphorical'.[42] They argue that, because of these scientific insights, philosophy cannot remain the same and that thousands of years of philosophical speculation, conducted *a priori*, have reached a terminus in which philosophy itself must now be radically reconfigured to address modern scientific findings.

More specifically, they contend that a series of changes needs to take place in our *very concept of reason itself*. Most importantly, for present purposes, they argue that reason is not disembodied: '[Reason] arises from the nature of our brains, bodies and bodily experience. This is not just the innocuous and obvious claim that we need a body to reason; rather it is the striking claim that the very structure of reason itself comes from the details of our embodiment'.[43] Not only this, but reason is *evolutionary* in the sense that our more abstract forms of thought do not discard the forms of perceptual and motor inference present in other animals. What makes human reason 'universal' (to the extent that it is) is not some transcendent quality of reason but the fact that we share commonalities arising from the embodiment through which the mind operates. In fact, empirical research reveals reason to be mostly unconscious, largely metaphorical and to have a large emotional component.[44] Accordingly, reason is not the completely conscious, literal, dispassionate human faculty that it has traditionally been presumed and understood to be in the Western tradition.[45] And importantly for present purposes, as an empirical matter, there is no mind/body split. There is no disembodied, transcendent mind. Reason never transcends the body. This means that there is, for example, no Kantian 'radically autonomous person'. Furthermore, reason is not strictly universal, because conceptual systems vary and become neurally embedded in the structure of our brains – meaning that thought is never truly free. For Lakoff and Johnson, not only are Cartesian and Kantian views rendered empirically inaccurate and therefore unsustainable, but utilitarian, phenomenological and poststructuralist views are also all rendered empirically unsustainable in their traditional forms.[46]

It is worth pausing at this point to reflect briefly on the relationship between these insights from cognitive science and the phenomenological perspective. It is clear that Johnson, in particular, aligns himself with a phenomenological perspective in the most general terms – its broad orientation. He states that the method he employs could be understood as a form of descriptive or empirical phenomenology, but that beyond that general alignment he is not identifying himself with any particular strand of the phenomenological tradition. However, he notes that, '[a]t the same time it will be obvious that some of my most important claims are anticipated in the work of philosophers who might legitimately claim allegiance to phenomenology of post-Husserlian varieties'.[47] Although it is quite legitimate to read Merleau-Ponty and Johnson's work as being mutually supportive, and Johnson's work as a further development of Merleau-Ponty's broad thesis concerning the embodied mind, there are important differences that must not be overlooked. Their arguments focus on slightly different things, in that Johnson arguably takes Merleau-Ponty's arguments into the more precisely focused domain of understanding the *ways* in which imagination links bodily and cognitive structures – utilising the insights of cognitive science to burrow deeper into the functioning of embodied mind. He insists, in fact, that a phenomenological account

> does not simply terminate with a description of structures of experience and understanding; instead it uses that description as the basis of a very powerful *explanation* of the process involved in making semantic

> connections among systematically related meanings... how non-propositional image-schematic structures [revealed by cognitive science] can be metaphorically projected to structure our abstract reasoning in on-going problematic situations of life, art or science.[48]

While Merleau-Ponty's philosophy insists on embodied perception as primary, Johnson's project is to understand more precisely using the insights of cognitive science, exactly *how* the body is *in the mind*, how embodiment is resonant in mind's typical patterns, structures and modalities of perception. Johnson explores the ways in which basic concepts such as scale, balance or force, or cycles emerge directly from our experience as 'contained' embodied beings. He suggests that we develop, on the basis of our embodiment and its incidents, schemata for understanding our world – general knowledge structures – that are then invoked in all higher level reasoning. For example, as Williams and Bendelow succinctly put it, the 'verticality' schema arises from our tendency to use an 'up-down' orientation in relating to experience meaningfully. The verticality schema is 'grasped repeatedly on a daily basis from perceiving a building and standing upright, to climbing stairs. This schema is an abstract representation or analogue of our embodied verticality experiences that are grounded in our every day lives and being in the world'.[49] Johnson argues that schemas such as the verticality schema are imaginative experiential structures, intrinsically grounded in the reality of embodiment, and integral to rationality because they are integral to meaning. Similarly, we develop 'metaphors' based on our physical experience. The contents of a glass of water when filled can be seen to rise – the level goes up – yielding, along with a myriad other such experiences and observations – the pervasive metaphor that 'more is up': 'More and up, in other words, are metaphorically connected in our experience in a way that provides a physical basis for more abstract understandings of quantity'.[50]

One key difference between traditional phenomenological accounts and the account of the embodied mind produced by cognitive science is the influence, in cognitive science, of the cognitive unconscious. We have no direct access to the operation of the cognitive unconscious (and therefore to most of our thought). This means that phenomenological reflection cannot, through introspection alone, discover a complete understanding of mind and the nature of experience. Phenomenological reflection, though it focally explicates the structure of human experience, accordingly needs to be supplemented by empirical research into the cognitive unconscious[51] if it is not merely to privilege a metaphysics limited to that which is either conscious or accessible to consciousness.

Taken together, the work of Merleau-Ponty, Johnson and Lakoff provides the foundation for constructing a strong argument that dualism is not only inadequate as a view of reality, but radically inaccurate. The insights of cognitive science render the notion of disembodied mind empirically unsustainable. Given the traditional and longstanding link between disembodiment, rationality and science, this is not without its irony. What emerges from these writings and their implications is the compelling nature of our corporeal engagement with the world and the role of that embodied engagement in the generation of meaning, imagination and reason.

The fundamental interrelationality that flows from the ethesiological nature of embodiment, stressed by Merleau-Ponty, is also implicated in scientific study of the nature of justice and the biological foundations of law itself.[52] We have already seen how law, through its adoption and promotion of a quintessentially disembodied rationality (in actuality, however, quasi-disembodied) reflects a largely suppressed relationship with human embodied existence. This suppressed relationship is complex and full of contradictions. First, law presupposes embodiment as the foundation of law's enforceability: law acts on human bodies,[53] meaning that despite the body's attenuated role in the delineation of the liberal legal subject,[54] the body operates, in a sense, as a suppressed premise. Secondly, law, when it addresses bodies, utilises a series of constructions of the body (the body as machine, property, autonomous, bounded, commodified etc)[55] in its scheme of legal categories and relations, while suppressing the full implications of embodied materiality, which remains theoretically attenuated in the construction of legal subjectivity. When liberal law has a body in mind in relation to the holder of legal rights, for example, it is the 'bounded heterosexual male body', an 'immutable' body, operating precisely as 'a means of denying bodily integrity to women (and to men who refuse to behave like "true" men who are deemed to lack clear boundary definition)'.[56] While, therefore, partial and ideologically shaped constructions of the body operate in law, they tend to support rather than detract from the implications of the quasi-disembodiment of law's discourse as rationality, or its construction of the legal person as quasi-disembodied.

One argument not often factored into discussion of the complex relationship between law and the body is the argument that the very nature of law itself emerges from 'biological foundations'. A range of studies seems to locate the impulses that found justice (and law) in embodied biological mechanisms shared by humans with non-human primate species. In his introduction to *The Sense of Justice: Biological Foundations of Law*,[57] Masters argues that the assumption that human social behaviour transcends natural constraints (an assumption implicit in the notion of disembodied reason) is coming under increasing pressure from evidence that proves that humans cannot be set apart from other natural species in quite the way that traditional legal and social theory presuppose. Just as Lakoff and Johnson argue that the findings of cognitive science falsify central Western philosophical assumptions about human nature, Masters argues that 'behavioural ecology demonstrates that similar considerations shape the social behaviour of non-human as well as human groups, and cognitive neuroscientists and evolutionary psychologists have shown that the structure and functioning of the human central nervous system are often inconsistent with widespread beliefs about human behaviour'.[58] Distinguishing his perspective carefully from any kind of biological reductionism, Masters argues that the human species has evolved and operates in complex combination with particular, identifiable 'processing mechanisms and physiological systems'.[59] The sense of justice, and the nature of law, just like the nature of rationality, cannot, in the light of such evidence, continue to be understood as phenomena abstracted from either human embodied nature or indeed nature itself.

A key theme that emerges from this diverse body of research, for the purposes of this book, is, again, the centrality of embodiment. Although this is not the explicit focus of Masters and his co-writers, the centrality of embodiment emerges in two main senses, both highly relevant to the present argument. First, embodiment is operatively decisive in the evolution of the sense of justice (and, by implication, law – the relationship will be more fully defended shortly). This is due to the importance of neurochemical processes and neuroanatomical structures in the operation of the sense of justice. Secondly, embodiment is clearly reflected in the structure of the sense of justice as a quintessentially interrelational phenomenon emerging from the embodied interaction of primates.[60] McGuire, for example, argues that moralistic aggression (the tendency to get angry and want to exact revenge for a failure in reciprocity) has been observed as a fundamental feature of human interaction, as well as being widely observed in non-human primates. From a biological perspective, such moralistic aggression is a feature of a 'strongly predisposed or species-characteristic human trait'.[61] This trait is regulated by the central nervous system, and exists across cultures – as we might indeed predict if such a trait reflects something of our embodied behavioural architecture. Thus, it has been shown that humans are 'predisposed' to judge the behaviour of others as being either just or unjust and to respond with anger when a behaviour is judged or perceived as being unjust. McGuire gives a simple example that captures the essence of what this sense of justice reflects: 'At considerable personal cost, I am helpful to a friend who, when asked to reciprocate, refuses to do so without providing an explanation for the refusal. In this situation, it is highly likely that I will experience anger and want to retaliate'.[62] This type of reciprocal expectation, and its accompanying moralistic aggression, is also noted in non-human primate species in relation to behaviours such as grooming.[63] MacGuire's argument that moralistic aggression underlies the sense of justice is repeatedly supported by other theorists writing from differing disciplinary backgrounds.[64] The broad convergence of their findings suggests that the sense of justice (and injustice) quintessentially concerns how we respond to defeated expectations, and emerges as a 'combination of emotion and cognition resulting from a balancing or matching of experience with expectations'.[65]

Law rests upon biological foundations in at least three identifiable senses relevant to this book. First, there is the sense in which law and justice have long been interwoven despite not being coterminous.[66] If the sense of justice has identifiable roots in the biology of bodies and the embodied interaction of primates and humans, then it would be unsurprising to find that law too has foundations emerging, in part, from embodied biology – whether indirectly (through the concept of justice) or even directly. Gruter, for example, argues that the origins of *legal* behaviour have their roots in human evolution – that '[h]omo sapiens, in effect, evolved as a species that created laws, modified them, and followed them', and that these behaviours reflect non-human primate behaviours that can be viewed as the precursors of rule-following behaviour.[67] She argues that much non-human primate behaviour can be seen as pre-legal, in the sense that it is behaviour that forms the indispensable foundation of human rule-following behaviour.[68] Human law is different in degree, although it has some crucial distinctions – such as social machinery for the sanctioning of deviant behaviour,[69] systemic organisation (such as the union of primary and secondary rules in Hart's terms[70]), the use of abstract rules relying on language and so forth. But human law nonetheless reflects the same origin in evolutionary legal behaviour. Gruter argues that it is highly likely that, during the early evolution of our species, 'dispositions favouring rule-making and rule-following behaviour were selected and became an integral part of the species genome'.[71] Viewed in this way, rule-making and rule-following behaviour became absorbed bodily as part of our genetic coding as a predisposed and quintessentially embodied response to the world. Law emerges in this light as a response of embodied biological organisms to the presence of embodied others in interaction in a material world – as a response to the need for control, co-ordination and the management of expectations (a central part of the sense of justice). While this is not reducible to a simple biological mechanism, it is clear that biology, and embodiment, played a crucial evolutionary role in the genesis of legal behaviour.[72]

Secondly, theories of law cannot, in the light of all that we have already discussed, rationally be divorced from conceptions or models of the mind – which, it should now be clear, means the embodied mind with its characteristic information processing capacities, developed through identifiable evolutionary mechanisms the foundations of which we still share with our primate cousins. Thirdly, law can be conceptualised as being a particularly apt way of accounting for the 'bystander' role in a triadic notion of justice. In chimpanzee behaviour, for example, the bystander plays a central role.[73] Similarly, in human society, laws address bystanders as well as participants. Masters makes the point that 'evolutionary theory suggests that the elemental situation is essentially a triad. This is particularly important because only with a third party or bystander is it possible to extend cooperation through the mechanisms of indirect reciprocity'.[74] He points out that this triadic structure is reflected in the law's role as intervener in disagreements over the violation of rules and laws. Moreover, he argues, this essentially triadic structure can be seen to underlie the sense of justice in modern states. The 'logic of the triad', as he puts it, points us to the question of why people feel injustice when they see others unjustly treated.

This consideration brings us neatly back to our earlier reflections on interrelationality – that central implication of embodiment so emphasised by Merleau-Ponty. Law and justice emerge from these reflections as being mechanisms intimately related to the socio-biological evolution of human beings as embodied beings living in shared socio-material space and formed – intercorporeally in Merleau-Ponty's radical sense – by an engagement with each other and the world that is so intimate that behaviour patterns are internalised as part of our very encoding, and passed down through bodies and social structures to undergird the unfolding of law and justice as aspects, in turn, of an inescapably embodied interrelationality.

The role of the body as an aspect of law's foundation is not straightforward. But it is certainly challenging to the notion of law as a product of disembodied reason. Taken together, arguments about the biological foundations of law and the sense of justice, arguments from cognitive science about the precise ways in which the body shapes the mind even at the most abstract levels of reasoning, and Merleau-Ponty's rich philosophical exploration of the centrality of embodiment and its implications, all suggest strongly that Western disembodied reason is an unsupportable notion. Not only this, it is both scientifically and philosophically *redundant*. It is therefore irrational to continue to shape law and legal theory around a quasi-disembodied subject, utilising old binary assumptions that rely for their logic on an unsustainable mind/body split and its related oppositional bifurcations. We shall return to this point and its implications for the re-conceptualisation of the human rights universal and of legal subjects generally in the final chapter of this book. For now we need to turn to the centrality of embodied *vulnerability*, the second argumentative foundation of the theory of human rights to be offered here.

Embodied vulnerability

A key incident of human embodiment is human vulnerability. Merleau-Ponty's account beautifully accounts for the ethesiological, other-seeking nature of embodiment, as well as its radical emplacement in a physical, perspectivally-limited context – both aspects of embodiment with rich theoretical implications for a theory of human rights. It is worth noting, however, that Merleau-Ponty stands accused of leaving out of his account, in any explicit sense, the ambivalence attending our embodiment and of elevating the 'intentional and expressive body' but neglecting 'the other side of sensibility, that is, sensibility as a condition of affectability',[75] affectability being a 'condition of non-intentional, heteronomous and more or less *vulnerable* openness to the surrounding world'.[76] It will be argued shortly, however, that Merleau-Ponty's theory contributes a rich and unusual vein to a theory of vulnerability.

Vulnerability, in a complex and muted way, has, for some time operated in liberal legal and political theory – but in very much the same attenuated way as the body itself. It is possible, for example, to read a conception of mutual vulnerability into Hobbes's unappealing equality of the power of 'men' to kill in the state of nature, for example.[77] In a similar vein, Hart's famous invocation of vulnerability in defence of what he called a 'minimum content of natural law'[78] focuses primarily on the need for rules restricting the use of violence in killing or inflicting bodily harm. Vulnerability is conceived of, in other words, as vulnerability to bodily attack – a rather thin conception of vulnerability – which is linked, revealingly perhaps, to an equally thin (and unconvincing) conception of approximate human equality. In the context of discussing this, Hart actually uses Hobbes's famous language concerning life as 'nasty', 'brutish' and 'short'.[79] Hart also considers the 'contingent fact' of the limited resources available to human beings as a basis for the justification of the institution of property (though not necessarily individual property[80]) and links this to the human need for clothes, food and shelter (all quintessentially embodied concerns). Hart's argument might certainly be mined for a richer set of implications than he himself explicitly provides, but his operative conceptions of embodied vulnerability (as vulnerability to attack) and embodied need (which could be formulated as 'vulnerability' but is not, in terms, by Hart) are both refracted through the highly problematic lens of an approximate embodied individual equality as a 'natural fact'.[81] Hart's analysis, therefore, does not appear to transcend traditional liberal legal presuppositions, in particular of an implied, muted or radically limited conception of vulnerability (reflecting, moreover, the bounded, autonomous self and its traditional concerns), an unrealistic approximate individual equality that ignores (forecloses) structural dimensions of power, or the attenuated role of the body.

Fortunately, vulnerability is a concept that has of late, been increasingly invoked in discussions highly relevant, not only to the construction of human rights subjectivity[82] but to the construction of political subjectivity (and substantive political equality).[83] The term 'vulnerability', moreover, has featured increasingly in discussions of globalisation[84] – a context highly salient to the concerns of this book – particularly as the theme of vulnerability, linked to the theme of violence – has been defended as a powerful way of connecting the state-market shifts of globalisation to their material impact upon the embodied lives of the world's poor,[85] an analysis that could yet provide a very fruitful link to Hart's minimalist conception for the justification of legal institutions. And, more directly linked to the central argument of this book, Fineman has recently argued that the autonomous liberal subject of the classical liberal tradition should be replaced by 'the vulnerable subject'

– and that this subject, who is 'far more representative of actual lived experience and the human condition… should be at the center of our political and theoretical endeavours'.[86]

Turning then, to the construction of the 'vulnerable subject' of human rights, it seems theoretically essential to emphasise that our human vulnerability arises, inescapably from our human embodiment understood as a thoroughly incarnate reality. The body needs to move to centre stage with all its complexity – its ontic qualities in combination with the social construction of embodiment and to become absolutely focal to human rights theorisation. Fineman argues that we share a common and enduring vulnerability because we are embodied subjects whose bodies have certain characteristics such as a need for, *minimally,* nutrients, hydration, air and sleep. We have bodies that present us with the ever-present possibility of being harmed or injured, whether by accident or design. We are susceptible to disease. We are mortal – our lives could be taken from us by attack, accident, illness or the like. We are vulnerable to the material realities of our environment – whether a flash flood, a drought, a chemical leak, a pandemic or a flu virus. Hart's thesis could be expanded to include this wider set of concerns and located within a more critical use of the concept of vulnerability to deconstruct ideological closures linked to liberal suppositions. In fact, Fineman hints at just such a critical role for a universal vulnerability thesis when she exposes the way in which our common vulnerability has been unfairly characterised as the particular condition of identified social groups, and associated with forms of victimhood (this especially affects the construction of female subjectivity in international human rights law, as noted in the last chapter[87]), dependency or even pathology.[88] In the light of this, it is all the more important, especially in the light of the urgent concerns at the heart of this book, to employ vulnerability as a critical concept explicitly founded on incarnate embodied life as a common ontic condition of being human, and to use this embodiment-centred critique to explicitly resist the ideological deployment of vulnerability as the foundation of a set of (predictably) stigmatised subjectivities.

Vulnerability, as an ontic matter, unites human beings, not only with each other in a way that invites critique of substantive inequalities and their related structural impediments to adequate protection, but unites us, as a species, with all other carbon-based life-forms and the eco-systems of which we are a part. The vulnerability thesis has vast theoretical potential, particularly because vulnerability need not be conceived of as a monolithic concept. The vulnerabilities of different entities will have differing nuances, interplay, orders of seriousness and complexity. The wider implications of the vulnerability thesis lie beyond the precise focus of the present work but suggest very rich future research questions. Returning, however, to the key concerns of this book, it is true to say that vulnerability can be theorised as a condition of corporations. However, corporate vulnerability, as was argued in Chapter 2, is not of the same order or kind as human embodied vulnerability, and nor is corporate embodiment on all fours with the human incarnate life.[89] There are very strong theoretical, conceptual and normative reasons for arguing that the corporation should not be understood as a human being, even if it can feasibly be understood as a person, both legal and moral.[90] Accordingly, while specific vulnerabilities of the corporate form might be conceived of as the foundation of *corporate* rights subjectivity, this rights subjectivity, it is suggested, should not be conceived of as *human* rights subjectivity. In the human rights context, a human vulnerability thesis focused on the inexorable ontic primacy of human material embodiment suggests that the quasi-disembodied universal possessor of human rights, so conveniently continuous with the structural and ideological features of liberal law that favour the corporate form, can be directly challenged by the production of a universal human subject explicitly understood to be the *human embodied vulnerable subject*. This, it is suggested, provides the best ethical and conceptual foundation (both necessary and sufficient) for a coherent notion of human rights (perhaps especially in the UDHR paradigm, for reasons that will become clearer in the next chapter).

The most sustained study of embodied vulnerability as being the proper foundation for human rights is that offered by Turner in his recent book, *Vulnerability and Human Rights*.[91] His account provides many rich insights and opportunities for reflection and critique, and will thus form the basis of this part of the argument – to be supplemented where appropriate. A few preliminary observations are in order. It should be noted from the outset that Turner's intention is to offer a sociological study of human rights.[92] His account combines the concept of human vulnerability with the notion of institutional precariousness in order to defend the universalism and importance of human rights. The account developed in this book, by contrast, will focus predominantly on human embodied vulnerability as the basis of a legal theoretical approach to the reinvigoration of human rights as constructs uniquely concerned with the legal, quasi-legal and trans-legal protection of human beings. Accordingly, while Turner's sociological account focuses on a significant cluster of social and economic rights and 'rights of the body' this account will argue that embodied vulnerability offers a suitable, conceptually compelling and direct theoretical foundation for *all* categories of human rights, including civil and political rights (which Turner only links *indirectly* to embodied vulnerability). Additionally, Turner reads vulnerability through the lens of suffering and pain – emphasising that 'suffering is inevitable and misery is universal' and that 'we suffer because we are vulnerable, and we need, above all else, institutions that will give us some degree of security'.[93] While it is certain that vulnerability is the root of our capacity for suffering, it will be argued here that vulnerability is also the source of multiple forms of wellbeing and joy, and the basis of empathy and intimacy in a way that moves beyond merely seeking 'security' in a world of risk to a wider, richer set of possibilities. Accordingly, a rather different view of vulnerability will be offered here – as, indeed, will a rather different view of suffering and pain.

Having made these opening remarks, we can now introduce Turner's broad thesis concerning vulnerability as the foundation of human rights. Drawing an introductory distinction between the social rights of citizens and individual human rights, Turner argues that, unlike social rights (which frequently require contributions from citizens in the form of taxation, or other contributions to society through work, public duty or parenting), human rights are 'rights enjoyed by individuals by virtue of being human – and as a consequence of their shared vulnerability'.[94] His stated purpose is to challenge the legacy of positivism and cultural relativism and to 'promote a sociological approach that starts with the idea of embodiment and human vulnerability. Human rights can be defined as universal principles, because human beings share a common ontology that is grounded in a shared vulnerability'.[95]

Turner takes as his starting point Ignatieff's attack on relativism, and what Turner identifies as 'close to' an ontological argument in support of universalism provided in Ignatieff's second essay in *Human Rights as Politics and Idolatry*.[96] In an argument in which Ignatieff suggests that human rights need to be understood as the basis for deliberation, as a shared vocabulary from which we begin to discuss how we should treat one another (rather than as any kind of trumps), Ignatieff concludes by suggesting that, in this deliberation, 'the ground we share may actually be quite limited: not much more than the basic intuition that what is pain and suffering for you is bound to be pain and humiliation for me. But this is already something'.[97] Turner, alighting on this, suggests that it is our 'capacity for suffering that creates a significant basis for universalism',[98] and he sets out to elaborate Ignatieff's argument in order to develop a defence of universalism based on the notion of human embodiment – asserting that the foundation to human rights is our 'common vulnerability'.[99] He continues:

> Human beings experience pain and humiliation because they are vulnerable. While humans may not share a common culture, they are bound together by the risks and perturbations that arise from their vulnerability. Because we have a common ontological condition as vulnerable, intelligent beings, human happiness is diverse, but misery is common and uniform. This need for ontological security provides a strong moral argument against cultural relativism and offers an endorsement of rights claims for protection from suffering and indignity. While liberal theory is largely about the political dimension of human rights, ontological insecurity indicates a cluster of salient social and economic rights... that are fundamentally connected with human embodiment.[100]

This quotation captures the essence of a central part of Turner's argument. Before addressing any further implications of his insightful work for our study of embodied vulnerability, it is useful to pause and reflect on what we have already encountered to this point.

First, it is already clear from the argument thus far presented that conceptualising human embodied vulnerability as being the ultimate relevant commonality underlying universalism is a potent way of capturing an ontic reality that unites all human beings in a community of living flesh. The incarnate reality of our common existence is, moreover, inherently open to context – and this means that human vulnerability, in day to day terms, is differentially experienced, or is – as was also argued above – particular as well as universal – just like the body itself. This differential experience of vulnerability in context raises a host of social justice considerations in a rich, substantive sense – certainly in a more substantive manner[101] than the empty formality of the liberal subject of rights can. Indeed, as we have seen the liberal 'man' was constructed, certainly within liberal law, precisely to mask such substantive social injustices and a result muted the potential reach of universalistic rights logic. Turner's assertion that the foundation of human rights must be our common embodied vulnerability is profoundly continuous, therefore, with both the concerns of this book and Fineman's important exhortation that we should reconceptualise the liberal political subject as a vulnerable subject.

It cannot be stressed enough that the centrality of human embodied vulnerability is a *crucial* insight for the theory of human rights. Focusing on the empirical reality of the incarnate nature of the human being brings us into direct connection with our basic materiality and its implications: The human body is 'affectable'. It can be radically compromised. We die if we cannot gain the necessary nutrients that our bodies require. We need to drink clean water. We suffer, and sometimes even die, if we cannot breathe sufficiently clean air. We can be killed. We can be made to suffer pain. Our skin, as a living, breathing organ, is a porous, receptive interface between the 'external' environment, and our complex system of blood, bones, organs, cells and molecules. In relation to the theorisation of international human rights, therefore, focusing on the centrality of embodied vulnerability brings *both* embodiment *and* vulnerability to the fore of our thinking.

It is worth emphasising that the power of this insight is not rendered redundant by the privileging of the discourse of the gene or the emergence of views presenting the body as a flow of information, or even by, for example, poststructuralist reconfigurations of the body as 'fluid, multiple, fragmented and dispersed'.[102] Despite the power of such alternate discursive constructions of the body there is a strong human rights-based case for emphasising the concomitant, continuing and possibly ever-more-urgent importance of an account of human rights based on embodied vulnerability. It may be increasingly important, in other words, to resist certain forms of body-dissipating discourse lest the lived human body be muted in its critical power *all over again*, in new ways that produce and reproduce social exclusions, reconfigured dualisms and human suffering. For Baxi, human rights languages find their fulcrum point 'at the surface of lived, and embodied, human anguish'.[103] Embodied vulnerability, it is suggested, is a vital concept of resistance to the tendency of human rights to be open to influences that suppresses their potential for radical humanitarian critique.[104] The quasi-disembodied construction of the human rights beneficiary (and its related concept, the legal subject), in particular, is directly challenged by a notion of human rights that foregrounds embodied vulnerability. And, in relation to the argument of this book concerning the urgent need to challenge the incremental invocation of corporate legal humanity through the corporate exploitation of human rights, embodied vulnerability supplies a (possibly *the*) crucial distinction between the corporation and the human being for the purposes of human rights attribution.

Secondly, it should be noted that vulnerability need not be understood simply as the capacity for suffering, nor treated merely as synonymous with suffering/pain, cathartic and important as the voices of suffering are in the genesis of human rights claims. (Turner seems to conceptualise vulnerability as suffering/pain/the capacity for suffering although he draws a distinction, for the purposes of his argument, between suffering and pain, which we shall attend to below.) However, at its best, embodied vulnerability can be taken further than this, and conceptualised as both a source and expression of a radical interrelationality. As Merleau Ponty's rich theorisation suggests, we are inescapably embodied beings whose bodies are in an intrinsically open, sensing, feeling, desiring, libidinal, expressive circuit with the world. This openness is highly nuanced in its implications. While vulnerability studies typically emphasise the affectability of the body in terms of the damage that can be visited upon it or the risks, insecurity etc that attend our lives, it is suggested that the body's openness can be reflexively employed to enrich the concept of vulnerability itself.

The openness – the ethesiological nature – of the living body, once fully appreciated, might provide the foundation for a vulnerability thesis that allows us to *embrace* vulnerability as a dynamic interrelational concept highly suggestive of richer human bonds not only with human beings, but of humans with the world itself. Vulnerability might re-emerge from such a theorisation as a potent concept that necessitates an expansive awareness of context, interaction, and interplay in the constitution of subjectivities – including legal subjectivities – thus opening law to a range of considerations hitherto systemically suppressed. (Moreover, such a thesis, taken in its widest sense, could open a very fruitful avenue for the reformulation of the relationship between the theorisation of human rights and other forms of legal rights. While the broader ambit of such a thesis awaits exploration in future work,[105] in the present context, the thesis offers a rich theoretical foundation for the redirection of human rights to human beneficiaries *without necessitating* the dismissal of the important rights claims of non-human, other-than-human, or post-human entities – including corporations.[106])

Returning to our reflections on human embodied vulnerability and Turner's thesis, it is suggested that human vulnerability should be conceptualised as more than the capacity for suffering – though it is certainly, minimally, the foundation of that capacity. Related to this point, Turner does conceptualise vulnerability as the root of a form of empathy and as the root of our need for social institutions, as related to social connectedness, but his conceptualisation of the world is rather Hobbesian.[107] He sees the world as being full of risk and brutishness. For him, then, it is our shared 'insecurity' in the face of a precarious existence that draws us together. Turner, in short, renders vulnerability and suffering/pain as virtually synonymous and locates them in a world of conflict and risk. While there is, of course, some deep truth in this position, it nonetheless seems to downplay the more positive aspects of vulnerability as the basis for intimacy, understood as being more than the suffering-based attempt to build a common security in a world of risk. Instead of imagining society as a pact of the insecure and suffering-prone, huddling together in the face of a dark, frightening world of risk and conflict, it is possible to move beyond this minimal, 'defensive' view of vulnerability, as argued above. In its place, or supplementing its insights, we can conceive of vulnerability as a quintessential embodied openness to each other and to the world to develop a political consciousness of standing in shared space. We could construct a worldview that embraces a more inclusive, harmonious set of aspirations, a vision of possible worlds transcending pessimistic Hobbesian assumptions. Vulnerability can thus be understood as a core component of an alternative view of human relations – as far more than our capacity to suffer/feel pain, and as far more than a synonym for suffering.

Thirdly, the statement made by Ignatieff concerning the assumption that 'what is pain and humiliation for you is bound to be pain and humiliation for me', and Turner's even stronger assertion that 'misery is common and uniform', invokes a questionable uniformity in the experience of suffering and pain. Turner is concerned to posit a universalism based on common vulnerability (cast as our common capacity for pain and suffering). He seeks to argue that relativism, in this light, is found wanting. Conceding that a critic might object that suffering is variable and thus cannot support a common standpoint in the way that this view of universalism suggests, Turner's response is to focus more precisely on pain: 'Whereas bankruptcy, for example could involve some degree of variable psychological suffering, a toothache is a toothache'.[108] However, while pain may well be less variable than suffering, pain, like suffering, is not immune from cultural influence. Pain is not uniform because pain is 'decisively shaped or modified by individual human minds and specific human cultures',[109] as Morris has shown. Pain is historically, culturally and psychosocially constructed – it is 'always more than a matter of nerves and neurotransmitters'.[110] A toothache is not just a toothache. A toothache will be variably experienced because nerve pathways are not the totality of the story. Pain is both deeply internal to the individual, uniquely experienced in that sense, and inescapably culture-soaked: 'We learn how to feel pain and what it means';[111] and '[w]hen we fall into pain, we also fall into a net of already constructed meanings'.[112]

Accordingly, although there can be a cross-cultural understanding of suffering related to embodiment, and a profound commonality attends the fact that we can all suffer and feel pain (in the usual course of events), it seems misleading to suggest that pain is uniform enough to defeat a relativist claim in a way that suffering is not. This does not matter, however. Turner simply does not need to establish a uniformity of pain or suffering to ground a universal basis for human rights in our shared ontic condition. The common given of our embodiment, and vulnerability as a key incident of that embodiment, is a solid enough ground for a universal. The cross-cultural implications of this human commonality are not undermined by the admission that it is variably experienced. The non-uniformity of misery/suffering/pain (Turner's 'vulnerability') cannot and does not detract from our basic ontic commonality. In fact, the admission that our common experience of misery/suffering/pain varies on cultural and/or individual grounds can actually enhance the case for an ethic of true respect: 'I understand that we are different. I understand that what is pain and humiliation for you is not bound to be pain and humiliation for me. Notwithstanding this, based on my own experience of pain and humiliation, I can imaginatively empathise with your position – respecting you beyond our differences, to understand that you, like me, are vulnerable'.

The acknowledgement of the experiential variation of vulnerability, in other words, diminishes nothing in the force of embodied vulnerability as being the proper foundation of human rights. Moreover, variation seems to be quintessentially human. Recognising the openness of vulnerability and its incidents to cultural and individual variation merely adds an acknowledgment of another universal human truth: our radical particularity (including the particularity related to our relationships with culture). None of this removes our fundamental ontic commonality. We are all embodied and share a key incident of that embodiment: vulnerability. It is simply not necessary to establish the uniformity of suffering/pain/misery (or indeed vulnerability itself) in order to found the human rights universal on human embodied vulnerability.

Moving on to the other relevant feature of Turner's account for present purposes, we noted earlier how Turner suggests that vulnerability, or 'ontological insecurity', implies a particular cluster of social and economic rights. He suggests, related to this, that 'the vulnerability thesis can be further criticized because it is very relevant to some human rights, but not to others'.[113] Certainly, there is no question that civil and political rights are less directly related to, for example, the need for nourishment, housing and medical care than are certain economic, social and cultural rights – or that needs for minimal shelter, nourishment and health form a crucial foundation for healthy bodies without which other less directly connected human rights claims become, to say the least, compromised.[114] However, it is argued that such a critique of the vulnerability thesis would overlook the important fact that embodied vulnerability provides the foundation of all categories of human rights. This will be more fully elucidated in the next chapter. But for now, it is worth noting that civil and political rights presuppose embodied vulnerability just as much as economic, social and cultural rights do – although the element of vulnerability may be less *directly* interwoven with survival/health issues.

Turner, rather than placing civil and political rights directly on the theoretical foundation of embodied vulnerability, defends the link by emphasising the relationship between 'poor socioeconomic conditions and health outcomes', and research revealing that human health is impacted by inequality of income and democratic participation. He suggests that 'it would not be difficult to show that human beings cannot successfully enjoy social rights to health care in societies that severely curtail civil and political liberties'.[115] While this is undoubtedly true, it is not necessary to link sickness and inequality to establish a foundation for civil and political rights in the notion of human embodied vulnerability. Rights such as rights to freedom of peaceful assembly and association presuppose embodiment, carving out the terms on which embodied personalities can communicate political opinion to other embodied personalities in shared social and civic space, in a way that also presupposes mutual vulnerability. This will be more fully argued in the next chapter, but at this point it is important to note that, while Turner is right to posit a strong and direct relationship between embodied vulnerability and certain socio-economic rights, it is a mistake to think that civil and political rights can only be indirectly founded on embodied vulnerability by linking inequality and sickness. Embodied vulnerability offers a more all-embracing theoretical foundation for human rights than Turner's sociological account seems to imagine.

Interim reflections on the implications of embodiment and vulnerability for international human rights law

This chapter has argued that, contrary to the liberal legal view of rationality and legal subjectivity as disembodied (quasi-disembodied), the human legal subject, despite being conceptualised in law as either abstract (P1) or quasi-disembodied (P3 and, to differing degree, P2), remains inescapably embodied. (The embodiment implicated in human vulnerability is, moreover, a far richer acknowledgment of the body and the implications of embodiment than the P2 liberal conception of the universal bearer of human rights supplies.) Accordingly, the gap between the legal subject and the human being explored in earlier chapters, which stems from law's disembodied rationality (and which serves ideological purposes as a mechanism of gendered, raced and class-based social exclusion) is unmasked as being a gap mediated by *an impossibility*. The inescapable centrality of human embodiment to philosophy, the nature of reason and the nature of law, revealed in the combination of philosophical and scientific arguments offered earlier in this chapter, strongly suggests that a disembodied view of reason is not only impossible, but also – and profoundly ironically – *irrational*.

Vulnerability, a key incident of human embodiment, has particular resonance for human rights law and discourse. Embodied vulnerability offers a powerful theoretical foundation for all of the categories of rights enshrined within the UDHR paradigm, as will be more fully argued in the next chapter. Equally, embodied vulnerability offers a devastating critique of the closures of the traditional prevailing abstract (quasi-disembodied) universal subject of human rights. Moreover, an insistence that human rights subjects be reconceived as being *both* embodied *and* vulnerable problematises corporate international human rights discourse. Corporations lack the foundational qualification for legitimate entitlement to beneficiary-status in international human rights law: *human embodied vulnerability*.

7
Embodied Vulnerability and the Universal Declaration of Human Rights

We have already noted the paradoxical interplay between disembodiment and embodiment (and its related themes) in the context of discussing the French Declaration of the Rights of Man and the Citizen and the emergence of the modern discourse of rights. We have also noted the sense in which the dominant conception of the rights-bearer as an autonomous and rational subject has produced forms of closure in rights discourse, paying particular attention to the way in which the central case universal rights-bearer is an *abstract entity*: either 'man' (in the French Declaration) or the 'human being' in the UDHR. This abstractionism, it has been suggested, plays (and continues to play) a central role in the production of the quasi-disembodiment of liberal legal theory, and is a key mechanism in the production of a system of legal rights in which the corporation is arguably the perfect fit for the quintessential legal subject, radically continuous with liberal law's analytical and ideological closures. In the light of the role of disembodiment in the construction of the human rights universal and the legal subject of human rights, it is now time to explore the role of embodied vulnerability in the UDHR paradigm, and the extent to which it can be said that embodied vulnerability undergirds a rather different theoretical reading of universal human rights discourse – one in which the corporation would appear to be disqualified as a suitable beneficiary of human rights protections.

Although the paradoxes surrounding rights discourse are legion, invoking, as has already been seen, complex relations between human rights, liberalism (which comes in different, contested forms,[1] although the dominant form has been the target of sustained critique (in this book and elsewhere)) and capitalism,[2] a further crucial and under-theorised paradox in human rights law and theory concerns the role of human embodiment. It has already been argued that embodiment is the inescapable and essential foundation of both rationality and law – and that vulnerability is a key ontic condition of embodiment in a material world. This chapter will explore more fully the role of embodied vulnerability in international human rights discourse. Specifically, it will examine the relationship between embodied vulnerability and the UDHR paradigm, to establish the case for embodied vulnerability as the proper foundation of all categories of human rights.

But before analysing the various categories of rights and their theoretical relationship to embodied vulnerability, there is a particularly revealing paradox which we need to attend to. This is the notable disjunction between the disembodiment invoked by the abstract conception of the human rights-bearer (discussed in Chapter 5) and the role of embodiment in the very genesis of rights discourse, both in the eighteenth century and at the end of the Second World War.

Empathy, rights and embodiment: The eighteenth century

We earlier noted the role of emotion and the emergence of empathy in the societal shifts that birthed the notion of the rights of man.[3] It is important to revisit that argument briefly here, in order to reveal and develop an important thematic continuity between early rights discourse and international human rights discourse concerning the role and centrality of embodied vulnerability.

Hunt has recently made a historical case for the fact (often overlooked) that human rights depend on emotion as much as reason (which, recall, is in any case quintessentially embodied and affective[4] despite the assumptions operative in the ideology of rationality associated with quasi-disembodiment). Hunt argues that the most important quality of human rights is, indeed, that they require a 'certain widely shared "interior feeling"'.[5] She demonstrates that the rise of rights discourse coincided with, and is directly related to, the rise of the epistolary novel in the mid-eighteenth century, a development which opened the interiority of human aspiration and vulnerability to the public imagination producing a certain disposition towards others and giving the self new content. This resulted in the development of an unprecedented level of social empathy.[6] Alongside this, a contiguous shift in attitudes to torture reflected shifting public sensibilities concerning the infliction of pain, instigated by the emotional impact of certain high profile torture cases, especially the notorious 'Calas affair'.[7] In short, Hunt's historical survey of the period reveals that the rise of the novel, the rise of the anti-torture movement and the genesis of the rights of man emerged as interrelated phenomena within an identifiable and relatively focused time-frame in the mid-eighteenth century – the 1760s.[8] More precisely, Hunt's argument suggests that what emerged in the mid-eighteenth century was a new sensibility capable of (and necessary for) founding rights as instantiations of a vision of human commonality.

Reading Hunt's historical account it is also clear that embodiment played a vital role in these crucial shifts towards a more empathic socio-political understanding of others. Likewise, the eighteenth century notion of autonomy, also foundational to the genesis of rights (like the new empathy a prerequisite for their conceptual formation), originated from shifts in the understanding of *embodied* relations: 'Autonomy and empathy are cultural practices, not just ideas, and they are therefore quite literally embodied, that is, they have physical as well as emotional dimensions'.[9] The period saw, for example, the democratisation of portraiture through which ordinary bodies were celebrated and made available for public viewing.[10] It is notable, in fact, that the new experiences and catalysts on which Hunt's account focuses are *predominantly embodied*. The historical changes Hunt traces amount to nothing short of a radically changed understanding of bodies and (embodied) selves. Embodiment – and a reconceptualisation of its meaning – were both necessary preconditions for empathy. The genesis of a new social empathy required 'a new concern for the human body'[11] and the impartation of new meanings to the body (decisive, for example, in the discourse of the anti-torture movement[12]). Hunt concludes that torture ended *precisely because* a new framework of pain and personhood emerged in which 'individuals owned their bodies, had rights to their separateness and to bodily inviolability, and recognized in others the same passions, sentiments and sympathies as in themselves'.[13]

While, as we have seen in earlier chapters, some of these assumptions concerning the 'bounded' autonomous self and 'self-ownership' were hyper-extended in problematic ways in liberal theory,[14] these important assumptions concerning the body played a vital and predominantly unacknowledged role in the construction of a new self and the generation of the related humanistic empathy crucial to the public acceptance of what we can broadly conceive of as a nascent human rights discourse in the eighteenth century. Interestingly, women played a crucial role in the development of empathy as a public reality through both novels and portraiture,[15] but their role deeply reflects the problematic suppositions of Western dualism. Women were viewed as personifications of emotion and sentiment. Hunt suggests, tellingly, that the compelling nature of the female heroines of the novels reflects the fact that each novel centred on the heroine's longing for independence, and the fact that her 'quest for autonomy could never succeed'.[16] Women in the mid-eighteenth century, unsurprisingly, were not proto-beneficiaries of the new rights-based order. They were neither fully autonomous nor regarded as fully rational,[17] and were embedded in emotionality and confined to the restricted sphere of domestic relations.

Hunt's historical account seems to bear out the argument in this book that the quasi-disembodiment inherent in the abstraction of the bearer of the rights of man functions as both gendered and exclusory. Although Hunt does not address abstraction or disembodiment in the terms in which they have been discussed in the present work, it is nonetheless clear, in the light of her analysis, that the abstract 'man' of the French Declaration of the Rights of Man and the Citizen stands in a profoundly paradoxical relationship to the role of the body in the production of the social and political empathy that underlay the genesis of those same rights. The elevation of the ordinary body, its sufferings, its longings (in which women were symbolically central), and the related changes in embodied social relations were crucial in laying the empathetic foundations for rights discourse to flourish. So too was the increasing sense of bodily separation to the related development of the notion of autonomy.[18] Yet, despite the body's role, despite the centrality of women in the genesis of the social empathy that rights relied upon for their critical energy, the abstract 'man' of the Declaration was 'empty' – 'abstract'[19] – rational, fully autonomous and quasi-disembodied, possessing, nonetheless, as we have seen, a paradoxically gendered morphology. The template of the quasi-disembodied proto-beneficiary of the rights-based order was one that women could not, and arguably can never,[20] fit. The template is also racist and exclusionary along class lines. We should note that the man of colour, the man without property and certain minority group men also struggled to find themselves fully accepted as instances of the 'universal' man of rights.[21] Even when women were eventually accounted for as rights-bearers, as we have seen there were ongoing and intractable tensions and exclusions related to the quasi-disembodiment of the human rights universal. These remain problematic to this day.

Empathy, rights and embodiment: The universal declaration of human rights

The predominantly unacknowledged role of embodiment and vulnerability in the genesis of rights is a much more pressing theme in relation to the UDHR paradigm than in relation to the French Declaration. In the UDHR paradigm, human rights were explicitly conceptualised by the drafters of the UDHR as a direct reaction to the murderous (embodiment-centred) bio-politics of the Nazi regime. The President of the Third Committee made unambiguous reference to 'the barbarous doctrines of Nazism and fascism',[22] and all the delegates agreed that 'the pattern of gross human rights abuses which occurred during World War II was *the major impulse* behind the drafting of the Declaration'.[23] The central focus of the international community on Nazi human rights abuses gives embodiment and its related vulnerability a *pivotal* role in the origins of international human rights discourse, notwithstanding the fact that the philosophical abstractionism of the universal bearer of human rights produces a P2 legal subject whose full embodiment is complexly suppressed. It is arguable, in fact, that given the decisive role of embodied vulnerability in the genesis of international human rights law (to be traced more fully below) the fractious relationship between embodiment and quasi-disembodiment in law and liberal rights discourse becomes its most haunting, ambivalent and revealing. That an order of rights with ascendant contemporary ethical status, critical reach and discursive power – an ascendancy drawing directly from a humanitarian critical reaction to the most horrific, wholesale embodied abuse of human beings – should now, some mere 60 years later prove so conducive to colonisation by disembodied jural entities and formations of capital to the point where the protective potential of the entire UDHR paradigm for human beings stands dramatically imperilled, is stark testimony, it is suggested, to the far reaching implications of liberal legal closures (both analytical and ideological) and their associated capacity to both disguise and produce ongoing and violent forms of exclusion.

The role of embodiment in the genesis of the UDHR is powerfully captured in the images of the time. As the Second World War ended, photographs and news reel coverage of the horrors perpetrated by the Nazi regime delivered a now almost unimaginable shock to the public imagination.[24] The traumatic revelations contained in the news reels after the war were captured by the haunting and nightmarishly painful visibility of corpses: corpses piled high, in pallid, ravaged mounds at Auschwitz and other concentration camps – and the possibly even more unbearable images of the ghostly living bodies of the emaciated, skeletal survivors in their ragged camp uniforms.[25] Embodied vulnerability could hardly have been made more savagely obvious. Images of ravaged bodies, living and dead alike, played a central, symbolic and profoundly cathartic role in summarising and making visible the monstrous horror of the Third Reich.

At the Nuremburg Trials, and in the publicity and discussion of the time, the Third Reich was revealed as having been animated by a murderous biopolitics – a politics quintessentially centred on the control and ultimate destruction of embodied life. The Nazi bio-political campaign initially centred on the elimination of bodily imperfections. Indeed, the first victims of the Nazi 'purification' agenda were 'deformed' 'retarded' children.[26] But this was a step, as the historical records show, towards the 'purification' of the German nation from the biologically 'inferior' races; most notably, the Jews. The Nazi regime systematically and emphatically denied the ontic commonalities between human beings in order to excise, in central respects, the humanity of its victims. The news reel audiences and the wider public at the end of the war, whose minds were not conditioned by the 'applied biology'[27] of the Third Reich, instantly recognised, however, as unmistakably human, all-too-human in their vulnerability, their fellow human beings in the ravaged stillness of death and the exposed vulnerability of bodily privation and abuse.[28]

Thus, although the UDHR enshrines the species being at its heart as an abstract human, and has profound philosophical and textual continuities with the earlier French Declaration,[29] the UDHR is radically distinguished from the French Declaration by the fact that it arose as an outraged response to a bio-political campaign of mass extermination. Accordingly, the protection of human embodied vulnerability (and the conditions for the flourishing of embodied vulnerable human beings) forms the fundamental underlying concern beneath the entire UDHR paradigm. This claim will be substantiated here through two main arguments. First, an argument drawing out the links between the Nazi regime, embodied vulnerability and the drafting of the UDHR will be constructed using Morsink's valuable analysis of the contemporaneous statements of the UN Assembly delegates responsible for the drafting process.[30] Secondly, a broader conceptual argument will be offered linking embodied vulnerability, in more general terms, to each existing category of human rights in the UDHR lexicon.

The first argument will suggest that embodied vulnerability is fundamental to Morsink's analysis (even though he does not use the terminology) and that embodied vulnerability (implicitly and explicitly evoked by the drafters of the UDHR in their response to the Nazi holocaust and its antecedents in Nazi legal and political organisation) forms a central part of the entire matrix from which the UDHR emerged and is fundamental to both its existence and content. The second argument will suggest that embodied vulnerability is either central to, intimately related to, or logically presupposed by all categories of rights contained in the UDHR. The arguments offered here can thus be taken independently or jointly in support of the conclusion that embodied vulnerability is foundational to the UDHR paradigm.

These arguments will, of course, be added to Turner's sociological argument for the centrality of embodied vulnerability to human rights, introduced in the last chapter. However, Turner's *indirect* linkage between embodied vulnerability and civil and political rights will be supplemented by the analysis offered here. It will be argued that embodied vulnerability provides the direct theoretical foundation for all categories of human rights in the UDHR paradigm. Moreover, it is the argument of this book that embodied vulnerability should, as a normative matter, be recovered and reasserted as foundational to human rights in both conceptual and ethical terms. It will be argued in Chapter 8 that embodied human vulnerability should form a core part of human rights jurisprudence and function as a key factor in legal reasoning about human rights. Importantly, for the purposes of facing the challenge of corporate humanity, human embodied vulnerability should be viewed as the foundational and essential qualifying characteristic of human rights beneficiaries.

Embodied vulnerability, Nazi horrors and the UDHR

As noted above, the UDHR was fundamentally a response to the horrors of the Second World War and the Nazi Holocaust. The Second World War was a war in which there were 60 million deaths, most of them civilian, and, of those, at least six million people were killed simply on the basis of their biological identification as Jews. The UDHR was adopted three years after the end of the war by the Third General Assembly of the United Nations – and the decisive imprint of the war and the Nazi regime on the genesis of the Declaration is revealed by Morsink's analysis of the deliberations of the delegates to the drafting committees of the UDHR.[31] While Morsink's analysis on some individual points is not entirely compelling, he nonetheless provides enough strong evidence to carry his central thesis: that the UDHR was written in conscious response to Nazi violations, and that many of the articles of the UDHR can be directly linked to specific Nazi strategies and rights violations.

One important difference between the UDHR and the French Declaration is the emphasis in the UDHR on affirming the *unity of the human race as a species*. This emphasis is pivotal, and implies the centrality to the entire UDHR scheme of a common human ontic condition. While it is not necessary, in taking this position, to defend some essential notion of 'human nature', or to endorse any particular metaphysical position on the source of rights, it is nonetheless minimally clear that, to focus on what the '*human family*' shares as a *commonality*, is to invoke an *inclusive species-notion* that focuses on the capacities and vulnerabilities of humanity as a whole. This inclusive species-notion was a direct response to the bio-politics of the Nazi regime. Hitler's notion of the state was deeply bio-centric and racist – drawing distinctions between human beings on grounds of embodied biological differences. The body, in Nazi Germany (and, as we shall shortly see, modern politics more generally) was thoroughly politicised. For Hitler, however, the state was itself an organic body of which he was the head[32] – and beyond which the individual had no independent existence. Crucially, this organic conception of the state was a species-specific conception embracing only a sub-segment of humanity. In Hitler's words the Nazi state was an 'organization of a community of physically and psychologically similar living beings for the better facilitation of the maintenance of *their species*'.[33] According to Nazi ideology, the human race was comprised of five races or species, with the Aryan race being the superior race. Hitler argued that '[t]he German Reich as a state must embrace all Germans and has the task, not only of assembling and preserving the most valuable stocks of basic racial elements in this people, but slowly and surely raising them to a dominant position'.[34] In the light of this decisive hierarchical separation of the human race, and the consciousness of the drafters in response to it, the insistence in the preamble of the UDHR that the recognition of the 'inherent dignity and of the equal and inalienable rights of all members of the human family' are vital and should be read as an insistence on a fundamental *species commonality*.

The deliberate counterpoint between these assertions and the Nazi State is further emphasised by the preamble's immediate reference to the 'barbarous acts which have outraged the conscience of mankind'. Morsink argues that the affirmation of the fundamental commonality of the human race was a conscious aim of the drafters of the Declaration.[35] Thus, although the philosophical and textual continuities between the French Declaration and the UDHR are clear, and despite the role of embodiment in the genesis of eighteenth century rights discourse, the distinct impact of the shock delivered by the Holocaust, reflected overtly in the preamble to the UDHR, plays a unique and decisive role in shaping the UDHR. Consequently, an appreciation of the context of the Holocaust and the Nazi regime is crucial to understanding the humanitarian, vulnerability-centred impulse that drives the UDHR.

It is important to note that despite the philosophical continuities between the UDHR and the earlier French Declaration, philosophy actually played a radically submerged role in the reasoning of the UDHR drafters. While the delegates naturally used the language available to them (with its influential philosophical and historical provenance) they 'did not need a philosophical argument in addition to the experience of the Holocaust' to justify the UDHR.[36] The trauma of the suffering and abuse inflicted by the Nazi regime during the war was considered to be a self-evident justification for the UDHR on the basis of an outraged and empathetic reaction based inescapably on human embodied commonality. While perhaps more developed and sophisticated, this approach carries striking echoes of the triadic notion of justice discussed in the last chapter in the context of introducing the biological foundations of law. Morsink argues that the UDHR drafters simply did not *need* philosophical argument in addition to the Holocaust. He states, in fact, that the Commission had a distinct 'lack of interest in philosophical arguments about human rights'[37] even when presented with them by a UNESCO report. Moral outrage, shock in the face of barbarity, and a strong affirmation of the unity of the human family – a direct response to the targeting of selected groups on bio-political grounds by the Nazis – these were the underlying drivers of the UDHR drafting mission. Morsink concludes that '[n]o philosophical argument can be as strong as moral repulsion of gross violations of human dignity. Indeed, I have shown that the delegates did what they did because they wanted to avoid another Holocaust. The justification for the Universal Declaration lies, therefore, in this shared abhorrence of what the Nazis did to their victims'.[38]

A reading of the UDHR in its inaugural context supports the contention that the UDHR is directly premised on a universally shared human ontic vulnerability. While the body's role in the inauguration of an unprecedented level of socio-political empathy in the emergence of rights in the eighteenth century is clear from Hunt's work, the body's role in the UDHR is even more potent. The UDHR insists on the ontic commonality of human beings as a *species* in overt, direct and oppositional reaction to the subdivisions within human embodied nature drawn by Nazi theory and practice. The UDHR carries *at its heart* a visceral awareness of a common human vulnerability – an awareness that was starkly and tragically lit by the fires of Auschwitz and Treblinka.

Morsink argues, moreover, that many of the individual articles of the UDHR can be directly linked to the precise contours of the Nazi Holocaust and its antecedent legal and political justifications and strategies. He divides the UDHR rights into four categories: (1) rights dealing with personal security; (2) procedures of democratic government; (3) legal rights and (4) rights such as the right to citizenship and to leave and enter countries – rights which he designates as being 'international' rights.[39] We shall shortly look in turn in detail at each category of specific rights contained in the UDHR, and demonstrate how embodied vulnerability can be seen to underpin or be intimately related to each one. First, however, we must contextualise our reading of the specific UDHR rights by examining Morsink's analysis of the preliminary Articles 1 and 2.

Articles 1 and 2

> *Article 1:* All human beings are born free and equal in dignity and rights. They are endowed with reason and conscience and should act towards one another in a spirit of brotherhood.
>
> *Article 2:* Everyone is entitled to all the rights and freedoms set forth in this Declaration, without distinction of any kind, such as race, colour, sex, language, religion, political or other opinion, national or social origin, property, birth or other status. Furthermore, no distinction shall be made on the basis of the political, jurisdictional or international status of the country or territory to which a person belongs, whether it be independent, trust, non-self-governing or under any other limitation of sovereignty.

Opening his analysis, Morsink firmly embeds Articles 1 and 2 of the UDHR in a reaction to Hitler's organic state – emphasising the importance of protecting the individual against absorption into the state, and defending the intrinsic value of the human being. Though Morsink emphasises that the UDHR reflects the importance of the *individual* throughout, and that this is most generally reflected in the first two articles, it should also be noted that the first two articles emphasise the *commonality* of the human family. Morsink cites Mr Cassin, the French delegate, who explained that his draft of Article 1 alluded to the three 'fundamental questions of liberty, equality and fraternity'[40] (with their clear link to the French Revolution) because they had been forgotten during the war and that 'connecting the ideas of equality and fraternity, he [Mr Cassin] wanted to stress "the fundamental principle of the unity of the human race..." because Hitler had "started asserting the inequality of men before attacking their liberties"'.[41]

Article 1 stresses human commonality with the phraseology 'all human beings are born...'. Clearly what the article has in mind is a living human being as a species being, organic and embodied. Embodiment pervades this article, not only as an inherent incident of human materiality, but also emphasised in the reference to *birth* – in the normal course of events a profoundly incarnate event, intensely physical for both mother and infant and deeply symbolic of the ineradicable intercorporeality of human life discussed in Chapter 6. (We should note, however, the exclusion of the unborn child (by clear implication) from the article. This is a matter of great complexity, of course, but it points to certain qualifying assumptions for human status consistent with the P2 conception of the legal person, introduced in Chapter 3 of this book.)

Article 1 then proceeds to proclaim freedom and equality of dignity and rights – making reference to reason, conscience and the 'spirit of brotherhood'. Morsink argues that these references were not 'mere enlightenment reflexes – they are deep truths rediscovered in the midst of the Holocaust'.[42] However, we can nevertheless discern in this formulation, and despite the emphasis on organic commonality, echoes of the gendered influence of the enlightenment quasi-disembodied 'neutral universal' human rights-bearer discussed in Chapter 5. Article 1 proclaims a fundamental commonality, therefore, in which embodied and quasi-disembodied elements co-exist – an inherently paradoxical formulation that only becomes fully apparent in the light of a critical reading of abstract neutrality. The way in which the elements co-exist, and the nature of what is privileged, will depend upon how dignity, freedom and rationality etc are interpreted, but the reference to rationality, in particular, has, as we already know from preceding argument, a complex potentiality for systematic exclusion – a possibility signalled rather less obliquely by the gendered linguistic closure of the term 'brotherhood'.[43]

Article 2 reinforces the inclusory intent of Article 1 by making explicit a fundamental principle of non-discrimination in which certain explicitly enumerated grounds of discrimination are effectively prohibited. This principle of non-discrimination is also directly aimed at countering Hitler's denial of human commonality. Indeed, Morsink argues that the Nazi attack on human equality directly led to Communist insistence on the inclusion of a strong non-discrimination value in the UDHR.[44] In fact, the Soviet-inspired Sub-Commission on the Prevention of Discrimination and the Protection of Minorities drafted most of the first paragraph of the article. Article 2 of the UHDR insists that 'everyone' is entitled to all the rights and freedoms set out in the Declaration 'without distinction of any kind'. Forbidden grounds of discrimination are then enumerated: 'race, colour, sex, language, religion, political or other opinion, national or social origin, property, birth or other status'. Morsink makes the argument that, for the Soviets, the enshrining of a strong non-discrimination principle was conceptualised precisely as a way of combating any resurgence of Nazism or fascism: 'Article 2 then was inspired by the horrors of Nazi discriminatory racism, and it was the Soviet delegation that repeatedly called that connection to mind, even if in the end the Soviets felt the Declaration did not go far enough'.[45]

Rights of personal security: Articles 3, 4 and 5

Moving onto Morsink's first category of specific rights of the UDHR, Morsink links Article 3, the right to 'life, liberty and security of person', directly to Nazi practices, including euthanasia (on which the Human Rights Commission had a UN report available)[46] and the deprivation of liberty under Nazi law. Article 4, the prohibition against 'slavery or servitude', included 'servitude' because the word is wider in implication than slavery, and (in the words of Mr Cassin) the status of persons deported to Germany 'was certainly worse than that of ancient slaves'.[47] The word 'servitude' was intended to cover the Nazi trafficking in women and children and the ill-treatment of prisoners of war.[48] Article 5, the prohibition against torture, likewise directly addresses the experience of Nazi barbarity – and a range of inhumane practices – including inhumane medical experimentation.[49]

All of these articles concerning the security of the person quite naturally focus on embodied vulnerability. The practices of euthanasia, the deprivation of liberty, slavery, servitude, torture, ill-treatment, trafficking and medical experimentation all exert their coercive force primarily on the body. The body is central to the infliction of degradation and the 'violation of dignity' (to borrow a concept used in the discourse of the Declaration itself) involved in such practices.[50] Not one of these practices is even possible without the body's vulnerability and affectability in a material world.

Democratic rights: Article 21

Turning to Morsink's second category of UDHR rights, those concerned with democratic government, embodied vulnerability is also very much at stake. Morsink recalls that Hitler rejected the notion of majority rule, defending instead 'the personality principle' of leadership. As Fuhrer, Hitler was the personification of the will of the German people. When he came to power he systematically destroyed democratic government, replacing it with rule by emergency decrees. Through the first of these, the Decree for the Protection of the German People, 'the democratic rights of freedom of opinion and expression and of assembly and association were abolished'.[51] The Nazi destruction of democratic rights, freedoms, processes and machinery was fundamental to the formulation of Article 21 of the UDHR, which guarantees democratic government by requiring every nation to establish the machinery of the democratic state. This article has been the target of critique aimed at exposing the Western liberal suppositions of the UDHR. But Morsink defends the article by insisting that the drafters of the UDHR had no trouble agreeing its terms in the light of the experience of Nazi Germany, noting that '[t]he destruction of the right to participate meaningfully in the government of one's country was Hitler's first step toward violating all the rest of the rights that later became part of the Declaration'.[52]

The need for genuinely protective democratic institutions can quite easily be linked to the fundamental insecurity that stems from human embodiment. When a tyrannical state acts against its population, the remorseless logic of tyranny ultimately targets embodied vulnerability. The protective mechanisms of democracy can thus be directly linked to our embodied vulnerability, but the relationship between our human vulnerability, state power and institution building is complex (as we shall see below when we briefly discuss Agamben's argument concerning the common focus of totalitarianism and democracy on the bio-political). However, as Turner argues, it is our biological vulnerability that leads to the need for the creation of political institutions to provide for our collective security – institutions that are, in turn, precarious[53] and paradoxical.[54] Indeed, Hitler's assault on democracy underlines both institutional precariousness and our related vulnerability. Democracy can be conceptualised as one complex, paradoxical but important institutional attempt to mediate vulnerability as an ontic incident of our embodiment. Certainly, the notion of democracy as a protective institutional arrangement is clearly reflected by the concerns of the UDHR drafting committee with violations of the rights that followed – and were facilitated by – the dismantling of the German democratic framework. Article 21 can accordingly be understood as resting on the theoretical foundation of embodied vulnerability and the related importance of institutional design in the deflection of some of the more negative implications of that vulnerability.[55]

Legal rights: Articles 6 to 12

Turning to his third category of rights, legal rights, Morsink emphasises that legal rights, such as the right to a legal personality (Art 6), to equality before the law (Art 7), to fundamental constitutional rights (Art 8), to an independent judiciary (Art 10), to the presumption of innocence in criminal trials (Art 11), to privacy (Art 12), and the rejection of arbitrary arrest and detention (Art 9), cover nearly one-quarter of the entire UDHR.[56] These rights can be linked to the argument immediately above concerning the need for institutional protection of embodied vulnerability. The stripping away of juridical personality, for example, was used in Nazi Germany as a way of declaring a Jew legally dead – radically removing the protection of juridical status – a technique of power that the UDHR drafters clearly had in mind.[57] Likewise, equality before the law can be seen as a right aimed at the prevention of the discriminatory abuse of people – and in Nazi Germany a fundamentally racist inequality was extolled as an inherent part of the legal system. Equality before the law is a form of institutional protection that, once explicitly withdrawn by Nazi law, left embodied difference starkly revealed as a newly legitimated source of special vulnerability – the extreme vulnerability that comes when a class or group or individual is rendered naked to legally sanctioned privation putatively justified by their membership of a category. That this strategy in Nazi Germany was ultimately about the bodily control of persons is abundantly clear. It is, for example, amply reflected in the Law for the Protection of German Blood and German Honour, a law forbidding marriage between Jews and citizens of German or related kinds of blood. As Morsink succinctly notes, '[h]ere is the essence of *Mein Kampf* put into legalese'.[58]

Agamben has argued that such law brought to an extreme point a separation, underway since the First World War, between the idea of birth and nationality. This separation, Agamben argues, was reflected in a wave of juridical measures in European states for the mass denaturalisation of large portions of their own populations, a trend ultimately rendering citizenship something to be deserved or earned. The Nazi laws were the most extreme instantiation of this trend. Indeed, Agamben points out that one of the few rules assiduously observed by the Nazi regime during the implementation of Hitler's 'Final Solution' was that the Jews could be sent to the concentration camps only after they had been fully denationalised – that is, 'stripped even of the residual citizenship left to them after the Nuremburg Laws'.[59] The Jews were literally made juridically and politically bare. Likewise, arbitrary arrest and detention, the absence of effective remedies before an independent judicial tribunal, the lack of the presumption of innocence, and similar legal deficiencies in the Nazi regime meant that human beings were grossly unprotected: *physically* vulnerable to state predation, terror and abuse. This unprotected vulnerability implicitly underlies the concerns of the UDHR drafters and links legal rights with the justification concerning the focus on democracy in the UDHR.

Morsink concludes that his brief survey of the rationale behind the legal rights enunciated in the UDHR makes it clear that 'these rights are intricately interwoven with the machinery of the modern democratic state and that they were voted into the Declaration in part as a protest to Nazi Germany'.[60] Rights to legal personality, equality before the law and the like have decisive importance for the protection of embodied human beings. It is ironic, then, in the light of our analysis in preceding chapters, to note the limitations imposed by the quasi-disembodiment inherent in the liberal notion of legal personality on that protective potential, and the problematic gap that legal disembodiment creates between the living human being and the legal entity or construct taken to represent the human being. This irony is particularly acute in the light of the role of legal personality in protecting embodied vulnerability.

International rights: Bio-politics, sovereign power, bare life and the challenge for human rights: A critical reading of Article 14 UDHR

The final category of rights that Morsink discusses is what he calls 'international rights'. It is with this category of rights that we arguably hit an *explicit* major failure in the drafting of UDHR in relation to the protection of embodied vulnerability (notwithstanding the way in which it is possible to read embodied vulnerability as being the ethical heart of the UDHR in any event). A set of revealing dilemmas surround Article 14, the right to asylum – and arguably reflects a profound problem – namely the paradoxical relationship between citizenship and human rights protection – a relationship that presents a major lacuna in the theory of human rights.[61]

Given the commitment to protecting members of the human family without distinction evinced by Articles 1 and 2 of the UDHR, one might reasonably expect that human beings should receive international legal protection on the basis of their humanity. This would reflect the intuition that, of all legal discourses, human rights should provide the concepts and language for the insistence that each embodied, vulnerable human being ought to be protected as such, pure and simple. But matters are not so simple. It was Hannah Arendt who lamented, in the clearest of terms, the failure of human rights to provide this most intuitive level of protection and concern. She notes in *The Origins of Totalitarianism*[62] that the 'rights of man', which are supposed to exist as inalienable rights independent of any government, leave nothing to protect a human being once citizenship is removed. She points out that the very figure who should *embody* the rights of man, the refugee, reveals instead that, without the support of citizenship, the concept of human rights reaches a terminal crisis, breaking down 'at the very moment when those who professed to believe in it were for the first time confronted with people who had indeed lost all other qualities and specific relationships – except that they were still human'.[63] Certainly, history forces the conclusion that effective human rights regimes require stable states and the institutionalisation of national citizenship.[64] But history also reveals the violation implicit in the withdrawal of citizenship and the urgency of adequate protection for vulnerable human beings – *qua* human beings – in the face of such withdrawal. And of all human beings the refugee and asylum seeker present us with the image of the human being requiring protection *qua* human being.

Morsink notes that most of the delegations present had no difficulty voting for most of the rights in the UDHR. Most of the rights were deeply continuous with constitutional rights with which they were all familiar but none of the constitutions of the member states contained 'international rights'. These rights, such as the right to move between countries (Article

13), the right to asylum (Article 14) and the right to citizenship (Article 16), are, he rightly suggests, the 'real test cases for any list of human rights'.[65]

While the right to leave and return to a country was granted by the drafters of the UDHR, the right is rendered meaningless without the right to enter another country. Article 14 of the UDHR declares that '[e]veryone has the right to seek and to enjoy in other countries asylum from persecution'. Morsink comments that the drafters, by using the words 'to enjoy' rather than the more robust 'to be granted', failed a pivotal test. One explanation for this critical failure to protect human vulnerability adequately with a robust right to enter countries when people are persecuted in their own is explained by factors that, some 60 years on, in a globalised age, will hardly surprise the average observer. Mr Wilson, the UK delegate, expressed the motivation in remarkably clear terms when he pointed out that, firstly, not all states would assume the obligation to grant asylum, and that 'one of the most jealously guarded rights of a state was the right to prevent foreigners from crossing its border'.[66] Unsurprisingly, in the light of the wartime experience, the representative from the World Jewish Congress argued that the right to asylum is implicit in the very concept of the right to life, and that the right to escape makes no sense without a right to be received elsewhere. He argued that the deprivation of such a right had resulted in thousands of deaths for the refugees of Germany.[67] This, too, was Arendt's point. The refugee – the quintessentially vulnerable human being of human rights – is left unprotected at the very moment when protection is most needed. The reason, it seems, is that the matter of asylum directly challenges national sovereignty over the territorial control of borders. While it may be true that a flood of refugees places difficult pressures on the internal life of a nation, it is also true that '[a]n article about the right to receive asylum is ... the real meeting place of national sovereignty and international human rights'.[68] For embodied, vulnerable human beings the world remains obdurately bordered. Asylum seekers and refugees still test the outer limits of the 'human' of international human rights law. All too often human rights law simply fails to protect vulnerable humanity in its most exposed position beyond the outer margins of any given political community. What Article 14 reveals, then, is a troubling lacuna into which embodied vulnerable human beings, without the protection of citizenship, fall, notwithstanding the lessons of Nazi Germany.

As already indicated, the relationship between citizenship and human rights is a complex, challenging and under-theorised one. However, Agamben's reading of the relationship between politics and 'bare life' alerts us to a related and vital strand of critique to which we must briefly attend. For, it reveals a provocative link between the lacuna of Article 14 and a troubling contiguity between totalitarianism and democracy that is pertinent to an age that has witnessed the first 'humanitarian wars' conducted in the name of human rights[69] and witnessed the fact that 'more human rights violations have been committed in this rights-obsessed age than at any other point in history'.[70] Foucault brilliantly pointed out that, in the modern world, and as a prerequisite for the capitalist state, the body has been radically enclosed within politics. Foucault names this enclosure 'bio-power', by which he means the increasing inclusion of human natural life in the mechanisms of power, with the result that, although '[f]or millennia man remained what he was for Aristotle: a living animal with the additional capacity for political existence; modern man is an animal whose politics calls his existence as a living being into question'.[71]

Agamben has augmented Foucault's argument by insisting that, throughout the entire history of Western thought about political sovereignty, sovereignty has always been constituted as power over life. But this power over life has remained submerged, or merely implicit, largely because the notion of the sacred has been imbricated with the notion of sovereignty. Agamben identifies an obscure figure of Roman law – *homo sacer* – as the key by which the meaning of political power, whether totalitarian or democratic, reveals its true structure. *Homo sacer* is a man who could not be sacrificed, but could be killed without punishment. He is 'bare life' – a man without political existence – included in the juridical order solely in the form of his exclusion. That is to say, his *capacity to be killed*.[72] Politics is constituted by the original exclusion of *homo sacer*. *Homo sacer* lives beyond the law, in a zone of indistinction between *bios* (a public life worthy of respect and inclusion) and *zoe* (mere biological existence).

Agamben argues that modern politics confuses *bios* and *zoe*, rendering biological life a strategic mechanism in the calculation of state power. The Jew living under Nazism is, when seen in this light, merely the 'privileged negative referent of the new biopolitical sovereignty'[73] – a paradigm case of *homo sacer*. The dimension, he insists, in which the extermination of the Jews as 'lice' (Hitler's word) took place 'is neither religion nor law, but biopolitics... [and i]f today there is no longer any one clear figure of the sacred man, it is perhaps because we are all virtually *homines sacri*'.[74] Politics in modernity is 'entirely transformed into bio-politics', and because of this – and only because of this – was it possible for politics to become totalitarian to a degree never before known,[75] as it did in the Third Reich.

Agamben points out a contiguity between totalitarianism and democracy by arguing that every decisive political event in history has been double-sided. The liberties and rights won by individuals 'always simultaneously prepared a tacit but increasing inscription of individuals' lives within the state order, thus offering a new and more dreadful foundation for the very sovereign power from which they wanted to liberate themselves'.[76] This thesis has some continuity with the critical comments made in earlier chapters concerning the links between rights and positivism in the philosophy of Hobbes, and the elements of closure and critique in the history of natural right and rights. But it also points to a more radical paradox yet.

This is the paradox inherent in the fact that the French Declaration was the place where Agamben claims that bare natural life was explicitly identified as being the source and bearer of rights but immediately disappeared into the citizen, and in the process, was invested with the principle of sovereignty. In other words, it was with the declaration of rights that a new biopolitical order was inaugurated. Birth and national belonging were unified. This, in turn, can be linked, by the same bio-political thread, to Nazism and the concentration camps, wherein the hidden gap between birth and nation became fully visible:

> The fiction implicit here is that *birth* immediately becomes *nation* such that there can be no interval of separation [*scarto*] between the two terms. Rights are attributed to man (or originate in him) solely to the extent that man is the immediately vanishing ground (who must never come to light as such) of the citizen. Only if we understand this essential historical function of the doctrine of rights can we grasp the development and metamorphosis of declarations of rights in our century. When the hidden difference [*scarto*] between birth and nation entered into a lasting crisis following the devastation of Europe's geopolitical order after the First World War, what appeared was Nazism and fascism, that is, two properly biopolitical movements that made of natural life the exemplary place of the sovereign decision.... Fascism and Nazism are, above all, redefinitions of the relations between man and the citizen, and become fully intelligible only when situated – no matter how paradoxical it may seem – in the biopolitical context inaugurated by national sovereignty and declarations of rights.[77]

Agamben's thesis has disturbing implications. It points to a radical gap between embodied vulnerability and the protection offered by citizenship. This is why the asylum seeker or the refugee is such a disturbing figure. The refugee functions as a 'limit concept', calling into question our most deeply embedded political assumptions, our fundamental categories 'from the birth-nation to the man-citizen link, and that thereby makes it possible to clear the way for a long-overdue renewal of categories in the service of a politics in which bare life is no longer separated and excepted, either in the state order or in the figure of human rights'.[78]

Hunt's work on the role of embodiment and empathy in the genesis of natural rights reminds us that the notion of natural human life and embodiment in the genesis of rights discourse remains both paradoxical and interpretively open. The French Declaration may have enshrined the rights of men as an incident of birth, fusing birth and nation as Agamben argues. But it is by no means clear that what the drafters had in mind was 'bare life'. If Hunt's analysis of the rise of rights discourse is historically accurate, embodied vulnerability evoked empathy and a sense of human commonality that sits in paradoxical relation to the closures operative in rights discourse at the moment of institutionalisation: the closures incipient in the abstraction employed in the designation of the central rights-bearer and the privileging, first and foremost, of a particular social group. But embodied vulnerability also sits in a complex relation to the closure invoked by Agamben's notion of bare life. Agamben's thesis forces the conclusion that any defence of human rights based on embodied vulnerability must somehow, in future theorisation, capture a new politics, a radical re-imagination of the role of the body that refuses to name embodied life as 'bare life' – a view that perhaps captures embodied vulnerability as being a new limit concept with ethical, political content. In other words, embodied vulnerability will need to be conceptualised as more than mere biology.

One highly plausible and valuable reading of the human rights contained in the UDHR is as a set of critical constructs based on the affirmation of human ontic commonality, empathetic identification, and a radical humanitarian critique of the reduction of human beings to 'bare life'. This valuable strand of UDHR discourse is, however, immediately betrayed by the crucial failure of nerve in the face of national sovereignty and state interests over the control of state borders. Embodied vulnerability could, however, be used to critique precisely the exteriority of *homo sacer* as 'bare life' and to insist on the radical politico-juridical interiority and value of all human beings, irrespective of their citizenship status.

The lacuna at the heart of the UDHR thus presents a paradigmatic and haunting case of Agamben's challenging analysis. The UDHR, even as it attempts to reject the bio-political logic of Hitler's totalitarianism, evinces a key failure to protect the refugee and asylum seeker – thus failing to transcend the very bio-political limit that Agamben identifies. Article 14 recreates the refugee and the asylum seeker as our contemporary *homo sacer* whose vulnerable figure returns, incessantly, to haunt those who imagine that our current conception of human rights is a sufficient answer to the violent exclusions of our age. Morsink concludes that this failure means that, in the UDHR itself, 'the lesson learned from the Holocaust was once again lost'.[79]

In the light of this haunting lacuna, the right to citizenship becomes particularly important as a remedial measure. Yet it hardly answers the fundamental human rights dilemma that Arendt pointed out. Yet again, it was the experience of the war that meant that the right not to be left stateless was high on the agenda for the drafters of the UDHR. The records show that the Nazis first stripped those whom they wished to exterminate of nationality, and that the removal of citizenship was a decisive moment[80] in the engineering of the Jews' physical incarceration and extermination. Making Jews stateless made them completely vulnerable, not just in Germany, but in the neighbouring countries that shipped Jews back to Germany. Statelessness achieved two pivotal aims. In the words of Eichmann, statelessness made it 'impossible for any country to inquire into [the fate of the Jews], and it enabled that state in which they were resident to confiscate their property'.[81]

Currently, to be without citizenship is to stand politically disconnected as an outsider to the international order – an exception, unaffiliated 'bare' humanity, rootless in a juridical lacuna. This is why, crucially, Agamben's challenge must be taken up. There must be no such thing in this world as 'bare life' judged unworthy of protection, life or flourishing, regardless of citizenship status. Embodied vulnerability may achieve this, but only if the radical implications of human ontic commonality are fully embraced and accepted as being the basis of an ethical and political empathy. That an urgent engagement with the bio-political dilemma haunting contemporary rights discourse is pressing cannot be doubted in the face of ongoing, wholesale violations of human vulnerability – sometimes in the name of human rights themselves. There is a very real sense in which human rights in the current context are in danger of forming a dangerously ascendant and valorised tool of a globalised bio-politics, or even a globalised thanato-politics. The battle for human rights meanings has arguably never been more urgent.

Some concluding remarks

Morsink's analysis reveals a strong case to support his insistence that the experience of Nazi Germany is epistemically fundamental to the entire UDHR. The whole of the UDHR, along with certain groups of rights within it, can be read as a repeated attempt to ensure that the horrors of Nazi Germany would not be repeated and that there would be a regime of rights capable of protecting human beings as *species beings*. When viewed in this light, the significant lacuna surrounding the right to be granted asylum seems all the more ironic, although Agamben's thesis explains this with chilling force. It is unsurprising that the UDHR fails fully to respect embodied vulnerability at precisely the point that national sovereignty is most at stake. The complex convergence between human rights and citizenship points to the very real sense in which sovereignty is itself constituted precisely by the power to govern bodies. Embodied vulnerability, in that sense, underlies the power of the state, as much as it underlies the reaction – the directly related reaction – to state power that rights discourse invokes.[82] The asylum seeker or refugee is the very instance of the human being who should embody human rights as *species* rights. Yet it is at this point precisely that rights discourse breaks down, signalling the failure of human rights to extend meaningfully beyond the notion of citizenship. This limitation, in the light of Agamben's complex argument about the foundations of sovereignty and the politicisation of bare life, seems to be an inherent part of the paradox of rights as they are currently constituted.

Turner is correct, in the light of this, to argue that we need to attempt to maintain some kind of distinction between what he calls the social rights of citizens, and the human rights of persons – and equally correct to insist that human rights should be conceptualised as resting on human embodied vulnerability. It is crucial that we establish embodied vulnerability as a value that takes us beyond the designation of some human beings, or even all of us, as 'bare life' in the calculations of modern market-driven politics. That these are pressing issues is clear from the fallout of globalisation and new wars in which warfare is both thoroughly mechanised and selectively privatised. The wholesale distortion of the UDHR paradigm, identified by Baxi, indicates the very real prospect that international human rights are genuinely in danger of losing their ethical force and their critical humanitarian potential.

Stepping back from these reflections, it is time to return to the central insistence of this book that embodied vulnerability should be taken to be conceptually and ethically foundational to international human rights discourse. Agamben's provocative thesis raises the question as to whether embodied vulnerability can supply a theory capable of resisting the biopolitical reduction of human beings to bare life. There are related questions also as to whether embodied vulnerability can move us beyond the closures of legal discourse in human rights, and whether the legal subject of human rights can be reconstituted in such a way as to provide protection to living human beings and communities in a context in which state power has become increasingly imbricated with the interests of global corporate capital. It will be argued later in this chapter that the answer to all these questions is that it can, and it must. But for now it is necessary to continue and conclude the argument concerning the capacity of embodied vulnerability to found the entire lexicon of UDHR rights.

Embodied vulnerability and the UDHR rights: Conceptual issues

Turner has argued that embodied vulnerability is the foundation of human rights. However, his sociological perspective leads him to focus on a cluster of salient socio-economic rights and merely to found civil and political rights *indirectly* on embodied vulnerability by linking health with democracy. While Turner's work is valuable and deeply insightful, it will be argued here that embodied vulnerability can be understood to be the foundation of all categories of human rights, not just on the basis of the role of embodied vulnerability in the genesis of the UDHR, but as a conceptual matter.

i. Economic, social and cultural rights

The list of rights contained in the UDHR is further elaborated in later treaties that sit firmly within the UDHR paradigm, most notably the ICCPR[83] and the ICESCR.[84] We should note, before proceeding, that, while all categories of human rights are treated as interdependent and indivisible,[85] it is well known that certain complexities surround the implementation of economic, social and cultural rights.[86] Indeed, compared to civil and political rights, economic, social and cultural rights are relatively neglected.[87] The traditionally perceived dichotomy between ICCPR and ICESCR rights reflects the legacy of the Cold War debates at the time the Covenants were being drafted. But the relative neglect of economic, social and cultural rights also implicates the privileging, within the international legal order, of a certain form of liberalism that as we have seen, tends to be antithetical in crucial respects to inclusory human rights values.[88] It has even been famously argued by Cranston that economic and social rights are not truly human rights.[89] Donnelly counters Cranston's argument in terms that strongly imply embodied vulnerability, though nowhere does he use the term. For example, in attempting to establish the relative lack of importance of economic, social and cultural rights, Cranston selects the right to periodic holidays with pay. Donnelly counters with the point that such a right, if denied, could 'indeed be a serious affront to human dignity; [the denial of such a right] was, for example, one of the most oppressive features of unregulated nineteenth century capitalism'.[90] Two points should be made about Donnelly's response. First, it should be noted that Donnelly's argument implicitly links human dignity with a defence of embodied vulnerability (a link to be more fully introduced in the next chapter). Clearly, there are a whole set of health-related, well-being-related considerations that make paid rest from employment pressing in relation to the protection of the human person – and Donnelly characterises the lack of such a right as a potential threat to 'dignity', in a context where it is relatively clear that the underlying issue at stake can just as meaningfully (if not more so) be understood to be embodied vulnerability and its need for protection. The second point to note is that the example chosen by Cranston was clearly an attempt to trivialise the nature of the rights at issue. Indeed, Donnelly notes that the right to periodic holiday with pay is not a typical economic, social and cultural right. Yet, even this less central right can be defended on grounds of embodied vulnerability.

When we turn to the central case of socio-economic rights we find that, as a set of rights, they focally embrace core human needs and issues intimately related to embodied flourishing and survival. The right to an adequate standard of living (defined as adequate food, clothing and housing) (Article 11), the right to work (Article 6) and to be able to work under just and humane conditions (Article 7), the right to social security (Article 9), rights concerning health (Article 12) and education (Article 13) – all invoke the centrality of embodiment. Of these, education may seem more remotely related. But in fact it is a prerequisite, in many cases, for the effective enjoyment of other rights, such as the right to work, which, in turn, relates to the right to an adequate standard of living. The underlying concern for social inclusion and collective empowerment indicated by the rights to cultural participation (Article 15) and to join and form trade unions (Article 8) can be directly related, again, to the vulnerabilities and needs of embodied beings inter-relating in socio-economic contexts wherein isolation renders human beings relatively defenceless in the face of risk and uncertainty. This point is reflective of the wider argument concerning the link between embodied vulnerability and the establishment of social institutions (including effective democracy) to mediate that vulnerability,[91] and rights as mechanisms through which to express and ensure a level of protection in a context in which our social institutions themselves turn out to be relatively precarious, as Turner has argued.[92] His sociological argument focuses quite naturally on the 'special importance of the International Covenant on Economic, Social and Cultural Rights, namely, those rights that are directly connected with human need and the protection of human life'.[93] At its core, however, his argument links embodied vulnerability with the concept of human need – both physical and social – underlining the strength of the connection between social, economic and cultural rights[94] and the notion of embodied vulnerability.

It can convincingly be concluded, then, that economic, social and cultural rights focus predominantly on embodied needs and the socio-cultural means for their protection. The predominant thrust of the ICESCR is socio-economic. This is despite the fact that the title of the Covenant refers to 'cultural' rights and Article 15(1) recognises 'the right of everyone ... to take part in cultural life'. Cultural rights in fact have tended to be dealt with in relation to the ICCPR. Arguably, it is precisely the socio-economic character of ICESCR rights that makes them more complex to institute than the civil and political rights of the ICCPR. This is because ICESCR rights are conceived of as being more programmatic and perhaps more suitable to the democratic process than to judicial determination.[95] It is also arguable that these difficulties reflect the underlying fact that the key aim of the ICESCR is the eradication of socio-economic deprivation and disempowerment – an aim focally concerned with embodied vulnerability and far less ideologically compatible with mainstream liberal assumptions than are civil and political rights. The preamble to the Covenant firmly recognises the basis of the rights proclaimed in the 'inherent dignity of the human person', and it stresses the ideal of human beings 'enjoying freedom from fear and want' – conditions that can only be achieved if everyone may 'enjoy his economic social and cultural rights, as well as his civil and political rights'. It is clear, therefore, that embodied vulnerability provides a direct foundation for ICESCR rights and Turner quite rightly highlights and embraces the importance of this fact.

ii. Civil and political rights

Turner suggests that his thesis concerning embodied vulnerability can be criticised on the ground that, while it is highly relevant to socio-economic rights, it is not a convincing argument in relation to civil and political rights. To counter this objection to his vulnerability thesis, Turner establishes an *indirect* link between embodied vulnerability and civil and political rights. He argues that '[i]t would not be difficult to show that human beings cannot successfully enjoy social rights to health care in societies that curtail civil and political liberties'.[96] Turner's argument at this point has a degree of resonance with our earlier reflections on Nazi Germany and Hitler's destruction of democratic rights as a prelude to the wholesale violation of important civil and political rights and liberties. However, Turner's argument is somewhat different. Instead of linking the importance of democracy and civil and political rights directly to the protection of embodied vulnerability, he takes a detour. The structure of his argument is as follows:

> Reason 1: Embodied vulnerability directly undergirds socio-economic rights.
>
> Reason 2: Poor socio-economic conditions and health outcomes are linked.
>
> Reason 3: Evidence from health research shows a relationship between health, income inequality and democratic participation in society.
>
> Interim Conclusion: A link can be 'forge[d]' between 'social conditions, health, and liberal political rights'.[97]
>
> Conclusion: Embodied vulnerability is the indirect foundation for civil and political rights.

While this argument provides a strong rationale for the centrality of participatory democracy to human flourishing, it is nonetheless the case that embodied vulnerability offers a richer and more direct foundation for civil and political rights than Turner's health and democracy argument suggests.

One direct link between embodied vulnerability and the enjoyment of civil and political rights has already been mentioned and is closely related, in any case, to Turner's linkage between democracy and health. The implication of the view taken by the drafters of the UDHR is that democracy, and the political structure of democracy, are important protections – along with important civil and political rights – that provide a politico-legal bulwark between the unrestrained power of the state and the embodied vulnerability of the population. This certainly seems to be the implication of the lessons drawn from the Nazi regime, and explains the importance in the UDHR of rights such as the right to legal personality, to citizenship, to democratic participation, equal protection of the law and so on. A wide range of rights broadly understood to be civil and political rights can thus be directly linked to embodied vulnerability in precisely this way, without needing to rely on the more remote two-step link between such rights and socio-economic rights.

However, it is also the case that the presupposition directly operative beneath many civil and political rights is precisely that of embodied vulnerability, although admittedly the presupposition is more evident in respect of some rights than others. In the case of some civil and political rights the protection of embodied vulnerability is overt and decisive. Embodied vulnerability is directly and focally at stake in the case of the right to life (Article 3 UDHR; Article 6 ICCPR); the right to liberty and security of the person (Article 3 UDHR; Article 9 ICCPR); the right to protection against slavery (Article 4 UDHR; Article 8 ICCPR); the right to protection against torture (Article 5 UDHR; Article 7 ICCPR); the right to protection against arbitrary arrest, detention or exile (Article 9 UDHR; Article 9 ICCPR); the right to freedom of movement (Article 13 UDHR; Article 12 ICCPR); the right to marry and found a family (Article 16 UDHR; Article 23 ICCPR); and the right to humane treatment when deprived of liberty (Article 10 ICCPR). Embodied vulnerability is also the presupposition operative in important civil and political rights that mediate the ways in which people communicate with each other in physical and social space. Such rights include the right to freedom of assembly (Article 20 UDHR, Article 21 ICCPR) and the right to freedom of association (Article 20 UDHR; Article 22 ICCPR).

Embodied vulnerability is also pervasive in the right to freedom of opinion and expression, (Article 19 UDHR; Article 19 ICCPR) albeit in a less obvious way perhaps. First, the right to freedom of opinion and expression directly protects embodied personalities from multiple forms of coercion on the basis of their opinions, beliefs or expression. Secondly, the right to freedom of expression is often considered an invaluable and first line of defence against the general erosion of liberties and democratic freedoms and is therefore fundamental to the effectiveness of democracy's protection of embodied vulnerable people. Indeed freedom of expression is often the most highly regarded of democratic rights. Thirdly, Scarry's invaluable study of bodily pain reveals an intimate structural link between embodiment, speech and the political.[98] Recalling that embodied vulnerability is the target at stake in torture and the coercive power of dictatorship and tyranny, Scarry argues that the deliberate infliction of pain destroys a sufferer's language. Her provocative thesis links speech, pain and the body in an intimate triadic structure at the very heart of the operation of political power. Interestingly, Scarry also demonstrates how the torturer's speech is also degraded in the process of inflicting bodily pain, matching the reversion to pre-linguistic sounds of the tortured: 'the person inflicting pain reverts to a pre-language, uncaring noises remembered in the accounts given by former political prisoners'.[99]

In the light of the direct link between free expression and the foundations of democracy and of Scarry's thesis, freedom of speech can be directly related to embodied vulnerability in the very structure of political power. Language, moreover, is central to the construction of embodied human reality as a more general matter. There is a direct relationship between speech, bodily freedom and our ability to inhabit the world. Tellingly, Scarry argues that the undoing of language by the imposition of pain contracts and then eliminates the space around the embodied person: '[t]hrough his ability to project words and sounds out into his environment, a human being inhabits, humanizes, and makes his own a space much larger than that occupied by his body alone. This space, always contracted under repressive regimes, is in torture almost wholly eliminated'.[100] Freedom of expression is intimately bound up with the spaces created by speakers and the forging of political, social, cultural and physical spaces around our embodied vulnerability. Freedom of expression, in this light, has a mutually supportive relationship with the prohibition on torture, structurally united in an intimate relationship with the human being as a vulnerable, speaking subject.

Finally, antidiscrimination rights can also be seen to have a profound and intimate relationship with embodied vulnerability. Such rights reflect the historical record of the forms of targeted vulnerability produced by the tragic and deplorable human tendency to employ embodied difference as a foundational pretext for the imposition of inequalities, hatreds and exclusions. Hitler's strategy of targeting the Jews is a classic case, as is the notion of apartheid – for a long time regarded as the paradigm international human rights abuse. And, as the argument in earlier chapters made clear, embodied difference was historically indispensible to exclusory distinctions drawn between white, male bodies and the bodies of women and 'others' whose morphology differed from the submerged beneficiary of liberal law (even if this morphology was complex in its relationship to legal disembodiment). Ideologies of difference such as racism, sexism, heterosexism and so on project their orders of meaning onto our embodied form. It is our bodies that are encoded with meanings based on 'colour' or 'sex'. The notion of embodiment is fundamental to discourses of hatred and liberation alike. Embodied vulnerability is both presupposed by, and a core protective concern of, anti-discrimination rights.

Summary

Based on the foregoing analysis it can be convincingly argued that both the main categories of human rights established in the UDHR paradigm can be read as an extended defence of human embodied vulnerability. The rights contained in the UDHR, the ICCPR and the ICESCR (which together form the 'International Bill of Rights') simply make *no conceptual sense without pre supposing a vulnerable living body*. Materiality and incarnate presence undergird international human rights law. For most of the human rights we have discussed, the relationship between embodied vulnerability and the right in question is relatively direct. On closer scrutiny, even those rights less obviously inhabited by embodiment – such as the right to a legal personality – can be seen to have at their core a concern for the protection of the embodied person. This fact is particularly attested to by the analysis of the central concern of the drafters of the UDHR to learn from the lessons of Nazi Germany.

What, then, are the implications of this focus on embodied vulnerability in the UDHR? Can an embodiment-centred human rights ethic be constructed from embodiment and vulnerability as ontic conditions of humanity? It is now time to turn to the ethical implications of embodied vulnerability for human rights law and theory.

Towards the ethical reconstruction of human rights and the human rights subject

Embodied vulnerability has emerged from our reflections as a key ontic incident of humanity. Against the disembodiment implicit in Western rationalism and legal theory it has been argued that embodiment is inescapable. Moreover, the notion of disembodied rationality is not only damaging, but profoundly *irrational*. The impossibility of legal disembodiment results in a gap between legal subjectivity and human beings. While this gap is problematic and requires interrogation in many legal contexts, it is especially unsuitable in the international human rights context. We have also seen how vulnerability is a key incident of embodiment and has clear (if sometimes ambivalent) links to the social origins and conceptual underpinnings of human rights. It has been argued that the notion of embodied vulnerability underpins the entire UDHR paradigm. But this claim should not be oversimplified. As has been stressed before, the relationship between disembodiment and embodiment in human rights law is complex. Even within a reading of the UDHR paradigm that emphasises embodied vulnerability as its true foundation we can see a highly significant lacuna invoking the complex relationship between citizenship and human rights. In turn, this can in turn be linked to the possibility that human rights themselves can be understood or exploited as instantiations of a form of bio-politics in which human embodied vulnerability becomes reduced to something approaching Agamben's concept of 'bare life'. These complexities are unlikely to disappear. Human rights as concepts are open to multiple interpretations and even, as we have seen, wholesale interpretive exploitation in the service of a neoliberal capitalist ideology which is arguably profoundly antithetical to the humanitarian, embodiment-centred impulse that first gave international human rights their life.

Embodied vulnerability itself is open to interpretive difficulties. It is clear, for example, as already conceded, that embodied vulnerability, if taken as a general concept, does not, without more, distinguish between human beings and animals. (It is also possible to conceive of posthuman entities, or the corporation itself, as in different and nuanced senses, both embodied and vulnerable – although some distinctions were drawn early in this work between the corporation and the vulnerable materiality of the human being in this respect.) It must be stressed again that it is no part of the argument of this book that animals should be prevented from having basic rights. It is no part of the argument of this book that corporations should be prevented from having legal rights. The notion of vulnerability, understood more broadly, could be extended, in fact, to provide a very powerful theoretical explanation of what underlies the impulse towards the extension of legal subjectivity to persons, animals, entities, and even the environment itself, for example. Again, these are arguments for another book. However, it *is* the argument of this book that the emergence of corporate legal humanity and the subversion of the UDHR paradigm into a paradigm of trade-related market-friendly human rights, with all the concomitant dangers for human beings, means that it is now *crucial* to redirect the energy and language of *human* rights towards *human* beings and away from corporations.

We have seen that human beings are highly vulnerable in particular and recognisable ways. Human beings organise themselves in complex social systems, building institutions for their protection to mediate the effects of embodied vulnerability.[101] Frequently these institutions are themselves precarious, and frequently they fail to protect human beings. On a critical reading, institutions feed on the embodied vulnerability of human beings in the very construction of power, as Foucault saw. And as we have just seen, Agamben adds to Foucault's concept of bio-power a notion of the biopolitical, insisting, moreover, that there is 'no return from the [concentration] camps [as the paradigm of modern politics] to classical politics… we are not only, in Foucault's words, animals whose life as living beings is at issue in their politics, but also – inversely – citizens whose very politics is at issue in their natural body'.[102]

Given the centrality of the human body to the political and to the construction and mediation of power, and given the transnational near-capitulation of state power to the interests of corporate capital, it could hardly be more important or timely to ask whether embodied vulnerability, explicitly utilised as a legal and political value, might offer a tentative beginning in the project of ethically reconstructing and redirecting human rights. It seems vital to devise a human rights ethic that is critical of the reduction of human beings to mere biological bodies (biological bodies frequently merely 'the bodies in the way' of profit, progress or whatever other political or economic goal is at stake – whether that be in the case of a Bhopal or the bombing of countries in the name of 'humanitarian war'). Perhaps an insistence on the inseparability of the relationship between embodied vulnerability and human rights – and beyond them, law and politics more generally – might offer a way of instigating a different kind of politics – a radical politics of interrelationality and compassion. It seems minimally clear that embodied vulnerability cannot achieve this without some kind of defence of its ethical implications.

Levinas and the 'ethics of alterity'

The concept of interrelationality (or, in Merleau-Ponty's philosophy, intercorporeality) reveals our radical interconnection with each other and the world. It is suggested that embodied interrelationality contains the promise of a profound and compassionate openness to each other and the world, if embraced as a positive value and fully explored. Our shared ontic commonality, and the vulnerability at its core, the range of implications that flow from the affectability of the body, has the potential, once fully theorised and utilised as the basis of new forms of legal and political subjectivity, to quite literally, change worlds. Turning, again, to the specific task of redirecting human rights, the work of Levinas beautifully draws out some of the rich potential implications inherent in the philosophical foundations offered to human rights theory by adopting the work of Merleau-Ponty. While Merleau-Ponty emphasises the radical interrelationality of embodied life, Levinas constructs what we could call an 'an ethics of interrelationality' in which the 'other' presents a unique ethical demand premised upon both uniqueness and vulnerability.

Levinas, in fact, insists that the prime philosophical question is not ontological, but *ethical*:[103] the first question is not the question of being, but the question of how 'being justifies itself'.[104] His ethics, the 'ethics of alterity', is committed to the absolute primacy of the 'other' – both in the sense that the other is always *prior* to the self, and in the sense that the other is resolutely irreducible to either the self, an extension of the self, or the *alter ego*. Levinas's insistence on an ethics of alterity, it is suggested, is a particularly useful philosophical counterpoint to the process and implications of the 'othering' that, as we have seen, lies at the heart of bio-political exclusion. Using Levinas's central insight we can insist that 'othering' as a mechanism of exclusion and reduction should be confronted by an ethic which points towards a radical acknowledgement of the uniqueness, the irreplaceability, the singularity of the other, combined with an absolute refusal to objectify the other. For Levinas, the other, in this rich sense, is our starting point: our ethical north – always *prior*: the other is, indeed, the precondition of our very existence, our language and our law.[105]

The conceptual dependence of Levinas's theory on the notion of embodied vulnerability is underlined by the fact that for Levinas, the other is summed up by the 'face'. For Levinas, the face is the archetypical carrier of absolute presence – the unique presence of the embodied vulnerable other that compels us to an ethical response to the other in all of his or her uniqueness and vulnerability. Douzinas, capturing the poignant and compelling potency of the insight, argues that for Levinas, '[a]lterity remains outside, quasi-transcendental, unique, frail like the face of a child that demands that I accept my responsibility. The face is a fundamental ontological fact which ... cannot be systematised'.[106] This last point has particular importance for human rights theory. A central element of our critique of international human rights law has been its construction (in line with longstanding Western intellectual tradition) of the universal bearer of human rights as an abstract entity. In the light of embodied vulnerability, refracted through the lens of Levinas's passionate ethic of alterity, the abstract universal is fully exposed and unmasked for all its pallid, quintessentially inadequate normativity. The other is not an abstract, empty rights-bearer – the quasi-disembodied mask-like abstraction so compatible with the corporate exploitation of human rights discourse. This view of the other takes embodied particularity seriously in concrete terms. And this unique, embodied other has, not a mask, but a living face.

For Levinas, a face in suffering commands us, demands something – delivers an ethical imperative: 'do not kill me', 'give me sanctuary' and so forth. Such a command is issued directly, in an embodied, present way. This is emphatically not the other of the disembodied universal of liberalism or the liberal legal subject. This other is simply not reducible to an interchangeable unit of political, legal or economic reference, nor is it yet the other as 'bare life'. This other is incarnate, 'always a unique, singular person who has place and time, gender and history, needs and desires'.[107] In a sense, the face, for Levinas, becomes the specific carrier of the ethical implications of embodied vulnerability – issuing, in effect, an insistence on the ethical inclusion of every single living human being in a common fleshly, in*carnate* community, whose very commonality – or in the language of human rights – universality – is *precisely comprised* of the *irreducibly unique* 'members of the human family' (to borrow the terminology of the UDHR).

The implications of this ethics of interrelationality, moreover, have a traction that reaches into the heart of the construction of first person subjectivity. For Levinas, the face is the way in which the other presents herself as 'exceeding the idea of the other in me'.[108] The face of the other escapes any limits we place on it by our own preconceptions, projections or measure. Adams argues that, by expressing his or her radical alterity, the other 'confronts me with meaning beyond my autonomous capacity to construct it, calls me to become open in a conversation with a mystery beyond myself'.[109] The other overflows our conceptions and is totally significant, singular and ultimately incomprehensible. The other is, in this sense, absolutely proximate and absolutely non-identical with the self. When I am summoned by the ethical command of the other in all her singularity, I am also constituted as uniquely present, the one – for Levinas the only one – who can answer the command so directly addressed to me.[110] For Levinas, it is the subjection to the ethical command of the other that is the essence of the subject or self. To be a self is precisely to be summoned to respond from our unique singularity to the unique singularity of the other. Accordingly, our very identity is radically intersubjective, interrelational, and, importantly, premised on the embodied vulnerability of the other. Arguably, then, we are most summoned by the most vulnerable, giving the most vulnerable among us a special role in the constitution of our human subjectivity.

In a globalised age of increasing risk and violence,[111] where the most disempowered figure of humanity is presented by the haunting figure of the refugee who lays bare the lacuna at the heart of international human rights law, such an ethics invites a radically alternate conception of both the human rights community and its constitution. Embodied vulnerable refugees, who in their growing numbers are driven against the policed and defended territorial borders of states (even as those same borders are porous or non-existent for TNCs)[112] present an ethical summons to international human rights law and theory. International human rights law and theory urgently needs redirecting towards the most vulnerable humans of all. The human rights universal, particularly at the international level, requires a thorough reconceptualisation, and should be understood, not as abstract, but as concrete, breathing, thoroughly incarnate. The universal urgently needs to be understood in all his and her radical particularity, fully embodied, fully vulnerable. Accordingly, international human rights protection should extend, *archetypally*, to the human being *qua human being*: including, perhaps most especially, the human being without citizenship, the human being as juridically naked and excluded. These most vulnerable human beings among us provide, it is suggested, the bottom-line test for an adequate conception of international human rights subjectivity.

For Levinas, the ethics of interrelationality is shaped by the fact that the other presents himself as simultaneously more than and less than me. The other has 'height' in that she can 'present herself as a stranger without opposing me as obstacle or enemy' but also is 'less' than me in that it is the very destitution or vulnerability of the other that summons me to respond: '[t]he Other who dominates me in his transcendence is thus the stranger, the widow, and the orphan, to whom I am obligated'.[113] This compassionate, humanitarian energy needs to re-animate the discourse of international human rights – challenging corporate humanity and the corporate exploitation of human rights with a fundamental insistence on the inescapable centrality of human embodied vulnerability and an ethics building on the implications of that centrality. As Douzinas has pointed out, Levinas bases the ontology of alterity on the 'absolute proximity of the most alien'.[114] The proximity of the other has an ongoing dynamism in the constitution of subjectivity – because the other is continually challenging us, and, importantly, in turning to embrace the other, we become who we are. We are, most profoundly, our interrelating.

Summing up the implications of this for human rights, Douzinas comments that, 'unlike the ontological emphasis of liberalism and the abstract nature of the (legal) subject, [the metaphysics of the ethics of alterity] ... carries the strongest historical commitment to the unique needs of the concrete other'.[115] And, it is theoretically decisive, arguably, that we must emphasis that this concrete other is embodied and vulnerable as a matter of human *ontic commonality*. What we have *in common* as members of the human family is precisely our embodied uniqueness, our common human singularity, our common but differentially experienced vulnerability, held in radical interrelationality with each other and the world. Embodied vulnerability is a way of reconstituting the human rights universal in terms that defy the closures of traditional abstract readings: we are united by a *universal* constituted by an incarnate vulnerability expressed through our *particularity*. Such a conception leaves no room for a flattening empty sameness, but nor does it leave room for violent categorical distinctions between human beings that overlook our ontic commonality and its tender, quintessential affectability.

International human rights, on this reading, should be conceptualised as juridical instantiations of our shared duty to respond to the fundamental incidents of a human ontic commonality. This characterisation sits well with Hunt's analysis of the origins of rights in the eighteenth century, as well as the arguments offered here for the relationship between embodied vulnerability and the UDHR paradigm. It is also the case that contemporary human rights awareness, based on evidence that public opinion is indeed mobilised by a sense of moral proximity to distant others all over the globe, reflects the role of embodied vulnerability and a related empathy. If embodied vulnerability were to be recognised as the explicit theoretical foundation of international human rights law and theory, it would be rendered satisfyingly consistent with a fundamental strand of human rights history and reflect more closely the contemporary function of human rights in the public intuition. Human rights would stand, reinvigorated, on the foundation of a deeply humanitarian response to human vulnerability as embodied (speaking) beings, directly challenging the overextension of human rights discourse and its related reconstitution as a language of global corporate desire.

8

Embodied Vulnerability and the Limits of Privatisation: Reconsidering Property and Human Rights

Introduction

The argument thus far has two key implications for legal disputes concerning human rights claims. First, in relation to corporations, utilising embodied vulnerability as the foundation of human rights would indicate that corporations should not be accepted as an appropriate human rights beneficiary or be viewed as a human rights victim. That argument was explicitly made in Chapter 2, in the context of addressing arguments made by Addo in favour of corporate human rights, but is strongly supported by the arguments offered in Chapter 7 concerning the centrality of embodied vulnerability to the UDHR paradigm and its role in the reformulation of international human rights subjectivity. Secondly, embodied vulnerability as the foundation of human rights suggests that in human rights litigation, or litigation that includes a human rights claim or dimension, embodied vulnerability should play a decisive role in determining what is at stake between the parties. This second point will be more fully explored in this chapter. But in order to make the argument complete, it is necessary to address the relationship between property and human rights.

Property and the bifurcation of human rights discourse

In the earlier chapters of this book we introduced certain closures, often the target of critical theorists, related to the liberal construction of the legal person, and in particular, the sense in which persons and property, in liberal theory, emerge as mutually constitutive categories – so intimate is the ideological relationship between legal rights subjectivity and property ideology.[1] The problem of liberal legal closure arguably becomes more intense in relation to international human rights as human rights themselves become more technical and positivistic. In other words, the more that human rights become internalised by law the more they become subject to the disciplinary closures (both analytical and ideological) of legal and judicial reasoning. As this happens, there is a sense in which human rights as 'positive' law become further removed from human rights as a supra-legal category expressing a critical humanitarian concern for embodied human beings. In that sense, human rights become less able to critique law in the name of a human rights ethic. Douzinas has commented, driving at this, that with the 'extensive positivisation of human rights... the external division between legal and human rights has been replicated in the body of human rights themselves'.[2] This is a factor adding yet another dimension of complexity to human rights analysis, but this rupture between human rights as critique and human rights as law opens a space in which a redirected human rights ethics centred on embodied vulnerability may do some important critical work.

Human rights, as has been argued in this book, have always been paradoxical at best. Indeed, we have seen that human rights seem so fractured by ambivalence that we can speak meaningfully of their bifurcation into two distinct notions: 'modern' and 'contemporary', as Baxi has argued.[3] It should be noted that property played, and continues to play, a central and complex role in this bifurcation. In particular, the modern notion of human rights focally concerns an exclusory construction of property relations serving a quintessentially P3 human rights subject, as was argued earlier. One well-known line of criticism of human rights reflects the fact that the first development of the idea of 'subjective right' developed out of the idea of legal dominance over property.[4] A related line of criticism characterises human rights as *inherently* concerned with the ideological privileging of property interests, or as the very embodiment of 'an exclusionary conception of autonomy'.[5] On the other hand, a contrasting perspective on the relationship between property and human rights is reflected in the fact that it has often been assumed that human rights and property serve contrasting, or inherently contradictory, ends[6] – that human rights, in other words, are an inherently inclusory discourse, while property tends to be inherently exclusory. However, matters are even more complex than this. The truth of the matter is that while property is *predominantly* constructed as exclusory, and while human rights discourse is *putatively* inclusory, both discourses are in fact, normatively and interpretively open to contradictory constructions of their nature.[7]

It is especially important, however, to interrogate the nature of property in relation to human rights claims. In practice, human rights considerations seem to be most often outweighed by an assertion of property rights – either as a countervailing human right, or as a private law right. How we conceptualise property has, therefore, an important role to play in any argument concerning the redirection of human rights towards the foundation of human embodied vulnerability.

Property has played a central role in this book thus far, in various ways. We have seen that property is inescapably implicated in the ideological structuring of liberal law. Property is fundamental, for example, to the construction of the 'legitimated' forms of social and economic exclusion discussed in the early chapters of this book. We have already seen that the traditional liberal reading of property rights is inseparably linked to the privileging of the liberal legal subject and to that subject's dominant construction as bounded, atomistic and autonomous;[8] to the abstract quasi-disembodiment of the liberal subject of human rights;[9] to the related dominance of the P3 legal actor for whom the corporation is an almost perfect match;[10] to the ideological production of the criminal legal subject designed to protect the emergent interests of a rising capitalist propertied class in the nineteenth century in England and America;[11] to the simultaneous co-production of the corporate person in America;[12] to the influence of the changing needs of the dominant economic class that decided the fortunes of various theories of the corporation;[13] as well as to the wholesale exploitation by corporations of the American Bill of Rights.[14]

The links between an exclusory property right and the assertion of identifiable class interests are further reflected in the decisive and highly significant moment in which emergent capitalism redefined property rights in the enclosure movements. The poor were excluded from land previously held as commons, a moment that arguably reflects the focally embodied implications of the replacement of traditional values with capitalist competitiveness and its related economic imperative.[15] This problematically exclusory construction of property,[16] as we shall see, has a haunting contemporary and future relevance in relation to the 'propertisation' of water.

Property, despite its profound imbrication with exclusory liberal constructions, is a right of considerable complexity in the human rights context. While the UDHR undoubtedly has a continuing, intimate and problematic relationship with liberal legalism and its operative closures, it should be noted that while Article 17 of the UDHR endows 'everyone' with the 'right to hold property, alone or in association with others' that, while other rights in the UDHR are further elaborated in the ICCPR and the ICESCR, the right to property finds no further elaboration in these two covenants.[17] This in interesting, and perhaps signals a certain ambivalence concerning property rights in relation to the inherently more distributive concerns underlying socio-economic rights.

Given the deleterious implications for human beings of the uncritical elevation of the liberal private property right, any consideration of the role of embodied vulnerability in the context of human rights analysis must address directly the nature and role of property. Accordingly, this chapter will now explore the general possibility of reconceptualising property along lines more hospitable to the priority of embodied vulnerability as being the foundation of human rights. It will then consider how embodied vulnerability might, in practice, inform reasoning in relation to human rights claims when the interests of embodied vulnerable people or communities are confronted by private property interests, and the complexities that arise in such cases.

Property: A contested concept under increasing pressure[18]

Introductory reflections

The complexities surrounding property can, in part, be linked to a challenging confluence of factors both analytical and ideological. We shall shortly examine an important distinction between 'excludability' as an analytical component of the property right, and 'exclusion' – a recurring theme common to various ideological critiques of property. But it is worth pausing first to note that the tensions surrounding the property notion are, if anything, escalating. Property is a site of intense and growing contestation, particularly in the context of land and water rights – sites of legal interaction with a profound link to embodiment and to the mediation of relationships in material space.

In broad terms we can identify two kinds of tensions – tensions that are often thought of as being 'external' to property. The first is the pressure on property from environmental concerns. The second is pressure on property from human rights-orientated concerns. However, both these 'external' factors could, of course, and perhaps should, be made 'internal' to the property right as a strategic normative matter in a reconstituted theory of property – something we shall reflect on at various points in this chapter.

Environmental pressure on property relations

It is increasingly clear that reflection upon rights in relation to property (human rights or private law rights), especially rights relating to land and natural resources, cannot realistically avoid taking into account the environment. It is an obvious point, but one frequently overlooked in legal property discourse, that human beings cannot ultimately be separated from their environment. A core implication of our embodied materiality is that the environment is the inescapable, material location of our very existence. Our embodied existence is, moreover, as has been argued, inescapably intercorporeal – fundamentally interrelational. There is a sense in which the environment itself, along with us, possesses a distinctive ontic vulnerability and in which environmental vulnerability and human vulnerability are radically interrelated.[19] Not only do we, as human beings, share an essential interconnectedness as persons, but we are unavoidably emplaced within, and co-constituted with, the 'landscapes' or 'spaces' that we inhabit, in their social, discursive[20] and material dimensions. Serious reflection on human rights understood in such a way leads inevitably to reflection on the environment, a point made all the clearer by our growing awareness of the complex effects of globalisation and the pressures of climate change.

We understand, almost as never before, the radical continuities between our practices, the environment, and wellbeing. Indeed, the environment is part of our very existence as selves. We truly are intercorporeally enfolded with (to borrow Merleau-Ponty's language) the 'flesh' of the world:

> The environment is in immediate relation to me: there is no gap between us. In its totality (viewed as a microcosm or as a macrocosm) it mediates life and death, health and danger, joy and despair, imagery and companionship. We are set in it and we adapt to it, but we also adapt it to ourselves. Thinking of it in this way the image of the person-in-the-environment is dissolved by a relational, total-field image. The relationships between me and any other being are such that they belong to the basic definition of what we are. They are an essential component of what I am in myself.[21]

In short, taking embodied vulnerability and interrelationality seriously ultimately requires us to locate human rights discourse within a broader matrix of concerns reflecting ontic vulnerability and interrelationality as a more all-embracing theoretical discourse. This idea needs far fuller exploration and elucidation than space here permits. But it is worth stressing that human rights and environmental discourses share a set of profound commonalities beneath the undoubted complexity of their relationship.[22] Any reflection on the nature of the property right, whether conceived of as a human right or as ideologically oppositional to human rights (depending on one's starting points, definitions and commitments), will need, increasingly, to be placed alongside or within the matrix of environmental concerns and regulations. The complex relationship between human rights, property and the environment yields a plethora of debates and contestations that present rich possibilities for further theoretical exploration and elucidation.[23]

'Property v human rights'

In addition to pressure from environmental considerations, there exists another set of tensions suggesting a complex interplay between property and human rights. It has already been suggested that both the notion of property and the notion of human rights are inherently interpretively and normatively open, and that human rights concerns could be reconstituted as 'internal' to property discourse. At present, however, a set of identifiable and growing tensions in the law concerning access to land are predominantly characterised as being tensions *between* property and human rights. In this characterisation of their relationship, property is conceptualised as a predominantly exclusory discourse that stands challenged by human rights to civil and political *inclusion* conceived of as a *counter-discourse* to property.[24] Our reflections thus far, however, would lead us to conclude that the real conflict is between an *exclusory construction* of property and an *inclusory construction* of human rights. After all, we have seen, quite clearly, that human rights are not inherently inclusory and that, in their 'modern' formulation – the formulation so intimately linked to liberal capitalism and the construction of the P3 legal subject of rights – human rights are radically open to exclusory interpretations and applications. For the sake of clarification, therefore, the simple formulation 'property v human rights' will not be accepted as an accurate characterisation of the tensions in play – despite the widespread use of this language in the relevant academic work on the subject.

In short, human rights are ambivalent concepts. Property is also interpretively open, although its plausibility structures tend to be dominated by an exclusory formulation. The 'modern' exclusory notion of human rights (E/R) is inescapably linked to the exclusory formulation of the traditional private property right (E/P). Thus, the contemporary tension between property and human rights is more accurately understood as a tension between E/P and an inclusory construction of human rights (I/R). An alternative formulation of property (I/P) will be suggested below in order to produce a theoretical unity between I/P and I/R. This will be offered as a counter-conception to both E/R and E/P. In other words, it may be possible to articulate an I/P-I/R theory that suggests limits, as a normative matter, to be applied to the exclusory interpretation and application of property rights and human rights *alike*.

Human rights and property formulations	
E/R	Exclusory human rights formulation
E/P	Exclusory property formulation
I/R	Inclusory human rights formulation
I/P	Inclusory property formulation

i. The privatisation of public space

A particularly dense site of E/P v I/R contestation (arguably linked to the broader transnational trend towards privatisation and the partnership between the state and capital discussed in Chapter 1) is the phenomenon, especially marked in several leading common law jurisdictions, of the increasing tendency to privatise public space.[25] Much of the relevant academic writing focuses on this subject.

Turning to the nature of E/P, exclusion is – and has long been – a central theme in liberal Anglo-American common law conceptualisations of property. Firstly, the effective physical exclusion of persons from land was given a long-standing and central juris-generative role by the common law, which traditionally employed a pragmatic analysis of *de facto* exclusory power as the foundation from which it generated *de jure* entitlements. Such analysis raises at least three objections. First, there are potential philosophical objections to using an empirical assessment to found a normative claim. Normative arguments could be rallied in defence of empirically sustained possession as the foundation of a legal right – such as, for example, an argument that *de facto* exclusory control facilitated and was evidenced by stewardship and husbandry of the land in question rather than the visceral assertion of naked social power. But, in general, the traditional common law analysis presents a more prosaic reality implying, as Gray has argued, that '[i]n some deep sense the sustained exercise of exclusory power is perhaps all there really is to the grand claim of proprietary ownership'.[26] Secondly, the common law analysis seems uncritically to endorse existing power relations, irrespective of their potential injustice. Thirdly, it seems likely that such an analysis is ideologically linked to identifiable (and predictable) forms of social exclusion that are thereby legitimated.[27]

Exclusion has also been central to the common law in another sense – one that, for present purposes, lies closer to the disparity between E/P and I/R reflected in the increasingly difficult tensions between traditional liberal property discourse and the more inclusive concerns that tend to find articulation as 'human rights concerns'. The common law property right *once established* has long been given an exclusory construction archetypically expressed as the relatively arbitrary, almost unqualified power of exclusion that the possessor or owner of land could traditionally exercise – and, in the jurisdiction of England and Wales, still can. The common law property right has, therefore, an exclusory totalitarian potential – even though this has never been entirely absolute.[28] It is the continuing nature of the exclusory power of the private landowner that has given rise to particularly illustrative tensions in a range of common law jurisdictions concerning the private control of public space.

The E/P construction of property is under increasing pressure in this context. Gray and Gray have recently argued that the notion of property as being uncontrolled exclusory power is 'nowadays untenable', precisely because it threatens the more inclusory 'fundamental values of community and democracy'.[29] They continue:

> It may not be going too far to suggest that the theme of exclusion will bulk large in the social history of the next 20 or 30 years; that fairly huge outcomes will turn on whether we attribute continued vitality to the unqualified exclusory function of 'property' or choose instead to fashion our property thinking to accord with more inclusive, more integrative visions of social relationship.[30]

At stake in the E/P v I/R debate is the nature of society itself. It is increasingly apparent that 'contemporary society is witnessing a decline in the amount of space that can meaningfully be called "public"'.[31] This phenomenon results in an acute tension between the land owner's right to exclude and democratic interests in, for example, freedom of expression.[32] Not only are there issues concerning the question of unimpeded access to such space, but also an expanding set of concerns about the power of private landowners to control public behaviour.[33] While in many jurisdictions these more inclusory concerns find expression in the form of reasonable rights of access to quasi-public space,[34] of which the city-centre shopping complex is the ultimate example, in the jurisdiction of England and Wales the landowner/possessor's relatively unqualified exclusory power remains firmly installed in the cognitive structure of the common law. Accordingly, the jurisdiction makes a particularly salutary case study because it reveals, as it were, the inner logic of the liberal private property right in its traditional formulation.

City centres have special significance as sites of civic social interaction and participation. In the city-centre context, the traditionally conceived exclusory power of private landowners presents a genuine threat to social and civic inclusion and to the successful deployment of important civil and political rights.[35] In the jurisdiction of England and Wales the raw and revealing logic of the traditional exclusory common law formulation of the liberal property construct is reflected in the case of *CIN Properties Ltd v Rawlins*.[36] The result in that case effectively confirmed the power of a private corporate actor to, in effect, banish a group of citizens from the centre of their own home town – an exile with serious implications for their ability to gain employment and to participate in any way in the social and commercial relationships of their local civic life. Commenting on the implications of the case, Gray and Gray ask whether it can 'be the case that an insidious culture of exclusion – which has the potential to become a dominant social phenomenon of the years ahead – has already begun to take hold of us'.[37]

The *Rawlins* case centred on the Swansgate Shopping Centre in Wellingborough – a complex covering some 12 acres of space. The council had originally granted outline planning permission on condition that there was to be a complete pedestrianisation of the new shopping mall. CIN Properties built the centre, and were subsequently granted a lease for a term of 125 years. Clause 3(15)(b) of the lease included a covenant that the lessee should permit full pedestrian access to the common parts of the mall during certain specified hours. The defendants in the case were a group of young men who lived locally and often visited the mall. Gray and Gray point out that the majority of the young men were black and unemployed, and that the private security firm policing the space allegedly taunted the boys with names like 'chimpanzees' and tried to have them arrested for trivial matters such as whistling in public.[38] CIN alleged that the youths caused a nuisance and sent a solicitor's letter purporting to revoke their licence to enter the centre – banning them in perpetuity from entering 'for any reason whatsoever'.[39] A trial for public order offences against the youths failed. Later, when the youths continued to frequent the mall, CIN brought an action against them, seeking an injunction to enforce the privately imposed ban on entry. The defendants claimed that they had a right, in common with all other members of the public, to enter the centre. At first instance, the Recorder found that the defendants did have, as members of the public, an equitable licence to use the malls, but that the licence was revocable for good reason. On appeal, however, this argument was not accepted. The case was remitted back to the county court to be continued on the basis that CIN had the right to determine any licence that the defendants might have to enter the shopping mall. This outcome effectively gave legal vindication to the right of a private corporate landowner 'to exile a group of citizens permanently from a sizeable portion of their own town'.[40] Accordingly, the case (which at the date of writing remains the leading authority on this issue) presents, in a raw form, the problematic implications of the traditional exclusory property right. There are a host of such cases across the common law world centring on precisely this problem. The jurisdiction of England and Wales, however, is distinguished by its retention of a more classical exclusory interpretation of the property right.[41]

As noted above, the *Rawlins* case raises troubling issues surrounding the potential control of private landowners over public access to quasi-public space and, accordingly, over the exercise of important rights of political expression.[42] It was argued in Chapter 7 that embodied vulnerability is presupposed by the rights of expression, assembly and protest. In the case of the private landowner's power of exclusion the presupposition of embodied vulnerability is rendered *focal*, since the root of the power of exclusion rests on the affectability of the physical body and the ability obdurately to border social space precisely by exploiting this affectability. Law acts upon the body. The bordering of the world is profoundly dependent on the visibility and vulnerability of bodies, whether those borders are national borders or the more subtle borders of the socio-political and geographical spaces mediated by the rules of land law and tort. To unite these considerations with our earlier critical analysis of the inclusions and exclusions operative in the submerged P3 construct of liberal law, it is instructive to reflect on the ideological links between citizenship and property.

There is strong evidence to suggest that full civic inclusion and property rights are ideologically coupled. Green, for example, has argued that a study of the idealised landowner/citizen construct of liberal law reveals an intimate connection between 'private' land ownership and 'public' citizenship. This argument gains immediate plausibility from the fact that the right to vote, for a long time, actually rested on land ownership.[43] The historical intertwining of active citizenship with private property ownership suggests their mutual operation as gateways of inclusion and exclusion.[44] It is not too difficult, moreover, to discern in this linkage the privileging of the P3 legal actor. Green's reading of adverse possession claims in the traditional law of unregistered title reveals radical (and unsurprising) continuities with P3. For, Green's analysis reveals the construct of an 'ideal English landowner' who is also 'the citizen'.[45] The contours of this construct emerge from Green's analysis as '...an adult Anglo-Saxon male, and at least of average mental and physical competence. He is the heterosexual father of the family. He sees himself as a free and rational individual who makes a permanent mark on the world'.[46] The landowner/citizen, moreover, invests his physical, intellectual and emotional energies in the land – his bounded autonomous self reflected precisely by his assertion of exclusive control over the land within his boundaries.[47]

It is highly significant that the characteristics of the ideal landowner as a permanent, rational and self-interested countryman precisely match those of the ideal citizen – and the two constructs are in fact, one. The ideal citizen is traditionally the same person as the landowner – 'the man with a fixed stake in his country'.[48] Moreover, the traditional liberal 'citizen' and the 'ideal landowner' perform the same function. Both operate as gateway concepts reflecting the primacy of P3 legal subjectivity, determining, by corollary, the familiar legal outsiders univocally identified by critical theorists, including those theorists addressing the exclusions operative in international human rights law. And, although the direct link between land ownership and active citizenship was eventually severed by the granting of suffrage to non-landowners, the link persists at a submerged level,[49] just as the analysis thus far in this book would lead us to expect.

The decisive and continuing importance of the notions of landowner and citizen as interconnected gateways of inclusion and exclusion rests, in significant part, on the inescapability of land and its primal relationship with our basic embodiment. This, in turn, relates to our sense of location and dislocation, both social and geographical. The nature of our social participation – expressed through our physical presence in civic spaces, or attenuated by our physical exclusion from such spaces – reflects the almost visceral sense in which law acts on the embodied speaking human subject, sculpting the nature and shape of the political community in the process. An appreciation of the link between land ownership and citizenship, and the ideological pattern of their imbrication, opens up renewed understanding of the depth of the abuse visited on the embodied being in acts of exclusion. The abuse suffered by the excluded, whether the refugee as the archetypical 'external outsider', who represents the brutal lacuna at the heart of international human rights law, or the citizen relegated to a secondary place as in 'internal outsider' in the face of the landowner/citizen's legal privilege of exclusionary power, reflects the disruption of an embodied relationship with land as 'space' or 'place', and the particular vulnerability that can flow from this.

Our human ontology means that we are always and everywhere embodied, a fact rendering our relationship with physical space a decisive aspect of our interrelationality with each other and the world. Turner, relying on Heidegger,[50] takes this one step further, arguing that 'emplacement' – a notion reflecting the temporality of being in space, *located* (*'Dasein' or 'there-being'*) – is crucial to our sense of human identity, continuity and security. He suggests that the disconnection of body and place, the disruption our sense of place through our physical removal by force, whether as a result of exile, deportation, land seizure, or imprisonment, is an archetypal human rights abuse.[51] The permanent exile of a group of citizens (non-idealised citizens who do not fit the P3 template) from their own town centre in *Rawlins*, read through such critique, stands revealed as a profound exclusion the socio-political significance of which extends beyond mere embodied exclusion. The exclusion, however, is nonetheless radically dependent upon embodied vulnerability. The dilemmas attending the privatisation of public space highlight, in yet another context, the centrality of embodied vulnerability as the ontic foundation of our political and legal lives. This demands that we give fuller attention to the potential role of embodied vulnerability in legal and political theory more generally. In this light, the relationship between embodiment and land, and between embodiment and space, is rendered central to an adequate theory of human rights – placing the need for renewed engagement with the meaning of the property right in a new and critical normative context.

ii. Access to rural space

In the jurisdiction of England and Wales, the relatively recent Countryside and Rights of Way Act 2000 can be understood as a limited acknowledgement that the traditional conception of a landowner's power of territorial exclusion is inappropriate to large areas of rural space,[52] even in this archetypically exclusory common law property jurisdiction. The most interesting aspect of the Act, for present purposes, is the reasoning behind it in relation to 'social equity',[53] and the fact that the Act is explicitly directed at 'improving public health and reducing social divisions'.[54] The incipient discourse underlying such considerations is arguably one of *embodied inclusion*. The links drawn between access to rural space, the enjoyment of the rural environment and the inclusive logic of social equity place freedom of embodied presence on the landscape centre-stage in an intimate relationship with participatory concerns. Furthermore, the logic behind the Act implies the influence of distributive justice values related to access issues. The Act raises, albeit in a muted way, the radical interconnection between human rights issues and environmental issues noted earlier. In turn, this interconnection hinges, on the relationship between rural landscapes, access, embodiment and wellbeing. This nascent discourse is also arguably reflected in the Marine and Coastal Access Bill 2008, one of the key aims of which is the provision of a long distance route around the coast of England with public access for recreational purposes, especially walking. It may not be going too far to suggest that it is possible to discern, in the form of these developments, the rather tentative emergence of a different kind of discourse in relation to rural spaces and the common law property construct – a context-sensitive gradation of the application of the private property right.

Re-imagining property as a claim for access and inclusion seems essential to creating a future in which the notions of citizenship and access to (and use of) land can converge in non-exclusory forms, forms more likely to be consistent with an inclusory formulation of human rights. The Countryside and Rights of Way Act, and the reasoning behind it, appear to conceptualise the citizen as a human being with an embodied and primal need for physical access to land in the form of scenic space, and to relate that to a notion of physical and social health linked to social equality. It is clear that access to scenic space is understood to have a direct relationship with the reduction of social divisions. In short, it seems possible to discern not only the embryonic stirrings of an inclusive vision of the citizen in psychological terms and one that presupposes the role of embodied vulnerability – but also a related and more nuanced, context-sensitive formulation of the private property right itself. The traditional exclusory land owner/citizen construct identified by Green seems internally dislocated, albeit minimally as yet, by a re-conceptualisation of the relationship *between* landowners and citizens.

Equality of inclusion in rural space represents, moreover, a particularly critical incursion into the legal ideology that has traditionally elevated the characteristics of the P3 legal actor as being the quintessential liberal legal subject. It is highly significant that Green's analysis of the ideal landowner/citizen places him within an idealised cartography of rural England, located in a mythical golden age.[55] This location, moreover, is in no sense random. For, according to Rennie Short:

> [a]t its simplest the countryside becomes the image of the country, indeed the 'country' has the double meaning of 'rural land' and 'native land'. It becomes the scene of national harmony, peace and stability ...

> the countryside has become the embodiment of the nation ... a combination of nature and culture which best represents the nation-state.[56]

This peculiarly English manifestation and location of the idealised landowner/citizen/P3 liberal subject, and the predictable set of exclusions accompanying it, are amply reflected in the troubling contemporary reality of rural racism, a reality that relies on a continuing association between 'Englishness', rural land and whiteness.[57] This is clearly reflected, for example, in the magazine of the Campaign against Racism and Fascism[58] published in April/May 2001, which exposes the problematic ongoing and well-established connection between the idealised white English landowner, his ideological location and racial exclusion. In that magazine, Bark argues, in the context of exploring the extent of racist and nationalist feeling in the countryside, that:

> [g]enerally the flight from the city to rural areas has been well documented, and some (not only fascists) have called this a 'white flight'. When this is coupled with the very English 'love of tradition' in the form of romantic notions of Englishness and the English landscape constructed around the exclusion of 'others', there is a snowballing effect.[59]

In the same publication, the newsletter of the National Civil Rights Movement comments on an alarming rise in racist incidents in rural locations, suggesting that Home Office figures at the time revealed a 358 per cent increase in reported racist incidents in Devon and Cornwall, the second highest in the country. In addition, the same publication notes that an *Observer* special national feature reported that racist attacks were ten times more likely to take place in rural as opposed to urban areas. A black person could well be the only one in a town of 25,000 people, and a black family may be the only one within a radius of 25 square miles in a rural location.[60]

These realities suggest the powerful contemporary significance of the hidden ideological exclusions present in the English relationship with land. The link between white P3 landowner/citizens and the ideological significance of rural location combines to engender in a corresponding social reflex, the real exclusion of black citizens in rural areas, designating them as outsiders identified by their embodied difference – an embodied difference that becomes an inevitable target for hate-crime. Unsurprisingly, the link between the P3 liberal construct and the process of 'othering' invoked by such exclusions in rural locations has been shown to be inescapably linked with the elevation of a white, heterosexual, masculinist norm from which the 'other' deviates.[61] Land, as much as law itself, emerges as a profoundly contested and highly significant medium of socio-political interaction in which the ideological privileging of the P3 liberal subject has ongoing relevance. The significance of such exclusory formulations of our relationship with land is underscored by the inescapability of our human embodiment and its implications concerning our inability ultimately to be disconnected from the embodied dimensions of place and space. In this light, the limited but significant stirring of a more inclusive notion of access to rural land, such as under Countryside and Rights of Way Act 2000, is a welcome sign of the potential emergence of an alternative discourse of equality, access and embodied life – even if, at this stage, its impact is rather muted. That Act, and the reasoning behind it, point, however, to the potential for developing a specifically embodiment-centred theory of civic inclusion – even in England and Wales.

Excludability and exclusion: Separating the analytical from the ideological

Liberal law and legal theory, as we have seen, have consistently submerged the full implications of human embodiment in order to construct a rationalistic scheme of justice based on the formal homologies between liberal subjects. That rationalism has also been revealed as central to the ideological protection of property interests. The conflict between E/P and I/R can only, it is suggested, be rendered less problematic if property itself is reconceptualised along such lines that will render it an inclusory I/P construct. However, before this important theoretical argument can be made, we must first identify the conceptually necessary element of 'excludability' in the property construct and separate it from its extension in the traditional forms of social exclusion identified here.

Private property, as we have seen, plays a central ideological role in liberal law and in the construction of the liberal legal subject. The complexities underlying the nature of the exclusions at stake in the private property construction, however, require us to draw a distinction between 'excludability'[62] – which is conceptually necessary to make sense of a 'property' claim at all[63] – and the overly-exclusive socio-legal application of the concept of excludability, exemplified archetypically in the traditional English common law which traditionally extends to the private property owner a theoretically near-absolute power of exclusion.[64] Analytical clarification of the difference between excludability and exclusion, accordingly, becomes important for separating the conceptually necessary incidents of a property claim from a problematic discourse of exclusion and control potentially at odds with countervailing, embodiment-centred human rights values. This analytical clarification will shortly prove useful in the context of assessing the nature of disputes concerning the human right to water.

Turning to this task, then, it is important to note that property is a complex, non-monolithic concept. There is no one single straightforward definition of property for all available purposes. For present purposes we will broadly define 'property' as a social and legal institution for organising human relationships concerning land and other things and resources, both in terms of their allocation and use.[65] Understood as such, property is a characteristic human institution. The impulse to 'propertise'[66] seems, in fact, innate: '[I]n one of the earliest phrases articulated by almost every human child, there lies the strongest affirmation of [the] internalised concern to appropriate. The phrase, "It's mine" is one of the earliest affirmations of our human concern to delineate "mine" from "yours", possibly as part of delineating "me" from "you" and "it"'.[67] (In this sense, the psychology of possession has a relatively obvious continuity with one particular reading of our embodiment).[68] At the simplest level, in order to say that something is 'mine', as distinct from 'yours', I must claim the power or the right to exclude you – conceptually at least – from some aspect of the particular relationship that I have with that thing. 'Mine' is defined as meaning 'not yours' – for relevant purposes, in this case, the attribution to me, as opposed to you, of the thing in question. Accordingly, 'excludability', or the ability to delineate or ring-fence the thing in question in some way or another, is a conceptually necessary feature of my property claim.

Before we examine the notion of excludability further, we should note two points. First, it is possible to imagine societies that have no property concept at all (although such societies are unknown in practice)[69] – societies for which excludability simply would not feature as an aspect of social organisation.[70] It is also possible to imagine societies that have a social institution of property, but whose property concept does not encompass all things – for example, their relationship with land. The Aboriginals of Australia provide an example of a generally non-exclusory relationship with land, providing a direct contrast with the conventional liberal legal conception of a private property right over land.[71] These two points demonstrate that excludability is not a necessary feature of human social organisation, despite the fact that it is a conceptually necessary feature for a property relationship.

Gray has argued that excludability is analytically foundational to private property.[72] His work provides a very useful and detailed clarification enabling us to link property meaningfully to human rights and embodied vulnerability. An embodiment-centred reading of human rights can be conceptualised, in the light of Gray's analysis, as forming a moral limit capable of contextualising and attenuating property claims. We should note that 'unpropertised' resources remain outside property, available for use and enjoyment by all.[73] Critically, a resource can only be 'propertised' if it is 'excludable'; and a resource is only 'excludable' if it is 'feasible for a legal person to exercise regulatory control over the access of strangers to the various benefits inherent in the resource'.[74] This gives us a way of understanding what is conceptually necessary for a successful property claim – and a way of drawing nuanced distinctions between *types* of excludability. Thus, Gray argues that the notion of excludability 'imports a hidden structure of rules which critically define the legal phenomenon of private property',[75] and that a resource may be *non-excludable* for physical, legal or moral reasons. Importantly, a resource cannot be propertised if it lacks the quality of excludability on *any* of these grounds.[76]

Physical non-excludability 'arises where it is not possible or reasonably practicable to exclude strangers from access to the benefits of a particular resource in its existing form'.[77] The essence of this claim is that no one can claim property in a resource in respect of which it is physically unrealistic to hope to exercise consistent, long-term control over access. For example, in the illustrative case chosen by Gray, *Victoria Park Racing*,[78] the plaintiff attempted to prevent races and starting prices being radio-broadcast by the defendant, who observed the racecourse from a raised wooden platform on neighbouring land and announced the races and starting prices for unauthorised off-course betting purposes. The plaintiff's claim failed, among other reasons, because of his failure to prevent 'visual intrusion' on the land using physical means. Accordingly, the particular resource at stake, 'the spectacle', was, at the time the case arose for determination, *physically non-excludable*.[79] *Legal non-excludability* concerns an analogous failure successfully to use legal means to protect a resource from strangers, using, for example, intellectual property rules or protective contractual terms.[80] The crucial issue is whether the claimant has managed to call into play the relevant legal trespassory rules,[81] to protect his claim in relation to the resource in question, thus delineating and asserting legal excludability.[82]

Moral non-excludability reveals, Gray argues, the moral limits to property. These moral limits, moreover, often concern values centring on human wellbeing and flourishing – issues close to the heart of human rights discourse:

> [C]laims of 'property' may sometimes be overridden by the need to attain or further more highly rated social goals ... It is no accident that the goals to which 'property' defers often relate to fundamental human freedoms. It is in the definition of moral non-excludables that the law of property most closely approaches the law of human rights ... Moral non-excludables are essentially concerned with the furtherance of constructive interaction, purposive dialogue and decent (or 'moral') communal living.[83]

Moral non-excludability is arguably an especially important concept for it reflects a key interface at which exclusory liberal legal property conceptualism comes into direct tension with countervailing values of inclusion, distributive justice, participatory norms, the needs of embodied human beings and the environment. In other words, it is in the notion of moral excludability that we can locate and negotiate the boundary between E/P and I/R.

To the degree that it rests upon excludability, the liberal private property construct possesses a conceptually necessary feature of a property claim. However, the interpretation and application of excludability is frequently problematic in the liberal legal paradigm. We have already seen this exemplified through our brief consideration of the English common law management of law concerning land, which we used as an archetypical prism through which to reflect on the strong impulse in liberal property law towards a high degree of exclusory control which has been linked to a predictable set of social exclusions. These exclusions are still visible and operative, observable not just in the context of human relationships with land and the questions of access to civic and rural space, but in relation to human rights law more broadly, including international human rights law. This we saw in our study of critical accounts of exclusions operative in the UDHR paradigm in Chapter 5. Such exclusions, and their provenance in classical liberal capitalist ideology, have important continuities with neo-liberal discourse that continues to favour an exclusory property paradigm beneath the rhetoric of a market-driven world order. Arguably, the global ascendance of corporations is also reflected in the wholesale privatisation, corporatisation and commodification of municipal law and political culture. This is reflected, as we have seen, in the expanding corporate control of public space, facilitated by a transnational wave of privatisation. But it can also be seen, with intense clarity, in the intractable tensions surrounding water law, as we shall shortly see.

Given that E/P and I/R are in profound conflict in these and related arenas, and given the strong link between E/P and E/R in the modern human rights paradigm, it becomes important to determine how we might reconceptualise property as I/P and relate it to embodied vulnerability, in order to produce a property construct capable of being sensitive to I/R values. We shall briefly reflect on this before focusing on the human right to water as a particularly illuminative case study.

Re-imagining property: Inclusion, propriety and rights as 'what is due'

The legal frameworks governing property and human rights are both open, to differing degrees, to inclusory and exclusory impulses concerning our relationships with each other and the landscapes we inhabit – both literal and social. It has already been argued that property and human rights are normatively and interpretively open. This means that, despite the fact that both can be united by a set of exclusions that can meaningfully be read as continuous – both in historical and ideological terms – it is also possible to imagine reconceptualising property so as to render it theoretically harmonious with the inclusory human rights impulses that emerge from the 'contemporary' (I/R) notion of human rights (introduced in Chapter 5).

The idea of reconceptualising property as an inclusory notion is not a new one, although it is an idea that stands, as Gray has suggested, in need of revitalisation.[84]

Property as a claim for access and inclusion

While discussing the notion of 'equitable property', Gray revisits two theoretical examinations of the reconceptualisation of property which place a 'central emphasis on the need to ensure access to certain human goods as a vital precondition of securing freedom, dignity and the flourishing of the human spirit'.[85] The works in question are C.B. Macpherson's *The Political Theory of Possessive Individualism*,[86] and Charles Reich's seminal article 'The New Property'.[87]

Macpherson argues that in the seventeenth century certain key shifts in the conception of property took place. First, he suggests, property became primarily a thing rather than a right, and this reification of property was accompanied by the rise of a capitalist market economy and a related 'replacement of old limited rights in land and other valuable things by *virtually unlimited rights*'.[88] Secondly, Macpherson argues that the meaning of property was reduced to private property. This had the effect of obscuring the previously important concept of common property to the point where it 'drops virtually out of sight'.[89] So complete, indeed, was the conceptual movement towards the private property paradigm that common property became treated as 'a contradiction in terms'.[90] Thus, as Gray puts it, for Macpherson, there was a problematic tension between two

> opposed views of the institutional function of property. On one view, property comprises essentially a right to exclude strangers from privately owned resources while, on an older and more expansive view, property had once consisted of a right *not to be excluded* from participation in the goods of life.[91]

It is this tension that we urgently need to recapture and retheorise in the globalised context. To the degree that property is conceived of as being exclusively E/P it will almost inevitably obscure important I/R considerations that can be treated as external to the property right and, if history is any reliable guide, normally will be overborne by E/P interests. The theoretical usefulness of Macpherson's analysis is that it challenges the exclusory discourse of private property rights with an alternative inclusory discourse of community-orientated rights of access and participation – reimagining property itself in I/P terms. Interestingly, Gray notes that, in later writings, Macpherson links this challenge explicitly to the protection of human rights: 'Macpherson was later to contend that, without this reinvigoration of the property concept, we risk a disastrous contradiction of the "democratic concept of human rights"'.[92] Macpherson seems, in other words, to have attempted to reconceptualise property as I/P in order to render it as compatible, or continuous, with something analogous to or approaching an I/R conception of human rights.

Macpherson's vision suggests the usefulness of placing a greater emphasis on the rightful limitations on property rights emerging from a more explicit contextualisation of property rights within a broader matrix of complementary and competing justice-based considerations and to the wider social impact of property rights. There is, however, also merit in elevating the ideas of common and communitarian property to a higher status in our social consciousness. Such a shift that could serve a potentially important political and rhetorical role, in redirecting conceptions of property towards a more inclusive frame of social reference, turning the mind towards *non-individualistic* conceptions of property relations and reflecting the inescapable interrelationality of embodied life.

Macpherson, on this point, is accused by Harris of making an unwarranted analytical leap from the idea of 'common property' to 'the assertion that all universal rights to everything are property rights of individuals'.[93] It is not necessary to repeat this analytical leap, with its irreducible individualism, here. Common property, as a concept, should not be overextended. The idea of 'universal rights to everything', rather than suggesting individual property rights, suggests, if anything, the *absence* of property. For, if all have universal rights to everything, there is no sense in which property, in the sense of 'excludability', operates at all. Common property, understood in this sense, is not strictly a proprietary conception at all since common 'property' remains in the commons, available for use and enjoyment by all – inherently 'unpropertised'. A re-emphasis on common property however, could provide an important conceptual mechanism for the curtailment of over-extended exclusory claims by asserting, in effect, the *limits* of property in the face of other important interests. An emphasis on the 'commons', for example, has been used by commentators as an alternative counter-commodification strategy to human rights arguments in the context of natural resources in order to resist commodity-based property relations.[94] Such strategies need not obscure conceptually necessary aspects of excludability in the boundary function of property, but they do openly acknowledge the possibility and desirability of having property 'no-go' zones. The recovery of the idea of the commons forms, it is suggested, a vital part of the argumentative arsenal against the constant expansion of E/P claims and a crucial zone of protection for embodied life. This crucial notion is arguably, for example, what underlay, in intuitive terms, the resistance of the people of Bolivia to the privatisation of water. This particularly revealing case will be discussed further shortly, but we can note briefly that the simple refusal of the people of Bolivia to accept that water should be commodified in this way is arguably a clear instance of the notion of moral non-excludability in operation – an insistence that rainwater, at least, remain in the commons.

Harris, examining Macpherson's argument for the re-imagination of property, argues that Macpherson in essence invokes property as a label for certain aspirational inclusory rights.[95] For Harris, this strategy is mistaken, because, despite the apparent rhetorical advantage gained by the 'prestige'[96] accorded to 'property rights', the strategy is 'wholly implausible', precisely because, in modern consciousness, the rhetoric of human rights has more prestige than property. It may be the case that human rights discourse has more prestige than property. But it is clear from the arguments examined in this book that human rights discourse is profoundly ambivalent in its implications and that one significant strand of its discourse, intimately associated with the historically absolutist E/P conception of property, is profoundly inhospitable to I/R claims. In fact, the analysis here suggests that the E/R-E/P conception (with its conceptual intimacy with quasi-disembodiment, the P3 liberal legal person and the corporation) is the ultimate source of the openness of the UDHR paradigm to interpretive colonisation by the current commodified property-driven paradigm of global corporate capital interests.

Harris is therefore mistaken to criticise Macpherson on the ground that human rights discourse has more prestige than property discourse as a language for Macpherson's aspirational vision of inclusion and access. E/P is so foundational to E/R that its role needs to be made explicit, and then strategically reformulated – even if predominantly rhetorically – as a *property construct*. Given the unique status of property in liberal legal law and theory, it becomes essential to reticulate with property discourse *directly* and to make claims in the language of I/P *as well* as I/R. Accordingly, Macpherson's utilisation of property as a mechanism for making aspirational inclusory claims is perhaps more strategically vital now than ever it was. However, we should note that Macpherson criticises excessively individualistic conceptions of property in defence of the democratic concept of human rights. Yet his critique is uncritical in relation to the inherently contestable normative content of human rights themselves. Macpherson seems to assume something like an I/R conception of human rights. We know, however, that human rights are slippery, contestable, bifurcated constructs. As a result, there can be no simple assumed opposition between individualised property rights and human rights, as if property will *always* be E/P and human rights *always* I/R. Both property and human rights are normatively contestable and interpretively open. Both need addressing.

Macpherson's insight concerning the importance of placing an explicit emphasis on common and communitarian property has one particularly important virtue: it raises our awareness of the collective, distributive dimensions of property institutions and relations. Such a conception, moreover, sits well with an emphasis on our fundamental interrelationality and the nature of human embodiment. Although embodied vulnerability turns us most obviously to the human being as an embodied personality, and thus to our relationship with physical space and the natural resources upon which our survival and flourishing depend, the notion of inter-relationality, and the importance of embodied vulnerability, can also be used to reconceptualise the exclusory property zones erected around notionally 'virtual' spaces, such as zones of intellectual property law. These zones rarely, if ever, remain 'virtual' in their impact and consequences. Nothing in law will be inherently beyond the theoretical reach of an examination based on the centrality of embodied vulnerability. And arguably nothing propertised or propertisable will be inherently beyond the reach of reconceptualisation along I/P lines. Using the language of I/R alone to achieve this, or to challenge E/P, will fail to address adequately the overarching and decisive nature and role of property, in the construction, interpretation and application of law, including human rights law.

Reich's argument supporting the recognition of a 'new property' involves the application of protections traditionally accorded to older property forms to modern entitlements, embracing such things as welfare payments, pensions, salaries, licences, and subsidies. Despite disappointments in relation to the unfolding of his vision for 'new property' which could embrace such interests, Gray points out that Reich is 'an unreconstructed Reichian'[97] who would expand the scope of his 'new property' to include even environmental rights.[98] Again, this is an important analytical application of the property construct. Harris believes that it is entirely possible to 'support any or all of Reich's remedial proposals without any expansion in the concept of property'.[99] Without moving beyond the scope of this chapter to consider the analytical structure of property in depth, it seems relatively safe to endorse Reich's call for an the extension of the kinds of interests that property can be taken to protect. Such a call makes a strong intuitive appeal to inclusory justice. Moreover, including environmental rights within property discourse along I/P lines seems a vital element in reconceptualising the relationship between human rights and the environment – an important and often overlooked aspect of the battle for human rights meanings.

Property as 'propriety' and rights as 'What is Due'

Gray and Gray have argued that 'property' is a 'spectrum concept'.[100] In their view, the allocation of socially approved user power represented in someone's 'property' in a resource crucially depends, in the final analysis, 'upon collective perceptions of the social permissibility or public merit attributable to various kinds of competing user of the resource in question'. Accordingly, '[i]n this way a deep sub-text of 'propriety' has always pervaded the social and legal definition of 'property'.[101]

Arguably, this vision of property brings us almost full-circle to our earlier considerations in relation to the question of moral excludability as being the point at which property notions most closely approach human rights. It also seems to represents a site at which cross-currents of inclusion and exclusion could shift their balance in relation to each other. Property, conceptualised as propriety in relation to the allocation of socially valuable access to resources and as a right to participatory inclusion in the goods of life, provides, it is suggested, a most conducive theoretical foundation for importing more explicitly inclusory concerns into legal thought about property. Moreover, the notion of propriety seems to relate closely to the conception of rights as being 'what is due' in terms of the just outcomes in any co-ordination challenges or conflicts of interests between persons or social groups in relation to valuable goods or resources – in other words, to an I/R formulation and theorisation of human rights. An emphasis on rights as being 'what is due' arguably facilitates an important conceptual shift towards a potentially collective, justice-based context for rights-claims. The conception of rights as 'what is due' has the advantage of providing a relatively clear theoretical link between I/R and the notion of property as I/P.

Finnis, in *Natural Law and Natural Rights*,[102] has argued that the language of rights is treated by those who use it in the context of assessing the justice of law as being a claim in relation to the value of certain freedoms and benefits considered to be foundational to the maintenance of the life, security, development and dignity of the human individual. For Finnis, the core notion of rights underlying such formulations is the notion of fundamental or basic needs – or, as Finnis prefers, 'basic aspects of human flourishing'.[103] Finnis suggests, that

> [i]n short, the modern vocabulary and grammar of rights is a many-faceted instrument for reporting and asserting the requirements or other implications of a relationship of justice *from the point of view of the person(s) who benefit(s) from* that relationship.[104]

The relationship between rights as what is due in the interests of justice, and human well-being in relation to fundamental needs, sits in obvious relationship with the notion of human embodied vulnerability. As argued in Chapter 6, our needs and multiple forms of human flourishing stem from our embodied nature and its affectability. We can further finesse Finnis's expression and argue that human rights are *what is due, in justice, to embodied vulnerable human beings* – and that legal human rights are, in this light, the jural instantiations of what is due, in justice, to embodied vulnerable human beings. This I/R conception (a conception that, while it operates from the beneficiary or 'victim' viewpoint', does not intrinsically excise the rights of others, the notion of responsibility or the notion of social or environmental context) can be intimately related to the notion of property as propriety – a notion in which property is radically contextualised by social and environmental context, collective considerations and the implications of our collective and individual embodied vulnerability.

Although Finnis goes on to suggest that the modern conception of rights is more subtle than the pre-modern sense of rights as being 'what is due', it seems important to recapture something of the incipient inclusory emphasis in the earlier formulation. Emphasising or re-invigorating the notion of rights as being 'what is due' in the context of common ontic vulnerability, with its complex sets of associated needs and modes of flourishing, re-orientates rights consciousness towards the shared moral space within which law mediates our various (sometimes conflicting) interests. By adopting this reorientation, we can achieve a vital justice-based contextualisation of rights claims without sacrificing the analytical utility of the 'differentiation and precision'[105] provided by modern rights-talk with its conceptual distinction drawn between rights and duties. A conception of rights as being 'what is due' arguably more closely links rights to both a wider pattern of justice and to the idea of related responsibilities or duties – thus addressing the problem of any inappropriate[106] over-emphasis on rights as being over-individualised exclusory demands. In short, rights as 'what is due' seems to direct rights discourse towards a framework of analysis naturally quite amenable to inclusive, community-oriented values. In the light of the ever present reality of exclusory constructions of rights, the very real dangers of self-interest (particularly democratically unaccountable private corporate self-interest), and the much lamented tendency for rights-talk to disintegrate into atomised (increasingly consumerist and trivialised[107]) formulations, a re-discovery and re-theorisation of rights as 'what is due' (and human rights as what is due, in justice, to embodied vulnerable human beings) seems urgent. The normative content of rights (the normative content of 'what is due'), is, of course, still inherently open. But notwithstanding this, it is suggested that a reorientation of human rights discourse along the lines discussed here will tend quite naturally to lift the focus of rights-talk away from individual demands and an E/R formulation towards a wider context and an I/R formulation.

The theoretical correlation between property as propriety and rights as 'what is due' supports the argument that both property and human rights are mutually capable of embracing more inclusory concerns. However, the ever-present problem of exclusory constructions of both property and human rights suggests that neither is free from continually shifting ideological cross-currents between exclusory and inclusory impulses. This ideological contestation between inclusion and exclusion is profoundly important. Inclusion is far more than an ideal. It is arguably a foundational normative pre-condition for the democratic legitimacy of political systems and, arguably, of law itself.[108] Given the harmful effects of neo-liberal globalisation and a transnational wave of privatisation, inclusion has never been a more compelling or urgent issue than it is today.

Even the private property construct itself, when cast in this light, can and should be seen as a nuanced, context-sensitive, graded conception – one, moreover, with a direct relationship to embodied vulnerability. For example, in relation to the traditionally undifferentiated nature of the common law property conception, one modest contribution to the task of rendering E/P property relations amenable to I/R based concerns would be the theorisation of a more context-sensitive, graded version of the private law property right, once granted. Meaningful distinctions can be drawn between a property owner's domestic space, privately owned 'public' spaces, and privately owned tracts of rural countryside. The right of exclusion in relation, for example, to the property owner's intimate domestic space has a direct relationship with the protection of the property owner's own embodied vulnerability, and the dignity and privacy related to that. Hence, it can be taken to support, in most cases, the normative acceptability of the application of excludability to protect this important, intimate space. By contrast, the case where a private landowner asserts the right to exclude others from vast tracts of rural land is less defensible on face value (though there may be other acceptable reasons for limitation where they apply, for example, on environmental grounds). The right of exclusion can, in other words, be nuanced and subjected to considerations relevant to the protection of embodied vulnerability and other important values (inclusive, human rights based, democratic, environmental) as appropriate. This I/R limit on E/P could, however, and perhaps should, be theorised as increasingly interior to the property concept, framing this more attenuated, context-sensitive application of excludability as an *I/P* conception: *property reformulated* as a right not to be excluded from important spaces, places, resources and goods.

A case study: The right to water

Bringing all of these considerations together, water offers a highly symbolic and instructive case study.[109] Water is a paradigm example, perhaps *the* paradigm example, of a realm where propertised and commodified relations concerning natural resources come into obvious conflict with human rights claims based on embodied vulnerability. Water is set, in some ways, to become the most symbolic and contested battleground, between E/P-E/R and I/R, and arguably presents a clear case of a resource ripe for an I/P reimagination of the property relations clustered around it. Contestation over the right to water, in fact, can be conceptualised as the ultimate 'frontier issue', the most decisive interface between the logic of economic rationality in a globalised world economy, and a logic based on embodiment-centred human rights impulses. Water presents a 'rhetorically and symbolically powerful... threshold to defend against ever-encroaching commodification and the spread of economic rationality',[110] possessing a 'symbolic resonance'[111] that perhaps no other natural resource invokes to the same degree. The right to water's iconic status in relation to battles over the discursive formation of human rights discourse as it comes into direct contact with commodified market logic – arguably the fundamental issue invoked by Baxi's thesis concerning the interpretive distortion of the UDHR paradigm in the context of globalisation – makes it the most instructive available case study. Indeed, many regard water as being the site of an 'intuitive "last bastion" against privatisation'.[112]

Water is particularly apt in the context of the concerns of the present book because it is primarily at the international or global level that problems associated with water rights, access, distribution, management, control and so forth most clearly arise. It is at the international level that the controversy over private sector involvement in water service delivery reaches a pitch of fierce intensity. In the context of globalisation, the closely related problem of north-south distributional justice takes political centre-stage. Morgan comments that, in the light of existing market inequalities between the global south and north, water serves to draw attention to such inequalities in a particularly focused way.[113] In her view, the disputation over water, in a central and important sense, is ultimately linked to the wider issue of placing appropriate limits on capitalism itself.[114] In fact, currently, just three transnational corporations effectively dominate the entire global water market, providing water services to 300 million individuals in over 200 countries. This reflects the emergence of an increasingly integrated global water regime in which public aid supplements private sector investment by multinational corporations.[115]

Arguably, no case is more instructive or symbolic than the notorious *Bechtel v Bolivia* case, already touched upon above. That case clearly suggests an inherent relationship between water supply and embodied vulnerability, and a related tension between corporate commodification and embodiment-centred human rights discourse. In the late 1990s, under pressure from the World Bank which threatened to withhold debt relief and other development assistance, the government of Bolivia was forced to privatise the public water system of Cochabamba, the country's third largest city.[116] There was only one bidder for the contract, International Water, a consortium which included the Bechtel Corporation, a US based transnational corporation.[117] The consortium was granted a 40 year lease to take over the control of Cochabamba's water supply through a subsidiary, Aguas del Tunari.[118] Within a very short space of time, a matter of weeks, the subsidiary imposed water rate rises of more than 50 per cent on average. This meant that families living on the minimum wage were charged for up to 25 per cent of their monthly income for water alone.[119] Not only this, the legal framework meant that collecting rainwater became subject to a paid permit system – effectively making illegal the unpermitted collection of rainwater.[120] This state of affairs graphically reflects the systemically coherent but profoundly counter-intuitive outcome of the application of the untrammelled logic of corporate commodification to a contractual regulatory framework designed to control access to this most natural and basic of resources. Morgan argues that this outcome can perhaps best be understood as stemming from the interaction between two competing frameworks – one reflecting the idea that rainwater is quintessentially in the commons in an unmediated relationship with human beings, and the other, reflecting the idea that water is transmuted into a service susceptible to regulation by a technical infrastructure. Understood in this light, Morgan argues, from the point of view of the service provider, 'requiring a permit for rainwater collection may seem a normal part of an exclusivity clause in the regulatory framework'.[121]

Baxi's thesis arguably finds its ultimate epitome in this starkly illustrative case. The fact that the free collection of rainwater could be made subject to a contractual, commodity-based regulatory regime that effectively rendered the direct natural relationship between embodied human beings and rainwater subject to legal control (in effect, to propertisation through the application of legal excludability) betrays the genuine danger to human beings and communities of the dominance of commodified, corporation-serving logic in international legal discourse. Such logic reaches conclusions profoundly antithetical to human embodied survival and flourishing – even, in some cases, resulting in outbreaks of disease and widespread death.[122] International human rights discourse, to the degree that it internalises the globalised logics of commodification, becomes colonised, in effect, by a logic that knows no inherent or internal limit to its potentially destructive or even fatal impact upon embodied vulnerable human beings. The longstanding bifurcation of human rights discourse that we have identified takes on, in such a light, particularly destructive and hyper-extended implications. It becomes virtually synonymous with a commercial discourse having the potential to constitute a thanato-discourse in which the pursuit of profit fully obscures embodied vulnerability and all of its juridico-ethical implications.

One way of understanding the mass street protests that this counter-intuitive legal position produced in Bolivia is that they embodied a clash between the cold, untrammelled economic logic of commodification and a countervailing visceral response fully reflecting human embodied vulnerability and the related intuition that water, particularly rainwater, should be morally non-excludable. Despite the fact that the rather stark discursive dichotomy between perceptions of water as a 'commodity' and water as a 'human right' implied by such an observation is by no means straightforward in the context of the emergent regulatory framework of global water welfarism, the underlying conflict remains clear at the conceptual level. Admittedly, in the context of regulatory frameworks the underlying conflict between the logics of commodification and embodiment-centred human rights impulses becomes more complex and frequently less dichotomous. For, amongst other things, they are mediated by shifting assumptions, practices of routinisation, and a dense network of legislative and regulatory rules and practices that make analysis truly challenging.[123] Nevertheless, it is clear that the intuitive bottom-line remains a rather intractable clash – one that is centred on the dissonance between commodification and embodied vulnerability.

Revealingly, and reflective of arguments concerning the selective hollowing out of the role of the state in the globalised context discussed in Chapter 1, the Bolivian government, faced by widespread popular protests, took the side of the corporation, declaring martial law and deploying repressive police power against the protestors. The potent symbolism of the might of state power summoned against the bodies of human beings protesting, bodily, in incarnate, visceral, physically expressed outrage at the unfairness of the regulatory scheme, could not be more instructive. State power, which focally relies on bio-power as Foucault so compelling argued,[124] fundamentally exploits the affectability of bodies – their inherent vulnerability. In this case, embodied vulnerability was exploited by state coercion in the service of private corporate interests as the police (armoured by riot gear and weapons) bore down on the assembled protestors. In the event, more than 100 protestors were injured, and one boy was killed.[125] In the end, again revealing the inescapable importance of embodiment to politics, the protestors made the material situation so uncomfortable and dangerous that the corporation's management abandoned the project. However, Bechtel retaliated by filing a claim with the International Centre for the Settlement of Investment Disputes, a part of the World Bank Group, seeking damages from the Bolivian government. Again, a legally decisive contrast between the disembodiment of corporations and the embodiment of human beings is captured in this tale. For the corporation, as a jural entity for which borders are ultimately porous in a globalised world system, exploited its advantage by establishing a 'post office box presence' in the Netherlands – a country, which unlike the US, had a bilateral investment treaty with Bolivia. Anderson and Grusky comment that '[e]ven the Dutch government was ambivalent about whether the corporate shell created by Bechtel should be entitled to take advantage of the treaty, but the ICSID tribunal accepted jurisdiction anyway'.[126] The acceptance of the 'corporate shell', an effortless jurisdictional extension of the disembodied corporate form, as the basis for asserting jurisdiction amply reflects a facet of the pivotal distinction between corporations and human beings that forms a central part of the argument of this book.

Embodied vulnerability, water, and corporate responsibility: Signs of embodiment-centred jurisprudence?

Of all of the countries in the world, South Africa presents the most salient context for exploring the potential role of embodied vulnerability in relation to water rights. This is because South Africa, almost uniquely, has made a formal constitutional commitment to enshrining a human right to water – presenting, as Morgan has argued, a 'formal opportunity, rarely present in cross-national terms, for human rights to balance commodification'.[127] Additionally, South Africa presents a context in which political resistance to the structures of neo-liberal globalisation can, again uniquely perhaps, draw on a strong national political will to supplement and exploit the constitutional commitment to a human right to water. This means, according to Morgan, that there is an opportunity for 'social movements to play a co-equal role with powerful market actors in debates over how markets should be embedded in political and social contexts'.[128] The strong commitment to human rights in the South African constitution is, however, set against a market-led strategy, embraced shortly after the ANC government came to power. This resulted in a legislative framework strongly influenced by the interests of international capitalism – and a concomitant seesawing between the needs of investors and the human rights dimension of water welfarism.[129]

Against this unique backdrop, then, it is invigorating to read the judgment of Tsoka, J. in the case of *Mazibuko v the City of Johannesburg*.[130] This case is particularly crucial because it demonstrates the way in which human rights discourse can be converted into a form of activism centred upon a legal fight for human rights meanings – as well as for the legal assertion of minimum human rights standards in the context of water commodification. The constitutional commitment of South Africa to a human right to water embodies, in this sense, a potent justice-based conception of water that promises a conceptualisation of the issue that is capable of forming a jurisprudential spearhead against the ruthless logic of market-based rights discourse. The case, before it was heard, was anticipated by Bond and Dugard for its potential to reveal 'how far constitutional and legal strategies can advance the decommercialisation and water rights-as-justice cause'.[131] The answer provided by the judgment, it seems, is that human rights-based arguments can form a very potent strand of critique indeed against overly trade and market-friendly conceptions. The decision suggests that the critical, inclusive strand of human rights energy is still capable, even in this globalised age, of delivering a robust critique to the closures now familiar to us. Moreover, it will be seen that this critical energy is sustained, fundamentally, by embodied vulnerability – even though that language was not used (as the case framed the issue as a combination of access to water and the right to human dignity).[132]

The background to the case was that, before 2001, all of the residents of Johannesburg, except the residents of the impoverished township of Phiri in Soweto, were entitled to an unlimited supply of water on credit. The residents of Phiri were only entitled to such supply at a flat rate. Johannesburg Water (the corporation delivering the commercialised water service) agreed in 2001 to provide every household in the City of Johannesburg with six kilolitres of free water per month per household or account holder. However, the resident's of Phiri were to have their free water dispensed by a prepayment meter system – and once the amount had been supplied, the supply would automatically be cut off. After that, the account holder would have to buy water credits for water until the next free entitlement accrued. The residents of the township were acknowledged by the court to be mostly poor, uneducated, unemployed and 'ravaged by HIV/AIDS'.[133] Mazibuko and five other applicants from the township of Phiri asked the court, among other things, to declare the disconnection of their unlimited water supply, and the installation, introduction and continued use of the pre-paid water meters, unlawful and unconstitutional[134] and to order that Johannesburg Water should provide everyone in Phiri with 50 cubic litres of water per day and provide the option of a metered supply to be installed at the cost of the City.[135] The applicants were supported by the Centre on Housing Rights and Evictions (COHRE) as *amicus curiae*.

The main substantive basis of the challenge to the prepayment meters and the policies of the water company was based on the constitutional commitment to the human right to water. The reasoning of the judge both reveals the centrality of the right to water to human rights as an entire category, and underlines, albeit without explicitly using the terminology, the fundamental basis of human rights in embodied vulnerability. The right to water was affirmed by Tsoka J. as being foundational to human rights, as 'a common denominator' and, in particular, as 'interconnected and interrelated' with socio-economic rights. This juridical elevation of the right to water parallels arguments in relation to the special place of water in conflicts concerning human rights discourse and the commodification of resources necessary to human survival and flourishing. Importantly, in the reasoning of Tsoka J., the pre-eminent role of the human right to water formed the indispensible interpretive context for his constitutional legal assessment of the introduction of the prepayment meters.[136]

Having established the foundational status of the right to water as a human right, the judge's reasoning moved seamlessly to an analysis of the discriminatory implications of the denial of the right to water – explicitly linked to the denial of 'the right to lead a dignified human existence'.[137] The linking of dignity and equality in the South African constitutional jurisprudence, as reflected in this element of the court's reasoning, is a familiar theme. Although dignity has often been criticised for its ambiguity,[138] or even vacuousness, as a concept it has nonetheless been vigorously defended, not least in the South African context, for its capacity to underpin an approach to equality that moves away from the rather empty formalism of liberalism to specify a substantive meaning to equality – one, moreover, that is capable of moving beyond individualism to embrace the important tension between individual and community needs.[139]

Dignity is, moreover, dependent, in analytical terms, on embodied vulnerability. The judge's reasoning, inescapably in the context of the case, reflects this. His reasoning in relation to the amount of water that should constitute the core substantive content of the human right to water employs embodiment and its ontic incidents, particularly vulnerability, at an almost axiomatic level. The judgment addresses, for example, the number of bodies in any given domestic space that can be sustained by the quantities of water at issue; the requirements for lavatory flushing; the relationship between climate, bodily function and dehydration; basic sanitation requirements; and the need for food to be washed. More specifically, the judgment discusses the role of water (related *explicitly* to dignity in this context) in the case of HIV/AIDS sufferers – such as in relation to food hygiene; the avoidance of disease transmission; the avoidance of skin infection; the taking of medicines; the ease of eating for those suffering from mouth ulcers or thrush; the mixing of baby formula; the required frequency of lavatory flushing in the terminal stages of the disease; soiling and laundry requirements and so on. All of these highly specific considerations point resolutely to the absolute dependence of the judicial arguments concerning dignity and the right to water upon an underlying (albeit unarticulated) conception of human embodiment and human vulnerability.[140] At paragraph 79 of the judgment the link between embodied vulnerability and dignity is most succinctly implicit. The potentially fatal implications of a commodified water discourse that fails to take embodied vulnerability into account is also made clear and given clear analytical weight in the same paragraph:

> To expect the applicants to restrict their water usage to compromise their health by limiting the number of toilet flushes in order to save water, is to deny them the right to health and to lead a dignified lifestyle. It is common cause that the people suffering from HIV/AIDS need more water than those not afflicted by the illness. Such persons require water regularly to wash themselves, drink, wash their clothes and cook. Their caregivers are also constantly expected to wash their hands. In this context waterborne sanitation is a matter of life and death.[141]

The judge declared both the forced installation of a prepayment water meter system and the pre-payment meter system used to be unconstitutional and unlawful, and he ordered that the residents of Phiri township be supplied with a free basic water supply of 50 cubic litres per person per day with the option of a metered supply installed at the cost of the City of Johannesburg. This outcome, and the analytical content of the reasoning in the judgment, arguably strike a unique jurisprudential blow in the battle for human rights meanings in the face of the commodification of water supplies. The judgment does so, in conceptual terms, by employing the twinned concepts of equality and dignity. But the reasoning makes it clear that dignity is, in the context of this case at least, radically dependent in analytical terms, upon the inescapability of human embodied vulnerability.

It is likely that the mutual reticulation between dignity, equality and vulnerability goes much further, in theoretical terms, than the circumstances of this particular case. For example, Fineman has recently presented a compelling theoretical argument linking equality to vulnerability. She has argued that equality needs to escape the formal limits that reflect the ideological commitments of liberal individualism (which has been linked in this book with quasi-disembodiment and the radical decontextualisation of the self). It needs to find expression as 'a universal resource... [and related to this] [w]e must begin to think of the state's commitment to equality as one rooted in an understanding of vulnerability'.[142] Fineman draws careful links between vulnerability and equality, claiming that she wants to employ the term 'vulnerability' for its potential to describe 'a universal, inevitable, enduring aspect of the human condition that must be at the heart of our concept of social and state responsibility'.[143] For Fineman, embracing vulnerability in this sense frees the notion from its limited and negative associations to produce a 'powerful conceptual tool' with the potential to provide a substantively rich and nuanced notion of equality.[144] Fineman's theoretical defence of the intimacy between vulnerability and the potential for a more inclusive and meaningful concept of equality can be linked, through reflections such as those contained in the South African equality discourse, to a defence of dignity; and dignity can, in turn, be linked to the notion of embodied vulnerability. Fineman clearly locates vulnerability in embodiment in terms profoundly continuous with the notion of embodied vulnerability employed in the present work,[145] emphasising, as was stressed in Chapter 6, the fact that embodied vulnerability is differentially experienced and that the differential experience of vulnerability is socially, economically and politically mediated.[146] She also, in terms compatible with Turner's work, endorses the idea of institutional vulnerability – arguing that the implications of this are that vulnerability, employed as a tool of theoretical analysis, needs to possess both institutional and individual components.[147] Importantly, one of the constructs rendered most problematic by the vulnerability thesis is the liberal subject. And, although Fineman does not explicitly say so, it is clear that one related implication of her thesis is the idea that the quasi-disembodiment of the liberal legal subject is rendered inadequate by a theory of embodied vulnerability. To insist on embodiment as the inescapable ground upon which vulnerability arises carries a set of related implications promising a far richer theorisation of the political and legal subject. For Fineman, the vulnerable subject is a 'more accurate and complete universal figure to place at the heart of social policy'.[148] When vulnerability is emphatically seen to arise from embodiment, and when bodies and their inherent openness and affectability are placed at the heart of the subject of human rights law, a quite different conception of the universal human rights subject emerges – one that necessitates a radical redirection of human rights reasoning and theorisation.

The case of the human right to water raises these theoretical issues with particular clarity. The reasoning in the South African constitutional case of *Mazibuko* implicitly invokes, it is suggested, a highly salient and promising link between equality, dignity and embodied vulnerability that suggests a rich seam for future theoretical exploration. Minimally, the case affirms that corporate social responsibility can be legally enforced and jurisprudentially justified by an analysis intimately related to, and analytically dependent upon, the undoubted centrality of embodied vulnerability to the human condition. It shows the jurisprudential scope for judicial interpretations of human rights meanings that render them a form of critique and resistance to the trade-related, market friendly conceptions to which they are increasingly in danger of becoming reduced to in our globalised world.

Concluding thoughts

It has been argued in this chapter that E/P has clear links to E/R – and that the conflict between the logics of exclusion (implicated in private property discourse, privatisation, corporatisation and commodification) and inclusory discourses emerging from embodiment-centred reactions to this can be understood, and often are, in E/P-E/R v I/R terms. In this sense, I/R forms a limit on the property concept. It operates as an instance of moral excludability, reflected in a countervailing I/R conception of human rights discourse. The *Mazibuko* case reflects just such a moral excludability. Physical excludability, combined with legal excludability, operated there as key elements of a propertised relation with the supply of water. But around the pre-payment meter scheme at issue in the case, and the denial of adequate free water supply, moral excludability broke down. This in turn led to a judicial redefinition, in effect, of the proper scope and application of physical and legal excludability to the resource-supply structure in question. The property right was re-applied, subject to a limit based on moral excludability, implicitly centred on embodied vulnerability operating as the foundation of dignity and inextricably linked with questions of substantive equality.

Another way of conceptualising the result in the *Mazibuko* case, however, would be to argue that the property right became more nuanced – that E/P was reconstituted in limited I/P terms to imply that a minimal core to the human right to water provided a reformulation of the property right itself. Irrespective of which of these two views is more satisfying in purely analytical terms, it is arguable that there is a clear strategic advantage to making property itself the site of an embodiment-centred reconceptualisation in rhetorical terms.

Moving beyond E/P, it has been argued by some that it is better to take resources of water beyond property constructs altogether, and to address the perceived shortcomings of the human right to water as a concept of resistance to privatisation by embracing a concept of the 'commons'.[149] This approach seems to rely on an essentially E/R characterisation of human rights, viewing them as individualistic, overly state-centric and compatible with the private sector provision of water supply. It also seems to rest on the idea that because of this, the human right to water presents 'a limited strategy for those seeking to refute water privatisation'.[150] However, the *Mazibuko* case suggests the strategic importance of *retaining* a human rights based critique of commodification and of E/P constructions of property relations. An I/R conception of human rights – preferably coupled with an I/P property conception, and with I/R and I/P theoretically established on a foundation of embodied vulnerability – has the virtue of direct reticulation with the central constructs of the dominant paradigm. While this permits a direct battle to take place over the discursive meanings of human rights and property, it by no means discounts or excludes the strategic importance of the role of a notion of a global commons. The notion of a global commons, in fact, adds an invigorating environmental dimension to the matrix of concerns involved – providing, for example, an alternative meaning the human right to life.[151] In fact, all of these argumentative strategies – the use of I/R, the potential for I/P and the role of a non-propertised commons – can be seen to rest on the global salience of vulnerability as an overarching theoretical construct. Understood in this way, the vulnerability thesis is capable of linking human rights and environmental concerns, and property rights and the notion of the commons, in a common theoretical framework.[152]

The brute fact is that, in the battle to protect vulnerable human beings against the perils and dangers of untrammelled corporate commodification, we need every strategic and rhetorical device at our disposal. We urgently need to redirect the language, discourse and theory of human rights – as well as human rights law reasoning – towards human embodied vulnerability. This, it is suggested, is now urgent in the light of far reaching and deleterious implications of the emergence of corporate legal humanity.

9
Some Brief Conclusory Thoughts and Future Research Directions

The compelling thesis, offered and defended by Baxi, that the UDHR paradigm is now, in effect, re-rendered as a paradigm of trade-related market-friendly human rights, is deeply troubling and has potentially very dark implications for the capacity of human rights discourse to protect human beings and communities in an age of increased vulnerability and risk. Moreover, this vulnerability most profoundly and negatively affects precisely those human beings and communities most in need of human rights protection – those least able, for social, political, physical, economic or other reasons to ameliorate the most serious aspects or implications of human embodied vulnerability, as we saw in the highly symbolic case of the human right to water in the last chapter.

In an age where corporate global dominance is widely accepted as a (for some, *the*) central reality of the contemporary global order, and where globalisation itself carries levels of unprecedented risk and presents a growing set of threats to human survival and flourishing, it seems a particularly serious mistake to conceptualise conglomerations of capital as human rights beneficiaries. Genuine dangers attend the corporate colonisation of the language and discourse of human rights, and it may be that the result is the eventual absence of any genuinely distinctive language or concept with which to protect vulnerable human beings and communities *from* such powerful legal and economic actors.

Accordingly, and on the basis of the arguments presented throughout this work, three explicit conclusory claims can now be made: First, it is suggested that it is now time to dismantle and reject the notion of corporate legal humanity. Specifically, corporations should not be conceptualised as being appropriate human rights beneficiaries or as putative human rights 'victims'. Secondly, international human rights law, in particular (but human rights more generally) should be understood as being focused on the embodied vulnerable human being. International human rights law, accordingly, should be understood as protecting human beneficiaries, understood in all the radical particularity of fully embodied life. Thirdly, in line with this, international human rights protection should extend, *archetypally*, to the human being *qua human being*. That is to say that the revealing lacuna in international human rights law concerning the human being without citizenship must be closed. The refugee, the asylum seeker, those who stand most juridically naked, these human beings arguably provide the bottom-line test for an adequate conception of international human rights subjectivity, as a foundation of embodied vulnerability suggests. In short, unless and until we redirect human rights towards a focused, protective and humanitarian core, the entire discourse, arguably, stands imperilled.

The corporate colonisation of human rights discourse is arguably instructive in relation to an emergent set of dangers linked to the semantic overstretching of human rights language. Currently, some claims made in the name of human rights seem so hyper-inflated that there is now a troubling rights-scepticism even among the general public. It is by no means clear, at this point, that human rights can even survive.[1] And that is, arguably, a prospect that should give us particular pause for thought in a context in which the logics of commodification shape and dominate virtually every social sphere and in which such logics have demonstrably resulted in the profound immiseration, exploitation and suffering of some of the most vulnerable human beings on earth.

A brief aside on an important emergent and future challenge

The reinvigoration and redirection of human rights is a matter of immense urgency but faces some genuine difficulties. The corporate colonisation of rights discourse is a particularly challenging one, but there are others. While there is undoubted danger in any uncritical elevation of human rights discourse as the ascendant ethical language of our age in its present bifurcated and complex form, the language remains a global language of claim with enormous potential. This very potential, however, leads to some complex challenges and potential dangers. If, a 'human rights' claim is, rightly or wrongly, regarded as the ultimate argumentative or ethical trump card, then virtually any or all claimants for inclusion in the legal and political community will seek to formulate their claim for inclusion or privileging in such terms. However, some genuine dangers attend this.

The rhetorical appeal of human rights is not always an aid to their effectiveness as a protective category. The semantic overstretching of human rights, if anything, diminishes their power and focus. Central to this particular concern is the widespread and possibly even increasing tendency to conflate claims for legal subjectivity with human rights claims. This conflation is related, of course, to the problematic and paradoxical anthropomorphism at the heart of liberal legal theory – an anthropomorphism which also haunts theories of corporate personality with obfuscating effects. Yet, strangely, those most critical of the exclusions inherent in anthropomorphism sometimes invoke it, in a way that may ultimately not achieve what they hope for.

For example, some thinkers defend the extension of the language of rights to a range of putative claimants including 'animals, plants and perhaps even inanimate objects'.[2] While there is a sense in which such arguments, to the extent that they 'invoke human rights [and they sometimes do], can be interpreted as claim that the *kind* of protection afforded by human rights should be extended to non-human entities', or as a 'kind of shorthand reference to a normative argument',[3] certain dangers nonetheless attend the linguistic extension of human rights arguments in this way. Such extension reveals the almost inevitable sense in which humanity and legal subjectivity are viewed as mutually co-constituting, even by those most critical of the exclusory results of such a conflation. There is a deep irony in this position. Those who wish to extend legal rights to animals, the environment itself, elements of it (and in the future, AIs, robots etc) frequently and rightly criticise the deep anthropomorphism of law. But simply to extend an overworked notion of humanity, or 'human rights', to putative non-human claimants of legal subjectivity seems to run the risk of a parallel and hyper-inflated anthropomorphism. Animal rights claims become human rights claims. Legal subjectivity becomes human legal subjectivity. The human, in other words, swallows the legal world.

Such conflation, moreover, comes accompanied by two very real dangers that serve neither the putative claimants of legal subjectivity, nor human beings. First, there is the very real danger that the special and distinctive qualities and characteristics of non-human legal subjects (whatever the moral status of such subjects) may be muted or lost beneath the overwhelming anthropomorphism of legal subjectivity thus constituted or evoked. This carries a genuine risk of inadequate respect and protection for the diverse ontic qualities, the particular context-sensitivities, the dynamic, changing and distinctive needs and vulnerabilities of non-human entity or group in question. Secondly, if the meaning of humanity expands to embrace almost everything to the point where the distinctiveness of entities is muted, there is also a directly related diminution in the power of legal subjectivity to protect the human being – a danger starkly illustrated by the case of corporations trading on the conflation between legal subjectivity and humanity.

It should also always be remembered that law, despite its problematic anthropomorphism, has failed to account for the living human being in vitally important respects. Legal anthropomorphism is of an attenuated and somewhat mutilated kind. The analysis of quasi-disembodiment and the ideological tilt of liberal law offered in this book amply reveals that if the notion of 'humanity' expands through the conflation of humanity with legal subjectivity, then the systemic limitations of 'juridical humanity' as currently constituted, far from offering adequate protection to the particularities of concrete, socially-contextualised, embodied living beings, tends to operate as a source of exclusion, suppression, distortion and selective invisibility. In short, legal anthropomorphism excludes, in very real and complex ways, those most vulnerable human beings and communities who find themselves, in a decisive sense, legal and discursive *outsiders* precisely *because* of a notion of hyper-inflated thoroughly *quasi-disembodied* anthropomorphic legal subjectivity.

The conflation of legal subjectivity and humanity is a conceptual confusion, the dangers of which are starkly presented by the case of corporate 'humanity'. The study undertaken in this book seems to imply the likelihood that invoking the conflation between humanity and legal subjectivity will not be particularly helpful or productive, for example, an attempt to defend animal rights. Accordingly, and in the interests of genuinely protecting human *and* non-human rights claimants, the theoretical task of separating legal subjectivity and humanity is now urgent. If we wish to construct forms of legal subjectivity that accord full respect to the ontic characteristics of, say, animals and a range of other potential rights beneficiaries, then calling for a hyper-extension of the anthropomorphism inherent in existing formulations of legal 'human' subjectivity is not, on past performance, a promising way forward.

What we now require is a theory of legal subjectivity that is responsive to commonalities and distinctions, to disembodiments and embodiments, to the complexities of context, and to the complexity and dynamism of the multiple and intersecting inter-relationships between, and clusterings of, a wide range of characteristics and entities. We need to design a theory of legal subjectivity, in other words, that extends the circle of legal subjectivity without hyper-extending the notion of humanity, or the intimately related concept of human rights. Such work lies beyond the remit of this book but will be attempted by the author in a forthcoming publication, *Law, Persons and Vulnerability: A New Theory of Legal Subjectivity*.

Embodied human vulnerability and the UDHR – 'Minding the gap'

Returning to corporations, it is most revealing that when we speak of corporate 'human rights' exploitation, we speak of entities that *already possess legal subjectivity*. Corporations are already constituted as legal persons. Theirs is a claim for a particular form of legal subjectivity – a human rights legal subjectivity. This is especially revealing. It takes place in a context where the complex closures and ideological structures of liberal law mean that liberal law itself is already tilted to the advantage of the corporation. The corporation is, in a very real sense, as we have seen, the paradigmatic liberal legal person writ large, in both analytical and ideological terms.

In this light, the corporate human rights claim, in particular, is an attempt to extend a set of corporate structural advantages into the very heart of a discourse ostensibly centred on the notion of humanity. And once international human rights law is inhabited by corporations as discursive 'insiders', the perilous consequences of conflating legal subjectivity and humanity become especially clear.

Fortunately, the UDHR paradigm, as we have seen, also yields an alternative conception of the foundation of human rights, and presents, perhaps, a critical legal space in which human embodied materiality can be embraced as a central theoretical and ethical value. It is possible to argue that the UDHR is premised precisely upon human embodied vulnerability, notwithstanding the UDHR's complex links to the limitations of a quasi-disembodiment reflecting the thin, abstract anthropomorphism of liberal law. Legal subjectivity and humanity seem capable of some degree of separation when placed over the fulcrum concept of human embodied vulnerability. Accordingly, we can employ embodied vulnerability to confront the gap between law's person and the real human being, precisely by attending to the ways in which law suppresses embodied materiality and its full implications.

The critical gap thus opened up provides a space in which new theorisations of the relationship between legal subjectivity, humanity and other forms of life and existence can be undertaken. In this gap, the embodied life of animals, the sensitive materiality of eco-systems, and so on, emerge, liberated from a flattening legal hyper-anthropomorphism. This, in turn, might open new possibilities for the development of a discourse of fundamental rights for a range of putative beneficiaries that does not need to be limited to the language of 'human rights', and arguably should not be conceptualised as such. Clearly, these concerns raise very complex issues and will have to await future theorisation, but *minimally*, at this stage, it is urgent to challenge the emergence of corporate legal humanity in the discourse of human rights.

Redirecting international human rights law and theory towards a foundation of human embodied vulnerability has a range of implications: first, and importantly, the corporation immediately looks less like a 'natural' beneficiary of human rights. Secondly, human vulnerability becomes a theoretical value capable of extension beyond international human rights law into the human rights law of domestic legal systems. Thirdly, human embodied vulnerability suggests the need for, and fruitfulness of, a related re-conceptualisation of the human legal and political subject, holding out the hope, moreover, of a related and more substantive vision of political and legal equality. Fourthly, embodied vulnerability can be used to reconceptualise property relations, placing limits on the excludability implied in corporate privatisation discourse and the legal claims arising from it. Fifthly, human ontic vulnerability reveals a profound material interrelationality, not just between human beings as social beings, but between humans and other beings within a living order of existence that itself reflects many forms of ontic vulnerability. Sixthly, insisting on the centrality of embodiment to the human rights universal brings embodied human difference to centre stage.

This last implication holds out a particularly fascinating and rich set of further implications for human rights theory: it immediately problematises quasi-disembodiment and its related exclusions. It also carries radical implications concerning the rigidly binary construction of sex, which, as we saw, is inescapably implicated in the structure of liberal quasi-disembodiment. An embodiment centred human rights theory will necessarily, if it takes ontic materiality seriously, need to engage with the biological nature of sex differentiation as a spectrum-reality, rather than a socially imposed oppositional binary. Fausto-Sterling's radical work on this theme, for example, strongly suggests that we can expect that the destabilisation of a *presumed* biological binary will destabilise a central justification underpinning the binary construction of gender relations.

The implications of an embodiment-centred biological argument for a sexual continuum are, in Fausto-Sterling's words, 'profound', because 'if nature really offers us more than two sexes, then it follows that our current notions of masculinity and femininity are *cultural conceits*'.[4] Foregrounding embodiment may just allow us to theorise sex and gender in a way that embraces a set of shifting and mutable but profoundly embodied gender-identities, along with a related pluralisation of terminology.[5] If Otto was right, as we saw in Chapter 5, to suggest that as long as a binary construction of sex and/or gender continues to exist, the genuine and full inclusion of women in the human rights universal remains a conceptual impossibility, then foregrounding the human body itself as a challenge to our dimorphic construction of sex and/or gender promises a very rich terrain for a profoundly inclusive theorisation of the human rights universal. *Minimally*, what is indicated is the *inclusion of embodied difference* at the heart of the human rights universal. This directly challenges the flattening and exclusory quasi-disembodiment of the abstract universal human rights bearer.

Furthermore, it is clear that embodied vulnerability has the theoretical potential for resolving certain longstanding tensions in human rights theory concerning the relationship between the universal and the particular. Indeed, the body, in its materiality and vulnerability, provides the ultimate figuration of what is most universal and in the very same symbolic moment, most particular to each of us. The body invokes our embodied particularity, in a concrete sense. It provides the very content of an embodied universal – a universal filled with bodies in all their variety, capacity, incapacity and contexts. This too, awaits further and fuller theorisation but hints at the possibility of a truly universalist conception capable of embracing the *entire* 'human family' at the heart of the inaugural text of international human rights law.

In the meantime, challenging corporate humanity may just open an aperture through which to struggle for a more liberating set of possible human rights futures. In the service of this important goal, the discursive and theoretical reformulation of the iconic UDHR paradigm as being centred on human embodied vulnerability may provide a strategic first step.

Notes

Introduction

1 C. Harding, U. Kohl and N. Salmon, *Human Rights in the Market Place: The Exploitation of Rights Protection by Economic Actors* (Aldershot: Ashgate, 2008) at 2. The authors also emphasise in n 30 that this basis for the extension of human rights subjectivity to corporations is not limited to Europe.
2 See M. Ignatieff, *Human Rights as Politics and Idolatry* (Princeton: Princeton University Press, 2001 at 53, n 1 and n 2 and the references cited there.
3 U. Baxi, *The Future of Human Rights* (Oxford: Oxford University Press, 2006).
4 C. Harding, U. Kohl and N. Salmon, *Human Rights in the Market Place*, above n 1 at 2.

Chapter 1

1 Charted most clearly by U. Baxi, *The Future of Human Rights* (Oxford: Oxford University Press, 2006).
2 Defended as desirable by M. Addo, 'The Corporation as a Victim of Human Rights Violations' in M. Addo (ed.) *Human Rights Standards and the Responsibility of Transnational Corporations* (Hague: Kluwer, 1999) 187–196, but most fully explored in the context of the European Convention on Human Rights and Fundamental Freedoms by M. Emberland, *The Human Rights of Companies: Exploring the Structure of ECHR Protection* (Oxford: Oxford University Press, 2006). See also the extensive discussion of the exploitation of fundamental rights regimes by corporations and other economic actors recently provided by C. Harding, U. Kohl and N. Salmon, *Human Rights in the Market Place: The Exploitation of Rights Protection by Economic Actors* (Aldershot: Ashgate, 2008).
3 To use the language of a leading corporate human rights proponent, Michael Addo: See M. Addo, 'The Corporation as a Victim of Human Rights Violations', above n 2.
4 W. Twining, *Globalisation and Legal Theory* (London: Butterworths, 2000) at 7.
5 See J. Abu-Lughod, *Before the European Hegemony: The World System AD 1250–1350* (New York: Oxford University Press, 1989).
6 B. De Sousa Santos, *Toward a New Legal Common Sense: Law, Globalization and Emancipation* (London: Butterworths, 2002) at 165. Santos refers to a range of commentators committed to such a view: M. Featherstone (ed.) *Global Culture: Nationalism, Globalization and* Modernity (London: Sage, 1990); A. Giddens, *Sociology* (Oxford: Polity Press, 1990); M. Albrow and E. King (eds) *Globalization, Knowledge and Society* (London: Sage, 1990).
7 B. De Sousa Santos, *Toward a New Legal Common Sense*, above n 6 at 166.
8 U. Baxi, *The Future of Human Rights*, above n 1 at 235.
9 P. Kirby, *Vulnerability and Violence: The Impact of Globalisation* (London, Ann Arbor: Pluto Press, 2006).
10 T.W. Luke, 'New World Order or Neo-World Orders: Power, Politics and Ideology in Informationalizing Glocalities' (1995) 91 *Global Modernities* at 99–100, cited

by R. McCorquodale and R. Fairbrother, 'Globalization and Human Rights' (1999) 21 *Human Rights Quarterly* 735–766 at 738.

11 Paragraph 20 of the UN Document 'Norms on the Responsibilities of Transnational Corporations and other Business Enterprises with regard to Human Rights' (2003) UN doc E/CN/.4/Sub.2/2003/12/Rev.2 defines a TNC as 'an economic entity operating in more than one country or a cluster of economic entities operating in two or more countries – whatever their legal form, whether in their home country or country of activity, and whether taken individually or collectively'.

12 B. De Sousa Santos, *Toward a New Legal Common Sense*, above n 6 at 167.

13 R. McCorquodale and R. Fairbrother, 'Globalization and Human Rights', above n 7 at 737.

14 See, for example, the arguments offered by S. George, 'The End of Neoliberalism: Alternatives to Finance-Led Capitalism' at *Erofnungsrede auf der Konferenze Linke Auswege aus der Krise*, an international conference held in the Deutscher Bundestag, Berlin, 20–21 March 2009 (available at <http://www.ulla-loezter.de/article/362.susan_george_the_end_of_neoliberalism_alternatives_to-finance_led_capitalism.html> Date of last access: 27 May 2009).

15 S. Gill, 'Constitutionalizing Inequality and the Clash of Globalizations' (2002) 4 *International Studies Review* 47–65 at 49.

16 Ibid, at 50.

17 U. Beck, *Power in the Global Age* (Cambridge: Polity Press, 2005/2006) at 52.

18 See, for example, the conception of 'counter-hegemonic globalisation' offered by B. De Sousa Santos, *Toward a New Legal Common Sense*, above n 6.

19 C. Douzinas, *Human Rights and Empire: The Political Philosophy of Cosmopolitanism* (Abingdon: Routledge-Cavendish (Glasshouse), 2007), for example, at 190–192. See also A. Orford, 'Beyond Harmonisation: Trade, Human Rights and the Economy of Sacrifice' (2005) 18 *Leiden Journal of International Law* 179–213.

20 T. Evans and A.J. Ayers, 'In the Service of Power: The Global Political Economy of Citizenship and Human Rights' (2006) 10 *Citizenship Studies* 239–308, abstract.

21 U. Beck, *Power in the Global Age*, above n 17 at 52.

22 Ibid, at 75.

23 R. Shamir, 'Corporate Social Responsibility: A Case of Hegemony and Counter-Hegemony' in B. de Sousa Santos and C.A. Rodrigues-Garavito, *Law and Globalisation from Below: Towards a Cosmopolitan Legality* (Cambridge: Cambridge University Press, 2005) 92–117 at 92.

24 R.C. Longworth, 'Large Companies now Economically Bigger Than Some Countries', *Chicago Tribune* 15 Oct 1996, cited by McCorquodale and Fairbrother, above n 7 at 738. See also S. Anderson and J. Cavanagh, 'Top 200: The Rise of Global Corporate Power' *Institute for Policy Studies* http://www.ips-dc.org/reports/top200.htm. See also J. Dunning, *Multinational Enterprises in a Global Economy* (Reading, MA: Addison-Wesley, 1993).

25 R Shamir, 'Corporate Social Responsibility', above n 23 at 92.

26 B. De Sousa Santos, *Towards a New Legal Common Sense*, above n 6 at 168.

27 U. Baxi, *The Future of Human Rights* (2006), above n 1 at 234.

28 U Baxi, *The Future of Human Rights* (Oxford, Oxford University Press, 2002), at 147.

29 U. Baxi, *The Future of Human Rights* (2006) above n 1 at 234.

30 GA res. 2200A (XXI) 21 UN GAOR Supp. (No 16) at 52, UN Doc A/6316 (1966), 999 UNTS 171, entered into force Mar 23, 1976.

31 GA res. 2200A (XXI) 21 UN GAOR Supp. (No 16) at 49, UN Doc A/6316 (1966), 993 UNTS 3, entered into force Jan 3, 1976.
32 See, J. Morsink, 'World War Two and the Declaration' (1993) 15 *Human Rights Quarterly* 357–405. The implications of his argument are examined in Chapter 7 of this book.
33 B. De Sousa Santos, *Towards a New Legal Common Sense*, above n 6 at 260.
34 See N. Lewis, 'Human Rights, Law and Democracy in an Unfree World' in T. Evans, *Human Rights Fifty Years On* (Manchester: Manchester University Press, 1988).
35 J. Donnelly, *Universal Human Rights in Theory and Practice* (Ithaca: Cornell University Press, 1989) at 213, cited by Santos, above n 6 at 260.
36 See B. De Sousa Santos, *Towards a New Legal Common Sense*, above n 6 at 263.
37 Ibid, at 266.
38 For a timely discussion of the historical significance of the state of exception and its contemporary status, see G. Agamben, *State of Exception* (K. Attell (trans)) (Chicago and London: University of Chicago Press, 2005).
39 B. De Sousa Santos, *Towards a New Legal Commonsense*, above n 6 at 267.
40 T. Evans and A.J. Ayers, 'In the Service of Power', above n 20 at 290.
41 See B. De Sousa Santos, *Towards a New Legal Common Sense*, above n 6 at 263–265, where he lists violations in Europe, the Americas, Africa and the Middle East – commenting that the 'global panorama of human rights practices is very sinister, and gives little room for optimism' (at 265).
42 Ibid, at 268.
43 U. Baxi, *The Future of Human Rights* (2006) above n 1 at 239.
44 See the discussion offered by E. Altvater, 'Post-Neoliberalism or Post-Capitalism?' (2009) *Alternatives International* available at <http://www.alterinter.org/article2629.html?lang=fr> (Date of Last Access 27 May 2009).
45 U. Baxi, *The Future of Human Rights* (2006), above n 1 at 240.
46 U. Beck, *Power in the Global Age*, above n 17 at 117.
47 Ibid, at 117.
48 T. Evans and A.J. Ayers, 'In the Service of Power', above n 20 at 293.
49 U. Baxi, *The Future of Human Rights* (2006), above n 1 at 246.
50 U. Beck, *Power in the Global Age*, above n 17 at 118.
51 S. Gill, 'Constitutionalizing Inequality', above n 15 at 47.
52 Ibid, at 48.
53 See S. George, 'The End of Neoliberalism', above n 14.
54 U. Baxi, *The Future of Human Rights* (2006), above n 1 at 248.
55 Ibid, at 248–249.
56 See, for more, C. Beitz, 'Economic Rights and Distributive Justice in Developing Societies' (1981) 33 *World Politics* 321–346 (cited by Evans and Ayers, n 20 above).
57 T. Evans and A.J. Ayers, 'In the Service of Power', above n 20 at 291.
58 See the discussion of this offered by S. George, 'The End of Neoliberalism', above n 14.
59 U. Beck, *Power in the Global Age*, above n 17 at 123. An example of this and its attendant human rights tensions, is starkly illustrated by the case of the Bolivian water privatisation scheme, discussed in Chapter 8.
60 J.L. Richardson, 'Contending Liberalisms: Past and Present'(1997) 3 *European Journal of International Relations* 5–33 at 21.
61 U. Beck, *Power in the Global Age*, above n 17 at 120.
62 R. Nader, 'Introduction' in L. Wallach and M. Sforza, *The WTO: Five Years of Reasons to Resist Corporate Globalization* (New York: Seven Stories Press, 1999) at 7.

63 See, for more, U. Baxi, *The Future of Human Rights* (2006), above n 1, especially at 234–252 and 264–275.

64 U. Baxi, *The Future of Human Rights* (2006), above n 1 at 250.

65 T. Evans and A.J. Ayers, 'In the Service of Power', above n 20 at 293.

66 U. Baxi, *The Future of Human Rights* (2006), above n 1 at 256–257. For example, the right to health is thought best served by the over-protection of the research and development rights of the pharmaceutical and diagnostic industries and various forms of progress in female reproductive autonomy, sustainable development and the management of environmental challenges are all though best served by, among other things, the protection of corporate property interests in various technologies.

67 U. Baxi, *The Future of Human Rights* (2006), above n 1 at 258. There is a notable parallel here between market-friendly rights interpretations and national security discourse in that, post 9-11, human rights are frequently recast as obstacles to be overcome in the name of their own protection.

68 U. Baxi, *The Future of Human Rights* (2006), above n 1 at 258.

69 Ibid, at 258–261, citing U Baxi, 'Justice as Emancipation: The Legacy of Babasaheb Ambedkar' in U. Baxi and B. Parekh (eds) *Crisis and Change in Contemporary India* (New Delhi: Sage, 1995) 122–149.

70 C. Jochnick, 'Confronting the Impunity of Non-State Actors: New Fields for the Promotion of Human Rights' (1999) 21 *Human Rights Quarterly* 21 at 65. See also S. Joseph, 'Taming the Leviathans: Multinational Enterprises and Human Rights' (1999) 46 *Netherlands International Law Review* 171, 173–174; and also the reports of the Special Rapporteur to the Commission on Human Rights' reports on the dumping of toxic waste: Commission on Human Rights (20 January 1998).

71 D. Kinley and S. Joseph, 'Multinational Corporations and Human Rights: Questions about Their Relationship' (2002) 27 *Alternative Law Journal* 7–10 at 7.

72 U. Baxi, *The Future of Human Rights* (2002), above n 28 at 146–149.

73 U. Baxi, *The Future of Human Rights* (2006) above n 1 at 216–220.

74 Ibid, at 223.

75 G.W. Pring and P. Canan, *SLAPPs: Getting Sued for Speaking Out* (Philadelphia: Temple University Press, 1996) at 221, cited by U. Baxi, *The Future of Human Rights* (2006), above n 1 at 260.

76 D. Schneiderman, 'Constitutional Approaches to Privatization: An Inquiry into the Magnitude of Neo-Liberal Constitutionalism' (2000) 63 *Law and Contemporary Problems* 83–109 at 86, citing S. Gill 'Globalisation, Market Civilisation, and Disciplinary Neoliberalism' (1995) 24 *Millennium Journal of International Studies*, 399–423 at 412.

77 S. George, 'The End of Neoliberalism', above n 14.

78 Norms on the Responsibilities of Transnational Corporations and Other Business Enterprises with Regard to Human Rights, 26 August 2003, E/CN.4/Sub.2/2003/12/Rev.2 ('Norms').

79 See, for an account, S.R. Ratner, 'Corporations and Human Rights: A Theory of Legal Responsibility' (2001) 111 *Yale Law Journal* 443–545 at 457–459.

80 Under Article 25 of its founding document, the ICC only has jurisdiction over natural persons.

81 See T. Egede and C. Wells, 'An Annotated Bibliography of the Accountability of Multinational Corporations: A Review of International Human Rights Law',

Working Paper Series No 12, The Centre for Business Relationships, Accountability, Sustainability and Society. See also, M. Monshipouri, C.E. Welch Jr. and E.T. Kennedy, 'Multinational Corporations and the Ethics of Global Responsibility: Problems and Possibilities' (2003) 25 *Human Rights Quarterly* 965–989, and also P. Simons, 'Corporate Voluntarism and Human Rights: The Adequacy and Effectiveness of Voluntary Self-Regulation Regimes' (2004) 59 *Relations Industrielles/Industrial Relations* 101.

82 D. Kinley and R. Chambers, 'The UN Human Rights Norms for Corporations: The Private Implications of Public International Law' (2006) 6 *Human Rights Law Review* 447–497 at 448–449. Kinley and Chambers point out that 'in response to the promulgation of the Norms, business leaders were quick to reiterate and highlight both the benefits that corporate enterprise bring to all societies, and their voluntary efforts to regulate the few instances where corporations are responsible for bad business practices and human rights abuses. It was on these bases that business leaders mounted critiques, not only of the Norms document itself, but also of any expansion of the concept of corporate liability for human rights responsibilities that went beyond the current model of self-regulation through codes of conduct, social responsibility policies and the like' (at 449).

83 D. Kinley and R. Chambers, 'The UN Human Rights Norms for Corporations', above n 82 at 449–450.

84 Interim Report of the Secretary-General's Special Representative on the Issue of Human Rights and Transnational Corporations and Other Business Enterprises, 22 February 2006, E/CN.4/2006/97 ('Interim Report').

85 See U. Baxi, *Future of Human Rights* (2006), above n 1 at 278–281.

86 See Baxi's discussion of the norms in *Future of Human Rights* (2006), above n 1 at 276–302.

87 B. De Sousa Santos, *Towards a New Legal Common Sense*, above n 6 at 267.

88 T. Evans and A.J. Ayers, 'In the Service of Power', above n 20 at 294.

89 L. Panitch, 'Rethinking the Role of the State' in J.H. Mittelman (ed.) *Globalization: Critical Reflections* (Boulder: Lynne Reiner, 1995) at 95, cited by Evans and Ayers, above n 20 at 294.

90 See, for example, *Awas Tingni Community v Nicaragua*, case no. 79, Inter-Am CHR (Judgment of the Inter-American Court of Human Rights of 31 August 2001).

91 Article 28 declares that 'Everyone is entitled to a social and international order in which the rights and freedoms set forth in this Declaration can be fully realised', while Article 30 declares that nothing in the UDHR 'may be interpreted as implying for any State, group or person any right to engage in any activity or to perform any act aimed at the destruction of the rights and freedoms' set forth in it.

92 See S. Joseph, *Corporations and Transnational Human Rights Litigation* (Oxford: Hart, 2004) at 8–11 on the legal accountability of TNCs under International Human Rights Law. See also, S. Joseph, J. Scultz and M. Castan, *The International Covenant on Civil and Political Rights: Cases, Commentary and Materials*, 2nd edn (Oxford: Oxford University Press, 2004), 36–37.

93 U. Baxi, *The Future of Human Rights* (2006), above n 1 at 254.

94 S. Joseph, *Corporations and Transnational Human Rights Litigation*, above n 92 at 9.

95 Ibid, at 11.

96 O.F. Williams, 'The UN Global Compact: The Challenge and the Promise' (2004) 14 *Business and Ethics Quarterly* 755–774 at 755, emphasis added.

97 With 1,100 companies signing across the globe by 2004 (this now stands at 4,000 'businesses' around the world) http://www.unglobalcompact.org/ParticipantsAndStakeholders/index.html (last accessed 03 June 2008).

98 O.F. Williams, 'The UN Global Compact', above n 96 at 757.

99 See, for example, the text of a letter sent to Kofi Annan, the proposer of the Global Compact, by a group of leading scholars and activists – available at <http://www.commondreams.org/news2000/0725-08.htm> (last accessed 22 June 2007).

100 S. Tester and G. Kell, *The United Nations and Business* (New York: St Martin's Press, 2000) at 53, cited by Williams, 'The UN Global Compact', n 96 above at 762.

101 U. Baxi, *Future of Human Rights*, above n 1 at 109.

102 M. Monshipouri, C.E. Welch, Jr and E.T. Kennedy, 'Multinational Corporations and the Ethics of Global Responsibility', above n 81 at 967.

103 Apart from Baxi's work, see also the rather briefer account in R. McCorquodale and R. Fairbrother, 'Globalization and Human Rights', above n 10. See also M. Monshipouri *et al.*, 'Multinational Corporations and the Ethics of Global Responsibility', above n 81.

104 See, for example, the discussion of this increasingly pressing question in C. Gearty, *Can Human Rights Survive?* (Cambridge: Cambridge University Press, 2006).

Chapter 2

1 U. Baxi, *Future of Human Rights* (Oxford: Oxford University Press, 2006) at 253.

2 M. Emberland, *The Human Rights of Companies: Exploring the Structure of ECHR Protection* (Oxford: Oxford University Press, 2006) at 52–54.

3 J. Donnelly, *Universal Human Rights in Theory and in Practice*, 2nd edn (Ithaca NY: Cornell University Press, 2003) at 23. See further, 23–27 and 204–224.

4 A. Cassesse, 'The Impact of the European Convention on Human Rights on the International Tribunal for the former Yugoslavia' in P. Mahoney *et al.* (eds) *Protecting Human Rights: The European Perspective: Studies in Memory of Rolv Ryssdal* (Koln: Carl Heymanns Verlag, 2000) 213 at 213, cited in M.-B. Dembour, *Who Believes in Human Rights? Reflections on the European Convention* (Cambridge: Cambridge University Press, 2006) at 18, n 42.

5 F.J. Bruinsma and S. Parmentier, 'Interview with Mr Luzius Wildhaber, President of the ECHR' (2003) 21 *Netherlands Quarterly of Human Rights* 185 at 193, cited in M.-B. Dembour, above n 4 at 18, n 42.

6 J.B. Attanasio, 'Rapporteur's Overview and Conclusions: Of Sovereignty, Globalization and Courts' in T.M. Franck and G.H. Fox (eds) *International Law Decisions in National Courts* (New York: Transnational Publishers, 1996) at 383.

7 M. Emberland, 'The Corporate Veil in the Jurisprudence of the Human Rights Committee and the Inter-American Court and Commission of Human Rights' (2004) 4 *Human Rights Law Review* 257–275. Emberland has suggested that ECHR discourse and related human rights discourses could 'reinforce each other' in relation to an exploration of the collective and economic aspects of civil and political rights – but while this is undoubtedly true, affirming the collective and economic aspects of such human rights does not, in and of itself, establish the case for corporate human rights. See, for more, M. Emberland, *The Human Rights of Companies*, above n 2 at 204–205.

8 A.-M. Slaughter, 'Judicial Globalization' (2000) 40 *Virginia Journal of International Law Association* 1103–1124 at 1110.
9 M. Emberland, *The Human Rights of Companies*, above n 2 at 12.
10 Ibid.
11 Ibid, at 3.
12 Ibid, at 50.
13 Ibid, at 51.
14 Ibid, at 42.
15 Ibid.
16 Ibid, at 10, n 35.
17 A.-M. Slaughter, 'Judicial Globalization', above n 8 at 1109–1112.
18 Ibid, at 1113.
19 M. Emberland, *The Human Rights of Companies*, above n 2 at 14.
20 Ibid, at 198.
21 Ibid.
22 On the basis of a detailed analysis of *Agrotexim Hellas SA and Others v Greece* A 330-A (1995); (1996) 21 EHRR 250, and related cases and contexts.
23 Through a detailed analysis of the court's reasoning in each of the following cases: with regard to corporate commercial protection under Article 10(1), ECHR, *Autronic AG v Switzerland* A 178 (1990); (1990) 12 EHRR 485; with regard to corporate business premises being regarded as a 'home' within the meaning of Article 8(1), ECHR, in cases concerning searches and seizures, *Société Colas Est SA and Others v France* 2002-III 421; (2004) 39 EHRR 17; and with regard to corporate entitlement to monetary compensation for immaterial loss (Article 41, ECHR), *Comingersoll SA v Portugal* 2000-IV 355; (2001) 31 EHRR 772.
24 M. Emberland, *The Human Rights of Companies*, above n 2 at 155–196.
25 Ibid, at 156–196.
26 Ibid, at 199.
27 Ibid, at 200.
28 A.J. Dignam and D. Allen, *Company Law and the Human Rights Act 1998* (London: Butterworths, 2000) at 173, cited by C. Harding, U. Kohl and N. Salmon, *Human Rights in the Market Place: The Exploitation of Rights Protection by Economic Actors* (Aldershot: Ashgate, 2008) at 26 in the context of drawing a direct contrast between the ECHR and the ICCPR in respect of their differing approaches to corporate rights protection.
29 M. Emberland, *The Human Rights of Companies*, above n 2 at 4.
30 J. Finnis, 'The Priority of Persons' in J. Horder (ed.) *Oxford Essays in Jurisprudence, Volume IV* (Oxford: Oxford University Press, 2000) 10. 'Ukase' is an archaic term for an edict, which derives from the Imperial Russian term used for edicts issued by the Tzar.
31 118 US 394 (1886).
32 J. Finnis, 'The Priority of Persons', above n 29 at 9.
33 C.J. Mayer, 'Personalising the Impersonal: Corporations and the Bill of Rights' (1990) 41 *Hastings Law Journal* 577–663 at 621.
34 M. Emberland, *The Human Rights of Companies*, above n 2 at 206.
35 Ibid, at 27–28.
36 Ibid, at 26.
37 Ibid, at 27.
38 Ibid.
39 See, for example, H. Guradze, *Die Eurpaische Menshcenrechtsconvention. Konvention zum Schutze der Menshcenrechte und Grundfreiheiten nebst Zusatsprotokollen. Kom-*

mentar (Berlin: Vahlen, 1968) 43 and 45–46, cited by M. Emberland, *The Human Rights of Companies*, above n 2 at 27, n 6.
40 See M. Emberland, *The Human Rights of Companies*, above n 2 at 28–29.
41 Ibid, at 31–32.
42 Ibid, at 31.
43 M. Addo, 'The Corporation as a Victim of Human Rights Violations' in M. Addo (ed.) *Human Rights Standards and the Responsibility of Transnational Corporations* (Hague: Kluwer, 1999).
44 Ibid, at 187.
45 Ibid, at 187.
46 Ibid, at 187–188.
47 Ibid, at 188.
48 Indeed, Emberland comes close to conceding something similar at the very end of his book when he suggests that '[c]orporate human rights issues may be judged trivial when compared with alleged violations of an individual human being's dignity, security, or participation in political life' (See *The Human Rights of Companies*, above n 2 at 208). This triviality, it is suggested, rests upon the differences in the order of harms that living human beings and corporations are capable of suffering. It is the argument of this book that this difference should have decisive implications for the normative acceptability of corporate human rights claims – but that conclusion rests on arguments yet to be made.
49 M. Addo, 'The Corporation as a Victim of Human Rights Violations', above n 43 at 188.
50 W.N. Hohfeld, 'Nature of Stockholders Individual Liability for Corporation Debts' (1909) 9 *Columbia Law Review* 285 at 288, cited in J. Finnis, 'The Priority of Persons', above n 30 at 10.
51 P. Jones, 'Human Rights, Group Rights, Peoples Rights' (1999) 21 *Human Rights Quarterly* 80 at 83.
52 Ibid, at 85.
53 Ibid, at 86.
54 Ibid.
55 Ibid, at 88.
56 Ibid, at 107, emphasis added. (It will also, however, be argued in this book that human rights themselves contain conflicting moralities.)
57 M. Addo, 'The Corporation as a Victim of Human Rights Violations', above n 43 at 189.
58 Communication No. 455/1991 (UN Doc. CCPR/C/51/D/445/1991), reprinted in 1995, Vol 2(1) IHRR, 148 – cited by Addo.
59 M. Addo, 'The Corporation as a Victim of Human Rights Violations', above n 43 at 189.
60 *Allan Singer v Canada*, above n 58 at paragraph 11.2 (emphasis added).
61 [1990] 1 SCR 425.
62 *Irwin Toy Ltd v Quebec* [1989] 1 SCR 927.
63 He mentions Canada, Germany, the United States of America, and the ECHR: M Addo, 'The Corporation as a Victim of Human Rights Violations', above n 43 at 191.
64 Ibid, at 188–189.
65 Ibid, at 188–189 at 196.
66 Ibid, at 188–189 at 192.
67 Ibid, at 193 [emphasis added].

68 Ibid, at 196.
69 N. Stammers, 'Social Movements and the Social Construction of Human Rights' (1999) 21 *Human Rights Quarterly* 980 at 981.
70 Ibid, at 986.
71 U. Baxi, *The Future of Human Rights* (2006), above n 1 at 258.

Chapter 3

1 This was also intimated in the last chapter when we noted Emberland's response to the fact that human rights and human beings share such an intimate conceptual and linguistic bond that the idea of 'corporate human rights' seems oxymoronic.
2 See J. Morsink, 'World War Two and the Declaration' (1993) 15 *Human Rights Quarterly* 357–405 for a full discussion of the drafting process of the UDHR and its focal concerns.
3 M. Johnson, 'Preface' in M. Johnson, *The Body in the Mind: The Bodily Basis of Meaning, Imagination and Reason* (Chicago and London: Chicago University Press, 1987) at *x*.
4 V. Seidler 'Embodied Knowledge and Virtual Space' in J. Wood (ed.) *The Virtual Embodied* (London, Routledge, 1998) at 17, cited by B. Ajana, 'Disembodiment and Cyberspace: A Phenomenological Approach' (2005) *Electronic Journal of Sociology* (available at: http://www.sociology.org/content/2005/tier1/ajana.html. Last accessed 19 April 2007).
5 P. Halewood, 'Law's Bodies: Disembodiment and the Structure of Liberal Property Rights' (1996) 81 *Iowa Law Review* 1331–1393 at 1338.
6 G. Lakoff and M. Johnson, 'Kantian Morality' in G. Lakoff and M. Johnson, *Philosophy in the Flesh: The Embodied Mind and its Challenge to Western Thought* (New York: Basic Books, 1999) 415–439 at 439.
7 V. Seidler 'Embodied Knowledge and Virtual Space', n 4 above at 17.
8 J. Richardson, 'A Refrain: Feminist Metaphysics and Law' in J. Richardson and R. Sandland (eds) *Feminist Perspectives on Law and Theory* (London: Cavendish, 2000) 119–134 at 128.
9 P. Halewood, 'Law's Bodies', above n 5 at 1340, emphasis original.
10 P. Cheah, D. Fraser and J. Grbich (eds) *Thinking Through the Body of Law* (St Leonards: Allen and Unwin, 1996) at *xv*, cited by S.D. Sclater, 'Introduction' in A. Bainham, S.D. Sclater and M. Richards, *Body Lore and Laws* (Oxford: Hart, 2002) at 1.
11 P. Halewood, 'Law's Bodies', above n 5 at 1341.
12 C. Smart, *Feminism and the Power of Law* (London: Routledge, 1989). See her chapter 'Law, Power and Women's Bodies' for a fuller account of this argument.
13 For more on this, see Chapter 7 below, which links embodied vulnerability to the drafting process of the UDHR. The chapter also briefly introduces the historical role of the body in the generation of the empathy that underlay the birth of rights discourse in the eighteenth century – a point often overlooked but fully discussed by L. Hunt, *Inventing Human Rights: A History* (New York: W.W. Norton and Co, 2007).
14 P. Halewood, 'Law's Bodies', above n 5 at 1337.
15 C. Douzinas and A. Gearey, *Critical Jurisprudence* (Oxford: Hart Publishing, 2005) 127–128.

16 E.F. Keller, *Reflections on Gender and Science* (Yale, Yale University Press, 1985) at 79, cited by K. Green, 'Being Here – What a Woman Can Say About Land Law' in A. Bottomley (ed.) *Feminist Perspectives on the Foundational Subjects of Law* (London: Cavendish, 1996).
17 A. Bottomley, 'The Many Appearances of the Body in Feminist Scholarship' in A. Bainham, S.D. Sclater, and M. Richards, *Body Lore and Laws* (Oxford: Hart, 2002) at 134–135.
18 A.M. Jaggar and S.R. Bordo (eds) *Gender/Body/Knowledge: Feminist Reconstructions of Being and Knowing* (New Brunswick, NJ: Rutgers University Press, 1989) at 4.
19 S. Ahmed, 'Deconstruction and Law's Other: Towards a Feminist Theory of Embodied Legal Rights' (1995) 4 *Social and Legal Studies* 55–73 at 56.
20 N. Naffine, 'The Body Bag' in N. Naffine and R. Owens (eds) *Sexing the Subject of Law* (Sydney: Sweet and Maxwell, 1997) 79–93 at 84.
21 Ibid, at 56.
22 There is no reason to fear the extension of legal subjectivity to non-human entities – in fact, there are strong normative arguments for adopting a flexible, formal construct of legal personality capable of protecting a range of entities and beings. See, for further discussion, C.D. Stone, *Should Trees Have Standing? And Other Essays on Law, Morals and the Environment* (New York: Oceana, 1996). See also Naffine's insightful exploration of the legal subject in *Law's Meaning of Life: Philosophy, Religion, Darwin and the Legal Person (Legal Theory Today)* (Portland: Hart Publishing, 2009).
23 See, for an extended examination of the teleology of human rights as a transcendent critique of positive human rights law, C. Douzinas, *The End of Human Rights* (Oxford: Hart, 2000).
24 C. Douzinas, *The End of Human Rights*, above n 23 at 183, emphasis added.
25 N. Naffine, 'Who are Law's Persons? From Cheshire Cats to Responsible Subjects' (2003) 66 *Modern Law Review*, 346–367, at 356, abstract.
26 C. Douzinas, *The End of Human Rights*, above n 23 at 185.
27 This has long been the case. The law has a remarkable history of, and facility for, personification: See W.W. Hyde, 'The Prosecution and Punishment of Animals and Lifeless Things in the Middle Ages and Modern Times' (1916) 64 *University of Pennsylvania Law Review* 696–730. The imputation to animals of a form of criminal intent is surely a warning against the perils of anthropomorphism in the attribution of legal responsibility.
28 See U. Baxi, *Human Rights in a Post-human World: Critical Essays* (Oxford: Oxford University Press, 2007).
29 C.D. Stone, *Should Trees Have Standing?* Above n 22.
30 See G. Teubner, 'Rights of Non-humans? Electronic Agents and Animals as New Actors in Politics and Law' (2006) 33 *Journal of Law and Society*, 497–521. See also, for a discussion in the context of human rights theory, U. Baxi, 'The Post-human and Human Rights' in U. Baxi, *Human Rights in a Post-human World*, above n 28 at 197–239.
31 Post-human discourse already proclaims the impossibility of this: See D. Haraway, *Simians, Cyborgs, and Women: The Reinvention of Nature* (London: Free Association Books, 1991). Haraway concludes that 'we are all chimeras, theorized and fabricated hybrids of machine and organism: in short we are cyborgs' (at 150). However, this figuration does not and cannot detract from the fact that, as yet, most of us have a visibly human embodiment, and

a concomitant vulnerability, distinguishable in important ways, from the machines with which our lives are lived as 'hybrids'. Metaphorical hybridity takes nothing essential from our embodied vulnerability as human beings. Actual cyborgs certainly qualify the term 'human' in the term 'human rights', as Baxi argues (in *Human Rights in a Post-human World,* above n 28 at 204) but there is no reason why a nuanced post-human rights theory could not carefully calibrate any ethically and conceptually relevant distinctions between actual and metaphorical cyborgs and their characteristics.

32 A. Nekam, *The Personality Conception of the Legal Entity* (Boston: Harvard University Press, 1938).

33 Ibid, at 26.

34 'The subject is a creation of the law, an artificial entity which serves as the logical support of legal relations. Right and subject come into life together': C. Douzinas, *The End of Human Rights,* above n 23 at 233.

35 The term 'person' has almost inseparable links with the idea of the human person and related theories of human personality. Their intimate convergence has caused considerable complexity in the theory of legal personhood and explains, to some extent, the assumption that, to extend legal subjectivity, is to extend the definition of humanity, discussed above. For a range of discussions on the theory of persons and personality see A. Peacocke and G. Gillet, *Persons and Personality: A Contemporary Inquiry* (Oxford: Blackwell, 1987).

36 D.P. Derham, 'Theories of Legal Personality' in L.C. Webb (ed.) *Legal Personality and Political Pluralism* (New York: Cambridge University Press, 1958) at 7, adopting a distinction drawn by A. Kocourek, *Jural Relations* (Indianapolis: Bobbs-Merrill, 1928) at 291–292.

37 N. Naffine, 'The Nature of Legal Personality' in M. Davies and N. Naffine, *Are Persons Property? Legal Debates about Property and Personality* (Aldershot: Ashgate, 2001) at 52. See also R. Tur, 'The "Person" in Law' in A. Peacocke and G. Gillett (eds) *Persons and Personality,* above n 35 at 123.

38 D. Derham, 'Theories of Legal Personality', above n 36 at 5.

39 D. Kinley (ed.) *Human Rights in Australian Law: Principles, Practice and Potential* (Sydney: Federation, 1988) at 5 – cited by N. Naffine, 'The Nature of Legal Personality', above n 37 at 55.

40 See M. Davies and N. Naffine, *Are Persons Property?* above n 37, for an extended discussion of the mutually constituting relationship between personhood and property in law.

41 M. Davies and N. Naffine, *Are Persons Property?* above n 37 at 5.

42 See below at page 65 ff.

43 See P.W. Duff, *Personality in Roman Private Law* (Cambridge, Cambridge University Press, 1938) at 3.

44 M. Radin, 'The Endless Problem of Corporate Personality' (1932) 32 *Columbia Law Review* 643–667 at 645.

45 G.W. Keeton, *The Elementary Principles of Jurisprudence* (London: Sir Isaac Pitman and Sons, 1930) at 117, cited by N. Naffine, 'The Nature of Legal Personality', above n 37 at 57.

46 N. Naffine, 'The Nature of Legal Personality', above n 37 at 57.

47 M. Radin, 'The Endless Problem of Corporate Personality', above n 44 at 646, who suggests (at n 8) that the 'instances cited under *persona* in the Forcellini Lexicon make the uses of the word clear enough'.

48 W.H. Rattigan, *Roman Law of Persons* (London: Wildy and Sons, 1873) at 3, cited by N. Naffine, 'The Nature of Legal Personality', above n 37 at 60.
49 D. Derham, 'Theories of Legal Personality', above n 36 at 13.
50 A. Nekam, *The Personality Conception of the Legal Entity*, above n 32 at 48.
51 As documented, most famously, by H. Maine, *Ancient Law: Its Connection with the Early History of Society and its Relation to Modern Ideas* (London: John Murray, 1930).
52 C.B. Macpherson, *The Political Theory of Possessive Individualism: Hobbes to Locke* (Oxford: Clarendon Press, 1964).
53 See, for example, C.B. Macpherson, *Possessive Individualism* , above n 52 at 261. See also the discussion of property and personhood in liberal theory in M. Davies and N. Naffine, *Are Persons Property?*, above n 37, and Halewood's extensive discussion of the links between disembodiment and the structure of liberal property rights in P. Halewood, 'Law's Bodies', above n 5.
54 A. Nekam, *The Personality Conception of the Legal Entity*, above n 32 at 49.
55 Ibid, at 39.
56 Ibid, at 67, emphasis added.
57 N. Naffine, 'Who are Law's Persons?', above n 25.
58 Ibid, at 347.
59 Ibid, at 350.
60 Ibid, at 357.
61 Ibid, at 362.
62 Ibid, at 365.
63 Ibid, at 351. See also n 20 where she attributes the phrase 'defined into existence' to Natalie Stoljar.
64 H. Kelsen, *Pure Theory of Law* (Berkeley: University of California Press, 1967) 173–174.
65 Ibid.
66 N. Naffine, 'Who are Law's Persons?', above n 25 at 350.
67 A. Nekam, *The Personality Conception of the Legal Entity*, above n 32 at 40.
68 M. Radin, 'The Endless Problem of Corporate Personality', above n 44 at 647–649.
69 Ibid, at 650.
70 For more, see W.N. Hohfeld, 'Some Fundamental Legal Conceptions as Applied in Judicial Reasoning' (1913) 23 *Yale Law Journal* 16–59 and W.N. Hohfeld, 'Fundamental Legal Conceptions as Applied in Judicial Reasoning' (1917) 26 *Yale Law Journal* 710–770 and the useful discussion of Hohfeld's scheme in A. Halpin, *Rights and Law: Analysis and Theory* (Oxford: Hart Publishing, 1997).
71 M. Radin, 'The Endless Problem of Corporate Personality', above n 44 at 651.
72 See A. Norrie, *Crime, Reason and History: A Critical Introduction to Criminal Law* 2nd edn (London: Butterworths, 2001); M.J. Horwitz, 'Comment: The Historical Contingency of the Role of History' (1981) 90 *Yale Law Journal* 1057–1059 at 1057.
73 N. Naffine, 'The Nature of Legal Personality', above n 37 at 68 (emphasis added).
74 Ibid, at 69.
75 Ibid.
76 B. De Sousa Santos, *Toward a New Legal Common Sense: Law, Globalization and Emancipation* (London: Butterworths, 2002) at 41.
77 N. Naffine, 'Who are Law's Persons?' above n 25 at 358, quoting D. Kinley (ed.) *Human Rights in Australian Law*, above n 39 at 5.
78 N. Naffine, 'Who are Law's Persons?' above n 25 at 357.

79 Ibid, at 358.
80 Ibid, at 362.
81 Ibid, at 362.
82 Ibid, at 365. Interestingly, it has been drawn to my attention by Alice Belcher that an analogous 'rational economic man' can be regarded as interior to economics, functioning in a similar way to P3 in law, as an ideal actor, irrespective of how real people make their economic decisions.
83 N. Naffine, 'Who are Law's Persons?' above n 25 at 365.
84 Ibid.
85 For fuller discussion of the traditional liberal property construct in relation to human rights, see A. Grear, 'A Tale of the Land, the Insider, the Outsider and Human Rights' (2003) 23 *Legal Studies* 33–65. For an extended discussion of the links between the concept of the legal person and property in liberal theory, see M. Davies and N. Naffine, *Are Persons Property?*, above n 37.
86 N. Naffine, 'The Nature of Legal Personality', above n 37 at 56. Emphasis added.
87 Ibid, at 357, n 56.
88 F.H. Lawson, 'The Creative Use of Legal Concepts' (1957) 32 *New York University Law Review* 907, at 915.
89 M. Radin, 'The Endless Problem of Corporate Personality', above n 44 at 643.
90 S.A. Schane, 'The Corporation is a Person: The Language of a Legal Fiction' (1987) 61 *Tulane Law Review* 563–609.
91 D. Derham, 'Theories of Legal Personality', above n 36 at 10.
92 S.A. Schane, 'The Corporation is a Person', above n 90 at 565.
93 L. Moran, 'Corporate Criminal Capacity: Nostalgia for Representation' (1992) 1 *Social and Legal Studies* 371–391 at 373.
94 (1819) 17 US (4 Wheat) 581 at 636.
95 M. Radin, 'The Endless Problem of Corporate Personality', above n 44 at 643–644.
96 D. Derham, 'Theories of Legal Personality', above n 36 at 8.
97 F. Hallis, *Corporate Personality* (London: Oxford University Press, 1930), 138.
98 See D. Derham, 'Theories of Legal Personality', above n 36 at 10.
99 Ibid, at 11.
100 S. Schane, 'The Corporation is a Person', above n 90 at 566.
101 S.J. Stoljar, 'Corporate Theory Re-Examined' in S.J. Stoljar, *Groups and Entities: An Inquiry into Corporate Theory* (Canberra: Australian National University Press, 1973).
102 D. Derham, 'Theories of Legal Personality', above n 36 at 11.
103 F. Hallis, *Corporate Personality* above n 97 at 139.
104 Ibid, at 140.
105 S. Schane, 'The Corporation is a Person', above n 90 at 567.
106 F.W. Maitland, *Domesday Book and Beyond: Three Essays in the Early History of England* (Cambridge: Cambridge University Press, 1897) at *xxxvi*, cited by S.J. Stoljar, 'Corporate Theory Re-Examined', above n 101 at 185.
107 Ibid.
108 *Soloman v A Soloman & Co Ltd* [1887] AC 22.
109 R. Grantham and C. Rickett, 'The Bookmaker's Legacy to Company Law Doctrine' in R. Grantham and C. Rickett, *Corporate Personality in the Twentieth Century* (Oxford: Hart Publishing, 1998) at 1.
110 R. Grantham and C. Rickett, 'The Bookmakers Legacy', above n 109 at 5.
111 S.J. Stoljar, 'Corporate Theory Re-Examined', above n 101 at 185.
112 L. Moran, 'Corporate Criminal Capacity', above n 93 at 375.

113 The corporation cannot suffer the same order of harms as an embodied human being, and this point is implicitly acknowledged by Addo when he notes that corporations have no inherent capacity to 'suffer harms associated with human rights violations': M. Addo, 'The Corporation as a Victim of Human Rights Violations' in M. Addo (ed.) *Human Rights Standards and the Responsibility of Transnational Corporations* (Hague: Kluwer, 1999) at 188.
114 See C.J. Mayer, 'Personalising the Impersonal: Corporations and the Bill of Rights' (1990) 41 *Hastings Law Journal* 577–663; G.A. Marks, 'The Personification of the Business Corporation in American Law' (1987) 54 *The University of Chicago Law Review* 1441–1483 at 1464–1478. See also Federman's account of this process in C. Federman, 'Constructing Kinds of Persons in 1886: Corporate and Criminal' (2003) 14 *Law and Critique* 167–189.
115 M. Neocleous, 'Staging Power: Marx, Hobbes and the Personification of Capital', *Law and Critique* 14 (2003), at 156–157.
116 C. Federman, 'Constructing Kinds of Persons in 1886: Corporate and Criminal', above n 114 at 181–182, footnotes omitted.
117 For a fascinating discussion of how this ideological gender tilt emerges at the level of internalised social power relations within the corporate managerial contexts, suggesting a strong patriarchal control of corporate culture, see A. Belcher, 'Gendered Company: Views of Corporate Governance at the Institute of Directors' (1997) 5 *Feminist Legal Studies* 57–76.
118 M. Neocleous, 'Staging Power: Marx, Hobbes and the Personification of Capital', above n 115 at 164.
119 D. Derham, 'Theories of Legal Personality', above n 36 at 1.
120 Ibid, at 11.
121 M. Horwitz, 'Santa Clara Revisited: The Development of Corporate Theory' (1985) 88 *West Virginia Law Review* 173–224, cited by S. Schane, 'The Corporation is a Person', above n 90 at 567, n 16.
122 S. Schane, 'The Corporation is a Person', above n 90 at 568.
123 Ibid.
124 Ibid.
125 For more, see A. Grear 'A Tale of the Land, the Insider, the Outsider and Human Rights', above n 85. In purely rights-orientated terms, it is possible to conceive of property as a defensive boundary – against forms of oppression – and to see 'property in oneself' as a form of recognition of the right to bodily integrity. See J. McLean, Property as Power and Resistance' in J. McLean, *Property and the Constitution* (Oxford: Hart Publishing, 1999) 1–10 at 1; E.M. Wood, *The Origin of Capitalism: A Longer View* (London: Verso, 2002) at 108–109; D. Thompson (ed.) *The Essential E.P. Thompson* (New York: New Press, 2001) at 287–315. It is also possible to conceive of property as being a right not to be excluded from certain fundamental social goods. Such a re-conceptualisation of property is offered, for example, by C.B. Macpherson in *The Political Theory of Possessive Individualism*, above n 52 and by C. Reich, 'The New Property' (1964) 73 *Yale Law Journal* 733–787.
126 See, for a particularly illuminating account, J. Nedelsky, 'Law, Boundaries and the Bounded Self' (1990) 30 *Representations* 162–189.
127 M. Davies and N. Naffine, *Are Persons Property?* above n 37 at 1.
128 M. Davies and N. Naffine, 'Persons as Property: Legal and Philosophical Debates' at 1, fn 1, in *Are Persons Property?* above n 37.
129 M. Davies and N. Naffine, *Are Persons Property,* above n 37 at 2.
130 P. Halewood, 'Law's Bodies', above n 5 at 1333.

131 Ibid, at 1340.
132 Ibid, at 1342.
133 See for example the oft-quoted 'every man has a property in his own person; this nobody has any right to but himself. The labor of his body and the work of his hands, we may say, are properly his. Whatsoever then he removes out of the state that nature has provided and left it in, he has mixed his labor with, and joined to it something that is his own, and thereby makes it his property'. J. Locke, *Second Treatise* (edited by T. Peardon) (Indianapolis: Bobbs-Merrill, 1952) at 17.
134 M. Davies and N. Naffine, *Are Persons Property?*, above n 37 at 5.
135 P. Halewood, 'Law's Bodies', above n 5 at 1358.
136 M. Davies and N. Naffine, *Are Persons Property?*, above n 37 at 5.
137 K. O'Donovan, 'With Sense, Consent or Just a Con? Legal Subjects in the Discourses of Autonomy' in N. Naffine and R. Owens (eds) *Sexing the Subject of Law* (Sydney: Law Book Company, 1997) 46, cited by Davies and Naffine, *Are Persons Property?*, above n 37 at 5.
138 C.B. Macpherson, *The Political Theory of Possessive Individualism*, above n 52.
139 Ibid, at 3.

Chapter 4

1 M.J. Horwitz, 'The Historical Contingency of the Role of History' (1981) 90 *Yale Law Journal* 1057–1059, at 1057.
2 W. Chambliss and R. Seidman, *Law, Order and Power* (Reading, Massachusetts: Addison-Wesley Publishing Co, 1982).
3 A. Woodiwiss, *Human Rights* (Abingdon: Routledge, 2005) at 3–4.
4 M. Neocleous, 'Staging Power: Marx, Hobbes and the Personification of Capital' (2003) 14 *Law and Critique* 147–165, abstract.
5 Baxi, for example, argues that the paradoxes of human rights are so profound as to produce, in essence, two competing notions of human rights: modern and contemporary – distinguished, among other things, by their differing relationship to logics of inclusion and exclusion and to the imposition of human suffering. See, in relation to this, the discussion in Chapter 5 below and U. Baxi, *The Future of Human Rights* (Oxford: Oxford University Press, 2006) at 27–35.
6 M. Freeman, 'Beyond Capitalism and Socialism' in J. Dine and A. Fagan, *Human Rights and Capitalism: A Multidisciplinary Perspective on Globalisation* (Cheltenham and Massachusetts: Edward Elgar Publishing, 2006).
7 C. Douzinas, *The End of Human Rights* (Oxford: Hart Publishing, 2000) at 32.
8 Ibid, at 30.
9 See N. Stammers, 'Social Movements and the Social Construction of Human Rights' (1999) 21 *Human Rights Quarterly* 980–1008, especially at 996–1000. See also, M. Ishay *The History of Human Rights: From Ancient Times to the Globalization Era* (Berkeley: University of California Press, 2004) and L. Hunt, *The French Revolution and Human Rights: A Brief Documentary History* (New York: Bedford/St Martins Press, 1996).
10 J. Finnis, *Natural Law and Natural Rights* (Oxford: Clarendon, 1980) at 198.
11 Ibid, at 206.
12 Ibid.
13 Ibid, at 208, emphasis original.

14 C. Douzinas, *The End of Human Rights*, above n 7 at 59.
15 Ibid, at 60.
16 Ibid, at 61. He writes that 'Freedom and equality, not justice, will be the rallying cries of modern natural law'.
17 J. Finnis, *Natural Law and Natural Rights,* above n 10 at 206–207, citing F. Suarez, *De Legibus* I ii 5. For more on the historical steps leading to this shift see R. Tuck, *Natural Rights Theories* (Cambridge: Cambridge University Press, 1979), and B. Tierney, *The Idea of Natural Rights* (Atlanta: Scholars Press, 1997) Chapter 1. It has been argued that such formulations reflect late-medieval controversies over 'the rightful (required or permitted) control, ownership or use of persons and things' sparked by dilemmas produced by the Franciscan doctrine of renunciation: M. Freeman, 'Beyond Capitalism and Socialism', above n 6 at 7–12.
18 J. Finnis, *Natural Law and Natural Rights,* above n 10 at 207.
19 Ibid.
20 B. De Sousa Santos, *Towards a New Legal Common Sense: Law, Globalization and Modernity* (London: Sage, 1990) at 26.
21 C. Douzinas, *The End of Human Rights*, above n 7 at 48.
22 For a fascinating account of this process see C. Douzinas, *End of Human Rights*, above n 7 at 61–68.
23 Ibid, at 65.
24 B. De Sousa Santos, *Towards a New Legal Common Sense*, above n 20 at 37.
25 Ibid, at 30.
26 Ibid, at 30.
27 Ibid, at 34.
28 C. Douzinas, *The End of Human Rights*, above n 7 at 65.
29 Ibid, at 65.
30 B. De Sousa Santos, *Towards a New Legal Common Sense*, above n 20 at 37.
31 Ibid.
32 See R.W. Grant, *John Locke's Liberalism* (Chicago: University of Chicago Press, 1987).
33 C. Douzinas, *The End of Human Rights*, above n 7 at 70.
34 Ibid, at 73.
35 Macpherson argues that the state of nature in Hobbes is not about 'natural man' as opposed to 'civilised man' but is 'about men whose desires are specifically civilised [and] the state of nature is the hypothetical condition in which men as they now are, with natures formed by living in civilised society, would necessarily find themselves if there were no common power to overawe them all': C.B. Macpherson, *The Political Theory of Possessive Individualism: Hobbes to Locke* (Oxford: Oxford University Press, 1962) at 19.
36 T. Hobbes, *Leviathan* (R. Tuck (ed.)) (Cambridge: Cambridge University Press, 1996) at 86, cited by Douzinas, above n 7 at 74.
37 C. Douzinas, *The End of Human Rights*, above n 7 at 74.
38 B. De Sousa Santos, *Towards a New Legal Common Sense*, above n 20 at 33.
39 C. Douzinas, *The End of Human Rights*, above n 7 at 76.
40 Ibid, at 78. This is not to argue, however, that Hobbes should be read through the lens of contemporary legal positivism and its sustained analytical attempt to distinguish the normativity of law from morality. Hobbes' explanation of the authority and distinctiveness of law, as is implied in the account of his position here, rests on his 'reflections about political necessity': S. Coyle,

'Thomas Hobbes and the Intellectual Origins of Legal Positivism' (2003) 16 *Canadian Journal of Law and Jurisprudence* 243–269 at 244.

41 B. De Sousa Santos, *Towards a New Legal Common Sense,* above n 20 at 34.

42 Ibid.

43 S. Coyle, 'Thomas Hobbes and the Intellectual Origins of Legal Positivism' (2003) 16 *Canadian Journal of Law and Jurisprudence* 243–269 at 245.

44 B. De Sousa Santos, *Towards a New Legal Common Sense,* above n 20 at 34.

45 C.B. Macpherson, *The Political Theory of Possessive Individualism,* above n 35 at 46.

46 Ibid, at 84.

47 Ibid, at 86.

48 Ibid.

49 Ibid, at 96.

50 C. Douzinas, *The End of Human Rights,* above n 7 at 80–81.

51 See S. Coyle, 'Thomas Hobbes and ... Legal Positivism', above n 43 at 245–248.

52 C. Douzinas, *The End of Human Rights,* above n 7 at 81.

53 C.B. Macpherson, *The Political Theory of Possessive Individualism,* above n 35 at 106.

54 Ibid.

55 See C. Douzinas, *The End of Human Rights,* above n 7 at 81–82.

56 B. De Sousa Santos, *Towards a New Legal Common Sense,* above n 20 at 32.

57 Most famously by Macpherson. See C.B. Macpherson, *The Political Theory of Possessive Individualism,* above n 35. Macpherson's work has been criticised by historical contextualists (such as Dunn, Laslett and Skinner) who argue that Macpherson mistakenly attributes to Locke a conscious ideological support for liberal capitalism. However, Macpherson addressed this critique by explaining that his target was not Locke's intention but rather his operative 'unstated assumptions': See J. Townshend, *C.B. Macpherson and the Problem of Liberal Democracy* (Edinburgh: Edinburgh University Press, 2000) at 68.

58 J. Locke, *Second Treatise of Civil Government* s 124; P. Laslett (ed.) (Cambridge, Cambridge University Press, 1960).

59 B. De Sousa Santos, *Towards a New Legal Common Sense,* above n 20 at 35.

60 J. Dunn, *The Political Thought of John Locke* (Cambridge: Cambridge University Press, 1969) at 222. But note Macpherson's defence of his approach, arguing that his critique is aimed at the operative assumptions, the unstated reasoning, in Locke's theory, rather than Locke's intentions: See J. Townshend, *C.B. Macpherson and the Problem of Liberal Democracy,* above n 57 at 68.

61 N. Wood, *John Locke and Agrarian Capitalism* (California, University of California Press, 1984) at 113.

62 J. Tully, *A Discourse on Property: John Locke and his Adversaries* (Cambridge, Cambridge University Press, 1980) at *x*.

63 See his discussion in 'Locke, the Political Theory of Appropriation' in *The Political Theory of Possessive Individualism,* above n 35 at 194–222.

64 Ibid, at 199.

65 Ibid, at 209.

66 J. Locke, *Second Treatise,* above n 58 at section 36.

67 C.B. Macpherson, *The Political Theory of Possessive Individualism,* above n 35 at 203.

68 B. De Sousa Santos, *Towards a New Legal Commonsense,* above n 20 at 36, and C.B. Macpherson's discussion of Locke's overcoming of the initial limitations on property in *The Political Theory of Possessive Individualism,* above n 35 at 203–220.

69 C.B. Macpherson, *The Political Theory of Possessive Individualism,* above n 35 at 209.

70 Ibid, at 209.

71 Ibid, at 221. Emphasis added.
72 C. Douzinas, *The End of Human Rights*, above n 7 at 83.
73 C.B. Macpherson, *The Political Theory of Possessive Individualism*, above n 35 at 221.
74 B. De Sousa Santos, *Towards a New Legal Commonsense*, above n 20 at 39.
75 See, for more, J.L. Richardson, 'Contending Liberalisms: Past and Present' (1997) 3 *European Journal of International Relations* 5–33.
76 A. Norrie, *Crime, Reason and History: A Critical Introduction to Criminal Law* (London: Butterworths, 2001) at 17. Norrie points out that although in England this new vision of the social order was expressed in the language of possessive individualism, in Germany, at around the same time, liberal individualism reflected a slightly different emphasis, taking the form of the metaphysical philosophies of Kant and Hegel and conceptualised in terms of right and reason.
77 A. Norrie, *Crime, Reason and History*, above n 76 at 20.
78 See again, J.L. Richardson, 'Contending Liberalisms', above n 75 at 7–9. See also, for example, Macpherson's discussion of the Levellers: C.B. Macpherson, *The Political Theory of Possessive Individualism*, above n 35 at 154 where Macpherson notes that the Levellers saw 'riches and power as concomitant, and they denounced both' and that they were particularly opposed to the 'concentration of wealth and the consequent practical inequality of the right to acquire' (*ibid*). Wood suggests that, although such forces of resistance may have ultimately 'lost the battle against capitalist landlords', they nonetheless left a legacy of radicalism, 'still alive today in various democratic and anticapitalist movements' (E. Wood, *The Origins of Capitalism: A Longer View* (London: Verso, 2002) at 120.
79 B. De Sousa Santos, *Towards a New Legal Common Sense*, above n 20 at 39.
80 Ibid, at 40.
81 C. Douzinas, *The End of Human Rights*, above n 7 at 67.
82 See, on this, M. Foucault, *Discipline and Punish: The Birth of the Prison* (A. Sheridan, trans) (New York: Vintage, 1995); M. Foucault, *The History of Sexuality: An Introduction* (R. Hurley, trans) (London: Penguin, 1981).
83 B. De Sousa Santos, *Towards a New Legal Common Sense*, above n 20 at 41.
84 A. Norrie, *Crime, Reason and History*, above n 76 at 8.
85 Ibid, at 10.
86 Ibid, at 10, emphasis added.
87 Ibid, at 13. See also, for a discussion of the subversive possibilities of critical legal history, R.W. Gordon, 'Historicism in Legal Scholarship' (1981) 90 *Yale Law Journal* 1017–1056.
88 M. Horwitz, 'Comment: The Historical Contingency of the Role of History' (1981) 90 *Yale Law Journal* 1057 at 1057–1059, cited in A. Norrie, *Crime, Reason and History*, above n 76 at 7.
89 These 'enclosures' provided a radical redefinition of property rights, displacing traditional social land rights with a forceful imposition of exclusory control directly linked to the replacement of traditional values by a powerful economic motive and capitalist competitiveness. See E.M. Wood, *The Origins of Capitalism* (New York: The Monthly Press, 1999) at 67–94 – cited by L. Westra, 'Environmental rights and Human Rights: The Final Enclosure Movement' in R. Brownsword (ed.) *Global Governance and the Quest for Justice: Volume IV: Human Rights* (Oxford: Hart Publishing, 2004) 107–119 at 107.

90 A. Norrie, *Crime, Reason and History*, above n 76 at 20.
91 Ibid, at 18.
92 Ibid, at 20.
93 Ibid, at 21.
94 Ibid, at 21.
95 B. De Sousa Santos, *Towards a New Legal Commonsense*, above n 20 at 44.
96 See, for more, the discussion in W. Chambliss and R. Seidman, *Law, Order and Power*, above n 2.
97 A. Norrie, *Crime, Reason and History*, above n 76 at 23.
98 C. Douzinas, *The End of Human Rights*, above n 7 at 237.
99 Ibid.
100 P. Cheah, and E. Grosz, 'The Body of the Law: Notes Toward a Theory of Corporeal Justice' in P. Cheah, D. Fraser and J. Grbich, *Thinking Through the Body of Law* (St Leonards: Allen and Unwin, 1996) at 3.
101 C. Douzinas, *The End of Human Rights*, above n 7 at 238.
102 P. Schlag, *The Enchantment of Reason* (Durham: Duke University Press, 1998) at 127, cited by C. Douzinas, *The End of Human Rights*, above n 7 at 238.
103 C. Douzinas, *The End of Human Rights*, above n 7 at 238.
104 P. Schlag, *The Enchantment of Reason*, above n 102 at 31, cited by C. Douzinas, *The End of Human Rights*, above n 7 at 238.
105 C. Douzinas, *The End of Human Rights*, above n 7 at 234.
106 A. Norrie, *Crime, Reason and History*, above n 76 at 23.
107 C. Douzinas, *The End of Human Rights*, above n 7 at 232–233.
108 Ibid, at 235.
109 C. Nino, *The Ethics of Human Rights* (Oxford: Clarendon, 1993).
110 Ibid, above n 109 at 63.
111 Ibid, at 110, cited by C. Douzinas, *End of Human Rights*, above n 7 at 235.
112 C. Douzinas, *End of Human Rights*, above n 7 at 235.
113 Ibid, citing C. Nino, *The Ethics of Human Rights*, above n 109 at 110.
114 C. Douzinas, *End of Human Rights*, above n 7 at 236.
115 Ibid, at 241.
116 M. Neocleous, 'Staging Power: Marx, Hobbes and the Personification of Capital' (2003) 14 *Law and Critique* 147–165. Abstract.
117 Ibid, at 148.
118 The 1844 Act drew a distinction between joint stock companies and private partnerships, provided for full publicity, and provided for incorporation through the act of registration alone (for new companies with more than 25 members or transferable shares). The latter two Acts introduced limited liability, which could be attained by seven persons signing and registering a memorandum of association.
119 [1897] AC 22.
120 M. Neocleous, 'Staging Power: Marx, Hobbes and the Personification of Capital', above n 116 at 155.
121 R. Grantham and C. Rickett, 'The Bookmaker's Legacy to Company Law Doctrine' in R. Grantham and C. Rickett, *Corporate Personality in the Twentieth Century* (Oxford: Hart Publishing, 1998) at 5.

122 M. Neocleous, 'Staging Power: Marx, Hobbes and the Personification of Capital', above n 116 at 155.
123 Ibid, at 156.
124 Ibid, at 156.
125 Ibid, at 157.
126 Ibid, at 157, emphasis original.
127 Ibid.
128 C. Federman, 'Constructing Kinds of Persons in 1886: Corporate and Criminal' (2003) 14 *Law and Critique* 167–189.
129 This process is traced in detail by G.A. Marks, 'The Personification of the Business Corporation in American Law' (1987) 54 *The University of Chicago Law Review* 1441–1483.
130 G.A. Marks, 'The Personification of the Business Corporation in American Law', above n 129 at 1444.
131 C. Federman, 'Constructing Kinds of Persons in 1886: Corporate and Criminal', above n 128 at 167, citing I. Hacking, *Mad Travellers: Reflections on the Reality of Transient Mental Illness* (Charlottesville: University Press of Virginia, 1998), 48.
132 118 US 394 (1886).
133 117 US 241 (1886).
134 C. Federman, 'Constructing Kinds of Persons in 1886: Corporate and Criminal', above n 128 at 168.
135 Ibid, at 169, citing A. Hunt and G. Wickham, *Foucault and Law: Towards a Sociology of Law as Governance* (London: Pluto Press, 1998 [1994]), 95.
136 C. Federman, 'Constructing Kinds of Persons in 1886: Corporate and Criminal', above n 128 at 169.
137 Ibid, at 181.
138 See G.A. Marks, 'The Personification of the Business Corporation in American Law', above n 129.
139 See, for an example, S. Palmer, 'Critical Perspectives on Women's Rights: The European Convention on Human Rights and Fundamental Freedoms' in A. Bottomley (ed.) *Feminist Perspectives on the Foundational Subjects of Law* (London: Cavendish, 1996), 223–242 at 225–226.
140 J. Flynn, 'The Jurisprudence of Corporate Personhood: The Misuse of a Legal Concept' in W. Samuels and A. Miller (eds) *Corporations and Society: Power and Responsibility* (New York: Greenwood Press, 1987) at 139, cited by C. Federman, 'Constructing Kinds of Persons in 1886', above n 128 at 189.
141 M. Horwitz, 'Santa Clara Revisited: The Development of Corporate Theory' (1985) 88 *West Virginia Law Review* 173–224.
142 See G.A. Marks, 'The Personification of the Business Corporation in American Law', above n 129 at 1470.
143 C.J. Mayer, 'Personalising the Impersonal: Corporations and the Bill of Rights' (1990) 41 *Hastings Law Journal* 577–663.
144 Ibid, at 589, citing *Connecticut General Life Insurance Company v Johnson* 303 US 77, 90 (1938) (Black, J. Dissenting). Mayer cites Black as insisting that '[n]either the history nor the language of the fourteenth amendment justifies the belief that corporations are included within its protection' (at 85–86) – Mayer, n 61.
145 C.J. Mayer, 'Personalising the Impersonal: Corporations and the Bill of Rights', above n 143 at 603.

146 Ibid, at 615.
147 For example, Mayer discusses the case of *First National Bank of Boston v Belotti* 435 US 530 (1978), a case in which a consortium of Boston corporations raised a first amendment challenge to legislation that forbade corporate expenditure on a referendum on gradated income tax. Despite rulings in the Massachusetts legislature and Supreme Judicial Court holding that the tax did not materially affect the corporations, the Supreme Court nonetheless held that corporate political speech was protected speech, and struck down the legislation. See C.J Mayer, 'Personalising the Impersonal: Corporations and the Bill of Rights', above n 143 at 615–618 for further discussion on this and other first amendment cases.
148 Ibid, at 621.
149 Ibid.
150 Ibid, at 662.
151 C. Federman, 'Constructing Kinds of Persons in 1886', above n 128 at 170.
152 M. Neocleous, 'Staging Power', above n 116 at 163.
153 There is a vast and complex range of theories concerning the nature of the body and processes of embodiment. Profound challenges to the simple Cartesian opposition between body and mind present new and invigorating ways of conceptualising the body – even doing away with the notion of a body as a discrete and identifiable form at all – perhaps most (in)famously in the work of Deleuze and Guattari. However, it is my own conviction that the experiential reality of an identifiable, material body that can be made to suffer harm and death is an important reality that needs to be fully accounted for on ethical grounds. This argument will be developed more fully later in this book.
154 M. Emberland, *The Human Rights of Companies: Exploring the Structure of ECHR Protection* (Oxford: Oxford University Press, 2006) at 208.
155 T. Hartmann, 'Unequal Protection: The Rise of Corporate Dominance and the Theft of Human Rights', available at: http://www.thomhartmanncom/summary/shtml.
156 See M. Foucault, *Discipline and Punish*, above n 82.
157 See the discussion offered by M. Neocleous, 'Staging Power', above n 116 at 159–161.
158 P.A. French, 'The Corporation as a Moral Person' (1979) 16 *American Philosophical Quarterly* 207–215 at 211, cited by M. Neocleous, 'Staging Power', above n 116 at 161. See also, in relation to attempts to address this difficulty, the discussion offered by A. Belcher, 'Imagining How a Company Thinks: What is Corporate Culture? (2007) 11 *Deakin Law Review* 1–21. See also, J. Gobert, 'The Corporate Manslaughter and Corporate Homicide Act 2007 – Thirteen Years in the Making but was it Worth the Wait?' (2008) 71 *The Modern Law Review* 413–463.
159 See J. Coffee, 'No Soul to Damn: No Body to Kick': An Unscandalized Inquiry into the Problem of Corporate Punishment' (1981) 79 *Michigan Law Review* 386.
160 M. Neocleous, 'Staging Power', above n 116 at 163.
161 Interestingly, although the possibility of prosecution for corporate manslaughter has existed for some time cases often foundered but for one man, or very small companies where the 'controlling human mind' could easily be identified. In the UK, a recent attempt to move beyond the limitations of the discredited 'identification doctrine', a doctrine under which before a company

could be convicted of manslaughter an individual had to be identified as 'the embodiment of the company itself' (A. Belcher, 'Imagining How a Company Thinks, above n 158 at 3) demonstrates the genuine and ongoing complexities involved in constructing corporate criminal liability. The Corporate Manslaughter and Corporate Homicide Act 2007 has recently brought a welcome symbolic validation of the notion of corporate manslaughter in the United Kingdom, but the Act contains many deficiencies and, significantly, it has been noted that, just as was the case under the identification doctrine, the concept of causation operative in the Act will disproportionately advantage TNCs or other large corporations with diffused command structures: J. Gobert, 'The Corporate Manslaughter and Corporate Homicide Act 2007', above n 158 at 419. See his general discussion of the Act, and also, A. Belcher, 'Imagining How a Company Thinks' above n 158.

162 M. Neocleous, 'Staging Power', above n 116 at 163.

163 C.A. MacKinnon, *Towards a Feminist Theory of the State* (Cambridge, Mass: Harvard University Press, 1989) at 237.

164 See C. Pateman, *The Sexual Contract* (Stanford: Stanford University Press, 1988).

165 C.A. MacKinnon, 'Reflections on Sex Equality Under Law' (1991) 100 *The Yale Law Journal* 1281–1328 at 1281.

166 C.A. MacKinnon, 'Reflections on Sex Equality Under Law', above n 165 at 1282, citing: T. Hobbes, *Leviathan* (Blackwell's Political Texts ed. 1946) at 80–82; J. Locke, *The Second Treatise of Civil Government* (T. Peardon ed. 1952) at 49–50; J. Rousseau, *The Social Contract and Discourses* (G. Cole trans 1950) at 210.

167 L.M. Friedman, *The Legal System: A Social Science Perspective* (New York: Russell Sage Foundation, 1975) at 180.

168 N. Stammers, 'Social Movements and the Social Construction of Human Rights' (1999) 21 *Human Rights Quarterly* 980–1008.

169 C. Douzinas, *The End of Human Rights*, above n 7 at 109.

170 See, for archetypal examples, E. Burke, *Reflections on the Revolution in France* (J.G.A. Pockocke (ed.)) (London: Hackett, 1987); K. Marx, 'On the Jewish Question' in K. Marx, *Early* Texts (D. McLellan trans) (Oxford: Blackwell, 1971) 85–114; J. Bentham, 'Anarchical Fallacies; Being an Examination of the Declaration of Rights Issued During the French Revolution' in J. Waldron (ed.) *Nonsense upon Stilts* (London: Methuen, 1987) 46–76.

171 C. Douzinas, *The End of Human Rights*, above n 7 at 109–110.

Chapter 5

1 G.A. res. 217A (III) UN Doc. A/810 at 71 (1948).

2 C. Douzinas, *The End of Human Rights* (Oxford, Hart, 2000) at 239.

3 C. Douzinas, *The End of Human Rights*, above n 2 at 183, emphasis added.

4 L. Hunt, *Inventing Human Rights: A History* (New York: W.W. Norton and Co, 2007).

5 J. Nedelsky, 'Law, Boundaries, and the Bounded Self' (1990) 30 *Representations* Special Issue on 'Law and the Order of Culture', 162–189.

6 See, for example, C. Douzinas, *The End of Human Rights*, above n 2 at 23–84.

7 N. Stammers, 'Social Movements and the Social Construction of Human Rights' (1999) 21 *Human Rights Quarterly* 980–1008, especially at 996–1000.

8 See above, Chapter 4. See also, M. Ishay, *The History of Human Rights: From Ancient Times to the Globalization Era* (Berkeley: University of California Press,

2004); L. Hunt, *The French Revolution and Human Rights: A Brief Documentary History* (New York: Bedford/St Martins Press, 1996).

9 See C. Douzinas, *The End of Human Rights*, above n 2 at 96–100.

10 L. Hunt, *Inventing Human Rights: A History*, above n 4, Chapter 4 'There Will Be No End of It', 146–175.

11 L. Hunt, *Inventing Human Rights: A History*, above n 4 at 16.

12 L. Hunt, *The French Revolution and Human Rights*, above n 8 at 3.

13 Ibid, at 5.

14 Ibid. Emphasis added.

15 He once famously characterised the primitive passions as 'food, a female, and sleep', hardly a formulation reflecting the full equality or putative full liberal political agency of women: J. Rousseau, *The Social Contract and Discourses* (G. Cole trans 1950) at 210, cited by C.A. MacKinnon, 'Reflections on Sex Equality Under Law' (1991) 100 *The Yale Law Journal* 1281–1328 at 1282.

16 L. Hunt, *The French Revolution and Human Rights*, above n 8 at 4–12.

17 Ibid, at 16.

18 Ibid, at 10.

19 J. Scott, *Only Paradoxes to Offer: French Feminists and the Rights of Man* (Cambridge Mass.: Harvard University Press, 1996) at 8, cited by C. Douzinas, *The End of Human Rights*, above n 2 at 97.

20 L. Hunt, *The French Revolution and Human Rights*, above n 8 at 27.

21 Ibid, at 111.

22 Ibid, at 109.

23 Ibid, at 108.

24 Ibid.

25 T. Jefferson, 'Letter to Madison', Fontainebleu (October 28, 1785) in A. Koch and W. Peden (eds) *The Life and Selected Writings of Thomas Jefferson* (New York: Modern Library, 1944) at 389, cited by M. Ishay, *The History of Human Rights*, above n 8 at 108.

26 M. Davies and N. Naffine, *Are Persons Property? Legal Debates About Property and Personality* (Aldershot: Ashgate, 2001).

27 J. Scott, *Only Paradoxes to Offer*, above n 19 at 6.

28 See C. Douzinas, *The End of Human Rights*, above n 2 at 96–100.

29 See K. Green, 'Citizens and Squatters: Under the Surfaces of Land Law' in S. Bright and J. Dewar (eds) *Land Law: Themes and Perspectives* (Oxford: Oxford University Press, 1998) 229–256. 'Land was seen as a form of wealth that ensured the reliability of the owner. The permanence of land and its tangible reality were a guarantee of the owner's commitment since his wealth was physically a part of the nation': L.E. Klein, 'Property and Politics in the Early Eighteenth Century Whig Moralists: The Case of the *Spectator* in J. Brewer and S. Staves (eds) *Early Modern Conceptions of Property* (London: Routledge, 1995) at 305.

30 N. Arnaud-Duc, 'Women Entrapped: from Public Non-existence to Private Protection' in A.-J. Arnaud and E. Kingdom, *Women's Rights and the Rights of Men* (Aberdeen: Aberdeen University Press, 1990) at 9, cited by C. Douzinas, *The End of Human Rights*, above n 2 at 97.

31 S.P. Marks, 'From the "Single Confused Page" to the "Decalogue for Six Billion Persons": The Roots of the Universal Declaration of Human Rights in the French Revolution' (1998) 20 *Human Rights Quarterly* 459–514 at 460.

32 L. Hunt, *The French Revolution and Human* Rights, above n 8 at 3. The text of the American Declaration of Independence (1776) declares 'all men' to be 'created equal, [and] endowed by their Creator with certain unalienable Rights, [and] among these are Life, Liberty and the pursuit of Happiness'.

33 This claim will be more fully discussed in Chapter 7.
34 C. Douzinas, *The End of Human Rights,* above n 2 at 96.
35 D. Otto, 'Disconcerting "Masculinities": Reinventing the Gendered Subject(s) of International Human Rights Law in D. Buss and A. Manji (eds) *International Law: Modern Feminist Approaches* (Oxford: Hart Publishing, 2005) 105–129 at 105–106. Emphasis added.
36 C. Douzinas, *The End of Human Rights* above n 2 at 96.
37 As Kennedy has pointed out, this critical gaze extends beyond rights beneficiaries themselves to a range of related concerns: 'Attention is routinely given to previously under-represented rights, regions, modes of enforcement, styles of work': D. Kennedy 'The International Human Rights Law Movement: Part of the Problem?' (2001) 3 *European Human Rights Law Review*, 245–267 at 250.
38 For a range of feminist responses to international human rights law, see, for example: H.B. Holmes, 'A Feminist Analysis of the Universal Declaration of Human Rights' in C.C. Gould (ed.) *Beyond Domination: New Perspectives on Women and Philosophy* (Totowa: Rowman and Allanheld, 1984) 250–264; C. Bunch, 'Women's Rights as Human Rights: Toward a Re-Vision of Human Rights' (1990) 12 *Human Rights Quarterly* 486; A. Gallagher, 'Ending the Marginalisation: Strategies for Incorporating Women in the United Nations Human Rights System' (1997) 19 *Human Rights Quarterly* 283; C. MacKinnon, 'Crimes of War, Crimes of Peace' in S. Shute and S. Hurley (eds) *On Human Rights* (New York: Basic Books, 1993); H. Charlesworth, 'Midlife Crisis of the Universal Declaration of Human Rights' (1998) 55 *Washington Lee Law Review* 781–796; F. Beveridge and S. Mullally, 'International Human Rights and Body Politics' in J. Bridgeman and S. Millns (eds) *Law and Body Politics: Regulating the Female Body* (Aldershot: Dartmouth, 1995); K. Engle, 'International Human Rights and Feminism: When Discourses Meet' (1992) 13 *Michigan Journal of International Law* 517; H. Charlesworth, C. Chinkin and S. Wright, 'Feminist Approaches to International Law' (1991) 85 *American Journal of International Law* 613–645, and for a much more recent contribution, D. Otto, 'Lost in Translation: Re-Scripting the Sexed Subjects of International Human Rights Law' in A. Orford (ed.) *International Law and its Others* (Cambridge: Cambridge University Press, 2006).
39 This concept will be more fully discussed in Chapter 7.
40 GA res. 2200A (XXI) 21 UN GAOR Supp. (No 16) at 52, UN Doc A/6316 (1966), 999 UNTS 171, entered into force Mar 23, 1976.
41 GA res. 2200A (XXI) 21 UN GAOR Supp. (No 16) at 49, UN Doc A/6316 (1966), 993 UNTS 3, entered into force Jan 3, 1976.
42 D. Otto, 'Lost in Translation', above n 38.
43 Ibid.
44 Ibid, at 321.
45 J. Derrida, *Positions* (University of Chicago Press, 1981) at 41, cited by Otto.
46 The Brussels Declaration Concerning the Law and Customs of War, Brussels, 27 August 1874 (esp Art XXXVIII); Manual of the Laws and Customs of War on Land, Oxford, 9 September 1880 (esp Art 49); Convention Respecting the Laws and Customs of War on Land, 29 July 1899, 32 Stat 1803, Art XLVI; Conventions Respecting the Laws and Customs of War on Land, 18 October 1907, entered into force 26 January 1910, 36 Stat 2277 (esp Art XLVI); Preamble to the Constitution of the International Labour Organisation, as contained in the Treaty of Peace Between the Allied and Associated Power and Germany, Versailles, 28 June 1919, in force 10 January 1920, 2 USTS 43; Convention No 4: Convention Concerning the Employment of Women during the Night, Washington,

28 November 1919, in force 13 June 1921; Recommendation No 4: Recommendation concerning the Protection of Women and Children Against Lead Poisoning, Washington, 28 November 1919; Convention No 45: Convention Concerning the Employment of Women on Underground Work in Mines of All Kinds, Geneva, 21 June 1935, in force May 1937; Convention No 3: Convention Concerning the Employment of Women Before and After Childbirth, Washington, 28 November 1919, in force 13 June 1921; revised in 1948 (Convention No 103); International Agreement for the Suppression of the White Slave Traffic, Paris, 18 May 1904, entered into force 18 July 1805, 1 LNTS 83; International Convention for the Suppression of White Slave Traffic, Paris, 4 May 1910, 211 Consol TS 45; 1912 Gr Brit TS No 20; International Convention for the Suppression of the Traffic in Women and Children, Geneva, 30 September 1921, 9 LNTS 415; International Convention for the Suppression of the Traffic in Women of Full Age, Geneva, 11 October 1933, in force 25 August 1934, 150 LNTS 431; *Convention du 12 Juin 1902 pour regler les conflits de loi en matiere de marriage; Convention du 12 Juin 1902 les conflits de loi et de jurisdictions en matiere de divorce et de separation de corps; Convention du 12 juin 1902 pour regler la tutelle des mineurs.*

47 D. Otto, 'Lost in Translation', above n 38 at 325.

48 S. Wright, 'Economic Rights and Social Justice: A Feminist Analysis of some International Human Rights Conventions' (1988–9) 12 *Australian Yearbook of International Law* 241–264, at 241.

49 H. Charlesworth, 'The Mid-Life Crisis of the Universal Declaration of Human Rights', above n 38.

50 D. Otto, 'Lost in Translation', above n 38 at 330 citing M.E. Galey, 'Promoting Nondiscrimination Against Women: The UN Commission on the Status of Women' (1979) 23 *International Studies Quarterly* 273–302.

51 See J. Morsink, 'Women's Rights in the Universal Declaration' (1991) 13 *Human Rights Quarterly* 229–256 at 231, also cited by Otto.

52 D. Otto, 'Lost in Translation', above n 38 at 331.

53 J. Morsink, 'Women's Rights', above n 51 at 235–236.

54 Ibid, at 235.

55 D. Otto, 'Lost in Translation', above n 38 at 332.

56 Ibid.

57 See F. Beveridge and S. Mullally, 'International Human Rights and Body Politics', above n 38 at 248–254; C. Romany, 'State Responsibility Goes Private: A Feminist Critique of the Public/Private Distinction in International Human Rights Law' in R.J. Cook (ed.) *Human Rights of Women: National and International Perspectives* (Philadelphia: University of Pennsylvania Press, 1994) 85–115.

58 D. Otto, 'Lost in Translation', above n 38 at 333.

59 F. Beveridge and S. Mullally, 'International Human Rights and Body Politics', above n 38 at 255.

60 Mackinnon, for example, writing in 1993, argues that '[w]omen are violated in many ways that men are not, or rarely are; many of these violations are sexual and reproductive ... [T]his abuse occurs in forms and settings and legal postures that overlap every recognised human rights convention but is addressed, effectively and as such, by none. What most often happens to women escapes the human rights net. Abuses of women as women rarely seem to fit what these laws and their enforcing bodies have in mind': C. Mackinnon, 'Crimes of War, Crimes of Peace', above n 38 at 85, cited by F. Beveridge and S. Mullally, 'Body Politics', above n 38 at 255.

61 GA Res 34/180, 34 UN GAOR Supp. (No 46) at 193, UN Doc A/34/46, entered into force Sept 3 1981.
62 F. Beveridge and S. Mullally, 'International Human Rights and Body Politics', above n 38 at 255.
63 GA Res 2106 (XX) Annex, 20 UN GAOR Supp. (No 14) at 47, UN Doc A/6014 (1966), 660 UNTS 195, entered into force Jan 4, 1969.
64 This is a point noted in the Report of the Sub-Commission on Prevention of Discrimination and Protection of Minorities, in its forty-third session, Geneva, 5–30 August 1991, U.N. Doc. E/CN.4/Sub.2/1991/65 of 24 October 1991, at 145–146.
65 '[T]he underlying assumption of ...[CEDAW's] definition of discrimination is that men and women are the same': H. Charlesworth, C. Chinkin and S. Wright, 'Feminist Approaches to International Law', above n 38 at 631.
66 F. Beveridge and S. Mullally, 'Body Politics', above n 38 at 257.
67 Ibid, at 258.
68 D. Otto, 'Lost in Translation', above n 38 at 338.
69 CEDAW, Art 1.
70 CEDAW, Art 4(1).
71 Art 1 defines discrimination in such a way as to include the 'political, economic, social, cultural, civil or any other field', and is relatively comprehensive in its potential scope. Art 2 (e), additionally, requires State Parties to 'take all appropriate measures to eliminate discrimination against women by any person, organisation or enterprise' – a requirement arguably open to interpretation as embracing private as well as public actors. The injunction, in Art 2 (f), to 'take all appropriate measures, including legislation, to modify or abolish existing laws, regulations, customs and practices which constitute discrimination against women' also has the potential to reach beyond the public sphere into the more private recesses of traditional custom and practice.
72 N. Lacey, 'Feminist Legal Theory and the Rights of Women' in K. Knop (ed.) *Gender and Human Rights* (Oxford, Oxford University Press, 2004) 13–55 at 22, cited by D. Otto, 'Lost in Translation', above n 38 at 340.
73 Ibid, at 341–343.
74 Ibid, at 343.
75 C. Bunch, 'Women's Rights as Human Rights', above n 38.
76 CEDAW was criticised for the relative invisibility of gender specific violence in its concerns, but the CEDAW Committee did address the issue: General Recommendation No 12 (eighth session, 1990) GAOR, 44th Session, Supp. No 37, UN Doc A/44/38, 1989.
77 GA Res 48/104, 48 UN GAOR Supp. (No 49) at 217, UN Doc A/48/49 (1993).
78 D. Otto, 'Violence Against Women: Something Other Than a Human Rights Violation?' (1993) 1 *Australian Feminist Law Journal* 159–162.
79 Human Rights Committee, General Comment 28, Equality of Rights Between Men and Women (Article 3), UN Doc CCPR/C/21/Rev.1/Add.10 (2000).
80 D. Otto, 'Lost in Translation', above n 38 at 349.
81 Ibid, at 350.
82 See U. Baxi, *The Future of Human Rights* (Oxford, Oxford University Press, 2002) at 27–35.
83 Ibid, at 29.
84 Ibid, at 32.
85 Ibid, at 33.
86 Ibid, at 32, n 17.

87 A. Woodiwiss, *Human Rights* (Abingdon: Routledge, 2005) at 39. Interestingly, although the 1776 American Declaration of Independence makes no reference to property rights, listing the inalienable rights as 'life, liberty and the pursuit of happiness', it has been suggested that, by the time of the Constitution of 1787, there had been, in effect, a counter-revolution by propertied elites.
88 U. Baxi, *The Future of Human Rights* , above n 82 at 31.
89 Ibid, at 154.

Chapter 6

1 See Chapter 3 above, and, for example, the discussion in P. Halewood, 'Law's Bodies: Disembodiment and the Structure of Liberal Property Rights' (1996) 81 *Iowa Law Review* 1331–1393. For further discussion of persons and property in liberal theory see M. Davies and N. Naffine, *Are Persons Property? Legal Debates about Property and Personality* (Aldershot: Ashgate, 2001), and J. Nedelsky, 'Law, Boundaries and the Bounded Self' (1990) 30 *Representations* 162–189.
2 See S. Ahmed, 'Deconstruction and Law's Other: Towards a Feminist Theory of Embodied Legal Rights' (1995) 4 *Social and Legal Studies* 55–73, especially at 56.
3 S.J. Williams and G. Bendelow, *The Lived Body: Sociological Themes, Embodied Issues* (London: Routledge, 1998) at 1.
4 E.F. Keller, *Reflections on Gender and Science* (Yale: Yale University Press, 1985).
5 See Chapter 5 above, especially the discussion of feminist critique of international human rights law and the gender of the human rights universal. References for further reading can be found in that chapter.
6 See, for discussion of this Chapter 2 above, and for further reading, see especially M. Emberland, *The Human Rights of Companies: Exploring the Structure of ECHR Protection* (Oxford: Oxford University Press, 2006); M. Emberland, 'The Corporate Veil in the Jurisprudence of the Human Rights Committee and the Inter-American Court and Commission of Human Rights' (2004) 4 *Human Rights Law Review* 257–275; M. Addo 'The Corporation as a Victim of Human Rights Violations' in M. Addo (ed.) *Human Rights Standards and the Responsibility of Transnational Corporations* (Hague: Kluwer, 1999); U. Baxi, *The Future of Human Rights* (Oxford: Oxford University Press, 2006); C. Harding, U. Kohl and N. Salmon, *Human Rights in the Market Place: The Exploitation of Rights Protection by Economic Actors* (Aldershot: Ashgate, 2008), especially the chapter entitled '*The Sun*, Liverpudlians and 'The Truth': A Corporate Right to Human Rights?'. For an illuminating and related discussion of corporations and constitutional rights, see C.J. Mayer, 'Personalising the Impersonal: Corporations and the Bill of Rights' (1990) 41 *Hastings Law Journal* 577–663.
7 See Chapters 3 and 4 above.
8 See U. Baxi, 'Two Notions of Human Rights: "Modern" and "Contemporary"' in U. Baxi, *The Future of Human Rights*, above n 6 at 33–58.
9 G. Lakoff, *Women, Fire and Dangerous Things: What Categories Reveal About the Mind* (Chicago: University of Chicago Press, 1987) at 174.
10 G. Lakoff, *Women, Fire and Dangerous Things*, above n 9 at 174.
11 Ibid, at 175.
12 S.J. Williams and G. Bendelow, *The Lived Body*, above n 3 at 51.
13 'We never cease living in the world of perception, but we go beyond it in critical thought – almost to the point of forgetting the contribution of perception to our idea of truth... The perceiving mind is an incarnated mind': M. Merleau-

Ponty, 'An Unpublished Text by Maurice Merleau-Ponty: A Prospectus of His Work' in M. Merleau-Ponty, *The Primacy of Perception* (Evanston, Illinois: Northwestern University Press, 1964) at 3–11.

14 'The perceived world is always the presupposed foundation of all rationality, all value and all existence. This thesis does not destroy either rationality or the absolute. It only tries to bring them down to earth': M. Merleau-Ponty, *The Primacy of Perception*, above n 15 at 13.

15 M. Merleau-Ponty, 'An Unpublished Text', above n 13 at 4.

16 M. Merleau-Ponty, *The Phenomenology of Perception* (London: Routledge Classics, 2002) (First published by Routledge and Kegan Paul, 1962).

17 In M. Merleau-Ponty, *The Primacy of Perception*, above n 15 at 12–42.

18 M. Merleau-Ponty, 'An Unpublished Text', above n 13 at 6.

19 See, for a fuller defence of his view, for example, the argument presented in M. Merleau Ponty, 'Sense Experience' in M. Merleau Ponty, *The Phenomenology of Perception*, above n 16 at 240–282.

20 M. Merleau-Ponty, *The Phenomenology of Perception*, above n 16 at 62.

21 Ibid, at 235.

22 Ibid, at 239.

23 M. Merleau-Ponty, 'The Primacy of Perception', above n 13 at 15–16.

24 S.J. Williams and G. Bendelow, *The Lived Body*, above n 3 at 53.

25 Ibid.

26 W.W. Adams, 'The Primacy of Interrelating: Practicing Ecological Psychology with Buber, Levinas and Merleau-Ponty' (2007) 38 *Journal of Phenomenological Psychology* 24–61 at 40, citing M. Merleau-Ponty, *Nature: Course Notes from the College de France* (R. Vallier, trans) (Evanston, Illinois: Northwestern University Press, 2003) at 210 and 225.

27 W.W. Adams, 'The Primacy of Interrelating', above n 26 at 40.

28 M. Merleau Ponty, *The Phenomenology of Perception*, above n 16 at 500.

29 M. Merleau-Ponty, *The Visible and the Invisible* (J.M. Edie, ed.) (Northwestern University Press, 1968).

30 M. Merleau-Ponty, *The Visible and the Invisible*, above n 29, 'Translator's Preface' at *xl*.

31 Ibid, at 139.

32 Ibid.

33 W.W. Adams, 'The Primacy of Interrelating', above n 26 at 43.

34 S.J. Williams and G. Bendelow, *The Lived Body*, above n 3 at 53.

35 M. Merleau-Ponty, *The Visible and the Invisible*, above n 29 at 134.

36 Ibid, at 134–135.

37 W.W. Adams, 'The Primacy of Interrelating', above n 26 at 44.

38 S.J. Williams and G. Bendelow, *The Lived Body*, above n 3 at 53, emphasis removed.

39 W.W. Adams, 'The Primacy of Interrelating', above n 26 at 45.

40 Ibid.

41 M. Johnson, *The Body in the Mind: The Bodily Basis of Meaning, Imagination and Reason* (Chicago: Chicago University Press, 1987); G. Lakoff and M. Johnson, *Philosophy in the Flesh: The Embodied Mind and its Challenge to Western Thought* (New York: Basic Books, 1999).

42 G. Lakoff and M. Johnson, *Philosophy in the Flesh*, above n 41 at 3.

43 Ibid, at 4.

44 It has, in fact, been argued that reason and emotion are inescapably interlinked and that emotion performs an essential role in reasoning: A. Damasio, *Descartes' Error: Emotion, Reason and the Brain* (New York: HarperCollins, 1994).

45 G. Lakoff and M. Johnson, *Philosophy in the Flesh*, above n 41 at 4.
46 Ibid, at 4–7.
47 M. Johnson, *The Body in the Mind*, above n 41 at *xxxvii*.
48 Ibid, at *xxxviii*.
49 S.J. Williams and G. Bendelow, *The Lived Body*, above n 3 at 54.
50 Ibid, at 54–55.
51 G. Lakoff and M. Johnson, *Philosophy in the Flesh*, above n 41 at 5.
52 See the extensive set of essays from a range of academic disciplines, including legal theory, in R.D. Masters and M. Gruter, *The Sense of Justice: Biological Foundations of Law* (London: Sage Publications, 1992).
53 'Rationalist legal theory [has systematically underplayed] the mundane fact that in order for the law to function at all it must first and foremost have a hold over bodies': P. Cheah, D. Fraser and J. Grbich (eds) *Thinking Through the Body of Law* (St Leonards: Allen and Unwin, 1996) at *xv*, cited by S.D. Sclater, 'Introduction' in A. Bainham, S.D. Sclater and M. Richards, *Body Lore and Laws* (Oxford: Hart, 2002) at 1. For a discussion of the radical implications of law's bodily basis see G. Agamben, *Homo Sacer: Sovereign Power and Bare Life* (D. Heller-Roazen (trans)) (Stanford: Stanford University Press, 1995).
54 See P. Halewood, 'Law's Bodies', above n 1.
55 A. Hyde, *Bodies of Law* (Princeton: Princeton University Press, 1997). Hyde also discusses the construction of the legal penis and vagina, the construction of the racial body, of offensive bodies etc.
56 N. Naffine, 'The Body Bag' in N. Naffine and R. Owens (eds) *Sexing the Subject of Law* (Sydney: Sweet and Maxwell, 1997) 79–93 at 84.
57 R.D. Masters and M. Gruter, *The Sense of Justice*, above n 52.
58 R.D. Masters, 'Justice in Contemporary Legal Thought' in R.D. Masters and M. Gruter, *The Sense of Justice*, above n 52 at 4.
59 Ibid, at 8.
60 For more on both these themes, see M.T. McGuire, 'Moralistic Aggression, Processing Mechanisms and the Brain: The Biological Foundations of the Sense of Justice' in R.D. Masters and M. Gruter, *The Sense of Justice*, above n 52, 31–46.
61 M.T. McGuire, 'Moralistic Agression', above n 60 at 32.
62 Ibid, at 36.
63 See also, the discussion of moralistic aggression among chimpanzees in F.B.M. De Waal, 'The Chimpanzee's Sense of Social Regularity and its Relation to the Human Sense of Justice' in R.D. Masters and M. Gruter, *The Sense of Justice*, above n 52 at 241–255.
64 See the full range of contributions to *The Sense of Justice*, above n 52 and the references therein.
65 R.D. Masters, 'Toward a More Coherent Theory of Justice' in R.D. Masters and M. Gruter, *The Sense of Justice*, above n 52 at 290.
66 'Whatever its content during a particular period, the concept [of justice] has influenced the legal system and often set standards for judicial decisions.. Why do humans want their laws to be just? Why do we evade, disregard, or disobey laws we consider unjust?' M. Gruter, 'An Ethological Perspective on Law and Biology' in R.D. Masters and M. Gruter, *The Sense of Justice*, above n 52 at 95–105 at 96.
67 M. Gruter, 'An Ethological Perspective on Law', above n 66 at 96.
68 Ibid, at 97.

69 Ibid, at 98.
70 H.L.A. Hart, *The Concept of Law* (Oxford: Clarendon Press, 1994).
71 M. Gruter, 'An Ethological Perspective on Law', above n 66 at 98.
72 See the extensive discussion in P. Strahlendorf, 'Traditional Legal Concepts from an Evolutionary Perspective' in R.D. Masters and M. Gruter, *The Sense of Justice*, above n 52 at 128–160.
73 See F.B.M. De Waal, 'The Chimpanzee's Sense of Social Regularity', above n 63.
74 R.D. Masters, 'Toward a More Coherent Theory of Justice', above n 65 at 298.
75 V. Vasterling, 'Body and Language: Butler, Merleau-Ponty and Lyotard on the Speaking Embodied Subject' (2003) 11 *International Journal of Philosophical Studies* 205–223 at 214.
76 V. Vasterling, 'Body and Language', above n 75 at 214. Emphasis added.
77 'Nature hath made men so equal, in the faculties of body, and mind... the weakest has strength enough to kill the strongest...' T. Hobbes, *Leviathan* (R. Tuck (ed.)) (Cambridge: Cambridge University Press, 1996) at 86.
78 H.L.A. Hart, *The Concept of Law*, above n 70 at 193–200.
79 Ibid, at 195.
80 Ibid, at 196.
81 Ibid, at 195.
82 See A. Grear, 'Human Rights – Human Bodies? Some Reflections on Corporate Human Rights Distortion, The Legal Subject, Embodiment and Human Rights Theory' (2006) 17 *Law and Critique* 171; B. Turner, *Vulnerability and Human Rights* (Pennsylvania: Pennsylvania State University Press, 2006); A. Grear, 'Challenging Corporate Humanity: Legal Disembodiment, Embodiment and Human Rights' (2007) 7 *Human Rights Law Review* 511–543.
83 M. Fineman, 'The Vulnerable Subject: Anchoring Equality in the Human Condition' (2008) 20 *Yale Journal of Law and Feminism* 1–23.
84 Since the early 1990 the term 'vulnerability' has been used to measure a range of impacts on social wellbeing, whether economic vulnerability, social vulnerability, financial vulnerability or environmental vulnerability: See P. Kirby, *Vulnerability and Violence: The Impact of Globalisation* (London, Ann Arbor: Pluto Press, 2006) at 4–23.
85 P. Kirby, *Vulnerability and Violence*, above n 85 at *vii*. Kirby has offered the first direct analysis of the meaning of the term vulnerability in the context of globalisation studies, pointing out its analytical power for the conceptualisation of the wide and complex range of changing social realities driven by the globalisation dynamic: *Vulnerability and Violence*, at 13. The most salient advantages of the notion of vulnerability explored by Kirby for the purposes of the present book concern its analytical attention to an account of human experience that moves beyond merely material accounts of quantifiable inequalities and risks to reflect notions of wellbeing that capture the concerns of the poor with vulnerability and powerlessness, the erosion of the 'bonds of secure belonging' (at 22) and dimensions of psychological or cultural poverty, as well as a focus on the risks of damage, not just a measurement of existing damage, to the wellbeing of people and communities. Kirby's account pays analytical attention to issues of power by focusing on mechanisms for coping with risk, and it specifically emphasises violence as a dimension of vulnerability, in the sense that vulnerability is both the product of, and producer of, violence (at, for example, 3, 22, 27) that in the globalised world is increasing at a marked rate. For example, Kirby draws attention to the notion of 'new wars' and the privatisation of organised violence charted by Kaldor: M. Kaldor, *New and Old Wars: Organized Violence in a Global Era* (Cambridge: Polity Press, 2001).

86 M. Fineman, 'The Vulnerable Subject', above n 83 at 2.
87 D. Otto, 'Disconcerting "Masculinities": Reinventing the Gendered Subject(s) of International Human Rights Law in D. Buss and A. Manji (eds) *International Law: Modern Feminist Approaches* (Oxford: Hart Publishing, 2005) 105–129.
88 M. Fineman, 'The Vulnerable Subject', above n 83 at 8. Fineman cites constructions of children, women and minorities as 'vulnerable, pathological and in a perpetual state of victimhood' in n 20, referring to C. Knowles, *Family Boundaries: The Invention of Normality and Dangerousness* (New York: Broadview Press, 1996) at 108–109. See also, M. Fineman, *The Autonomy Myth: A Theory of Dependency* (New York: The New Press, 2003), especially at 33–35.
89 A fact that even Addo (a key proponent of corporate human rights) acknowledges – see Chapter 2 above.
90 For more on the corporation as a moral person see P.A. French, 'The Corporation as a Moral Person' (1979) 16 *American Philosophical Quarterly* 207–215 and for arguments that the corporation is not a moral person, and should not be regarded as a legal person see E. Wolgast, *Ethics of an Artificial Person: Lost Responsibility in Professions and Organisations* (Stanford: Stanford University Press, 1992) and M. Moore, *Law and Psychiatry: Rethinking the Relationship* (Cambridge: Cambridge University Press, 1984).
91 B. Turner, *Vulnerability and Human Rights*, above n 82.
92 Ibid, at 2.
93 Ibid, at 127.
94 Ibid, at 3.
95 Ibid, at 6.
96 M. Ignatieff, *Human Rights as Politics and Idolatry* (Princeton: Princeton University Press, 2001).
97 Ibid, at 95.
98 B. Turner, *Vulnerability and Human Rights*, above n 82 at 9.
99 Ibid.
100 Ibid.
101 See Fineman's argument concerning the substantive notion of equality that ripens on the foundation of the vulnerable subject as opposed to the autonomous liberal political subject: M. Fineman, 'The Vulnerable Subject', above n 83.
102 S.J. Williams and G. Bendelow, *The Lived Body*, above n 3 at 2.
103 U. Baxi *The Future of Human Rights*, above n 6 at 198.
104 See, for more, the arguments in Chapters 1 and 5. See also, U. Baxi, *The Future of Human Rights*, above n 6 and U. Baxi, 'Market Fundamentalisms: Business Ethics at the Altar of Human Rights' (2005) 5 *Human Rights Law Review* 1–26.
105 See A. Grear, *Law, Persons and Vulnerability: A New Theory of Legal Subjectivity* (forthcoming 2010/11).
106 As Harding, Kohl and Salmon recently concluded, reflecting on the centrality of material vulnerability to human rights (referring to the argument of the author in A. Grear, 'Challenging "Corporate Humanity"', above n 82) 'it may be argued that the "human" in "human rights" is a matter of material vulnerability, and that is a major element in the justification for some kind of special or higher regime of legal protection. Following that argument, it might then be the case that both human and non-human or organisational actors may assert basic rights, but that their respective rights *may not be of exactly the same nature, and so may be said to have a different currency*... a differing valuation for "real" (or perhaps "embodied") basic *human* rights on the one hand, and *corporate* basic rights on the other hand': C. Harding, U. Kohl and N. Salmon, *Human*

Rights in the Market Place: The Exploitation of Rights Protection by Economic Actors (Aldershot: Ashgate, 2008) at 232–233. Emphasis original.

107 B. Turner, *Vulnerability and Human Rights*, above n 82 at 26 – 'Such a theory of society embraces a set of Hobbesian assumptions in which life itself is vulnerable – that is, nasty, brutish and short' and 'in psychological terms, this shared world of risk and uncertainty results in sympathy, empathy, and trust, without which society would not be possible'.

108 B. Turner, *Vulnerability and Human Rights*, above n 82 at 35.

109 D.B. Morris, *The Culture of Pain* (Berkeley: University of California Press, 1991) at 1.

110 Ibid, at 2.

111 Ibid, at 14.

112 Ibid, at 19.

113 B.S. Turner, *Vulnerability and Human Rights*, above n 82 at 36.

114 Turner argues, for example, that 'a minimum level of good health is a material precondition for the enjoyment of human rights' (*Vulnerability and Human Rights*, above n 82 at 111). This seems absolutely unassailable as a proposition. But this does not mean that embodied vulnerability will only support rights addressing survival/health questions – or a focus on 'the rights of the body' (health and social rights).

115 D.B. Morris, *The Culture of Pain*, above n 109 at 37.

Chapter 7

1 J.L. Richardson, 'Contending Liberalisms: Past and Present' (1997) 3 *European Journal of International Relations* 5–33.

2 See, for a discussion of the complexity of the relationship between human rights and capitalism, M. Freeman, 'Beyond Capitalism and Socialism' in J. Dine and A. Fagan, *Human Rights and Capitalism: A Multidisciplinary Perspective on Globalisation* (Cheltenham: Edward Elgar, 2006) 3–27.

3 L. Hunt, *Inventing Human Rights: A History* (New York: W.W. Norton and Co, 2007), and the brief observations in Chapter 5, above.

4 See the discussion in the last chapter. And for a detailed exposition of the dependency of reason on emotion see A. Damasio, *Descartes' Error: Emotion, Reason and the Brain* (New York: Harper Collins, 1994).

5 L. Hunt, *Inventing Human Rights*, above n 3 at 27, citing D. Diderot and J. Le Rond d'Alembert (eds) *Encyclopedie ou Dictionnaire rasonne des sciences, arts, et des metiers* (Paris: 1751–1780) Vol 5 (1755) 115–116.

6 L. Hunt, *Inventing Human Rights*, above n 3, Chapter 1 'Torrents of Emotion'.

7 Ibid, Chapter 3 'Bone of their Bone'.

8 Ibid, 'Introduction'.

9 Ibid, at 29.

10 Ibid, at 85–92.

11 Ibid, at 82.

12 Ibid, at 108.

13 Ibid, at 112.

14 See J. Nedelsky, 'Law, Boundaries and the Bounded Self' (1990) 30 *Representations* 162–189; M. Davies and N. Naffine, *Are Persons Property? Legal Debates about Property and Personality* (Aldershot: Ashgate, 2001).

15 L. Hunt, *Inventing Human Rights*, above n 3, Ch 1 'Torrents of Emotion', 35–69 and at 90.

16 Ibid, at 59.
17 See J. Scott, *Only Paradoxes to Offer: French Feminists and the Rights of Man* (Cambridge Mass: Harvard University Press, 1996).
18 See Hunt's discussion of the genesis of the 'self-contained person' – with the felt need for control over bodily excretions and the lowering of the threshold of shame – changes signalling 'the advent of the self-enclosed individual, whose boundaries had to be respected in social interaction': L. Hunt, *Inventing Human Rights*, above n 3 at 82–85.
19 See C. Douzinas, 'Revolutions and Declarations: The Rights of Men, Citizens and a Few Others' in C. Douzinas, *The End of Human Rights* (Oxford: Hart Publishing, 2000) 85–107, especially 'The Emancipation of Abstract Man', at 96–100.
20 See the discussion in Chapter 5 and D. Otto, 'Disconcerting "Masculinities": Reinventing the Gendered Subject(s) of International Human Rights Law in D. Buss and A. Manji (eds) *International Law: Modern Feminist Approaches* (Oxford: Hart Publishing, 2005) 105–129.
21 See L. Hunt, *The French Revolution and Human Rights: A Brief Documentary History* (New York: Bedford/St. Martin's Press, 1996).
22 C. Malik, representative from Lebanon, rapporteur of all three sessions in which the UDHR was drawn up, and the president of the Third Committee: See U.N. GAOR, 3rd Sess., 181st–183rd plen.mtg. at 857, U.N. Doc A/C.3/SR.181–183 (1948), cited by J. Morsink, 'World War Two and the Declaration' (1993) 15 *Human Rights Quarterly* 357–405 at 357.
23 J. Morsink, 'World War Two and the Declaration', above n 22 at 357. Emphasis added.
24 Sadly, many of the images are now so familiar that their shock, in an age of media exposure to continuing mass atrocities, is muted.
25 See H. Caven, 'Horror in Our Time: Images of the Concentration Camps in the British Media 1945' (2001) 21 *Historical Journal of Film, Radio and Television* 205–253.
26 See R.J. Lifton, *The Nazi Doctors* (New York: Basic Books, 1986) at 255, cited by J. Morsink, 'World War Two and the Declaration', above n 22.
27 Rudolph Hess is attributed with saying that National Socialism was 'nothing but applied biology' in R.J. Lifton, *The Nazi Doctors*, above n 26 at 129.
28 H. Caven, 'Horror in Our Time: Images of the Concentration Camps in the British Media 1945', above n 25 and the relevant references therein.
29 S.P. Marks, 'From the "Single Confused Page" to the "Decalogue for Six Billion Persons": The Roots of the Universal Declaration of Human Rights in the French Revolution' (1998) 20 *Human Rights Quarterly* 459–514.
30 J. Morsink, 'World War Two and the Declaration', above n 22.
31 Ibid.
32 See J. Morsink, 'Hitler's Organic State and Articles 1 and 2' in J. Morsink, 'World War Two and the Universal Declaration', above n 22 at 359–366.
33 A. Hitler, *Mein Kampf* (trans R. Manheim) (Boston: Houghton Mifflin Co, 1971) at 150, cited by J. Morsink, 'World War Two and the Declaration', above n 22 at 361. Emphasis added.
34 A. Hitler, *Mein Kampf*, above n 33 at 398.
35 J. Morsink, 'World War Two and the Declaration', above n 22 at 362–363.
36 Ibid, at 358.
37 Ibid, at 397–398, n 216. Such was this lack of interest that the Commission decided not to circulate to its members a UNESCO report based on a

questionnaire to 150 philosophers and some organisations on 'The Bases of an International Bill of Human Rights' – evoking a concerned response from the UNESCO representative at the UN Commission of Human Rights. Morsink comments that there is no evidence that the concern expressed changed the Commission's lack of interest in philosophical arguments.

38 Ibid, at 398.
39 Ibid, at 359.
40 U.N. GAOR, 3rd Sess, above n 22 at 54.
41 J. Morsink, 'World War Two and the Declaration', above n 22 at 362, citing Mr Cassin, U.N. GAOR, 3rd Sess, above n 22 at 54.
42 J. Morsink, 'World War Two and the Declaration', above n 22 at 362.
43 For further discussion of these themes see F. Beveridge and S. Mullally, 'International Human Rights and Body Politics' in J. Bridgeman and S. Millns (eds) *Law and Body Politics: Regulating the Female Body* (Aldershot: Dartmouth, 1995); D. Otto, 'Lost in Translation: Rescripting the Sexed Subjects of International Human Rights Law' in A. Orford (ed.) *International Law and its Others* (Cambridge: Cambridge University Press, 2006).
44 J. Morsink, 'World War Two and the Declaration', above n 22 at 363.
45 Ibid, at 365. (We also know, however, that the dominant abstract reading of the universal has, notwithstanding the inclusion of such strong anti-discriminatory language, produced hierarchies and exclusions based on precisely such grounds – as we saw in Chapter 5.)
46 'Information Concerning Human Rights Arising from Trials of War Criminals' – in which the authors noted that the report was 'designed to serve the specific purpose of contributing to the task of the Commission of Human Rights in preparing an international bill of human rights or international declaration or convention on civil liberties': U.N. Doc. E/CN.4/W.20 at vi – cited by Morsink at n 54.
47 Mr. Cassin, U.N. GAOR, Comm'n on Hum. Rts Drafting Comm. 1st Sess., 13th mtg., at 2, U.N Doc E/CN.4/AC.1/SR13 (1947).
48 Mr. Cassin, *Third Committee Records* (U.N. GAOR, 3rd Sess. U.N. Doc A/C.3/ (1948) 84th–180th mtgs, at 217.
49 J. Morsink, 'World War Two and the Declaration', above n 22 at 369–370.
50 For a provocative discussion of the centrality of the body and the political consequences of deliberately inflicted bodily pain see E. Scarry, *The Body in Pain: The Making and Unmaking of the World* (Oxford: Oxford University Press, 1985).
51 J. Morsink, 'World War Two and the Declaration', above n 22 at 372.
52 Ibid, at 375.
53 See B.S. Turner, *Vulnerability and Human Rights* (Pennsylvania: The Pennsylvania State University Press, 2006) 1–5, 25–34.
54 See the discussion, shortly to be introduced, of the nature of sovereign power and the nature of modern politics as bio-politics in G. Agamben, *Homo Sacer: Sovereign Power and Bare Life* (D. Heller-Roazen (trans)) (Stanford: Stanford University Press, 1995).
55 See also M. Fineman, 'The Vulnerable Subject: Anchoring Equality in the Human Condition' (2008) 20 *Yale Journal of Law and Feminism* 1–23 and for a discussion of the importance of institutional design and the centrality of participation for the amelioration of vulnerability in a globalised context, P. Kirby, *Vulnerability and Violence: The Impact of Globalisation* (London, Ann Arbor: Pluto Press, 2006), especially Chapters 8 and 9.

56 J. Morsink, 'World War Two and the Universal Declaration', above n 22 at 375.
57 Ibid, at 376–377.
58 Ibid, at 377.
59 G. Agamben, *Homo Sacer*, above n 54 at 132.
60 J. Morsink, 'World War Two and the Universal Declaration', above n 22 at 380.
61 B.S. Turner, *Vulnerability and Human Rights*, above n 58 at 2–5.
62 H. Arendt, *The Origins of Totalitarianism* (New York: Harcourt Brace Jovanovich, 1979).
63 H. Arendt, *The Origins of Totalitarianism*, above n 62 at 299.
64 B. Turner, *Vulnerability and Human Rights*, above n 58 at 4.
65 J. Morsink, 'World War Two and the Universal Declaration', above n 22 at 381.
66 U.N. ESCOR, Comm'n on Hum.Rts., 3rd Sess., 56th mtg., at 10, U.N. Doc E/CN.4/SR.56 (1948), cited by Morsink at 383.
67 J. Morsink, 'World War Two and the Universal Declaration', above n 22 at 384.
68 Ibid, at 383.
69 See the discussion of this in C. Douzinas, *The End of Human Rights*, above n 19 at 129–141.
70 C. Douzinas, *The End of Human Rights*, above n 19 at 9.
71 M. Foucault, *The History of Sexuality: An Introduction* (R. Hurley (trans)) (New York: Random House, 1978) at 143.
72 G. Agamben, *Homo Sacer*, above n 54 at 9–11 and 71–115.
73 Ibid, at 114.
74 Ibid, at 114–115.
75 Ibid, at 120.
76 Ibid, at 121.
77 Ibid, at 128–130.
78 Ibid, at 134.
79 J. Morsink, 'World War Two and the Declaration', above n 22 at 385.
80 R.E. Conot, *Justice at Nuremburg* (New York: Harper and Row, 1983) at 169, cited by Morsink, at 391.
81 J. von Lang and C. Sibyll (R. Manhiem (trans)), *Eichmann Interrogated: Transcripts from the Archives of the Israeli Police* (New York: Farrar, Straus and Giroux, 1983) at 115.
82 G. Agamben, *Homo Sacer*, above n 54, especially 'Biopolitics and the Rights of Man', at 126–135; A. Woodiwiss, *Human Rights* (Abingdon: Routledge, 2005), especially, 'The Paradox of Human Rights' at 3–15.
83 GA res. 2200A (XXI) 21 UN GAOR Supp. (No 16) at 52, U.N. Doc A/6316 (1966), 999 UNTS 171, entered into force Mar 23, 1976.
84 GA res. 2200A (XXI) 21 UN GAOR Supp (No 16) at 49, U.N. Doc A/6316, 993 UNTS 3, entered into force Jan 3, 1976.
85 Article 5 of the Vienna Declaration declares all human rights to be 'universal, indivisible and interdependent and interrelated': Vienna Declaration and Programme of Action U.N. Doc.A/CONF.157/24 (Part 1) at 20 (1993), adopted 25 June 1993.
86 Such rights are 'notoriously politically sensitive since their effective elaboration requires the political branches to adjust their allocation and distribution of resources, sometimes at a highly systemic level, in response to judicial direction': B. Morgan, 'The Regulatory Face of the Human Right to Water' (2004) 15 *Journal of Water Law* 179–187.
87 S. Leckie, 'Another Step Towards Indivisibility: Identifying the Key Features of Violations of Economic, Social and Cultural Rights' (1998) 20 *Human Rights Quarterly* 81–124 at 81–83.

88 The neo-liberal policies of the World Bank and the IMF have resulted in wholesale violations of ESC rights in developing nations – especially the poorest. The 'commitment' of these institutions to human rights has been dismissed as 'lip service'. See D.D. Bradlow and C. Grossman , 'Limited Mandates and Intertwined Problems: A New Challenge for the World Bank and the IMF' (1995) 17 *Human Rights Quarterly* 411–442. On the inhospitality of the liberal legal order to human rights values in the context of liberalism's orientation towards capitalism – particularly in the globalised context – see U. Baxi, *The Future of Human Rights* (Oxford: Oxford University Press, 2006); S. Anderson and J. Cavanagh, *Top 200: The Rise of Global Corporate Power* (Washington DC: Institute for Policy Studies, 2000); G. Soros, 'The Capitalist Threat' (1997) 279 *Atlantic Monthly* 45–58.

89 M. Cranston, *What are Human Rights?* (New York: Taplinger Publishing, 1973).

90 J. Donnelly, *Universal Human Rights in Theory and Practice* (Ithaca NY: Cornell University Press, 2003) at 28.

91 B.S. Turner, *Vulnerability and Human Rights*, above n 58 at 27–34.

92 In fact, Turner argues that 'human and social rights are juridical expressions of social solidarity, whose foundations rest in the common experience of [human] vulnerability and [institutional] precariousness': B.S. Turner, *Vulnerability and Human Rights*, above n 58 at 26.

93 Ibid, at 10.

94 The ICESCR does not explicitly distinguish between or categorise the rights within it as economic, social or cultural. No clear divisions can be drawn between the rights on the basis of these categorisations, and many of the rights evince more than one of these dimensions. See, for more H. Steiner, 'Social Rights and Economic Development: Converging Discourses?' (1998) 4 *Buffalo Human Rights Law Review* 25–42, at 27.

95 For example, the brief view expressed in A. Neier, 'Social and Economic Rights: A Critique' (2206) 31 *Human Rights Brief* 1–3.

96 B.S. Turner, *Vulnerability and Human Rights*, above n 58 at 37.

97 Ibid.

98 E. Scarry, *The Body in Pain*, above n 50.

99 Ibid, at 43.

100 Ibid, at 49.

101 B.S. Turner, *Vulnerability and Human Rights*, above n 58 at 1.

102 G. Agamben, *Homo Sacer*, above n 54 at 188.

103 E. Levinas, *Totality and Infinity* (A. Lingis (trans)) (Pittsburgh: Duquesne University Press, 1969).

104 E. Levinas, 'Ethics as First Philosophy' in *The Levinas Reader* (S. Hand and M. Temple (trans)) (Malden, MA: Blackwell, 1984), 75–87 at 87.

105 C. Douzinas, *The End of Human Rights*, above n 19 at 349.

106 Ibid.

107 Ibid, at 348.

108 E. Levinas, *Totality and Infinity*, above n 103 at 50.

109 W.W. Adams, 'The Primacy of Interrelating: Practicing Ecological Psychology with Buber, Levinas, and Merleau-Ponty' (2007) 38 *Journal of Phenomenological Psychology* 24–61 at 33.

110 E. Levinas, *Ethics and Infinity* (R.A. Cohen (trans)) (Pittsburgh: Duquesne University Press, 1985) at 100.

111 See the discussion and evidence offered by P. Kirby, *Vulnerability and Violence*, above n 55 and also B.S. Turner, *Vulnerability and Human Rights*, above n 58.

112 See the discussion in Chapter 1.
113 E. Levinas, *Totality and Infinity*, above n 103 at 215.
114 C. Douzinas, *The End of Human Rights*, above n 19 at 350.
115 Ibid, at 351.

Chapter 8

1 See the discussion in Chapters 3 and 4, and the references therein, especially to M. Davies and N. Naffine, *Are Persons Property? Legal Debates about Property and Personality* (Aldershot: Ashgate, 2001); P. Halewood, 'Law's Bodies: Disembodiment and the Structure of Liberal Property Rights' (1996) 81 *Iowa Law Review* 1331–1393; J. Nedelsky, 'Law, Boundaries and the Bounded Self' (1990) 30 *Representations* 162–189.
2 C. Douzinas, *The End of Human Rights* (Oxford: Hart Publishing, 2000) at 244.
3 See the brief overview in Chapter 5. For more, see U. Baxi, *The Future of Human Rights* (Oxford, Oxford University Press, 2002) at 27–35.
4 See, for more E. Bloch, *Natural Law and Human Dignity* (D.J. Schmidt (trans)) (Cambridge, Massachusetts: MIT Press, 1988) and R. Tuck, *Natural Rights Theories* (Cambridge: Cambridge University Press, 1979), Chapter 1 – cited by C. Douzinas, *The End of Human Rights*, above n 2 at 244.
5 A. Woodiwiss, *Human Rights* (Abingdon: Routledge, 2005) at 13. Woodiwiss makes reference to the well-known arguments of Glendon concerning the impoverishment of rights-talk: M.A. Glendon, *Rights-Talk: The Impoverishment of Political Discourse* (New York: Free Press, 1996).
6 This is an understandable assumption, since there are clear tensions between an exclusory reading of the property right and countervailing human rights interests in, for example, democratic inclusion. This theme forms the core of much of the excellent work by Gray and Gray, some of which will be discussed in this chapter.
7 A. Grear, 'A Tale of the Land, The Insider, The Outsider and Human Rights' (2003) 23 *Legal Studies* 33–65.
8 J. Nedelsky, 'Law, Boundaries and the Bounded Self', above n 1.
9 P. Halewood, 'Law's Bodies: Disembodiment and the Structure of Liberal Property Rights', above n 1.
10 M. Davies and N. Naffine, *Are Persons Property? Legal Debates about Property and Personality*, above n 1.
11 A. Norrie, *Crime, Reason and History: A Critical Introduction to Criminal Law*, 2nd edn (London: Butterworths, 2001); C. Federman, 'Constructing Kinds of Persons in 1886: Corporate and Criminal' (2003) 14 *Law and Critique* 167–189; M. Neocleous, 'Staging Power: Marx, Hobbes and the Personification of Capital' (2003) 14 *Law and Critique* 147–165.
12 C. Federman, 'Constructing Kinds of Persons in 1886', above n 11.
13 G.A. Marks, 'The Personification of the Business Corporation in American Law' (1987) 54 *The University of Chicago Law Review* 1441–1483; J. Flynn, 'The Jurisprudence of Corporate Personhood: The Misuse of a Legal Concept' in W. Samuels and A. Miller (eds) *Corporations and Society: Power and Responsibility* (New York: Greenwood Press, 1987); M. Horwitz, 'Santa Clara Revisited: The Development of Corporate Theory' (1985) 88 *West Virginia Law Review* 173–224.

14 C.J. Mayer, 'Personalising the Impersonal: Corporations and the Bill of Rights' (1990) 41 *Hastings Law Journal* 577–663.

15 See, for more on this process, E.M. Wood, *The Origins of Capitalism* (New York: The Monthly Review Press, 1999), 67–94, cited by L. Westra, 'Environmental Rights and Human Rights: The Final Enclosure Movement' in R. Brownsword (ed.) *Global Governance and the Quest for Justice Volume IV: Human Rights* (Oxford: Hart Publishing, 2004) 107–119 at 107, in the context of an insightful argument linking the original capitalist exclusion and its effects to environmental degradation and the human right to life.

16 For discussion of the exclusory nature and impact of the dominant liberal conception of property in various contexts see K. Gray and S. Gray, 'Private Property and Public Propriety' in J. McLean (ed.) *Property and the Constitution* (Oxford: Hart Publishing, 1999) 11–39; K. Gray, 'Equitable Property' (1994) 47 *Current Legal Problems* 157–214; K. Gray and S. Gray 'Civil Rights, Civil Wrongs and Quasi-Public Space' [1999] *European Human Rights Law Review* 46–102; K. Green, 'Citizens and Squatters: Under the Surfaces of Land Law' in S. Bright and J. Dewar (eds) *Land Law: Themes and Perspectives* (Oxford: Oxford University Press, 1998) 229–256 and A. Grear, 'A Tale of the Land', above n 7.

17 U. Baxi, *The Future of Human Rights* (Oxford: Oxford University Press, 2002) at 145.

18 This section of the argument is based, in part, on the arguments offered in A. Grear, 'A Tale of the Land', above n 7.

19 This is the major premise underlying Westra's arguments concerning the environment and the human right to life – see L. Westra, 'Environmental Rights and Human Rights', above n 15. See also the range of relevant discussions relating human rights to the idea of 'ecological integrity' in L. Westra, K. Bosselmann and R. Westra, *Reconciling Human Existence with Ecological Integrity* (London: Earthscan, 2008).

20 'What space is depends on who is experiencing it and how. Spatial experience is not innocent and neutral, but invested with power relating to age, gender, social position and relationships with others. Because space is differentially understood and experienced it forms a contradictory and conflict-ridden medium through which individuals act and are acted upon.': C. Tilley *A Phenomenology of Landscape: Places, Paths and Monuments* (Oxford: Berg, 1994) at 11.

21 A. Primavesi, 'Faith in Creation' in A. Race and R. Williamson (eds) *True To This Earth: Global Challenges and Transforming Faith* (Oxford: Oneword Publications, 1995), 101–102.

22 See, for more: S. Coyle and K. Morrow, *The Philosophical Foundations of Environmental Law* (Oxford: Hart Publishing, 2004); A. Boyle and M. Anderson (eds) *Human Rights Approaches to Environmental Protection* (Oxford: Clarendon, 2003).

23 See *The Journal of Human Rights and the Environment*, especially Issue 1: 'Where Discourses Meet' (forthcoming, 2010) for a range of inaugural discussions of the relationship between human rights and environmental discourses.

24 This characterisation is reflected quite widely in the relevant literature – see for example, the work of Gray and Gray generally. It is also interestingly, as Gray recently remarked to me, reflected in the current judicial controversy in the jurisdiction of England and Wales concerning the degree to which the Human Rights Act 1998 should be viewed as having changed the legal landscape concerning the traditional conception of property rights in land, allowing the more 'open textured secular morality of the EHCR' to challenge traditional exclusory applications of property-reasoning. See K. Gray and S.F. Gray, *Elements of Land Law*

(Oxford: Oxford University Press, 2005) at 130–140 for a discussion of this issue and the relevant case law.

25 K. Gray and S. Gray 'Private Property and Public Propriety', above n 16.

26 K. Gray, 'Property in Common Law Systems' in G.E. van Maanen and A.J. van der Walt (eds) *Property Law on the Threshold of the 21st Century* (Antwerp: MAKLU, 1996), at 265.

27 This point is reflected in arguments identifying predictable classes of claimant traditionally unsuccessful in claims for inclusion in relation to the traditional property right – for example, gypsies whose nomadism places them in an analogous bracket to refugees in their relation to both land and the construction of the ideal citizen/landowner (to be discussed further below): *R v Environment Secretary, ex p Davis* (1989) 59 P & CR 306 (failure of adverse possession claim); *Buckley v United Kingdom* (ECHR) Case No 23/1995/529/615, 1996–iv; 23 EHRR 101. See, for further discussion, K. Green, 'Citizens and Squatters: Under the Surfaces of Land Law', above n 16 at 229 and the discussion of gypsy claims by S. Poulter, 'The Rights of Ethnic, Religious and Linguistic Minorities' (1997) 3 *European Human Rights Law Review* 254–264 at 261ff.

28 See K. Gray and S. Gray, 'Civil Rights, Civil Wrongs and Quasi-Public Space', above n 16 at 73.

29 K. Gray and S. Gray, 'Private Property and Public Propriety', above n 16 at 15.

30 Ibid.

31 B. Fitzpatrick and N. Taylor, 'Trespassers *Might* Be Prosecuted: The European convention and Restrictions on the Right to Assemble' (1998) 3 *European Human Rights Law Review* 298–300.

32 J. Rowbottom, 'Property and Participation: A Right of Access for Expressive Activities' (2005) 2 *European Human Rights Law Review*, 186–202.

33 '[I]t is increasingly the case that spaces to which the public have physical access are becoming the objects of heightened and more overt forms of private control. For example, the proliferation of closed circuit television cameras and other forms of private security in shopping malls, town centres and even residential areas': B. Fitzpatrick and N. Taylor, 'Trespassers *Might* Be Prosecuted, above n 16 at n 1. See also C.D. Shearing and P.C. Stenning, 'Private Security: Implications for Social Control'(1982–1983) 30 *Social Problems*, 493.

34 K. Gray and S. Gray, 'Civil Rights, Civil Wrongs and Quasi-Public Space', above n 16 at 57–60.

35 J. Rowbottom, 'Property and Participation', above n 32.

36 [1995] 2 EGLR 130.

37 K. Gray and S. Gray, 'Civil Rights, Civil Wrongs', above n 16 at 46.

38 Ibid, at 47.

39 Ibid.

40 K. Gray and S. Gray, *Elements of Land Law* (London: Butterworths, 2001) at 169.

41 Interestingly, the argument (rejected by the Court of Appeal: [1995] 2 EGLR 130 at 134E-J) in *Rawlins* employing the concept of an 'equitable licence' has since been hesitantly supported by the Court of Appeal in *Porter v Commissioner of Police of the Metropolis* [1999] All ER (D) 1129 though the Court considered itself bound to follow the precedent of *Rawlins*.

42 The implications of, and alternative to, this raw exclusory power are fully discussed in J. Rowbottom, 'Property and Participation', above n 32 and by Gray and Gray in 'Civil Rights, Civil Wrongs', above n 16. Whereas Gray and Gray favour the judicial development of a 'right of reasonable access' analogous to that developed in other common law jurisdictions, the English Court of Appeal

in *Porter v Commissioner of Police of the Metropolis* [1999] felt unable to follow that route. Rowbottom, by contrast, proposes the creation of a limited statutory right of reasonable access for the purposes of political expression and association.

43 We should note the deeply gendered nature of this link: it was only in 1928 in Britain that women were granted suffrage, and as late as 1944 in France.

44 K. Green, 'Citizens and Squatters', above n 16 at 230.

45 The memoirs of a woman born in 1907 reflect the ideological link and its hierarchies of exclusion with telling poignancy: 'At this time Grandah as a property owner had two votes and Father had none. Father did get the vote when general male franchise was introduced, but Mother had to wait until after the First World War': Mollie Prendergast, *My Memoirs* (Unpublished, 2000), at 6.

46 K. Green, 'Citizens and Squatters', above n 16 at 248.

47 Ibid, at 241.

48 Ibid, at 252.

49 Ibid.

50 M. Heidegger, *Being and Time* (Oxford: Blackwell, 1962).

51 B.S. Turner, *Vulnerability and Human Rights* (Pennsylvania: Pennsylvania State University Press, 2006) at 27.

52 Note that the Act concerns only access on foot (Countryside and Rights of Way Act 2000, Sch 2, para 1(a)). Access is subject to restrictions in relation to reasonable behaviour (Countryside and Rights of Way Act 2000, Sch 2 and s 2(1)(a)). Access rights only affect land designated as 'access land' by the Act.

53 *DETR Consultation Paper* (1998) paras 3.66–3.67.

54 *DETR Consultation Paper* (1998) para 3.50.

55 K. Green, 'Citizens and Squatters', above n 16 at 230.

56 J.R. Short, *Imagined Country: Society, Culture and Environment* (London: Routledge, 1991) at 34–35, quoted by K. Green, 'Citizens and Squatters', above n 16 at 230.

57 N. Chakrabarti and J. Garland (eds) *Rural Racism* (Cullompton: Willan Publishing, 2004) at 123. See also M.L. Stevenson, 'The Sociopolitical Implications of Rural Racism and Tourism Experiences' in J. Tribe and D. Airey, *Developments in Tourism Research* (Oxford: Elseveier, 2007) 171–184.

58 (2001) *Carf 61*.

59 T. Bark 'Racism, Nationalism and the Countryside Alliance' (2001) *Carf61* at 6.

60 National Civil Rights Movement Newsletter, Issue 5 in (2001) *Carf61* at 7.

61 See N. Chakarabarti and J. Garland, *Rural Racism*, above n 57 at 1–14 ('Introduction') and 17–35 ('Rurality and Racialised Others: Out of Place in the Countryside?' and the wide range of studies referred to therein).

62 Kevin Gray discusses this concept in the context of an analysis of *Victoria Park Racing and Recreation Grounds Co Ltd v Taylor* (1937) 58 CLR 479 in relation to its conceptual significance in the provision of vital clues to the identification of the 'propertiness' of property in relation to land: 'Property in Thin Air' (1991) *50 Cambridge LJ* 252–307 at 268–292.

63 See the extensive discussion of the conceptually necessary elements of a property institution in J.W. Harris, *Property and Justice* (Oxford: Clarendon Press, 1996), especially his discussion of trespassory rules and the ownership spectrum. The notion of 'excludability' as discussed by Kevin Gray (see footnote above) is utilised more fully below.

64 'This right of exclusion has a strong foundation in English Law. It is used as the point of divide between leases (estates) and licences (non-estate, and not even proprietary). The right to exclude is still upheld as an essential right of landowners. Even owners of what Gray labels 'quasi-public' property have a

right to exclude particular individuals on a selective basis, for any (or no) reason, notwithstanding that the public generally is invited onto the property': S. Bright, 'Of Estates and Interests: A Tale of Ownership and Property Rights' in S. Bright and J. Dewar, *Land Law: Themes and Perspectives* (Oxford: Oxford University Press, 1998) above n 16 at 529–546.

65 See J.W. Harris, *Property and Justice* , above n 63 at 3.

66 The term is Gray's. See K. Gray, 'Property in Thin Air', above n 62 at 268.

67 K. Gray, 'Equitable Property', above n 16 at 157. For further reading on the psychology of possession, see the references in 'Equitable Property', above n 16 at n 2.

68 Indeed, Nedelsky has argued from a critical perspective, that property depends upon a particular notion of the person as a 'bounded self' – an exclusionary and atomistic view of the human being that gives troubling ideological content to our embodied distinctness from other bodies. J. Nedelsky, 'Law, Boundaries and the Bounded Self', above n 1.

69 See Harris's chapter on 'Imaginary Societies' in J.W. Harris, *Property and Justice,* above n 63 at 15–22, together with his discussion on the ubiquity of property in the introduction, with the references cited there to A.I. Hallowell, 'The Nature and Function of Property as a Social Institution' in A.I. Hallowell, *Culture and Experience* (Pennsylvania: University of Pennsylvania Press, 1955), Chapter 12.

70 Societies without a concept of private property, moreover, could not have a notion of common property, because the concept of private property is logically prior to the notion of common property. Without a concept of private property, common property as 'property' makes no conceptual sense: J.W. Harris, *Property and Justice,* above n 63 at 15.

71 See, for example, *Milirrpum v Nabalco Pty Ltd* (1971) 17 FLR 141, at 270ff where Blackburn J suggests that the Aboriginals had 'a more cogent feeling of obligation to the land than of ownership of it', and that it was easier to say that 'the clan belongs to the land than that the land belongs to the clan'. In that case, the lack of a concept of a right to exclude others was a decisive obstacle to the founding of a conventional common law property claim (272 ff). See the discussion of this case and native title generally in the context of considering 'equitable property' in traditional country in K. Gray, 'Equitable Property', above n 16 at 181–188.

72 K. Gray, 'Property in Thin Air', above n 62 at 252.

73 Ibid, at 268.

74 Ibid.

75 Ibid, at 269.

76 Ibid.

77 Ibid.

78 *Victoria Park Racing and Recreation Grounds Co Ltd v Taylor* (1937) 58 CLR 479.

79 K. Gray, 'Property in Thin Air', above n 62 at 270. Note also Gray's insistence that the test of physical excludability be applied with care, because it only applies to the property in its existing form. 'Ultimately', he suggests, 'most resources can be physically insulated from access by strangers – if only through vast expenditures of money or imagination': K. Gray, 'Property in Thin Air', above n 62 at 272.

80 'The plaintiff who neglects to utilise relevant legal protection has failed, so to speak, to raise around the disputed resource the legal fences which were plainly available to him. He has failed to stake out his claim; he has failed in effect to propertise the resource', K. Gray, 'Property in Thin Air', above n 62 at 274.

81 See J.W. Harris, *Property and Justice*, above n 63 at 23–41 for how trespassory rules form part of the minimal structure of a property institution.
82 See the fuller discussion of contractual protection as a form of legal excludability, intellectual property protection and the implications for fiduciary law in K. Gray, 'Property in Thin Air', above n 62 at 274–280.
83 Ibid, at 281.
84 K. Gray, 'Equitable Property', above n 16.
85 Ibid, at 170.
86 C.B. Macpherson, *The Political Theory of Possessive Individualism: From Hobbes to Locke* (Oxford: Clarendon Press, 1962).
87 C. Reich, 'The New Property', 73 *Yale Law Journal* 733–787 (1964).
88 C.B. Macpherson, *Property: Mainstream and Critical Positions* (Toronto: Toronto University Press, 1978) at 7 (emphasis added).
89 Ibid, at 10.
90 Ibid.
91 K. Gray, 'Equitable Property', above n 16 at 167.
92 Ibid.
93 J.W. Harris, *Property and Justice*, above n 63 at 155.
94 For example, see K. Bakker, 'The "Commons" Versus "Commodity": Alter-globalization, Anti-privatization and the Human Right to Water in the Global South' (2007) 39 *Antipode* 430–455.
95 J.W. Harris, 'Is Property a Human Right?' in J. McLean (ed.) *Property and the Constitution* (Oxford: Hart Publishing, 1999).
96 C.B. Macpherson, 'Capitalism, and the Changing Concept of Property' in E. Kamenka and R.S. Neale (eds) *Feudalism, Capitalism and Beyond* (Canberra: Australian National University Press, 1975) at 119–122; C.B. Macpherson, *Property: Mainstream and Critical Positions* (Oxford: Blackwell, 1978), 205–206 – cited by J.W Harris, 'Is Property a Human Right?', above n 63 at 73.
97 K. Gray, 'Equitable Property', above n 16 at 168.
98 Ibid, at 169.
99 J.W. Harris, *Property and Justice*, above n 63 at 151.
100 K. Gray and S. Gray, 'Private Property and Public Propriety', above n 16 at 13.
101 Ibid.
102 J. Finnis, *Natural Law and Natural Rights* (Oxford: Clarendon Press, 1980).
103 Ibid, at 205.
104 Ibid, at 205–206.
105 The phrase is Finnis's, *Natural Law and Natural Rights*, above n 102 at 209.
106 The relationship between rights and duties is complex, and certainly an over-emphasis on duties would undermine certain fundamental human rights norms. However, it has often been argued that comtemporary rights discourse has under-emphasised duties and over-emphasised rights as being individualistic, atomised claims of self-interest. The debates surrounding the Banjul Charter, with its extensive emphasis on duties which move far beyond duties correlative to rights is instructive in this regard.
107 Consider, for example, Tesco Plc's plans to invoke human rights arguments against the ECJ ruling that it could not sell 'grey import' Levi Strauss jeans (*Zino Davidoff SA v A & G Imports Ltd, Levi Strauss & Co v another v Tesco Stores Ltd and another; Levi Strauss & Co and another v Costco Wholesale UK Ltd* (Joined Cases C 414/99–C 416/99 [2002] CMLR 1)): Tesco's plan was to invoke the right to freedom of expression, right of freedom to own and deal in property, and the right not to be discriminated against. For more see *Wall Street Journal*

(Europe) 18 December 2001, *Financial Times* 18 December 2001, *Republic*, 20 May 2002.

108 In relation to inclusion as a necessary pre-condition of law (in particular of criminal law) see A. Duff, 'Inclusion and Exclusion: Citizens, Subjects and Outlaws' (1998) 51 *Current Legal Problems* 241–266. Duff argues that any 'plausible interpretation' of the concepts of law and legal obligation entail certain essential conditions, one of which is a certain notion of inclusion: 'those bound by the law must be included within, as members of, a community whose law it is; and that notion of inclusion has normative substance' (at 242).

109 Morgan argues that water has a particular salience for public discourse: B. Morgan, 'Emerging Global Water Welfarism: Access to Water, Unruly Consumers and Transnational Governance' in F. Trentmann and J. Brewer, *Consumer Cultures, Global Perspectives* (Oxford and New York: Berg Press, 2006) at 383. Available at: http://seis.bris.ac.uk/~lwbmm/documents/Trentmann%20and%20Brewer%20book%20chapter%202006.pdf <date of last access 1 September 2008>.

110 B. Morgan, 'Water: Frontier Markets and Cosmopolitan Activism' (2004) 27 *Soundings: A Journal of Politics and Culture* 10–24 at 15.

111 B. Morgan, 'Water: Frontier Markets and Cosmopolitan Activism', above n 110 at 14.

112 Ibid, at 10.

113 Ibid, at 11.

114 Ibid, at 18.

115 Ibid, at 11. The three companies are Thames Water, Suez and Vivendi. While 85 per cent of the world's population is not supplied by these providers, their operations are significant and part of a rapidly consolidating, and contested, paradigm for water services delivery.

116 S. Anderson and S. Grusky, 'Challenging Corporate Investor Rule: How the World Bank's Investment Court, Free Trade Agreements, and Bilateral Investment Treaties have Unleashed a New Era of Corporate Power and What To Do About It', *Food and Water Watch*, April 2007.

117 B. Morgan, 'Water: Frontier Markets and Cosmopolitan Activism', above n 110 at 14.

118 T. Johnson, '"Water War": A Test-Case on Trade Transparency', *Miami Herald*, October 13, 2002, cited by S. Anderson and S. Grusky, 'Challenging Corporate Investor Rule', above n 116.

119 T. Johnson, 'Water War', above n 118.

120 B. Morgan, 'Water: Frontier Markets and Cosmopolitan Activism', above n 110 at 14.

121 Ibid, at 15.

122 See P. Bond and J. Dugard, 'Water, Human Rights and Social Conflict: South African Experiences' (2007) 1 *Law, Social Justice and Global Development Journal* http://go.warwick.ac.uk/elj/lgd/2008_1/bond_dugard/ <Date of last access: 1st September 2008>. The authors itemise the lethal effects of the privatisation or commercialisation of water in South Africa – see pages 7–8.

123 For a sophisticated account of these complexities, see B. Morgan, 'The Regulatory Face of the Human Right to Water' (2004) 15 *Journal of Water Law* 179–187.

124 See above, Chapter 7 at 152.

125 J. Schulz, 'Bolivia's War over Water', The Democracy Center, February 4, 2000, cited by S. Anderson and S. Grusky, 'Challenging Corporate Investor Rule' above n 116.

126 S. Anderson and S. Grusky, 'Challenging Corporate Investor Rule', above n 116 at 18.

127 B. Morgan, 'Global Business, Local Constraints: The Case of Water in South Africa' in N. Woods, *Making Global Self-Regulation Effective in Developing Countries* (Oxford: Oxford University Press, 2006) 201–226 at 203.
128 B. Morgan, 'Global Business, Local Constraints', above n 127 at 203.
129 B. Morgan, 'Emerging Global Water Welfarism', above n 109 at 397.
130 Case No. 06/13865 *Mazibuko and Others v The City of Johannesburg and Others*.
131 P. Bond and J. Dugard, 'Water, Human Rights and Social Conflict', above n 122.
132 *Mazibuko* at para 2.
133 Para. 4.
134 Para. 9.
135 Para. 11.
136 Paras. 157–158.
137 Paras. 159–160.
138 'Dignity', although a central value in human rights discourse, is, to say the least, multivalent: see C. McCrudden, 'Human Dignity', *University of Oxford Faculty of Law Legal Studies Research Paper Series*: Working Paper No. 10/2006. McCrudden argues that the use of the notion of dignity is widespread in legal discourse, whether instantiated in international or constitutional documents, judicial decision-making in the human rights context, or in transnational judicial conversation. Nevertheless, '[t]here is little common understanding of what dignity requires across jurisdictions. The meaning of dignity is therefore highly context specific, varying significantly from jurisdiction to jurisdiction and (often) over time within particular jurisdictions .... Dignity often provides a convenient cover for the adoption of interpretations of human rights guarantees that appear to be intentionally, not just coincidentally, highly contingent on local circumstances' (at 21).
139 See, for example, the arguments offered by E. Grant, 'Dignity and Equality' (2007) 7 *Human Rights Law Review* 299–329.
140 See paras 168–181.
141 Para 79.
142 M.A. Fineman, 'The Vulnerable Subject: Anchoring Equality in the Human Condition' (2008) 20 *Yale Journal of Law and Feminism* at 23.
143 Ibid, at 8.
144 Ibid, at 8–9.
145 Ibid, at 9.
146 Ibid, at 13–15.
147 Ibid, at 10.
148 Ibid, at 11.
149 For example, this is the argument presented by K. Bakker, 'The "Commons" Versus "Commodity"', above n 94.
150 P. Bond and J. Dugard, 'Water, Human Rights and Social Conflict', above n 122 at 11.
151 L. Westra, 'Environmental Rights and Human Rights', above n 15.
152 This does not preclude the fact that vulnerability needs to be theorised in a way that reflects species-specific nuances and forms of differentiation important to the design of legal regimes of protection and facilitation.

Chapter 9

1 Some of the issues related to this scepticism and a set of concomitant dangers to human rights are explored in C. Gearty, *Can Human Rights Survive* (Cambridge: Cambridge University Press, 2006).

2 See M. Diamantides, 'The Subject May Have Disappeared But Its Sufferings Remain' (2000) 11 *Law and Critique* 156.

3 A. Grear, 'Human Rights – Human Bodies? Some Reflections on Corporate Human Rights Distortion, the Legal Subject, Embodiment and Human Rights Theory' (2006) 17 *Law and Critique* 171 at 175, emphasis added.

4 A. Fausto-Sterling, *Sexing the Body: Gender Politics and the Construction of Sexuality* (New York: Basic Books, 2000) at 31, emphasis added. Her book presents a sophisticated and well argued critique of sexual dimorphism as a cultural imposition.

5 J. Hearn and D.H.J. Morgan, 'Men, Masculinities and Social Theory' in J. Hearn and D. Morgan (eds) *Men, Masculinities and Social Theory* (London: Unwin Hyman, 1990) at 8–10.

Bibliography

Abu-Lughod, J. *Before the European Hegemony: The World System AD 1250–1350* (New York: Oxford University Press, 1989).

Adams, W.W. 'The Primacy of Interrelating: Practicing Ecological Psychology with Buber, Levinas and Merleau-Ponty' (2007) 38 *Journal of Phenomenological Psychology* 24–61.

Addo, M. 'The Corporation as a Victim of Human Rights Violations' in Addo, M. (ed.) *Human Rights Standards and the Responsibility of Transnational Corporations* (Hague: Kluwer, 1999).

Agamben, G. *Homo Sacer: Sovereign Power and Bare Life* (D. Heller-Razzen (trans.)) (Stanford: Stanford University Press, 1995).

Agamben, G. *State of Exception* (Chicago and London: University of Chicago Press, 2005).

Ahmed, S. 'Deconstruction and Law's Other: Towards a Feminist Theory of Embodied Legal Rights' (1995) 4 *Social and Legal Studies* 55–73.

Ajana, B. 'Disembodiment and Cyberspace: A Phenomenological Approach' (2005) *Electronic Journal of Sociology*.

Albrow, M. and King, E. (eds) *Globalization, Knowledge and Society* (London: Sage, 1990).

Altvater, E. 'Post-Neoliberalism or Post-Capitalism?' (2009) *Alternatives International* available at <http://www.alterinter.org/article2629.html?lang=fr> (Date of Last Access 27 May 2009).

Anderson, S. and Cavanagh, J. 'Top 200: The Rise of Global Corporate Power' *Institute for Policy Studies* http://www.ips-dc.org/reports/top200.htm (date of last access: 1 July 2008).

Anderson, S. and Cavanagh, J. *Top 200: The Rise of Global Corporate Power* (Washington DC: Institute for Policy Studies, 2000).

Anderson, S. and Grusky, S. 'Challenging Corporate Investor Rule: How the World Bank's Investment Court, Free Trade Agreements, and Bilateral Investment Treaties have Unleashed a New Era of Corporate Power and What To Do About It', *Food and Water Watch*, April 2007.

Arendt, H. *The Origins of Totalitarianism* (New York: Harcourt Brace Jovanovich, 1979).

Arnaud-Duc, N. 'Women Entrapped: from Public Non-existence to Private Protection' in A.-J. Arnaud and E. Kingdom, *Women's Rights and the Rights of Men* (Aberdeen, Aberdeen University Press, 1990).

Attanasio, J.B. 'Rapporteur's Overview and Conclusions: Of Sovereignty, Globalization and Courts' in Franck, T.M. and Fox, G.H. (eds) *International Law Decisions in National Courts* (New York: Transnational Publishers, 1996).

Bainham, A., Sclater, S.D. and Richards, M. *Body Lore and Laws* (Oxford: Hart, 2002).

Bakker, K. 'The "Commons" Versus "Commodity": Alter-globalization, Anti-privatization and the Human Right to Water in the Global South' (2007) 39 *Antipode* 430–455.

Bark, T. 'Racism, Nationalism and the Countryside Alliance' (2001) *Carf61*.

Baxi, U. 'Justice as Emancipation: The Legacy of Babasaheb Ambedkar' in Baxi, U. and Parekh, B. (eds) *Crisis and Change in Contemporary India* (New Delhi: Sage, 1995) 122–149.
Baxi, U. and Parekh, B. (eds) *Crisis and Change in Contemporary India* (New Delhi: Sage, 1995).
Baxi, U. *The Future of Human Rights* (Oxford: Oxford University Press, 2002).
Baxi, U. 'Market Fundamentalisms: Business Ethics at the Altar of Human Rights' (2005) 5 *Human Rights Law Review* 1–26.
Baxi, U. *The Future of Human Rights* (Oxford: Oxford University Press, 2006).
Baxi, U. *Human Rights in a Post-human World: Critical Essays* (Oxford: Oxford University Press, 2007).
Beck, U. *Power in the Global Age* (Cambridge: Polity Press, 2005/2006).
Beitz, C. 'Economic Rights and Distributive Justice in Developing Societies' (1981) 33 *World Politics* 321–346.
Belcher, A. 'Imagining How a Company Thinks: What is Corporate Culture?' (2007) 11 *Deakin Law Review* 1–21.
Belcher, A. 'Gendered Company: Views of Corporate Governance at the Institute of Directors' (1997) 5 *Feminist Legal Studies* 57–76.
Bentham, J. 'Anarchical Fallacies; Being an Examination of the Declaration of Rights Issued During the French Revolution' in Waldron, J. (ed.), *Nonsense upon Stilts* (London: Methuen, 1987) 46–76.
Beveridge, F. and Mullally, S. 'International Human Rights and Body Politics' in Bridgeman, J. and Millns, S. (eds) *Law and Body Politics: Regulating the Female Body* (Aldershot: Dartmouth, 1995).
Bloch, E. *Natural Law and Human Dignity* (D.J. Schmidt (trans.)) (Cambridge, Massachusetts: MIT Press, 1988).
Bond, P. and Dugard, J. 'Water, Human Rights and Social Conflict: South African Experiences' (2007) 1 *Law, Social Justice and Global Development Journal* http://go.warwick.ac.uk/elj/lgd/2008_1/bond_dugard/ <Date of last access: 1st September 2008>.
Bottomley, A. (ed.) *Feminist Perspectives on the Foundational Subjects of Law* (London: Cavendish, 1996).
Bottomley, A. 'The Many Appearances of the Body in Feminist Scholarship' in Bainham, A., Sclater, S.D. and Richards, M. *Body Lore and Laws* (Oxford: Hart, 2002) 127–148.
Boyle, A. and Anderson, M. (eds) *Human Rights Approaches to Environmental Protection* (Oxford: Clarendon, 2003).
Bradlow, D.D. and Grossman, C. 'Limited Mandates and Intertwined Problems: A New Challenge for the World Bank and the IMF' (1995) 17 *Human Rights Quarterly* 411–442.
Brewer, J. and Staves, S. (eds) *Early Modern Conceptions of Property* (London: Routledge, 1995).
Bridgeman, J. and Millns, S. (eds) *Law and Body Politics: Regulating the Female Body* (Aldershot: Dartmouth, 1995).
Bright, S. 'Of Estates and Interests: A Tale of Ownership and Property Rights' in Bright, S. and Dewar, J. (eds) *Land Law: Themes and Perspectives* (Oxford: Oxford University Press, 1998).
Bright, S. and Dewar, J. (eds) *Land Law: Themes and Perspectives* (Oxford: Oxford University Press, 1998).
Brownsword, R. (ed.) *Global Governance and the Quest for Justice: Volume IV: Human Rights* (Oxford: Hart Publishing, 2004).

Bruinsma, F.J. and Parmentier, S. 'Interview with Mr Luzius Wildhaber, President of the ECHR' (2003) 21 *Netherlands Quarterly of Human Rights* 185.

Bunch, C. 'Women's Rights as Human Rights: Toward a Re-Vision of Human Rights' (1990) 12 *Human Rights Quarterly* 486.

Burke, E. *Reflections on the Revolution in France* (Pockocke, J.G.A. (ed.)) (London: Hackett, 1987).

Buss, D. and Manji, A. (eds) *International Law: Modern Feminist Approaches* (Oxford: Hart Publishing, 2005).

Cassesse, A. 'The Impact of the European Convention on Human Rights on the International Tribunal for the former Yugoslavia' in Mahoney, P. *et al.* (eds), *Protecting Human Rights: The European Perspective: Studies in Memory of Rolv Ryssdal* (Koln: Carl Heymanns Verlag, 2000) 213.

Caven, H. 'Horror in Our Time: Images of the Concentration Camps in the British Media 1945' (2001) 21 *Historical Journal of Film, Radio and Television* 205–253.

Chakrabarti, N. and Garland, J. (eds) *Rural Racism* (Cullompton: Willan Publishing, 2004).

Chambliss, W. and Seidman, R. *Law, Order and Power* (Reading, Massachusetts: Addison-Wesley Publishing Co, 1982).

Charlesworth, H., 'Midlife Crisis of the Universal Declaration of Human Rights' (1998) 55 *Washington Lee Law Review* 781–796.

Charlesworth, H., Chinkin, C. and Wright, S. 'Feminist Approaches to International Law' (1991) 85 *American Journal of International Law* 613–645.

Cheah, P. and Grosz, E. 'The Body of the Law: Notes Toward a Theory of Corporeal Justice' in Cheah, P., Fraser, D. and Grbich, J. *Thinking Through the Body of Law* (St Leonards: Allen and Unwin, 1996).

Cheah, P., Fraser, D. and Grbich, J. (eds) *Thinking Through the Body of Law* (St Leonards: Allen and Unwin, 1996).

Coffee, J. 'No Soul to Damn: No Body to Kick': An Unscandalized Inquiry into the Problem of Corporate Punishment' (1981) 79 *Michigan Law Review* 386.

Conot, R.E. *Justice at Nuremburg* (New York: Harper and Row, 1983).

Cook, R.J. (ed.) *Human Rights of Women: National and International Perspectives* (Philadelphia: University of Pennsylvania Press, 1994).

Coyle, S. 'Thomas Hobbes and the Intellectual Origins of Legal Positivism' (2003) 16 *Canadian Journal of Law and Jurisprudence* 243–269.

Coyle, S. and Morrow, K. *The Philosophical Foundations of Environmental Law* (Oxford: Hart Publishing, 2004).

Cranston, M. *What are Human Rights?* (New York: Taplinger Publishing, 1973).

Damasio, A. *Descartes' Error: Emotion, Reason and the Brain* (New York: Harper Collins, 1994).

Davies, M. and Naffine, N. *Are Persons Property? Legal Debates about Property and Personality* (Aldershot: Ashgate, 2001).

Dembour, M.-B. *Who Believes in Human Rights? Reflections on the European Convention* (Cambridge: Cambridge University Press, 2006).

Derham, D.P. 'Theories of Legal Personality' in Webb, L.C. (ed.), *Legal Personality and Political Pluralism* (New York: Cambridge University Press, 1958) at 7.

Derrida, J. *Positions* (Chicago: University of Chicago Press, 1981) at 41.

De Sousa Santos, B. *Towards a New Legal Common Sense: Law, Globalization and Modernity* (London: Sage, 1990).

De Sousa Santos, B. *Toward a New Legal Common Sense: Law, Globalization and Emancipation* (London: Butterworths, 2002).

De Sousa Santos, B. and Rodrigues-Garavito, C.A. *Law and Globalisation from Below: Towards a Cosmopolitan Legality* (Cambridge: Cambridge University Press, 2005).

De Waal, F.B.M., 'The Chimpanzee's Sense of Social Regularity and its Relation to the Human Sense of Justice' in Masters, R.D. and Gruter, M. *The Sense of Justice* (London: Sage Publications, 1992) 241–255.

Diamantides, M. 'The Subject May Have Disappeared But Its Sufferings Remain' (2000) 11 *Law and Critique* 156.

Dignam, A.J. and Allen, D. *Company Law and the Human Rights Act 1998* (London: Butterworths, 2000).

Dine, J. and Fagan, A. *Human Rights and Capitalism: A Multidisciplinary Perspective on Globalisation* (Cheltenham and Massachusetts: Edward Elgar Publishing, 2006).

Donnelly, J. *Universal Human Rights in Theory and Practice* (Ithaca: Cornell University Press, 1989).

Donnelly, J. *Universal Human Rights in Theory and Practice*, 2nd edn (Ithaca NY: Cornell University Press, 2003).

Douzinas, C. *Human Rights and Empire: The Political Philosophy of Cosmopolitanism* (Abingdon: Routledge-Cavendish (Glasshouse)), 2007.

Douzinas, C. *The End of Human Rights* (Oxford: Hart, 2000).

Douzinas, C. and Gearey, A. *Critical Jurisprudence* (Oxford: Hart Publishing, 2005).

Duff, A. 'Inclusion and Exclusion: Citizens, Subjects and Outlaws' (1998) 51 *Current Legal Problems* 241–266.

Duff, P.W. *Personality in Roman Private Law* (Cambridge: Cambridge University Press, 1938).

Dunn, J. *The Political Thought of John Locke* (Cambridge: Cambridge University Press, 1969).

Dunning, J. *Multinational Enterprises in a Global Economy* (Reading, MA: Addison-Wesley, 1993).

Egede, T. and Wells, C. 'An Annotated Bibliography of the Accountability of Multinational Corporations: A Review of International Human Rights Law', Working Paper Series No 12, The Centre for Business Relationships, Accountability, Sustainability and Society.

Emberland, M. 'The Corporate Veil in the Jurisprudence of the Human Rights Committee and the Inter-American Court and Commission of Human Rights' (2004) 4 *Human Rights Law Review* 257–275.

Emberland, M. *The Human Rights of Companies: Exploring the Structure of ECHR Protection* (Oxford: Oxford University Press, 2006).

Engle, K. 'International Human Rights and Feminism: When Discourses Meet' (1992) 13 *Michigan Journal of International Law* 517.

Evans, T. *Human Rights Fifty Years On* (Manchester: Manchester University Press, 1988).

Evans, T. and Ayers, A.J. 'In the Service of Power: The Global Political Economy of Citizenship and Human Rights' (2006) 10 *Citizenship Studies* 239–308.

Fausto-Sterling, A. *Sexing the Body: Gender Politics and the Construction of Sexuality* (New York: Basic Books, 2000).

Featherstone, M. (ed.) *Global Culture: Nationalism, Globalization and* Modernity (London: Sage, 1990).

Federman, C. 'Constructing Kinds of Persons in 1886: Corporate and Criminal', *Law and Critique* 14 (2003), 167–189.

Fineman, M. *The Autonomy Myth: A Theory of Dependency* (New York: The New Press, 2003).

Fineman, M. 'The Vulnerable Subject: Anchoring Equality in the Human Condition' (2008) 20 *Yale Journal of Law and Feminism* 1–23.

Finnis, J. *Natural Law and Natural Rights* (Oxford: Clarendon Press, 1980).
Finnis, J. 'The Priority of Persons' in Horder, J. (ed.), *Oxford Essays in Jurisprudence, Volume IV* (Oxford: Oxford University Press, 2000) 10.
Fitzpatrick, B. and Taylor, N. 'Trespassers *Might* Be Prosecuted: The European Convention and Restrictions on the Right to Assemble' (1998) 3 *European Human Rights Law Review* 298–300.
Flynn, J. 'The Jurisprudence of Corporate Personhood: The Misuse of a Legal Concept' in Samuels, W. and Miller, A. (eds), *Corporations and Society: Power and Responsibility* (New York: Greenwood Press, 1987).
Foucault, M. *The History of Sexuality: An Introduction* (Hurley, R. (trans.)) (New York: Random House, 1978).
Foucault, M. *Discipline and Punish: The Birth of the Prison* (Sheridan, A. (trans.)) (New York: Vintage, 1995).
Franck, T.M. and Fox, G.H. (eds) *International Law Decisions in National Courts* (New York: Transnational Publishers, 1996).
Freeman, M. 'Beyond Capitalism and Socialism' in Dine, J. and Fagan, A. *Human Rights and Capitalism: A Multidisciplinary Perspective on Globalisation* (Cheltenham: Edward Elgar Publishing, 2006).
French, P.A. 'The Corporation as a Moral Person' (1979) 16 *American Philosophical Quarterly* 207–215.
Friedman, L.M. *The Legal System: A Social Science Perspective* (New York: Russell Sage Foundation, 1975).
Galey, M.E. 'Promoting Nondiscrimination against Women: The UN Commission on the Status of Women' (1979) 23 *International Studies Quarterly* 273–302.
Gallagher, A. 'Ending the Marginalisation: Strategies for Incorporating Women in the United Nations Human Rights System' (1997) 19 *Human Rights Quarterly* 283.
Gearty, C. *Can Human Rights Survive?* (Cambridge: Cambridge University Press, 2006).
George, S. 'The End of Neoliberalism: Alternatives to Finance-Led Capitalism' at *Erofnungsrede auf der Konferenze Linke Auswege aus der Krise*, an international conference held in the Deutscher Bundestag, Berlin, 20–21 March 2009 (available at <http://www.ulla-loezter.de/article/362.susan_george_the_end_of_neoliberalism_ alternatives_to-finance_led_capitalism.html> Date of last access: 27 May 2009).
Giddens, A. *Sociology* (Oxford: Polity Press, 1990).
Gill, S. 'Globalisation, Market Civilisation, and Disciplinary Neoliberalism' (1995) 24 *Millennium Journal of International Studies*, 399–423.
Gill, S. 'Constitutionalizing Inequality and the Clash of Globalizations' (2002) 4 *International Studies Review* 47–65.
Glendon, M.A. *Rights-Talk: The Impoverishment of Political Discourse* (New York: Free Press, 1996).
Gobert, J. 'The Corporate Manslaughter and Corporate Homicide Act 2007 – Thirteen Years in the Making but was it Worth the Wait?' (2008) 71 *The Modern Law Review* 413–463.
Gordon, W. 'Historicism in Legal Scholarship' (1981) 90 *Yale Law Journal* 1017–1056.
Gould, C.C. (ed.) *Beyond Domination: New Perspectives on Women and Philosophy* (Totowa: Rowman and Allanheld, 1984) 250–264.
Grant, E. 'Dignity and Equality' (2007) 7 *Human Rights Law Review* 299–329.
Grant, R.W. *John Locke's Liberalism* (Chicago: University of Chicago Press, 1987).

Grantham, R. and Rickett, C. 'The Bookmaker's Legacy to Company Law Doctrine' in Grantham, R. and Rickett, C. *Corporate Personality in the Twentieth Century* (Oxford: Hart Publishing, 1998).

Grantham, R. and Rickett, C. *Corporate Personality in the Twentieth Century* (Oxford: Hart Publishing, 1998).

Gray, K. 'Property in Thin Air' (1991) *50 Cambridge LJ* 252.

Gray, K. 'Equitable Property' (1994) 47 *Current Legal Problems* 157–214.

Gray, K. 'Property in Common Law Systems' in Van Maanen, G.E. and Van der Walt, A.J. (eds), *Property Law on the Threshold of the 21st Century* (Antwerp: MAKLU, 1996).

Gray, K and Gray, S. 'Private Property and Public Propriety' in McLean, J. (ed.), *Property and the Constitution* (Oxford: Hart Publishing, 1999).

Gray, K. and Gray, S. 'Civil Rights, Civil Wrongs and Quasi-Public Space' [1999] *European Human Rights Law Review* 46–102.

Gray, K. and Gray, S. *Elements of Land Law* (London: Butterworths, 2001).

Gray, K. and Gray, S.F. *Elements of Land Law* (Oxford: Oxford University Press, 2005).

Grear, A. 'A Tale of the Land, the Insider, the Outsider and Human Rights', *Legal Studies*, 23 (2003), 33–65.

Grear, A. 'Human Rights – Human Bodies? Some Reflections on Corporate Human Rights Distortion, the Legal Subject, Embodiment and Human Rights Theory' (2006) 17 *Law and Critique* 171.

Grear, A. 'Challenging Corporate Humanity: Legal Disembodiment, Embodiment and Human Rights' (2007) 7 *Human Rights Law Review* 511–543.

Green, K. 'Being Here – What a Woman Can Say About Land Law' in Bottomley, A. (ed.), *Feminist Perspectives on the Foundational Subjects of Law* (London: Cavendish, 1996).

Green, K. 'Citizens and Squatters: Under the Surfaces of Land Law' in Bright, S. and Dewar, J. (eds), *Land Law: Themes and Perspectives* (Oxford: Oxford University Press, 1998) 229–256.

Gruter, M. 'An Ethological Perspective on Law and Biology' in Masters, R.D. and Gruter, M. *The Sense of Justice* (London: Sage Publications, 1992) 95–105.

Guradze, H. *Die Eurpaische Menshcenrechtsconvention. Konvention zum Schutze der Menshcenrechte und Grundfreiheiten nebst Zusatsprotokollen. Kommentar* (Berlin: Vahlen, 1968) 43 and 45–46.

Hacking, I. *Mad Travellers: Reflections on the Reality of Transient Mental Illness* (Charlottesville: University Press of Virginia, 1998).

Halewood, P. 'Law's Bodies: Disembodiment and the Structure of Liberal Property Rights' (1996) 81 *Iowa Law Review* 1331–1393.

Hallis, F. *Corporate Personality* (London: Oxford University Press, 1930).

Hallowell, A.I. 'The Nature and Function of Property as a Social Institution' in Hallowell, A.I. *Culture and Experience* (Pennsylvania: University of Pennsylvania Press, 1955).

Hallowell, A.I. *Culture and Experience* (Pennsylvania: University of Pennsylvania Press, 1955).

Halpin, A. *Rights and Law: Analysis and Theory* (Oxford: Hart Publishing, 1997).

Haraway, D. *Simians, Cyborgs, and Women: The Reinvention of Nature* (London: Free Association Books, 1991).

Harding, C., Kohl, U. and Salmon, N. *Human Rights in the Market Place: The Exploitation of Rights Protection by Economic Actors* (Aldershot: Ashgate, 2008).

Harris, J.W. *Property and Justice* (Oxford: Clarendon Press, 1996).

Harris, J.W. 'Is Property a Human Right?' in McLean, J. *Property and the Constitution* (Oxford: Hart Publishing, 1999).

Hart, H.L.A. *The Concept of Law* (Oxford: Clarendon Press, 1994).
Hartmann, T. 'Unequal Protection: The Rise of Corporate Dominance and the Theft of Human Rights', available at: http://www.thomhartmanncom/summary/shtml.
Hearn, J. and Morgan, D.H.J. 'Men, Masculinities and Social Theory' in Hearn, J. and Morgan, D. (eds), *Men, Masculinities and Social Theory* (London: Unwin Hyman, 1990).
Heidegger, M. *Being and Time* (Oxford: Blackwell, 1962).
Hitler, A. *Mein Kampf* (R. Manheim (trans.)) (Boston: Houghton Mifflin Co, 1971).
Hobbes, T. *Leviathan* (Tuck, R. (ed.)) (Cambridge: Cambridge University Press, 1996).
Hohfeld, W.N. 'Nature of Stockholders Individual Liability for Corporation Debts' (1909) 9 *Columbia Law Review* 285.
Hohfeld, W.N. 'Some Fundamental Legal Conceptions as Applied in Judicial Reasoning' (1913) 23 *Yale Law Journal* 16–59.
Hohfeld, W.N. 'Fundamental Legal Conceptions as Applied in Judicial Reasoning' (1917) 26 *Yale Law Journal* 710–770.
Holmes, H.B. 'A Feminist Analysis of the Universal Declaration of Human Rights' in Gould, C.C. (ed.), *Beyond Domination: New Perspectives on Women and Philosophy* (Totowa: Rowman and Allanheld, 1984) 250–264.
Horwitz, M.J. 'Comment: The Historical Contingency of the Role of History' (1981) 90 *Yale Law Journal* 1057–1059.
Horwitz, M. 'Santa Clara Revisited: The Development of Corporate Theory' (1985) 88 *West Virginia Law Review* 173–224.
Hunt, A. and Wickham, G. *Foucault and Law: Towards a Sociology of Law as Governance* (London: Pluto Press, 1998 [1994]).
Hunt, L. *The French Revolution and Human Rights: A Brief Documentary History* (New York: Bedford/St Martin's Press, 1996).
Hunt, L. *Inventing Human Rights: A History* (New York: W.W. Norton and Co, 2007).
Hyde, A. *Bodies of Law* (Princeton: Princeton University Press, 1997).
Hyde, W.W. 'The Prosecution and Punishment of Animals and Lifeless Things in the Middle Ages and Modern Times' (1916) 64 *University of Pennsylvania Law Review* 696–730.
Ignatieff, M. *Human Rights as Politics and Idolatry* (Princeton: Princeton University Press, 2001).
Ishay, M. *The History of Human Rights: From Ancient Times to the Globalization Era* (Berkeley: University of California Press, 2004).
Jaggar, A.M. and Bordo, S.R. (eds) *Gender/Body/Knowledge: Feminist Reconstructions of Being and Knowing* (New Brunswick, NJ: Rutgers University Press, 1989).
Jochnick, C. 'Confronting the Impunity of Non-State Actors: New Fields for the Promotion of Human Rights' (1999) 21 *Human Rights Quarterly* 21.
Johnson, M. *The Body in the Mind: The Bodily Basis of Meaning, Imagination and Reason* (Chicago: Chicago University Press, 1987).
Johnson, T. '"Water War": A Test-Case on Trade Transparency', *Miami Herald*, October 13, 2002.
Jones, P. 'Human Rights, Group Rights, Peoples Rights' (1999) 21 *Human Rights Quarterly* 80.
Joseph, S. 'Taming the Leviathans: Multinational Enterprises and Human Rights' (1999) 46 *Netherlands International Law Review* 171, 173–174.
Joseph, S. *Corporations and Transnational Human Rights Litigation* (Oxford: Hart, 2004).
Joseph, S., Scultz, J. and Castan, M. *The International Covenant on Civil and Political Rights: Cases, Commentary and Materials*, 2nd edn (Oxford: Oxford University Press, 2004).

Kaldor, M. *New and Old Wars: Organized Violence in a Global Era* (Cambridge: Polity Press, 2001).

Kamenka, E. and Neale, R.S. (eds) *Feudalism, Capitalism and Beyond* (Canberra: Australian National University Press, 1975).

Keeton, G.W. *The Elementary Principles of Jurisprudence* (London: Sir Isaac Pitman and Sons, 1930).

Keller, E.F. *Reflections on Gender and Science* (Yale: Yale University Press, 1985).

Kelsen, H. *Pure Theory of Law* (Berkeley: University of California Press, 1967).

Kennedy, D. 'The International Human Rights Law Movement: Part of the Problem?' (2001) 3 *European Human Rights Law Review*, 245–267.

Kinley, D. (ed.) *Human Rights in Australian Law: Principles, Practice and Potential* (Sydney: Federation, 1988).

Kinley, D. and Chambers, R. 'The UN Human Rights Norms for Corporations: The Private Implications of Public International Law' (2006) 6 *Human Rights Law Review* 447–497.

Kinley, D. and Joseph, S. 'Multinational Corporations and Human Rights: Questions about Their Relationship' (2002) 27 *Alternative Law Journal* 7–10.

Kirby, P. *Vulnerability and Violence: The Impact of Globalisation* (London, Ann Arbor: Pluto Press, 2006).

Klein, L.E. 'Property and Politics in the Early Eighteenth Century Whig Moralists: The Case of the *Spectator*' in Brewer, J. and Staves, S. (eds), *Early Modern Conceptions of Property* (London: Routledge, 1995).

Knowles, C. *Family Boundaries: The Invention of Normality and Dangerousness* (New York: Broadview Press, 1996).

Koch, A. and Peden, W. (eds) *The Life and Selected Writings of Thomas Jefferson* (New York: Modern Library, 1944).

Kocourek, A. *Jural Relations* (Indianapolis: Bobbs-Merrill, 1928).

Knop, K. (ed.) *Gender and Human Rights* (Oxford: Oxford University Press, 2004).

Lacey, N. 'Feminist Legal Theory and the Rights of Women' in Knop, K. (ed.), *Gender and Human Rights* (Oxford: Oxford University Press, 2004) 13–55.

Lakoff, G. *Women, Fire and Dangerous Things: What Categories Reveal About the Mind* (Chicago: University of Chicago Press, 1987).

Lakoff, G. and Johnson, M. *Philosophy in the Flesh: The Embodied Mind and its Challenge to Western Thought* (New York: Basic Books, 1999) 415–439.

Lang, J. von and Sibyll, C. *Eichmann Interrogated: Transcripts from the Archives of the Israeli Police* (New York: Farrar, Straus and Giroux, 1983).

Lawson, F.H. 'The Creative Use of Legal Concepts' (1957) 32 *New York University Law Review* 907.

Leckie, S. 'Another Step Towards Indivisibility: Identifying the Key Features of Violations of Economic, Social and Cultural Rights' (1998) 20 *Human Rights Quarterly* 81–124.

Levinas, E. *Totality and Infinity* (A. Lingis (trans.)) (Pittsburgh: Duquesne University Press, 1969).

Levinas, E. *Ethics and Infinity* (R.A. Cohen (trans.)) (Pittsburgh: Duquesne University Press, 1985).

Levinas, E. 'Ethics as First Philosophy' in Levinas, E. (Sittand and M. Temple (trans.)) *The Levinas Reader* (Malden, MA: Blackwell, 1984) 75–87.

Lewis, N. 'Human Rights, Law and Democracy in an Unfree World' in Evans, T. *Human Rights Fifty Years On* (Manchester: Manchester University Press, 1988).

Lifton, R.J. *The Nazi Doctors* (New York: Basic Books, 1986).

Locke, J. *The Second Treatise of Civil Government* (Peardon, T. (ed.)) (Indianapolis: Bobbs-Merrill, 1952).

Locke, J. *Second Treatise of Civil Governments* 124; P. Laslett (ed.) (Cambridge: Cambridge University Press, 1960).

Longworth, R.C. 'Large Companies now Economically Bigger Than Some Countries', *Chicago Tribune* 15 Oct 1996.

Luke, T.W. 'New World Order or Neo-World Orders: Power, Politics and Ideology in Informationalizing Glocalities'(1995) 91 *Global Modernities* at 99–100.

McGuire, M.T. 'Moralistic Aggression, Processing Mechanisms and the Brain: The Biological Foundations of the Sense of Justice' in Masters R.D. and Gruter, M. *The Sense of Justice* (London: Sage Publications, 1992) 31–46.

MacKinnon, C.A. *Towards a Feminist Theory of the State* (Cambridge, Mass: Harvard University Press, 1989).

MacKinnon, C.A. 'Reflections on Sex Equality under Law' (1991) 100 *The Yale Law Journal* 1281–1328.

MacKinnon, C.A. 'Crimes of War, Crimes of Peace' in Shute, S. and Hurley, S. (eds), *On Human Rights* (New York: Basic Books, 1993).

McLean, J. (ed.) *Property and the Constitution* (Oxford: Hart Publishing, 1999).

Macpherson, C.B. *The Political Theory of Possessive Individualism: Hobbes to Locke* (Oxford: Clarendon Press, 1962).

Macpherson, C.B. 'Capitalism, and the Changing Concept of Property' in Kamenka, E. and Neale, R.S. (eds), *Feudalism, Capitalism and Beyond* (Canberra: Australian National University Press, 1975) at 119–122.

Macpherson, C.B. *Property: Mainstream and Critical Positions* (Toronto: Toronto University Press, 1978).

Mahoney, P. *et al.* (eds) *Protecting Human Rights: The European Perspective: Studies in Memory of Rolv Ryssdal* (Koln: Carl Heymanns Verlag, 2000).

Maine, H. *Ancient Law: Its Connection with the Early History of Society and its Relation to Modern Ideas* (London: John Murray, 1930).

Maitland, F.W. *Domesday Book and Beyond: Three Essays in the Early History of England* (Cambridge: Cambridge University Press, 1897).

Masters, R.D. 'Justice in Contemporary Legal Thought' in Masters, R.D. and Gruter, M. *The Sense of Justice: Biological Foundations of Law* (London: Sage Publications, 1992).

Masters, R.D. and Gruter, M. *The Sense of Justice: Biological Foundations of Law* (London: Sage Publications, 1992).

Marks, G.A. 'The Personification of the Business Corporation in American Law' (1987) 54 *The University of Chicago Law Review* 1441–1483.

Marks, S.P. 'From the "Single Confused Page" to the "Decalogue for Six Billion Persons": The Roots of the Universal Declaration of Human Rights in the French Revolution' (1998) 20 *Human Rights Quarterly* 459–514.

Marx, K. 'On the Jewish Question' in Marx, K. *Early* Texts (McLellan, D. (trans.)) (Oxford: Blackwell, 1971) 85–114.

Mayer, C.J. 'Personalising the Impersonal: Corporations and the Bill of Rights' (1990) 41 *Hastings Law Journal* 577–663.

McCorquodale, R. and Fairbrother, R. 'Globalization and Human Rights' (1999) 21 *Human Rights Quarterly* 735–766.

McCrudden, C. 'Human Dignity', *University of Oxford Faculty of Law Legal Studies Research Paper Series*: Working Paper No. 10/2006.

McLean, J. 'Property as Power and Resistance' in McLean, J. *Property and the Constitution* (Oxford: Hart Publishing, 1999).

McLean, J. *Property and the Constitution* (Oxford: Hart Publishing, 1999).
Merleau Ponty, M. *The Phenomenology of Perception* (C. Smith (trans.)) (London: Routledge Classics, 2002) (First published by Routledge and Kegan Paul, 1962).
Merleau-Ponty, M. *The Primacy of Perception* (Evanston, Illinois: Northwestern University Press, 1964).
Merleau-Ponty, M. *The Visible and the Invisible* (J.M. Edie (ed.)) (Northwestern University Press, 1968).
Merleau-Ponty, M. *Nature: Course Notes from the College de France* (R. Vallier (trans.)) (Evanston, Illinois: Northwestern University Press, 2003).
Monshipouri, M., Welch, C.E. Jr. and Kennedy, E.T. 'Multinational Corporations and the Ethics of Global Responsibility: Problems and Possibilities' (2003) 25 *Human Rights* Quarterly 965–989.
Moore, M. *Law and Psychiatry: Rethinking the Relationship* (Cambridge: Cambridge University Press, 1984).
Moran, L. 'Corporate Criminal Capacity: Nostalgia for Representation' (1992) 1 *Social and Legal Studies* 371–391.
Morgan, B. 'The Regulatory Face of the Human Right to Water' (2004) 15 *Journal of Water Law* 179–187.
Morgan, B. 'Water: Frontier Markets and Cosmopolitan Activism' (2004) 27 *Soundings: A Journal of Politics and Culture* 10–24.
Morgan, B. 'Emerging Global Water Welfarism: Access to Water, Unruly Consumers and Transnational Governance' in Trentmann, F. and Brewer, J. *Consumer Cultures, Global Perspectives* (Oxford and New York: Berg Press, 2006).
Morgan, B. 'Global Business, Local Constraints: The Case of Water in South Africa' in Woods, N. *Making Global Self-Regulation Effective in Developing Countries* (Oxford: Oxford University Press, 2006) 201–226.
Morris, D.B. *The Culture of Pain* (Berkeley: University of California Press, 1991).
Morsink, J. 'World War Two and the Declaration' (1993) 15 *Human Rights Quarterly* 357–405.
Morsink, J. 'Women's Rights in the Universal Declaration' (1991) 13 *Human Rights Quarterly* 229–256.
Nader, R. 'Introduction' in Wallach, L. and Sforza, M. *The WTO: Five Years of Reasons to Resist Corporate Globalization* (New York: Seven Stories Press, 1999).
Naffine, N. 'The Body Bag' in Naffine, N. and Owens, R. (eds), *Sexing the Subject of Law* (Sydney: Sweet and Maxwell, 1997) at 79–93.
Naffine, N. and Owens, R. (eds) *Sexing the Subject of Law* (Sydney: Law Book Company, 1997).
Naffine, N. 'Who are Law's Persons? From Cheshire Cats to Responsible Subjects' (2003) 66 *Modern Law Review*, 346–367.
Naffine, N. *Law's Meaning of Life: Philosophy, Religion, Darwin and the Legal Person (Legal Theory Today)* (Portland: Hart Publishing, 2009).
National Civil Rights Movement Newsletter, Issue 5 (2001) in *Carf61* at 7.
Nedelsky, J. 'Law, Boundaries and the Bounded Self' (1990) 30 *Representations* 162–189.
Neier, A. 'Social and Economic Rights: A Critique' (2006) 31 *Human Rights Brief* 1–3.
Nekam, A. *The Personality Conception of the Legal Entity* (Boston: Harvard University Press, 1938).
Neocleous, M. 'Staging Power: Marx, Hobbes and the Personification of Capital' (2003) 14 *Law and Critique* 147–165.
Nino, C. *The Ethics of Human Rights* (Oxford: Clarendon, 1993).

Norrie, A. *Crime, Reason and History: A Critical Introduction to Criminal Law* 2nd edn (London: Butterworths, 2001).
O'Donovan, K. 'With Sense, Consent or Just a Con? Legal Subjects in the Discourses of Autonomy' in Naffine, N. and Owens, R. (eds) *Sexing the Subject of Law* (Sydney: Law Book Company, 1997).
Orford, A. 'Beyond Harmonisation: Trade, Human Rights and the Economy of Sacrifice' (2005) 18 *Leiden Journal of International Law* 179–213.
Orford, A. (ed.) *International Law and its Others* (Cambridge: Cambridge University Press, 2006).
Otto, D. 'Violence Against Women: Something Other Than a Human Rights Violation?' (1993) 1 *Australian Feminist Law Journal* 159–162.
Otto, D. 'Disconcerting "Masculinities": Reinventing the Gendered Subject(s) of International Human Rights Law' in Buss, D. and Manji, A. (eds), *International Law: Modern Feminist Approaches* (Oxford: Hart Publishing, 2005) 105–129.
Otto, D. 'Lost in Translation: Rescripting the Sexed Subjects of International Human Rights Law' in Orford, A. (ed.), *International Law and its Others* (Cambridge: Cambridge University Press, 2006).
Palmer, S. 'Critical Perspectives on Women's Rights: The European Convention on Human Rights and Fundamental Freedoms' in Bottomley, A. (ed.), *Feminist Perspectives on the Foundational Subjects of Law* (London: Cavendish, 1996), 223–242.
Panitch, L. 'Rethinking the Role of the State' in Mittelman, J.H. (ed.), *Globalization: Critical Reflections* (Boulder: Lynne Reiner, 1995) at 95.
Pateman, C. *The Sexual Contract* (Stanford: Stanford University Press, 1988).
Peacocke, A. and Gillet, G. *Persons and Personality: A Contemporary Inquiry* (Oxford: Blackwell, 1987).
Poulter, S. 'The Rights of Ethnic, Religious and Linguistic Minorities' (1997) 3 *European Human Rights Law Review* 254–264.
Primavesi, A. 'Faith in Creation' in Race, A. and Williamson, R. (eds), *True To This Earth: Global Challenges and Transforming Faith* (Oxford: Oneword Publications, 1995) 101–102.
Pring, G.W. and Canan, P. *SLAPPS: Getting Sued for Speaking Out* (Philadelphia: Temple University Press, 1996).
Race, A. and Williamson, R. (eds) *True To This Earth: Global Challenges and Transforming Faith* (Oxford: Oneword Publications, 1995).
Radin, M. 'The Endless Problem of Corporate Personality' (1932) 32 *Columbia Law Review* 643–667.
Ratner, S.R. 'Corporations and Human Rights: A Theory of Legal Responsibility' (2001) 111 *Yale Law Journal* 443–545.
Rattigan, W.H. *Roman Law of Persons* (London: Wildy and Sons, 1873).
Reich, C. 'The New Property' (1964) 73 *Yale Law Journal* 733–787.
Richardson, J. 'A Refrain: Feminist Metaphysics and Law' in Richardson, J. and Sandland, R. (eds), *Feminist Perspectives on Law and Theory* (London: Cavendish, 2000) 119–134.
Richardson, J.L. 'Contending Liberalisms: Past and Present' (1997) 3 *European Journal of International Relations* 5–33.
Romany, C. 'State Responsibility Goes Private: A Feminist Critique of the Public/Private Distinction in International Human Rights Law' in Cook, R.J. (ed.), *Human Rights of Women: National and International Perspectives* (Philadelphia: University of Pennsylvania Press, 1994) 85–115.
Rousseau, J. *The Social Contract and Discourses* (G. Cole (trans.)) (New York: E.P. Dutton, 1950) at 210.

Rowbottom, J. 'Property and Participation: A Right of Access for Expressive Activities' (2005) 2 *European Human Rights Law Review*, 186–202.
Samuels, W. and Miller, A. (eds) *Corporations and Society: Power and Responsibility* (New York: Greenwood Press, 1987).
Scarry, E. *The Body in Pain: The Making and Unmaking of the World* (Oxford: Oxford University Press, 1985).
Schane, S.A. 'The Corporation is a Person: The Language of a Legal Fiction' (1987) 61 *Tulane Law Review* 563–609.
Schlag, P. *The Enchantment of Reason* (Durham: Duke University Press, 1998).
Schneiderman, D. 'Constitutional Approaches to Privatization: An Inquiry into the Magnitude of Neo-Liberal Constitutionalism' (2000) 63 *Law and Contemporary Problems* 83–109.
Schulz, J. 'Bolivia's War over Water', *The Democracy Center*, February 4, 2000.
Scott, J. *Only Paradoxes to Offer: French Feminists and the Rights of Man* (Cambridge Mass.: Harvard University Press, 1996).
Seidler, V. 'Embodied Knowledge and Virtual Space' in Wood, J. (ed.), *The Virtual Embodied* (London: Routledge, 1998).
Shamir, R. 'Corporate Social Responsibility: A Case of Hegemony and Counter-Hegemony' in De Sousa Santos, B. and Rodrigues-Garavito, C.A. *Law and Globalisation from Below: Towards a Cosmopolitan Legality* (Cambridge: Cambridge University Press, 2005) 92–117.
Shearing, C.D. and Stenning, P.C. 'Private Security: Implications for Social Control' (1982–1983) 30 *Social Problems*, 493.
Short, J.R. *Imagined Country: Society, Culture and Environment* (London: Routledge, 1991).
Shute, S. and Hurley, S. (eds) *On Human Rights* (New York: Basic Books, 1993).
Simons, P. 'Corporate Voluntarism and Human Rights: The Adequacy and Effectiveness of Voluntary Self-Regulation Regimes' (2004) 59 *Relations Industrielles/Industrial Relations* 101.
Slaughter, A.-M. 'Judicial Globalization' (2000) 40 *Virginia Journal of International Law Association* 1103–1124.
Smart, C. *Feminism and the Power of Law* (London: Routledge, 1989).
Soros, G. 'The Capitalist Threat' (1997) 279 *Atlantic Monthly* 45–58.
Stammers, N. 'Social Movements and the Social Construction of Human Rights' (1999) 21 *Human Rights Quarterly* 980.
Steiner, H. 'Social Rights and Economic Development: Converging Discourses?' (1998) 4 *Buffalo Human Rights Law Review* 25–42.
Stevenson, M.L. 'The Sociopolitical Implications of Rural Racism and Tourism Experiences' in Tribe, J. and Airey, D. *Developments in Tourism Research* (Oxford: Elseveier, 2007).
Stoljar, S.J. 'Corporate Theory Re-Examined' in Stoljar, S.J. *Groups and Entities: An Inquiry into Corporate Theory* (Canberra: Australian National University Press, 1973).
Stone, C.D. *Should Trees Have Standing? And Other Essays on Law, Morals and the Environment* (New York: Oceana, 1996).
Strahlendorf, P. 'Traditional Legal Concepts from an Evolutionary Perspective' in Masters, R.D. and Gruter, M. *The Sense of Justice: Biological Foundations of Law* (London: Sage Publications, 1992) 128–160.
Teubner, G. 'Rights of Non-humans? Electronic Agents and Animals as New Actors in Politics and Law' (2006) 33 *Journal of Law and Society* 497–521.
Tester, S. and Kell, G. *The United Nations and Business* (New York: St Martin's Press, 2000).

Tilley, C. *A Phenomenology of Landscape: Places, Paths and Monuments* (Oxford: Berg, 1994).
Thompson, D. (ed.) *The Essential E.P. Thompson* (New York: New Press, 2001).
Tierney, B. *The Idea of Natural Rights* (Atlanta: Scholars Press, 1997).
Townshend, J. *C.B Macpherson and the Problem of Liberal Democracy* (Edinburgh: Edinburgh University Press, 2000).
Trentmann, F. and Brewer, J. *Consumer Cultures, Global Perspectives* (Oxford and New York: Berg Press, 2006).
Tribe, J. and Airey, D. *Developments in Tourism Research* (Oxford: Elseveier, 2007).
Tuck, R. *Natural Rights Theories* (Cambridge: Cambridge University Press, 1979).
Tully, J. *A Discourse on Property: John Locke and his Adversaries* (Cambridge: Cambridge University Press, 1980).
Tur, R. 'The "Person" in Law' in Peacocke, A. and Gillett, G. (eds), *Persons and Personality: A Contemporary Inquiry* (Oxford: Blackwell, 1987).
Turner, B. *Vulnerability and Human Rights* (Pennsylvania: Pennsylvania State University Press, 2006) 1–5, 25–34.
Twining, W. *Globalisation and Legal Theory* (London: Butterworths, 2000).
Van Maanen, G.E. and Van der Walt, A.J. (eds) *Property Law on the Threshold of the 21st Century* (Antwerp: MAKLU, 1996).
Vasterling, V. 'Body and Language: Butler, Merleau-Ponty and Lyotard on the Speaking Embodied Subject' (2003) 11 *International Journal of Philosophical Studies* 205–223.
Waldron, J. (ed.) *Nonsense upon Stilts* (London: Methuen, 1987).
Wallach, L. and Sforza, M. *The WTO: Five Years of Reasons to Resist Corporate Globalization* (New York: Seven Stories Press, 1999).
Webb, L.C. (ed.) *Legal Personality and Political Pluralism* (New York: Cambridge University Press, 1958).
Westra, L. 'Environmental Rights and Human Rights: The Final Enclosure Movement' in Brownsword, R. (ed.), *Global Governance and the Quest for Justice: Volume 4: Human Rights* (Oxford: Hart Publishing, 2004) 107–119.
Westra, L., Bosselmann, K. and Westra, R. *Reconciling Human Existence with Ecological Integrity* (London: Earthscan, 2008).
Williams, O.F. 'The UN Global Compact: The Challenge and the Promise' (2004) 14 *Business and Ethics Quarterly* 755–774.
Williams, S.J. and Bendelow, G. *The Lived Body: Sociological Themes, Embodied Issues* (London: Routledge, 1998).
Wolgast, E. *Ethics of an Artificial Person: Lost Responsibility in Professions and Organisations* (Stanford: Stanford University Press, 1992).
Wood, E.M. *The Origins of Capitalism* (New York: The Monthly Review Press, 1999).
Wood, E.M. *The Origins of Capitalism: A Longer View* (London: Verso, 2002).
Wood, N. *John Locke and Agrarian Capitalism* (California: University of California Press, 1984).
Woodiwiss, A. *Human Rights* (Abingdon: Routledge, 2005).
Woods, N. *Making Global Self-Regulation Effective in Developing Countries* (Oxford: Oxford University Press, 2006).
Wright, S. 'Economic Rights and Social Justice: A Feminist Analysis of some International Human Rights Conventions' (1988–9) 12 *Australian Yearbook of International Law* 241–264.

Index

abstraction, 44, 48, 53, 57, 59, 78, 81, 96, 99, 114, 120, 137, 154, 165
ahistoricism, 69, 77, 86
alterity, 163–7
American Convention of Human Rights, 24
animal rights, 47, 203
anthromorphism
  legal anthropomorphism, 1, 46, 52, 96, 202, 203, 204, 205, 216n27
artificial intelligences, 46
Auschwitz, 41, 141, 145

biopolitics, 141, 152
bio-power, 152, 163
biotechnology, 65
binary/ies
  body/women/emotion/nature, 43–4
  mind/men/reason/culture, 44
body
  affectability of, 126, 131, 132, 147, 164, 176, 194
  as boundary, 42, 44, 66, 123, 239n18
  and empathy, 98, 102, 138, 153
  materiality of, 4, 42, 66, 89, 91, 127, 131, 146, 206
  politicisation of, 100, 101, 109, 127, 140, 143, 160, 163
  and rights discourse, 98, 102, 106, 108, 109, 139
  as site of law's regulation and control, 42
  suppression of, 97, 111
body-mind dualism, 42, 66, 114, 116

capitalism
  global, 2, 9, 12, 19
  industrial, 63, 64, 80, 86, 94
  mercantile, 80
  neo-liberal, 8, 9, 26, 162, 184
  re-invention of, 8
caveats – preliminary, 4–5
citizenship
  and human rights, 95, 100, 150, 151, 155, 162
  and landownership, 102, 177, 178, 179
closure
  analytical, 2, 137, 141
  ideological, 2, 22, 56, 82, 98, 100, 128, 137, 141
cognitive science, 120–4
  cognitive unconscious, 122
colonialism, 111
commodification, 4, 17, 66, 184, 186, 191, 192–4, 197, 202
commons, the, 170, 186, 193, 199, 200
constitutionalism – new, 13–14, 17
contract
  elevation of, 59
Convention on the Elimination of all Forms of Discrimination against Women, 19, 108–9, 232n65, n76
Convention on the Elimination of all Forms of Racial Discrimination, 108
corporate
  accountability, 21
    difficulties of, 18–20
    exemption from International Criminal Court jurisdiction, 18
    norms on the Responsibility of Transnational Corporations, 18
    voluntarism, 18
  corruption, 16, 21
  dignity, 10, 90
  gender, 93
  global dominance, 21, 201
  human rights
    abuse, 12, 16, 18, 19, 35, 38, 75, 211n82
    conceptually inspired critique of, 29–31
    principle of derivative entitlement, 35–6
  immortality, 61, 64

corporate – *continued*
legal humanity, 1, 3, 4, 132, 163, 200, 201, 205
personality theory, 59–64
and economic/ideological imperatives, 64
fiction theory, 60–4
group theory, 61–4
natural entity theory, 61–4
personification, 63, 64, 84, 85, 87
persons, 1, 23, 25, 28, 33, 49, 53–4, 59, 85, 86, 89–91, 204
social responsibility, 20–1, 198, 211n82
UN Global Compact, 20–1
sovereignty, 12, 113
corporations
and the American Bill of Rights, 112, 170
artificiality of, 28, 32, 33, 61, 62–3, 90
as classical liberal actor writ large, 64, 68
global, 11, 16, 18, 20, 21
as human rights beneficiaries, 25, 26, 32, 37, 39, 90, 110, 201
as male, 63, 87
as paradigmatic legal person, 49, 96
as private-sector quasi-states, 6, 10
as 'victims' of human rights abuses, 2, 39, 201
criminal law, 79, 80, 85, 90–1

Declaration on the Elimination of Violence Against Women, 109
decontextualisation, 42, 197
democracy, 75, 148, 151, 152, 156, 159, 160, 175
developing world, 15, 16
dignity, 10, 57, 77, 90, 103, 130, 143, 145, 157, 185, 189, 196, 214n48, 250n138
and embodied vulnerability, 90, 191, 195, 196–8
disembodiment
as exclusion, 42, 44, 58, 98, 101, 104, 110, 112, 114, 140, 205
gender-privilege masked by, 44, 45, 82, 96, 101, 107, 114, 135
impossibility of, 44, 130, 136, 162
legal-, 41, 92, 95, 111, 149, 162
quasi-, 41–5, 59, 81, 96, 98, 99, 101, 102, 105, 112, 114, 140, 149, 205–6
dualism
body-mind, 42, 66, 114, 116
Cartesian, 41–2, 117, 227n153
public/private, 107, 109, 116
sex/gender, 105
male/female, 43

eco-system/s, 4, 47, 128, 205
embodied
mind, 117, 121, 122, 125
perception, 116, 117, 120, 122
vulnerability, 3–4, 5, 32, 39, 90, 105, 116, 126–35, 136, 140, 142, 145, 147–8, 153, 154, 156, 158, 159–60, 162, 165, 167, 168, 172, 178, 187, 193, 196, 205
and anti-discrimination, 161
and civil and political rights, 129, 134, 135, 156, 158–61
and economic, social and cultural rights, 134–5, 156–8
as foundational to human rights, 5, 32, 98, 113, 116, 129, 130, 135, 142, 156, 159, 168, 205
as fundamental to dignity, 90, 147, 157, 191, 196, 197, 199
and property, 4, 127, 169, 170, 179, 182, 183, 184, 188, 189, 191, 199
and substantive equality, 109, 127, 198–9, 205
embodiment
centrality of, 114, 115–26, 131, 136, 138, 142, 157, 166, 199, 205
and the environment, 128, 131, 171, 179, 183
inescapability of, 116, 117, 120, 126, 132, 135, 136, 144, 162, 171, 181, 197, 198
and interrelationality, 119, 123, 126, 163, 164, 172, 186, 188
and perception, 116–18, 120, 122
and reason, 43, 72, 82, 114, 116, 117, 120–3, 126, 129, 136, 169, 170, 179, 183, 197, 200
empathy, 98, 102, 129, 133, 138–40, 145, 155, 167
empiricism, 117

environment
human rights and, 8, 16, 20, 21, 32, 46, 88, 171–2, 200
ontic vulnerability of, 5, 171
property and, 171–2, 188, 189, 200
European Convention on Human Rights
corporate beneficiaries of, 23–31
links to European liberal project, 25
links to liberal capitalism, 25
pragmatism, 23, 28, 29
strategic importance of, 24
'excludability' and private property, 171, 181–3, 186, 191
legal, 181, 193, 199
moral, 183, 188, 199
physical, 183, 199
exclusion
body, 42, 44, 54, 98, 131, 176
indigenous peoples, 94, 111
people of colour, 94, 111, 161, 180
propertyless, 100, 102
women, 93, 94, 100, 102, 104–10, 161

feminism/ist, 87, 92, 104, 105, 106–8, 230n38
flesh, 55, 118–20, 131
chiasm, 119
French Declaration of the Rights of Man and Citizen, 103
French Revolution, 71, 101, 103
fundamental freedoms, 30, 207n2

gender
exclusion, 93–4, 104, 108, 110, 116, 135
hierarchies, 93, 103, 107, 110, 116
mainstreaming, 109
of corporation, 45, 67, 93, 96
of neutrality/objectivity, 44, 104, 244n20
genealogy of human rights, 32, 58
General Agreement on Tariffs and Trade (GATT), 16
globalisation
contemporary intensification of, 7, 8, 13
corporate dominance of, 9, 24
global capitalism, 2, 9, 12, 19
legal globalisation, 2, 26
neoliberalism, 2, 8, 9, 12, 26
rights-discourse and, 2, 7
group rights
collective conception of, 34–5
corporate conception of, 34–5
G20, 14, 15, 18

hegemony
capitalist, 9
corporate, 6, 9, 21, 24
historical contingency, 69, 78, 89, 93
Hohfeldian correlativity, 33, 38, 56
human
blurred boundaries of, 5, 47
commonality, 131, 134, 143–6, 153, 154, 164, 166, 167
human beings
artificiality of, in law, 32, 33, 37, 51, 53, 56, 60, 63
embodied vulnerability of, 3–4, 5, 32, 39, 90, 105, 116, 126–35, 136, 140, 142, 145, 147–8, 153, 154, 156, 158, 159–60, 162, 165, 167, 168, 172, 178, 187, 193, 196, 205
humanity
conflation with legal subjectivity, 1, 46, 47, 56, 203, 204
as construct, 4, 22, 39, 44, 48, 50, 55, 56, 63, 72, 90, 99, 105, 149
human rights
abuse, 11, 12, 18, 19, 31, 38, 109, 140, 161, 178, 211n82
beneficiaries, 2, 23–6, 34, 38, 39, 90, 110, 132, 142, 201
and citizenship, 17, 95, 102, 145, 150–1, 154, 155, 166, 202
colonisation of, 3, 6, 40, 95, 201, 202
co-option of, 16
council, 11
as critique of positive law, 84, 94, 169
discourse, 2–3, 7, 9, 10–18, 29, 45, 48, 58, 70, 95, 98, 101, 102, 108, 110, 113, 136, 138, 140, 154, 165, 169, 172, 183, 192, 193, 202
as exclusory/inclusory, 56, 58, 65, 70, 78, 99, 101, 102, 105, 110, 139, 169, 172–3, 179, 184, 190
genealogy, 32, 58, 96–113
interpretive distortion of, 12, 15, 19, 191
languages, 17, 110, 131–2

human rights – *continued*
law, 2, 4, 7, 11, 19, 20, 24, 26, 40, 41, 42–3, 45, 46, 48, 58, 95, 97, 104, 106, 115, 136, 164, 200, 201, 205
markets, 17
movements, 17
as 'obstacles' to their own promotion, 16
paradoxes, 102–4, 116, 137, 221n5
sociology of, 11
subjectivity, 113, 116, 127, 128, 129, 166, 168, 202, 204
supra-legal category as, 169
trade-related-market-friendly paradigm of, 2, 14, 15, 16, 163, 201
two notions of
contemporary, 110–13, 169
modern, 110–13, 115, 169
universal, 3, 9, 48, 58, 98, 102, 104, 105, 108, 109, 114, 129, 130, 134, 165–6, 198, 205, 206

idealism, 117
ideology, 2, 14, 18, 21, 41, 82, 103, 106, 162, 168, 179, 184
individualism
liberal, 52, 79, 197, 224n76
possessive, 9, 59, 67, 80, 102, 224n76
inequality, 14, 76, 77, 81, 135, 159, 224n78
intercorporeality, 118, 120, 146
interrelationality, 119, 123, 126, 132, 163–4, 172, 186, 205
International Covenant of Civil and Political Rights, 11, 36, 104, 156, 157, 158, 160, 170
International Covenant of Economic, Social and Cultural Rights, 11, 104, 156, 157, 158, 170, 242n94
international human rights law
embodied vulnerability and, 136, 140, 164, 167, 201, 205
quasi-disembodiment and, 58, 95, 96–113
International Monetary Fund (IMF), 8, 9, 14, 15, 18, 242n88

jurisprudence
of the person, 53, 54

justice
as abstract, 43
as fairness, 43, 70
as formal, 43, 78, 79

Kantian moral theory, 42

landowner/citizen, 177, 178, 180
laissez-faire, 15, 17
law
biological foundations of
moralistic aggression, 124
rule-making/following, 125
closures of, 22, 48, 68, 94, 113, 115, 137, 204
as rationalising enterprise, 68–9, 77, 80, 84, 115
legal
anthropogenesis, 1, 46
anthropomorphism, 1, 46–7, 52, 96, 202, 203–5
disembodiment, 41, 92, 95, 111, 149, 162
entity, 34, 49, 50, 53–4, 55, 78, 149
humanity, 1, 3, 46, 96, 115, 132, 163, 200, 205
interiority, 58
personality, 29, 34, 45–59, 59–64, 96, 97, 148, 216n22
person/s
assumed convergence with 'human being', 45, 49, 217n35
as mask/role, 51, 78, 97
naturalist conception of, 50–1, 57–60
positivist conception of, 50, 51, 53, 55, 56–60, 73, 78
P1, 54–66
P2, 54–66
P3, 54–66
subjectivity
of capital, 63
conflation with 'humanity', 1, 46–7, 202, 203–4
subject/s
corporate, 63
human, 50, 129, 177
liberal
capitalism, 25, 68, 73, 77–8, 81, 89, 95, 113, 173
links to legal positivism, 73, 78

individualism, 52, 79, 197, 224n76
legal rationality, 41, 82, 114
subject of rights, 52, 68, 81–4, 95, 131
liberalism
classical, 30, 58, 127, 184
European, 26, 27, 31, 111

market
morality, 74
rationality, 17
society, 67, 74, 75
materiality, 4, 5, 22, 41, 42, 55, 56, 62, 63, 66, 82, 118, 123, 131, 205, 206
materialisation
and ideology, 55, 56, 64, 104

national interest, 11, 12, 22
national security, 11, 12, 22, 210n67
nation-state
'end of', 13, 14
'progressive state', 13, 14
'soft-state', 13
natural law, 46, 70–2, 76, 127
'natural' legal persons, 47
as a liberal construction, 96, 168
natural man, 58, 73, 77, 99, 110, 222n35
natural right, 70, 76, 94, 152
natural rights, 58, 69, 70–3, 75, 94–5, 99, 101, 110, 153
naturalist theory of persons, 50, 57, 58
Nazi
regime, 140–3, 149, 159
holocaust, 11, 32, 40, 142, 144–5, 154
neoliberal/ism
disciplinary, 9, 10, 14
globalisation, 2, 8, 9, 12, 26
NGOs, 17, 37
North American Free Trade Agreement (NAFTA), 16
Nuremburg International War Crimes Tribunal, 141, 149

perception
embodied nature of, 116–18, 120, 122
perspectival nature of, 117–18
primacy of, 117, 122
person/s
corporate, 1, 23, 25, 28, 33, 49, 53–4, 59, 85, 86, 89–91, 204
criminal, 58, 84, 85, 86, 90, 91
history of 'person', 48–54
juridical/legal persons, 1, 23, 40, 42, 47, 49–51, 54–9, 80, 81, 82, 89–95, 148, 166, 202, 203, 204
as 'mask', 51, 78, 97
property and persons, 51, 58, 64, 65–7, 85, 99, 101, 112, 168, 170, 172–3, 182
personification
and capital, 63–4, 84
phenomenology, 117, 121
positivism, 44, 57, 73, 74, 77–81, 94, 130, 152, 222n40
possessive individualism, 9, 59, 67, 80, 102, 224n76
post-9/11, 8, 11, 22
posthumanism, 5, 46, 47, 132, 162
power, 1, 6, 9, 10, 12–13, 15, 38–9, 46, 47, 51, 56, 63, 69, 73, 75, 78, 84, 91, 94, 101, 127, 148, 150, 152, 159, 163, 174, 176, 194, 202
privatisation
of public space, 174–8
'propertisation', 170, 193
property
common, 185, 186, 247n70
communitarian, 186, 187
a contested concept, 171–80
and embodied vulnerability, 4, 127, 169, 170, 179, 182, 183, 184, 188, 189, 191, 199
and 'excludability'
legal, 181, 193, 199
moral, 183, 188, 199
physical, 183, 199
as exclusory, 65, 169–70, 172–3, 174–6, 183–4, 188, 190, 243n6, 244n16, n24
as inclusory
and human rights, 169, 173, 175, 179, 184–5, 190
as 'propriety', 184, 188–91, 244n16
-owners
citizenship links with, 177–8, 179
privileging of, 58, 115, 169
private, 57, 65, 76, 80, 115, 170, 173, 177, 179, 181, 182, 185, 190, 247n70
reasonable rights of access to, 175, 185
reconceptualising, 170, 184–5

poverty, 15, 110, 230n85
public/private divide, 107, 109, 116

quasi-disembodiment
  in international human rights law, 58, 95, 96–113
  of the liberal legal person, 187
  in western philosophy, 99, 104
quasi-public space, 175, 176
quasi-states, 6, 10

racism, 95, 111, 147, 161, 180
rationalism, 42, 44, 57, 68, 73, 81, 162, 181
re-distributive state – end of, 14
refugees, 112, 151, 166, 245n27
rights discourse
  ascendancy, 2, 101
  conflation with human rights discourse, 46
  corporate, 2, 7, 11, 32, 45, 48, 95, 202
  liberal, 140–1
robots, 46, 203

social construction, 4, 39, 48, 128
social contract theory
  Hobbes
    and positivism, 71–7
  Locke
    and property, 66, 71–7
social movements, 17, 39, 70, 94, 195
state-centrism, 12
state sovereignty, 11, 73
Strategic Law Suits Against Public Participation (SLAPPS), 17
structural adjustment, 15

Trade-related Intellectual Property Rights, 16
Trade-related Market-friendly Human Rights, 2, 10, 163, 201
TNCs
  ascendancy, 8, 184
transcendent critique, 70
transnational corporations, 2, 8, 10, 12, 14, 15–16, 18, 24, 35, 38, 192

United Nations (UN)
  Code of Conduct for Transnationals, 18
  Development Programme (UNDP), 15
  Global Compact, 20–1
  Norms on the Responsibilities of Transnational Corporations and Other Business Enterprises, 18
United States
  Bill of Rights
    corporations and, 28–9, 87–8, 170
Universal Declaration of Human Rights (UDHR)
  embodied vulnerability and, 156–61
  interpretive distortion of, 12, 19, 191
  lacuna at the heart of, 154, 166, 178
  paradigm, 10–14, 19, 22, 24, 39, 40, 48, 58, 98, 102–3, 140, 142, 163, 191, 205
  promotional nature, 10, 11, 18
  weaknesses of, 11, 12
universalism
  abstract, 43, 58, 82, 100, 101, 104, 107
  concrete, 166, 206
  gendered, 105, 107
  masculinist, 99, 100, 105, 106, 107, 108

vulnerability
  as affectability, 110, 126–7, 132, 147, 164, 176, 194, 198
  as distinct from suffering, 5, 129–30, 132, 133
  embodied nature of, 3–4, 5, 32, 39, 90, 105, 116, 126–35, 136, 140, 142, 145, 147–8, 153, 154, 156, 158, 159–60, 162, 165, 167, 168, 172, 178, 187, 193, 196, 205
  experiential variation of, 134
  as female, 110
  as foundational to human flourishing, 5, 159
  and human rights, 5, 22, 39, 105, 110, 116, 127, 130, 132, 135, 138, 140, 154, 159–60, 161, 167, 170, 172, 196, 198, 205
  of human rights, 22, 113
  and interrelationality, 119, 123, 126, 132, 163–4, 172, 186, 205
  as nuanced/non-monolithic, 132, 162, 190, 191
  and the ontic dimension, 4, 5, 128, 134, 144, 148, 155, 164, 166, 171, 178, 203, 205

and political subjectivity, 127, 164
and rights discourse, 153, 155, 167, 172, 201
and stigmatised subjectivities, 128
as universal, 128, 144, 167

water
human right to
centrality of, 196
regulation of, 193
welfarism, 193, 195
women
exclusion of, 93, 94, 100, 102, 104–10, 161
marginality of, 104–10
World Bank, 9, 15, 192, 194, 242n88
world economic order, 8
World Trade Organisation, 8, 15, 16, 18